NEW CENTURY BIBLE COMMENTARY

General Editors

RONALD E. CLEMENTS	MATTHEW BLACK
(Old Testament)	(New Testament)

The Book of REVELATION

THE NEW CENTURY BIBLE COMMENTARIES

EXODUS (J. P. Hyatt)
LEVITICUS AND NUMBERS (N. H. Snaith)*
DEUTERONOMY (A. D. H. Mayes)
JOSHUA, JUDGES, AND RUTH (John Gray)*
EZRA, NEHEMIAH, AND ESTHER (L. H. Brockington)*
JOB (H. H. Rowley)
PSALMS Volumes 1 and 2 (A. A. Anderson)
ISAIAH 1-39 (R. E. Clements)
ISAIAH 40-66 (R. N. Whybray)
EZEKIEL (John W. Wevers)*
THE GOSPEL OF MATTHEW (David Hill)
THE GOSPEL OF MARK (Hugh Anderson)
THE GOSPEL OF LUKE (E. Earle Ellis)
THE GOSPEL OF JOHN (Barnabas Lindars)
THE ACTS OF THE APOSTLES (William Neil)*
ROMANS (Matthew Black)*
1 and 2 CORINTHIANS (F. F. Bruce)
GALATIANS (Donald Guthrie)*
EPHESIANS (C. Leslie Mitton)*
PHILIPPIANS (Ralph P. Martin)
COLOSSIANS AND PHILEMON (Ralph P. Martin)*
1 PETER (Ernest Best)*
THE BOOK OF REVELATION (G. R. Beasley-Murray)

*Not yet available in paperback
 Other titles are in preparation

NEW CENTURY BIBLE
COMMENTARY

Based on the Revised Standard Version

The Book
of
REVELATION

G. R. BEASLEY-MURRAY

WM. B. EERDMANS PUBL. CO., GRAND RAPIDS

MARSHALL, MORGAN & SCOTT PUBL. LTD., LONDON

To
PAUL, ELIZABETH, STEPHEN, ANDREW
in gratitude for their
affection, understanding and encouragement
in all my labours

Copyright © Marshall, Morgan & Scott (Publications) Ltd. 1974
First published 1974 by Marshall, Morgan & Scott, England
Revised edition published 1978
Softback edition published 1981

Printed in the United States of America
for
Wm. B. Eerdmans Publishing Company
255 Jefferson Ave. S.E., Grand Rapids, Mich. 49503
and
Marshall, Morgan & Scott
A Pentos company
1 Bath Street, London ECIV 9LB
ISBN 0 551 00897 0

Library of Congress Cataloging in Publication Data

Beasley-Murray, George Raymond, 1916-
The Book of Revelation.

(New century Bible commentary)
Reprint of the ed. published by Marshall,
Morgan & Scott, London.
Includes indexes.
1. Bible. N.T. Revelation — Commentaries.
I. Title. II. Series.
BS2825.3.B24 1981 228.7'7 80-28252
ISBN 0-8028-1885-4 (pbk.)

CONTENTS

5

158227

ABBREVIATIONS

BIBLICAL

OLD TESTAMENT (*OT*)

Gen.	Jg.	1 Chr.	Ps.	Lam.	Ob.	Hag.
Exod.	Ru.	2 Chr.	Prov.	Ezek.	Jon.	Zech.
Lev.	1 Sam.	Ezr.	Ec.	Dan.	Mic.	Mal.
Num.	2 Sam.	Neh.	Ca.	Hos.	Nah.	
Dt.	1 Kg.	Est.	Isa.	Jl	Hab.	
Jos.	2 Kg.	Job	Jer.	Am.	Zeph.	

APOCRYPHA (*Apoc.*)

1 Esd.	Tob.	Ad.Est.	Sir.	S. 3 Ch.	Bel.	1 Mac.
2 Esd.	Jdt.	Wis.	Bar.	Sus.	Man.	2 Mac.
(= 4 Ezra)			Ep. Jer.			

NEW TESTAMENT (*NT*)

Mt.	Ac.	Gal.	1 Th.	Tit.	1 Pet.	3 Jn
Mk	Rom.	Eph.	2 Th.	Phm.	2 Pet.	Jude
Lk.	1 C.	Phil.	1 Tim.	Heb.	1 Jn	Rev.
Jn	2 C.	Col.	2 Tim.	Jas	2 Jn	

JEWISH WRITINGS

Babylonian Talmud Tractates quoted include

Aboth	Aboth
B.B.	Baba Bathra
Sanh.	Sanhedrin
Shab.	Shabbath
Ta.	Tamid

BIBLIOGRAPHY

i. Commentaries on the Book of Revelation

Allo E. B. *St. Jean, l'apocalypse* (Etudes Bibliques), Paris, 1921
Behm J. *Die Offenbarung des Johannes* (Das Neue Testament Deutsch), Göttingen, 5th edn, 1949
Bousset W. *Die Offenbarung Johannes* (Kommentar begründet von H. A. W. Meyer) Göttingen, 9th edn, 1906
Caird G. B. *The Revelation of St. John the Divine* (Black's New Testament Commentaries), London, 1966
Cerfaux L. and Cambier J., *L'apocalypse de St. Jean lue aux chrétiens*, Paris, 1955
Charles R. H. *A Critical and Exegetical Commentary on the Revelation of St. John* (International Critical Commentary), Edinburgh, 2 vols, 1920
Farrer A. M. *The Revelation of St. John the Divine*, Oxford, 1964
Glasson T. F. *The Revelation of John* (The Cambridge Bible Commentary), Cambridge, 1965
Hendriksen W. *More than Conquerors. An Interpretation of the Book of Revelation*, Grand Rapids, Michigan, 1939
Hobbs H. H. *The Cosmic Drama. An Exposition of the Book of Revelation*, Waco, Texas, 1971
Hort F. J. A., *The Apocalypse of St. John I–III*, London, 1908
Kepler T. S. *The Book of Revelation*, New York, 1957
Kiddle M. *The Revelation of St. John* (The Moffat New Testament Commentary), London, 1940
Ladd G. E. *A Commentary on the Revelation of John*, Grand Rapids, Michigan, 1972
Lilje H. *The Last Book of the Bible*, Philadelphia, 1957
Lohmeyer E. *Die Offenbarung des Johannes* (Handbuch zum Neuen Testament), Tübingen, 2nd edn, 1953
Lohse E. *Die Offenbarung des Johannes* (Das Neue Testament Deutsch), Göttingen, 1960
Moffatt J. *The Revelation of St. John the Divine* (The Expositor's Greek Testament), London, 1910
Morris L. *The Revelation of St. John* (Tyndale Commentaries), London, 1969
Newbolt M. R. *The Book of Unveiling. A Study of the Revelation of St. John*, London, 1952
Peake A. S. *The Revelation of John*, London, 1920
Preston R. H. and Hanson A. T. *The Revelation of St. John the Divine* (The Torch Bible Commentaries), London, 1949
Schlatter A. *Die Briefe und die Offenbarung des Johannes* (Erläuterungen zum Neuen Testament), Stuttgart, 1938
Scott C. A. A. *Revelation* (The Century Bible), Edinburgh, 1902

9

Swete H. B. *The Apocalypse of St. John* London, 3rd edn, 1909
Zahn T. *Die Offenbarung des Johannes* (Kommentar zum Neuen Testament, herausg. v. T. Zahn), Leipzig, Erlangen, 2 vols, 1924

ii. Other Literature

Barclay W. *Letters to the Seven Churches*, London, 1957
Bietenhard W. *Das tausendjährige Reich*, Zürich, 1955
Burkitt F. C. *Jewish and Christian Apocalypses*, Oxford, 1914
Bousset W. *The Antichrist Legend*, London, 1896
Farrer A. M. *A Rebirth of Images*, London, 1949
Feuillet A. *L'Apocalypse: l'état de la question*, Paris, 1963
Gunkel H. *Schöpfung und Chaos in Urzeit und Endzeit*, Göttingen, 1895
Holtz T. *Die Christologie der Apokalypse des Johannes*, Berlin, 1962
Leonertz R. J. *The Apocalypse of Saint John*, London, 1947
Niles D. T. *As Seeing the Invisible*, London, 1962
Oman J. *The Book of Revelation*, Cambridge, 1923
Porter F. C. *The Messages of the Apocalyptical Writers*, London, 1905
Prigent P. *Apocalypse 12: Histoire de l'exégèse* (Beiträge zur Geschichte der Biblischen Exegese), Tübingen, 1959
Ramsay W. M. *The Letters to the Seven Churches of Asia*, London, 1904
Rissi M. *Time and History, A Study on the Revelation*, Richmond, Virginia, 1966
    The Future of the World. An Exegetical Study of Revelation 19:11–22:15 (Studies in Biblical Theology, 2nd series), London, 1972
Rowley H. H. *The Relevance of Apocalyptic*, London, 2nd edn, 1947
Satake A. *Die Gemeindeordnung in der Johannesapokalypse* (Wissenschaftliche Monographien zum Alten und Neuen Testament), Neukirchen-Vluyn, 1966
Scott E. F. *The Book of Revelation*, London, 1939
Shepherd M. H. *The Paschal Liturgy and the Apocalypse* (Ecumenical Studies in Worship), London, 1960
Stauffer E. *Christ and the Caesars*, London, 1955
Torrance T. *The Apocalypse Today*, London, 1960
Welch A. *Visions of the End. A Study in Daniel and Revelation*, London, 1922

Charles R. H. *The Apocrypha and Pseudepigrapha of the Old Testament*, 2 vols, Oxford, 1913
Kittel G. and Friedrich G. (ed.) *Theologisches Wörterbuch zum Neuen Testament*, Stuttgart, 1933, E. T. Grand Rapids 1964 (cited as *TWNT*)
Strack H. L. and Billerbeck P. *Kommentar zum Neuen Testament aus Talmud und Midrasch*, 5 vols, München, 1922–8 (cited as Strack-Billerbeck)

INTRODUCTION

to

The Book of Revelation

INTRODUCTION TO THE BOOK OF REVELATION

I. THE FORM OF THE WORK

The unique place which the Book of Revelation occupies in the Bible and in Christian tradition has led many to look upon it as though it has no counterpart in literature by which it may be judged, or from which guide-lines can be supplied. This assumption has encouraged an undisciplined freedom in the elucidation of the book such as would be inadmissible in other types of literature, and it has made possible that chaotic diversity of interpretation for which the book is notorious. The unique character of the work is indisputable, but it is a mistake to consider it to be without analogy. Within the first five verses of the prologue John employs three different categories of composition in referring to his work. The first word he pens is the term 'revelation', the Greek word for which is *apocalypsis*, and this self-description of the book has given the name to the whole class of writings with which it is most closely related, namely the 'apocalypses'. In verse 3 John speaks of his work as a 'prophecy', and in verse 4 he proceeds as though he were writing an 'epistle', or letter of instruction (cf. also v. 11). John's book takes its unusual character from its combination in a unique fashion of all three of these forms. To relate the work to them will help us to grasp its message in the way John wished it to be understood.

i. The Revelation as an Epistle

The *letter* as a form of instruction became established in Greek literature before Christian times. Its popularity as a form of treatise was aided through the rise of a multiplicity of centres of learning in the Greek-speaking world, by which the virtual monopoly of scholarship formerly enjoyed by Athens was ended. The letters of counsel written by Aristotle to Alexander the Great and to Themison king of Cyprus were well known, and Epicurus wrote letters of instruction to his followers. Accordingly we find letters used in a similar way by philosophers, moralists, scientists, physicians, and even comedians. It is not surprising that Christian leaders adopted this mode of instruction from the earliest times of the Church. The New Testament letters were intended to be read during services of worship (cf. Col. 4 : 16). The same is true of the Book of Revelation, as is evident from its introduction (1 : 3) and conclusion (22 : 6ff.), the letters to the seven churches (chs. 2–3), the hymns and songs scattered through the book, and the nature of the work as a whole.

An important corollary of this feature of the work is the relation which the book was intended to have to a group of Christian people in a known area of the world at a particular time in history. Nothing could be further from John's mind than the statement which occurs in the opening paragraph of the *Book of Enoch*, that what the prophet saw was 'not for this generation, but for a remote one which is for to come'. The situation and the needs of the churches in proconsular Asia were as truly in John's mind while he wrote as, say, the situation of the nearby churches of Galatia was present in Paul's mind and spurred him to write to them in the manner that he did a generation or so earlier. The circumstances of John's contemporaries naturally did not create John's theology of judgment and redemption, any more than those of the Galatian churches gave rise to Paul's gospel. But just as Paul was compelled to adapt his message to the needs of the Galatians, so John was constrained to adapt the Christian hope to the situation which was developing in Asia Minor. Whatever the precise date of the book, it is evident that the clouds of persecution were darkening the churches' sky in the writer's time. For him it was apparent that to be a Christian was to share in 'the tribulation and the kingdom and the patient endurance' which is the lot of those who live in the fellowship of Jesus (1 : 9). He himself was suffering exile, presumably for no other reason than his activity as a leader of Christian churches. There are hints in the letters to the seven churches that similar difficulties were being experienced in at least some of the churches (e.g., 2 : 10, 13), and the whole book is written in the conviction that such persecution would become universal. From various passages (above all, ch. 13) it would appear that the current adulation of the Roman emperor was assuming serious proportions in Asia Minor. For John this fore-shadowed the movement of the Antichrist, of which prophecy, ancient and modern, spoke. He therefore wrote to the churches for whom he had special responsibility, warning them of the gravity of the issues, and drawing out in accordance with the teaching of

biblical prophecy the ultimate consequences of what was beginning to come to pass. This message was for his friends in the seven
churches and for all who would receive it. By giving it the form of
a letter he lent to his appeal the highest degree of urgency and
effectiveness.

ii. The Revelation as an Apocalypse

The heading is strictly tautologous, for *apocalypse* means revelation.
Yet it may be allowed to stand, for the term apocalypse is generally reserved for a particular class of writings, chiefly Jewish, which
claimed to reveal or unveil God's purpose in history. The works so
characterized found their classic representative in the book of
Daniel, which was the first complete work of this order, and whose
style was imitated in a succession of works produced during the
two centuries before and the century after the birth of Jesus.

The apocalyptic movement, as expressed in this literature, may
be regarded as the child of prophecy. As in prophecy, the great
theme of apocalyptic writings was the coming of the day of the
Lord and the kingdom of God. But the doctrine became more
systematized, even more transcendent, and reflection on the relation of that day to the processes of history led to the formulation of
a kind of philosophy of history, of which the all important factor
was God's sovereign purpose working towards its triumphant end
despite the resistance of evil powers. Unlike prophecy, apocalyptic
was literary rather than oral, composed in longer prose episodes
rather than in short poetic oracles. This facilitated the habit of
apocalyptic writers freely to borrow materials both from Old
Testament prophetic works and from other apocalypses. This was
not thought of as plagiarism; rather it was a product of their conviction that the word of the Lord would surely be fulfilled. Consequently the apocalyptists rewrote earlier prophecies, freshly
combined them, and applied them to the differing situations of
their times.

Perhaps the most striking characteristic of these writings is their
pseudonymity. Whereas prophecy was usually the direct utterance of a prophet, speaking openly on behalf of the Lord God of
Israel to the writer's contemporaries, apocalyptic writings were
commonly written in the name of ancient saints and heroes of
Israel's history. Accordingly we find several books ascribed to

Enoch, an *Apocalypse of Abraham* and a *Testament of Abraham*, *Testaments of the Twelve Patriarchs*, the *Assumption of Moses*, *Psalms of Solomon*, an *Apocalypse of Ezra*, two apocalypses ascribed to *Baruch* the scribe of Jeremiah, and several books purporting to be *Oracles* from the Sibyl, written for the benefit of pagans. The reasons for ascribing these books to men of earlier times are still the subject of debate. But whatever the truth may be, the motives at work were evidently the product of conditions and convictions prevailing in Israel's religious history and have little in common with forgery.[1]

Already in the prophetic writings of the Old Testament we find a strong tendency to use highly coloured poetic and symbolic language, as when Amos, in his opening oracle, writes:

> The Lord roars from Zion ... .
> the pastures of the shepherds mourn,
> and the top of Carmel withers (1:2).

And Micah declares that when the Lord steps forth out of his place,

> The mountains will melt under him
> and the valleys will be cleft,
> like wax before the fire,
> like waters poured down a steep place (1:4).

Conversely in the day when God reveals his judgment and delivers his people,

> The mountains shall drip sweet wine,
> and the hills shall flow with milk (Joel 3:18).

This is sheer poetry. But the prophets go beyond this, and in their oracles employ pictures drawn from ancient times. Consider for example the following:

> Awake, awake, put on strength,
> O arm of the Lord;
> awake, as in days of old,
> the generations of long ago.
> Was it not thou that didst cut Rahab in pieces,
> that didst pierce the dragon?
> Was it not thou that didst dry up the sea,
> the waters of the great deep;

---

[1] For an illuminating discussion of the issues, see D. S. Russell, *The Method and Message of Jewish Apocalyptic*, London, 1964, pp. 127ff.

> that didst make the depths of the sea a way
>   for the redeemed to pass over?
> And the ransomed of the Lord shall return,
>   and come to Zion with singing;
> everlasting joy shall be upon their heads;
>   they shall obtain joy and gladness,
>   and sorrow and sighing shall flee away (Isa. 51 : 9ff.).

Here is a prayer for God to act mightily as he did 'in the days of old'. The pagans in Babylon told of the slaying of the monster of the deep by a god of heaven, and that from its body the world was made. The prophet declares that the Lord of hosts is the only dragon-slayer, and he it is who made the heavens and the earth. He moreover slew another dragon, namely Egypt, when Israel languished in slavery, and he brought his people through the waters to the promised land (an apt comparison, since the 'dragon' was a sea monster). This he will do again, when he performs a further act of redemption in delivering his people from oppressors and bringing them into the inheritance of the kingdom of God. The prophet's language in this passage therefore entails the use of ancient near-eastern mythology, the prophetic typology of the second exodus, and a belief that the last things will be as the first. This kind of symbolic thought and language was taken over by the apocalyptists and developed to a degree unknown before. If sometimes it degenerated into an artificial and even banal style, it was capable of powerful and highly evocative expression, as in the seventh chapter of Daniel, and it comes to its height of development in the book of Revelation.

The closest modern parallel to this mode of communication is the political cartoon, which has gained an established place in the popular press all over the world. The purpose of a cartoon is to embody a message relating to a contemporary situation, whether it be of local, national, or international import. Many of the symbols employed by cartoonists are stereotyped. Some of their representative figures are human (like John Bull and Uncle Sam), others are animal (e.g., the lion for Britain, the bear for Russia, the eagle for USA), and occasionally the animals are given human faces, identifying leaders of the nations in their representative actions. Frequently the situations depicted are deliberately exaggerated, and even made grotesque, in order that the message may be made plain. But no one complains of that—except perhaps the

people represented. The effectiveness of the cartoon was illustrated about a year ago from the time of writing these lines: a
cartoon by Lowe relating to strikes which were affecting the production of newspapers so infuriated certain printers' employees,
they withdrew their labour so as to prevent the paper in which the
cartoon appeared from being distributed. Now it would be overpressing the parallel to suggest that the apocalyptists were religious
cartoonists, for much of their writing is not in picture form. But it
would not be misleading to compare their works with writings
frequently illustrated by drawings, and at times containing whole
chapters of strip cartoon. The book of Revelation uses the cartoon
method more consistently than any other work of this order.

It is important to observe that the symbols by which the contemporary political forces and the spiritual powers of heaven and
hell are portrayed were as traditional as Britannia and the
British lion, the Russian bear, and the Chinese dragon. For
example the monsters in Daniel 7, which emerge from the sea as
representations of world empires and culminate in the last antigod kingdom, are variants of the evil sea-monster Tiamat which
defied the gods of heaven. The earliest readers of the book will
have recognized the caricature immediately, and approved of the
judgment thereby implied as to the nature of the tyrannical empire of their day and its impending doom from the God of heaven.
This is the source of the portrayals of the antichristian empire and
ruler in the book of Revelation. Significantly the writer did not
draw immediately on the book of Daniel for his description of the
dragon with seven heads and ten horns, for not all the details are
contained in Daniel's descriptions. John drew on the living tradition about the monster, and he followed in the wake of the Old
Testament prophets and contemporary apocalyptists in applying
the symbol to the oppressor power of his day. What to the un-
initiated modern reader appears grotesque imagery, spoke with
power to John's fellow Christians. The same applies to other
symbols drawn from the stream of tradition, perhaps above all to
those linked with the typology of the second exodus, and those
relating to the city of God, wherein the images of Old Testament
prophecy and of contemporary non-Christian religious beliefs
flow together to produce a picture of unparalleled beauty and
power.

Here it is desirable to recall two features of Jewish apocalypses

which we have mentioned, in one of which John separates himself
from the rest and in the other of which he follows their procedure.
Unlike other apocalyptists, John writes in his own name, not under
a pseudonym. Consonant with this his book has no history under
the guise of prophecy. The latter was a by-product of a writer
assuming the name of a saint of ancient times, for if the venerable
'prophet' was to issue a prophecy concerning events contemporary
with the writer, it was necessary to bridge the period from the
times of the saint to his own day. John had no need of such a
device. He wrote in the name of the living Christ, not in the name
of an Enoch or Abraham or Elijah or Isaiah, and he believed
himself to be under the inspiration of the Holy Spirit, burdened
with a revelation wherein he was guided by an angel of God for
the Church of his own day. This fact so impressed Zahn that he
declared it sufficient to mark off John's Apocalypse from all others
as authentic in contrast to imitations.[1] This judgment would be
unfair to the motives which led to pseudonymity, but it points
to a characteristic which we shall have to consider later, namely,
John's consciousness of being a prophet of the Lord to whom 'the
word of God and the testimony of Jesus' had been committed with
authority.

That does, however, bring us to the feature which John shares
with other apocalyptists. He freely makes use of existing materials,
both prophetic and apocalyptic, which serve as vehicles for his
message. The realization that earlier visions were incorporated
into the Revelation led expositors and critics of a previous generation to believe that the book must have been composed of more
than one work. Such views did not take into account the manifest
unity of the Revelation as we have it, and the thoroughness with
which all extraneous elements have been made to subserve the
Christian message. One controlling hand, one master mind has
been at work to produce a vision of the end wherein many originally diverse elements have been worked into a panorama of
wonderful symmetry. For the understanding of the meaning of the
parts, it is often necessary to distinguish between the meaning
which the original oracle had and the purpose for which John used
it. In illustration the reader is referred to the commentary on
chapters 7, 11, 12, 17, 21. Perhaps the outstanding example of
John's method in this respect is the vision of chapter 12, wherein

[1] *Introduction to the New Testament*, vol. III, Edinburgh, 1909, pp. 386ff.

an international myth which embodied the beliefs, not to say
yearnings, of adherents of pagan religions for one who has power
to deliver from the evil forces of the universe, has been taken over
by a Jew and applied to the biblical promise of a Messiah. John by
the addition of a mere sentence or so has indicated the Deliverer's
identity, eliminated all rival claimants to the position of world-
redeemer, and shown how the hopes of the whole world and the
promises of God made known through the prophets reach their
fulfilment in the Lamb who was slain. No doctrinal declaration or
formal argument as to the relative merits of Jesus over against the
Babylonian Marduk or Greek Apollo or Egyptian Horus or Iranian
Saoshyant could have presented the belief in Jesus as Saviour and
Lord with such dramatic power as the cartoon of chapter 12. This
alone should vindicate John's method, if justification were needed.
Admission of this procedure, however, has for a corollary the
recognition that many of the details in John's pictures no longer
have relevance for him. It is the leading ideas in their new context to which attention has to be paid. The rest supply the scenic
background for his parables.

iii. The Revelation as Christian Prophecy

There will be at least some readers of this book who will question
whether the Revelation should be described as either *prophecy* or
Christian. For there is a trend of thought, more discernible on the
European continent than in the English-speaking world, which
draws the contrasts between the conceptual worlds of prophecy
and apocalyptic more sharply than we have done. Those who
follow it think of prophecy in terms of the declaration of God's
demand on man now in the light of his acts of judgment and grace,
but apocalypse they view as mainly concerned with cosmology—
with the appearance and content of the seven heavens, and the
programme of things to come, duly dated. On this reckoning
prophecy responds to the hunger of man for God, whereas apocalyptic answers the hunger of man for his curiosity about the
future to be satisfied. While the former can be Christian, the latter
is not.

The intention of this contrast is comprehensible, but such a
black and white statement of it over-simplifies the issues and rests
on an incorrect estimate of the evidence. John will not have been

unacquainted with those who sought to satisfy man's insatiable appetite for knowledge of the future. There were more fortune-tellers in his day than there are in ours, and to him the distinction between them and the prophet of the Lord will have been as night and day. It was the difference between false prophecy and true. The distinction between a desire to know the future for curiosity's sake and a willingness to heed warning and encouragement about things to come was clearly present in John's mind. It is assumed in the first and last beatitudes of his book, both of which are directed to encouraging people to hear and keep what is written therein (1 : 3, 22 : 7). One cannot 'keep' the judgments of God and the triumph of his rule and the descent of the city of God from heaven, but one can keep faith and obedience in the light of their advent. To inspire that obedience of faith is, on John's doubly reiterated statement, the purpose of his book. To minimize that element in John's motivation and in the actual content of the Revelation (for it extends beyond the two beatitudes into the entire work) is to do injustice alike to the book and its author.

Admittedly the keeping of faith and obedience, for which John wrote, is set in relation to the resistance to God which John saw at work in the world and in the light of God's purpose for man in his world. Anyone who believes that nothing can be known about the purpose of God in history and for humanity will be compelled to reject John's picture of the future in toto. The integrity of those who maintain such a viewpoint will naturally be respected, but they on their part should also recognize that in adopting such an attitude they distance themselves from the generality of the prophets, from Jesus and the apostles and the writers of the New Testament, and from the historic Church. The question whether it is the army which is out of step is neither irrelevant nor im-pertinent.

The opening words in John's work speak of it as both an 'apo-calypse' and a 'prophecy' (vv. 1–3). In writing it the author num-bers himself with the prophets of the Church (19 : 10, 22 : 9; see also 10 : 7, 11 : 18, 22 : 6). The content of the prophecy he des-cribes as 'the word of God and the testimony of Jesus Christ, even all that he saw'. That is, he claims it to be an authoritative revelation given through the medium of vision. Visions belong to the acknow-ledged media of prophecy. John will have reflected on those he experienced, and interpreted them by the aid of the symbolism

which had become established in apocalyptic literature and which
was part of the furniture of his mind. The doctrine embodied in
the revelation, however, has been determined through another
source, namely, the gospel as interpreted in the tradition of
Christian prophecy.

Here we recall that prophecy was no isolated phenomenon in
the Church, nor was the prophet the solitary figure which he
tended to be in Israelite history. Rather prophecy was constitutive
of the Church, with a significant role in the worship of the Church
and in the shaping of its thought. In contemporary Judaism a
favourite name for the Holy Spirit was 'the Spirit of prophecy',
for inspiration was the characteristic function of the Spirit. It was
quite natural therefore for Luke to represent the sending of the
Holy Spirit at the great Pentecost festival as the occasion when all
the Lord's people became prophets, seeing that the Holy Spirit
came upon them all (see Ac. 2 : 16ff., and cf. vv. 38f.). This did
not render needless the ministry of individuals specially gifted by
the Spirit for prophetic ministry. Luke calls attention to the prophets of Jerusalem, of whom Agabus was conspicuous (Ac.
11 : 27f., 21 : 10f.), and the prophets of Antioch, through whom
Paul and Barnabas were called for missionary service (Ac.
13 : 1ff.), and the prophet daughters of Philip (Ac. 21 : 9). Paul's
position was not very different from Luke's, in that he views prophecy as a gift to which all Christians can aspire, and for which all
should pray (1 C. 14 : 1, 39). But he also acknowledges some as
possessing the prophetic gift in special measure, and these rank
second only to apostles (1 C. 12 : 28). In Ephesians 2 : 20 the
prophets share with apostles the function of constituting a foundation for the Church, presumably in view of their role as bearers of
'the testimony of Jesus'.[1] The contribution of Christian prophecy
in the Church's formative years was evidently of major importance. It was not a phenomenon apart from the main stream of the
Church's life but a prime means of her witness.

John, then, sets himself in the context of the prophetic ministry
within the Church, and he claims that his message is one with the
prophetic testimony as a whole ('the word of God and the testimony

[1] Or, if the *NEB* is right, they jointly lay the foundation of the Church,
which is Christ. Since the task of apostles and prophets is to bear witness to
God's redemptive action and the revelation of his will in and through Christ,
the difference of interpretation is not so great as may at first appear.

of Jesus'). Was he justified in so doing? Despite dissentient
voices raised from time to time, the Church through the ages has
generally believed that he was (hence the place accorded to the
book in the Canon). In this judgment her instincts were better
than some of her reasons for it.

G. Friedrich has defined early Christian prophecy as 'speech
borne from the inspiration of charismatic preachers, through
which God's plan of salvation for the world and the Church is
made known, as also the will of God in the life of the individual
Christian'. He continues, '(The prophet) does not only say what
God purposes to do, he also proclaims what God wills to be done
by men ... The prophet exhorts the indolent and weary, as he
consoles those who are tempted and strengthens their courage.'[1]
Friedrich's definition accords strikingly with the nature of the
book of Revelation, and his statement of the aim of the prophet
can be amply illustrated from that book.

John's adoption of the style of an apocalyptist in no way hinders
him from thinking as a prophet. This appears with all clarity in
the letters to the seven churches, which in content (and even
style) are extraordinarily reminiscent of the prophetic oracles of
the Old Testament.[2] The doom song of chapter 18 could have
been lifted out of an Old Testament prophetic writing, and indeed
has been written in conscious reminiscence of similar Old Testament compositions. Apart from such obvious examples of prophetic writing, it is perhaps not unworthy of note that most of
John's work, even in its highly apocalyptic passages, consists of
series of prophetic-like oracles, strung together. This is immediately apparent from chapter 14, which is a group of seven little
oracles, giving almost an independent view of the end of the age.
It can also be seen in the section 19 : 1–21 : 8, which affords a
succession of short paragraphs, describing the praise of heaven at
the judgment on 'Babylon', the parousia, the kingdom of Christ,
the last judgment, and the new creation. The like applies to the
portrayal of the three series of messianic judgments, and the

---

[1] Article on prophecy, *TWNT* VI, pp. 849f.
[2] Lohse aptly compares the seven letters with the seven oracles of Amos,
chapters 1–2; *Offenbarung d. Johannes*, Göttingen, 1960, p. 21. Each letter commences with the formula 'the words of' = 'Thus saith (the Lord)'. The phrase
occurs elsewhere in the New Testament only in Acts 21:11, in the utterance of
the prophet Agabus.

episodes which punctuate them (6 : 1–8 : 5, 8 : 6–11 : 19, 15–16). From the standpoint of our present interest it is to be observed that while the imagery in many of these passages is luxuriant, the events so symbolized are seen 'as in a glass, darkly'. At times they are scarcely discernible through the haze. It is astonishing, in view of the nature of John's book, that his representation of the parousia in 19 : 11f. is so manifestly clothed in symbol, it is impossible to glean from it an idea of the event itself. All we can gather is that the Lord will 'come' and act in sovereign power to judge and reign. The brevity of John's description of the millennial kingdom in chapter 20 raises more questions than it answers, and the economy of language regarding the new creation in 21 : 1ff. is so stringent as to make it difficult to know what he really means by it. Even the lengthy description of the city of God in 21 : 9ff. proves, on examination, to be a succession of symbols, whose measurements and materials have exclusively to do with theology and not with architecture. Whoever maintains that the Revelation was written to satisfy curiosity has not really pondered the book. And he who seeks to compile from it a history-in-advance will be either disappointed or deceived, for it is not there to be written. John's visions of the end are those of an impressionist artist rather than the pictures of a photographer. For the most part they defy precision in application. But they convey sufficient to warn men of the end of state-idolatry, and enough about the kingdom of God, to encourage them to faith and adoration of God.

Granting that John's work may be classed as *prophecy*, to what extent is it *Christian*?[1] In the opinion of some, very little at all. To Bultmann the Revelation presents 'a weakly Christianized Judaism'. He views its eschatological outlook as entirely futurist, and the significance of Christ in it as mainly to provide a certainty to hope which Jewish apocalypses did not have.[2] Dodd similarly regarded the eschatology of the Revelation as virtually pre-Christian, on the ground that it relegates to a secondary place the essential features of the gospel, has a view of God below that of much Old Testament teaching, and gives a picture of a fierce

[1] For a fuller statement of this issue, see my article, 'How Christian is the Book of Revelation?' (in the *Festschrift* for L. L. Morris, *Reconciliation and Hope*, Exeter, 1974).

[2] *Theology of the New Testament*, vol. II, London, 1955, p. 175.

Messiah far removed from the Jesus of the primitive preaching.[1]
The three objections thus relate to the book's Christology, eschatology, and its view of God in relation to judgment. We shall briefly
examine these, from the aspect of their 'Christian' content.

The Christology of the Revelation, when compared with that of
other writings of the New Testament, is 'advanced'.[2] Constantly
the attributes of God are ascribed to Christ, as in the opening
vision of the first chapter, which is significantly a vision of Christ
and not of God. The lineaments of the risen Lord are those of the
Ancient of Days and of his angel in the book of Daniel (chs. 7 and
10). Christ is confessed as Alpha and Omega (22 : 13), as God is
also (1 : 8). The implications of the claim are drawn out in the
book as a whole, wherein Christ is presented as the mediator of
creation (3 : 14), as he is of redemption (ch. 5) and of the final
kingdom (19 : 11ff.). Strangely enough it is in the context of the
parousia that the Christ is called 'the Word of God' (19 : 13). If
the term calls attention to the function of the Christ to be the
bearer of the revelation of God in his person and action,[3] there is
nevertheless a fitness in its application to him who in his parousia
fulfils the purpose of the creation initiated through him. More
central is the concept of the Christ as the Lamb of God, which
reflects a highly original insight into the relation of Jewish and
Christian interpretations of the Messiah. Here the prophet has
taken a typical apocalyptic representation of the Messiah as the
young Warrior-Lamb, raised from the midst of God's flock to be
its leader and champion,[4] and transformed it by conjoining with
it the Christian conception of the crucified Christ, who has
wrought the world's redemption by the sacrifice of himself—God's
paschal lamb, through whom the greater exodus is wrought (ch. 5).
The kingdom which is to come is 'the kingdom of our Lord and of
his Christ' (11 : 15). In the closing vision of the city of God, therefore, God and the Lamb are united as Lord of the kingdom and
source of its blessedness. It is especially noteworthy that John
depicts the throne of God and the Lamb as the source of the river
of water of life in the city, thereby conveying the notion of a single

[1] *The Apostolic Preaching and its Development*, 2nd edn, London, 1944, pp. 40f.
[2] For a comprehensive treatment, see T. Holtz, *Die Christologie der Apokalypse
des Johannes*, 2nd edn, Berlin, 1971.
[3] Holtz, op. cit., p. 177.
[4] As in *Test. Jos.* 19:8ff.

throne, a single rule, and a single source of life. He adds, 'his servants shall worship him; they shall see his face, and his name shall be on their foreheads' (22 : 3f.). In the context it is difficult to interpret the pronoun 'his' as meaning anything other than 'God and the Lamb' as a unity (see the exposition). The Lamb remains the mediator of judgment and redemption, yet he is inseparable from the God who enacts his works of judgment and redemption through him.

This illustrates the inseparability of Christology from eschatology. In the Revelation the redemptive action of God through Christ is not an adjunct to the expectation of a future kingdom, but controls the understanding of the kingdom in the book. It results in an expectation of the future kingdom quite different from that in the Old Testament prophets and Jewish apocalypses. The future which is awaited is the revelation of that sovereignty which has its decisive beginning in the incarnation, death, and resurrection of Christ. The fulcrum of this book is not the parousia and the descent of the city of God, described in its closing visions, but the vision of God and the Lamb in chapters 4–5. This vision is in two parts, first of God exalted in his transcendent majesty, reigning in a heaven untroubled by the storms of history, and then of the Lamb through whom God makes his saving sovereignty effective in the universe. By delaying the vision of the Lamb to the second part, greater prominence is given to his action and to its universal consequences. The slain and risen Lamb has accomplished redemption, he has ascended the throne of God and commenced his reign with the Father. The turn of the ages, therefore, lies in the past. The exaltation of the Christ has taken place, and the acclamation of his sovereignty has been rendered by the hosts of heaven. Its acknowledgement by the whole creation, described at the conclusion of chapter 5, alone lies in the future. The succeeding chapters of the Revelation show that a special exercise of the divine sovereignty must take place before earth's rebellion is subdued and the universe acclaims its Lord; but this is the outworking of the central action of the vision. The remarkable feature of the vision in chapter 5 is its unitary nature. The process of redemption and the establishment of the sovereignty of God is an indivisible whole, so the divine intervention from the incarnation to the parousia is presented as a single act. This unheard-of concentration of the action of God in Christ is a different way of presenting the 'now' and the 'not yet' of the kingdom from that which is seen in other writers of the New Testament. It views the redemptive process *sub specie aeternitatis*, and bids us see that the victory of God in Christ is one, and that it has been won.

The clear statement of this viewpoint in the crucial vision of the Revelation suggests that it holds the key to the eschatology of the whole work. This is confirmed as we observe that the remaining visions flow from that of chapter 5 and develop its content. The Christ who takes from God the book of destiny in virtue of his achieved redemption, sets in motion the messianic judgments as he looses the seals one by one, and these lead to the coming of the kingdom, since the 'book' is either a document conveying God's covenant promise of the kingdom or a testament which bequeaths it. This principle of the Christ leading on the judgments of history to their goal in the kingdom of God is assumed in the remaining parallel series, and they in turn give way to the revelation of the city of God at the end. To place the weight of this interpretation of eschatology solely on the future is like trying to stand a pyramid on its apex. To view it as on a par with pre-Christian Jewish eschatology is simply untrue to the evidence. There is no analogy to the eschatological doctrine of Revelation chapter 5 in all Jewish apocalyptic, and that for a simple reason: it is an exposition of the gospel of the crucified and risen Christ, such as only a Christian prophet can give.

From the foregoing it will be apparent that the doctrine of God in the Revelation cannot be taken by itself, but must be viewed in the light of the Christology, soteriology, and eschatology of the book. The central vision of chapters 4–5 does not present us with the figure of the Redeemer alone. The conjunction of the two chapters shows us the God of creation as the God of redemption, accomplishing his sovereign and gracious will through the crucified and risen Christ. If Paul presents us with the gospel that God in Christ was reconciling the world to himself (2 C. 5 : 19), John yields a gospel of God in Christ redeeming the world for himself. It is God in Christ who delivers mankind, and God in Christ who judges mankind. This inevitably leads to a belief that God is revealed in the acts of Christ, and that Christ is the revelation of his Father (in the Revelation the concept of God as Father is exclusively reserved for his relation to Christ). As is the Christ, so is the Father; as the Father, so the Christ.

But where does the accent lie? In judgment, or in salvation? A just answer perhaps would be in the conjunction of both, though John would almost certainly view the latter as ultimate. This is illustrated if we ask why the Revelation was written. It was not written in order to hold threats of damnation before sinners, but to encourage saints to press on, despite all opposition, and to win the inheritance. The Revelation was written that men might enter the city of God, and the vision of the city is the true climax of the book—its goal, not simply its finis.

In this connection the question may be raised whether John's method of composition has not led many of his readers to misunderstand his concept of judgment in relation to the kingdom. For the three series of messianic judgments, represented under the imagery of the seals, trumpets, and bowl-cups, are almost certainly intended to portray from three different aspects a single, short period of judgment in history. Many readers, failing to recognize the parallelism, have received the impression that John narrates wave after wave of judgments in apparently sickening and senseless profusion, and so have gained an exaggerated estimate of the place of judgment in John's thought. The role of these events in the typology of the second exodus—judgments on another and more fearful Pharaoh (the Antichrist) who resists God and oppresses his people—is similarly overlooked. As in the book of Exodus so in the Revelation, the crucial event is not the 'plagues' but the redemption which leads to the new world.

If the question be asked whether a book in which the judgment of God prominently figures can be Christian, comparison must be made with other foundational Christian writings. It is easy, and tempting, to view the synoptic gospels in a generalized way and assume that Jesus spoke words of love alone and not of judgment; but that is to ignore so much of what Jesus said as to distort what remains. The Sermon on the Mount begins with beatitudes of the kingdom and concludes with a parable of judgment. Such a complementary presentation of kingdom and judgment is characteristic in the teaching of Jesus.[1] The contrast is sharpened almost to paradox in the Fourth Gospel, wherein the cross is viewed in terms of judgment, as truly as in the Revelation. This is apparent not only in such a striking saying as John 12:31f. (cf. Rev. 12:10),

---

[1] Consider, e.g., Mt. 8:11f; 11:5–24; 12:28–32, 38–42; 13:10–17, 24–30, 47ff; 18:1–9; 25:1–13, 14–30, 31–46.

but also in the central paragraph of John 3 : 16–21, wherein the judgment of the world is represented as taking place in the cross of Christ, and God's judgment is rooted in the love that gave the Son for incarnation and death.[1] The representations of judgment in the epistles of the New Testament are too numerous to warrant mention. How does the Revelation relate to all these? Its emphasis on judgment is undoubtedly more intense and prolonged than in any epistle or gospel. To no small extent that may have been due less to a divergence between John's theology and that of other New Testament writers than to the nature of his situation and the prospect which he believed the Church of his time faced. John contemplated a world giving its allegiance to the Antichrist and declaring war to the death on the Church. This he interpreted as the work of evil powers in their endeavour to make wickedness triumph in the world and so to frustrate the good purpose of God for it. For the 'destroyers of the earth' (11 : 18), who debased themselves to the likeness of the Devil whom they served (22 : 15), he foresaw annihilating judgment, unless they repented and listened to the eternal gospel (14 : 6f.). Accordingly he applied the teaching of the Church's prophetic tradition to the situation as he saw it unfolding. It is significant that where Paul deals in brief compass with the subject of apostasy under the Antichrist, he too adduces elements of the prophetic tradition and speaks of judgment from heaven in unusually severe terms (2 Th. 2 : 1–17). It was Swete's conviction that John's work is a revelation of the 'severity of God' rendered necessary by the nature of the times, and that it forms a needful complement to the revelation of God in the gospel and the epistles.[2] The corollary of that is the desirability of reading the Revelation in conjunction with the rest of the New Testament, and

[1] 'There would be no judgment at all were it not for the event of God's love.' (Bultmann on John 3:16ff. His exposition of the whole passage is deeply perceptive.)

[2] 'A revelation of the "severity of God" was needed by the Churches, which were hard pressed by the laxity of pagan life and the claim to Divine honours made by the masters of the Empire. The Apocalyptist meets the immoralities and blasphemies of heathendom by a fresh setting forth of the majesty of the One God and a restatement of His sole right to the worship of men. Thus he represents a view of the Divine Character which, apart from his book, would be nearly wanting in the New Testament, and supplies a necessary complement to the gentler teaching of the Gospels and Epistles.' (*The Apocalypse of St. John*, 3rd edn, London, 1909, p. clx.)

the rest of the New Testament along with the Revelation in order
to secure a balanced view. That, of course, is not unusual. The
Synoptic Gospels without the Fourth Gospel would be wanting;
the Fourth Gospel without the Synoptics would be misleading.
The epistles require supplementing by the gospels, and the gospels
by the epistles, if we are to gain a mature understanding of the
Christian Faith. The Revelation is the last book of the canon. If it
is the crown of biblical eschatology, it requires to be read in conjunction with the works which precede it; and they are incom-
plete without it.

2. THE CONTENT AND STRUCTURE OF THE REVELATION

The book commences with a brief prologue, stating its origin and
conveying the writer's customary greeting, together with a doxology to Christ and two prophetic sayings which announce the
theme of the book. This is followed by an account of John's vision
of the risen Christ on Patmos. The passage recalls and invites comparison with narratives in the Old Testament wherein the prophets recount their experiences of a call to the prophetic ministry.
Characteristically the object of a prophet's vision in the new age is
the risen Christ, not God in his solitary glory. And the occasion
probably indicates not the commencement of John's prophetic
ministry, but the commission to write this particular vision of the
kingdom.

The letters to seven churches in proconsular Asia follow in
chapters 2–3. These letters are set in every case in relation to the
vision described in chapter 1, to the situation of the church
addressed, and to the closing vision of the kingdom of Christ and
the city of God in chapters 20–22. By the generalization which
concludes each one, the messages to the individual congregations
are applied to all the churches—to the seven, and to those beyond
their circle in Christendom generally.

As the vision of the risen Lord in chapter 1 leads into the seven
letters and is related to them, so in chapters 4–5 a vision of heaven
is given which introduces the main body of the Revelation. This
vision of God and the Lamb, as we have already noted, supplies
the key to the theology of the entire work, but it also occupies a
key position in the structure of the book. It initiates the process of
events leading to the unveiling of the final kingdom (chs. 6–19),

and at the same time by the symbolism determines the series of messianic judgments which immediately follows (the seven seals which open the book of destiny, 6: 1–8: 5).

At this point a decision has to be made on how the remainder of the book is to be construed. Are chapters 6–19 to be viewed as a continuous narration of events leading to the parousia? Or are we to regard the three series of messianic judgments, set forth under the symbolism of the seals, trumpets, and cups of wrath, as parallel? The present writer is persuaded that the latter interpretation alone accords with the evidence. This is more apparent in the second and third series of judgments than in the first. The trumpet-judgments clearly bring us to the end of the age. At the sounding of the seventh trumpet voices in heaven proclaim, 'The kingdom of the world has become the kingdom of our Lord and of his Christ', and God is worshipped because 'thou hast taken thy great power and begun to reign . . . Thy wrath came, and the time for the dead to be judged, for rewarding thy servants . . .' (11 : 15ff.). Similarly when the seventh cup of wrath is poured out a voice from the throne of God declares, 'It is done!' (16 : 17). Had the first series of judgments concluded with a like unambiguity no one would have doubted that John was operating with a threefold representation of the signs of the end. But the seventh seal leads to an uncertain episode. 'When the Lamb opened the seventh seal, there was silence in heaven for about half an hour. Then I saw the seven angels who stand before God, and seven trumpets were given to them' (8 : 1f.). The prayers of the saints were presented on the altar before the throne (8 : 3ff.) and the narration of the seven trumpets begins. The impression is given that the seventh seal is opened in order to usher in the events heralded by the seven trumpets. This, however, is not John's intention. The opening of the sixth seal brings shattering catastrophes in the universe. 'There was a great earthquake; and the sun became black as sackcloth, the full moon became like blood, and the stars of the sky fell to the earth as the fig tree sheds its winter fruit when shaken by a gale; the sky vanished like a scroll that is rolled up, and every mountain and island was removed from its place.' The wicked call on the mountains and rocks, 'Fall on us and hide us from the face of him who is seated on the throne and from the wrath of the Lamb; for the great day of their wrath has come' (6 : 12ff.). This language permits one interpretation alone: the last day has come. The only thing that can now take place is the advent of Christ and all that accompanies it. Every clause of the passage cites standard prophetic anticipations of the day of the Lord. By utilizing them John makes it plain that the end has arrived and that the Lord is now to be unveiled in his kingdom. How then are we to interpret the episode of the seventh seal? It is a dramatic portrayal of the truth that the kingdom comes in answer to the prayers of God's people. This accounts for the silence of heaven: it takes place that the prayers of the saints may be solemnly offered on God's altar. Thereupon the fire of judgment falls upon the earth, and the saints are vindicated as they receive the kingdom.

The three series of judgments, therefore, describe under different images a single short period in history, namely, the time of the end which precedes the coming of Christ's kingdom. John's complex organization of these judgments is almost certainly due to the precedent of Leviticus 26, wherein Israel is warned of the consequences of apostasy: 'I will multiply your calamities seven times' (reiterated in vv. 18, 21, 24, 28). By triplicating his portrayal of the judgments John builds up to the advent of Christ in an awe-inspiring climax.

The descriptions of judgments however are themselves not allowed to proceed without interruption. They are interspersed with episodes of varying length, the chief intention of which is to shed light on what happens to the Church and on the nature of her task during the great distress. Between the sixth and seventh seals two visions are set, the one describing the sealing of the faithful for their protection in the time of trial, and the other their consolation in the coming kingdom (ch. 7). Another interlude occurs between the sixth and seventh trumpets, confirming John in his prophetic witness and depicting the Church's call to bear witness in her period of suffering (chs. 10–11). The longest interruption in the flow of the visions occurs in chapters 12–14. It sets the conflict between the Church and the state on the background of the age-long conflict between the powers of darkness and the God of heaven, and draws a vivid picture of the kind of pressure to which the Church is subject when Caesar demands what belongs to God. After the description of the judgments initiated by the outpoured cups of wrath (chs. 15–16), the prophet holds up once more his description of the coming of Christ and the kingdom in order to show the reader how the antichristian empire falls prey to its own forces of destruction (chs. 17–18). Then at last the revelation of Christ is portrayed, and all that is bound up with it in relation to his kingdom—the last judgment, the new creation, and the city of God (chs. 19–22).

An epilogue, summing up and pressing home the lessons of the book, brings the whole to a conclusion (22 : 6–25).

The structure of the book may therefore be tabled as follows:

1 : 1–8	Prologue
1 : 9–20	The Call of John to Prophesy
2–3	The Letters to the Churches
4–5	The Vision of Heaven
6 : 1–8 : 5	The Judgments of the Seven Seals
	ch. 7 *Interlude:* The Sealing of the 144,000 and the Triumph of the Countless Multitude
8 : 6–11 : 19	The Judgments of the Seven Trumpets
	10 : 1–11 : 13 *Interlude:* The Angel and the Little Scroll, The Two Witnesses
12–14	The Conflict between the Church and the Evil Powers
15–16	The Judgments of the Seven Bowl-Cups
17 : 1–19 : 10	The Reign and Ruin of the City of the Antichrist
19 : 11–22 : 5	The Revelation of Christ and the City of God
22 : 6–21	Epilogue

3. THE AUTHORSHIP AND DATE OF THE REVELATION

It is impossible to consider the authorship of the Revelation without taking into account its relationship to the Fourth Gospel, partly because of the tradition of the Church that ascribes all five Johannine writings to John the Apostle, and partly because of the peculiar differences and connections between the thought and style of the Revelation and the Gospel.

The issues were remarkably well grasped and expounded in the third century AD by Dionysius, bishop of Alexandria.[1] Dionysius

---

[1] His arguments are set forth at length by Eusebius, *History of the Church*, VII. 25.

was disturbed at the spread of millennial teaching in his diocese. He laboured to show first that the Revelation is not to be interpreted in a literal sense, and secondly, that, contrary to popular opinion, it was not written by John the son of Zebedee. Assuming that the Gospel was the work of the apostle, he adduced three considerations to demonstrate that the Apocalypse was written by a different author. First, while it is reasonable to believe that the author of the Revelation was named John, a prophet, he did not identify himself as the Beloved Disciple, or the brother of James, or an eyewitness and hearer of the Lord, as the Evangelist did. Many Christians have borne the name John, and there were two Christian leaders of that name in Asia, as is indicated by the existence of two tombs in Ephesus, each said to be the tomb of John. Secondly, there are many affinities of thought between the Gospel and Epistle of John. The two works begin in the same way and they have many terms in common, such as life, light, truth, grace, joy, the flesh and blood of the Lord, the love of God toward us, the promise of the Holy Spirit, 'the Father', 'the Son', etc. But the Revelation is utterly different from both books. 'It scarcely, so to speak, has a syllable in common with them.' Thirdly, the style of the Gospel and Epistle is different from that of the Revelation. The former are written in faultless Greek and show great literary skill in their diction and constructions, but the author of the Revelation employs inaccurate Greek usage and barbarous idioms, and even at times commits downright solecisms. 'I have not said these things in mockery,' Dionysius adds, 'but merely to establish the dissimilarity of these writings.'

This is a penetrating piece of criticism and in the main has secured the assent of most modern critics. The situation is nevertheless more complex than Dionysius recognized. For example, while it is now generally agreed that there is no reason to doubt that the name of the author of the Revelation was John, the motives which gave rise to pseudonymity are wholly absent from this book, the evidence of the two tombs of John is tenuous, and we cannot be so sure as Dionysius was that the author, as distinct from the authority behind the Fourth Gospel, was John the Apostle. The odd thing is that from some points of view a more plausible case can be made out for the authorship of the Revelation by John the Apostle than for that of the Gospel. The authority of John the Seer in the churches of Asia Minor was so great, his relationship with them so well established, it is unlikely that another Christian leader of that name lived in Ephesus at the same time. And the impression made by the Gospel as to the character of John the Apostle accords uncommonly well with what one might imagine of the Seer of Revelation.[1] On such a view differences between the Fourth Gospel and the Revelation affect the authorship of the Gospel rather than that of the Revelation.

The ideas of the Gospel and the Revelation certainly have marked differences, yet there are also striking contacts. The divergences noted by Dionysius are mainly (not entirely) correct, but his assertion that there is 'scarcely a syllable' in common between the two works is a strange exaggeration for a critically minded person to make. In these two works alone in the New Testament the Christ is called the Word of God. Admittedly there is a difference of emphasis in the use of the term, but this is not, as is often suggested, because it has a Greek meaning in the Gospel and a Hebrew meaning in the Revelation. Rather one must say that it has a more biblical ring in the Revelation, with a striking contact with its use in Wisdom 18 : 14ff., and a fuller significance in the Gospel, due to the writer's awareness of the widespread traditions of the Word in the ancient world.[2] The Lamb of God is a key concept of the Messiah in the Gospel as well as in the Revelation. The difference of terms (*amnos* Gospel, *arnion* Revelation) is secondary to the strong probability that in the Gospel as in the Revelation, but nowhere else in the New Testament, we have in this image a coalescence of the apocalyptic tradition of the Warrior-Lamb and the Christian understanding of the death of Christ as a fulfilment of the passover-Lamb typology. A glance in a concordance of the New Testament as to the use of the terms for witness or testimony (*martyreō* and *martyria*) and those for life, death, thirst, hunger, conquer, used in a spiritual or moral sense, points to a positive relationship in the area of soteriology between these two works unequalled in other New Testament Writings from different authors. These contacts are not merely verbal, but reveal a sharing

[1] See Swete, *Commentary*, pp. clxxx ff. He was inclined to accept the author of the Revelation as John the Apostle and wished to divorce the problem from that of the authorship of the Fourth Gospel.

[2] See especially, T. Boman, *Hebrew Thought compared with Greek*, London, 1960, ch. 4; O. Cullmann, *The Christology of the New Testament*, London, 2nd edn, 1963, part IV, ch. 1; C. H. Dodd, *The Fourth Gospel*, Cambridge, 1953, pp. 263ff; R. Bultmann, *The Gospel of John*, Oxford, 1971, pp. 19ff.

in some highly characteristic ways of thinking about Christ and his salvation.

It is in respect of style and language that Dionysius has his strongest point. These are so transparently different that supporters of the traditional identity of authorship have to search for an explanation of some sort. The obvious recourse is to suggest that the different styles are due to differences in the subject matter and in the nature of the Revelation and the Gospel. Some seek to strengthen this contention by postulating an early date for the Revelation (pre-AD 70), so giving time for the writer to improve his style. There are however few supporters of this latter hypothesis. In the opinion of most it is asking too much to suggest that the differences of theme could account for such features as, e.g., the absence from the Revelation of the attracted relative and of the genitive absolute, of the negative *mē* with the participle or the narrative use of *oun* (therefore), all of which are common in the Gospel. The careful examination by Charles of the style and grammar of the Revelation has shown that the author has a consistent way of writing, even if it is a unique one and entails many solecisms as judged by ordinary Greek. Everyone recognizes that behind the Revelation there lies a Semitic mind. But how that is related to the language and style of the book is disputed. Charles considered that the Seer *thought* in Hebrew and *wrote* in Greek.[1] H. H. Rowley held that the Seer's native language was Aramaic, and that it was the Aramaic syntax and grammar that dominated John's mind as he wrote in Greek.[2] C. C. Torrey advanced the view that the Seer actually *wrote* his work in Aramaic and that someone else, out of reverence for the word of his master, *translated* it very literally into Greek.[3] If this last position were to be adopted, no argument could be adduced from language and style as to the relation between the author of the Revelation and of the Gospel. In a problem of this kind the linguistic layman feels frustrated, but in the light of Aramaic studies on other books of the New Testament the present writer is inclined to look with suspicion on hypotheses involving the translation of whole works of the New Testament from Aramaic into Greek. Failing this escape-route, we are shut up to the recognition that the same person could not

---

[1] Commentary, vol. I. p. cxliii.

[2] A view intimated in a private communication to the writer.

[3] *Documents of the Primitive Church*, 1941, p. 158.

have penned the Gospel and the Revelation in their present form.

This conclusion appears to be confirmed by reflection on the different kinds of mind which produced the Gospel 'and the Revelation. Both books convey the impression of having been composed with utmost care. The Gospel contains material which seems to have been pondered for years, and which in all likelihood has been used in preaching by the evangelist over many years. The Revelation is the product of a mind soaked in the Old Testament —the allusions to the Old Testament text are too numerous to be indicated by the modern method of using heavy type for Old Testament quotations in the Greek text, and the Seer is so much at home in Jewish apocalyptic literature that he finds it natural to express his theological convictions in this mode of writing. To a degree beyond most literary works these writings manifest the personality, character, and way of thinking of their authors, and they indicate authors of very different cast of mind. How then are we to account for the close links between the two books? Their authors must have been well acquainted. The one could have been the disciple of the other, or they could have been disciples of a common master. Scholars are increasingly inclined to the latter view, believing that the common master was none other than the Beloved Disciple, John the son of Zebedee.

It is an attractive solution to the problem of the authorship both of the Fourth Gospel and of the Revelation, but it must be recognized that the authority of John the Seer in the churches of Roman Asia poses problems on that view; for then we must either take seriously the hypothesis of two Christian leaders named John in Asia Minor, and suppose the Apostle to have died a considerable time before the composition of the Revelation, or we must assume that the Apostle John never reached Ephesus, having died long before, and that Christian tradition from early times confused John the Seer with John the Apostle.

Readers who have trodden the familiar paths of speculation regarding the authorship of the Fourth Gospel will be aware that conjecture follows conjecture in this area, and it is not a profitable exercise. Swete, writing at the beginning of this century, wished to keep an open mind as to the authorship of the Revelation. Kiddle forty years later adopted a similar attitude, and added, 'The authorship of the Revelation may prove the one mystery of the book which will never be revealed in this world.'[1] Kümmel a generation after Kiddle stated, 'We know nothing more about the author of the Apocalypse than that he was a Jewish-Christian prophet by the name of John.'[2] Perhaps that is all we need to know. The issue of real importance regarding this book is not the identity of the author but the authenticity of the claim in its opening paragraph: 'The revelation *of Jesus Christ*, which God gave him . . .' That is settled not by the name of the writer, but by the nature of his work.

As to the date of the Revelation, two chief possibilities present themselves, namely, the end of the reign of Nero, *c.* AD 68, or the end of Domitian's reign, *c.* AD 95.

The earlier date has been favoured by some exegetes on the ground that 11 : 1f. presumes that Jerusalem has fallen into the hands of heathen aggressors but the temple shrine still stands. The enigmatic chapter 17 also yields a reasonable exegesis on this view, for 17 : 10f. speaks of seven emperors of the antichristian empire, who will be followed by an eighth who is one of the seven. Of these seven, five are past, the sixth is reigning, and the seventh will rule for a short time only. Reckoning from Augustus, the sixth emperor was Galba, who came to the throne in AD 68. John was scarcely in a position to know that Galba's reign would be so short, but he assumed that the seventh emperor also would not have a lengthy rule since the end was not distant. The fact that neither emperor did reign for long would, as Torrey observed, be no discredit to the prophecy.

Despite the attractiveness of this view there are many factors militating against it. From Irenaeus on, the tradition of the Church has maintained that John 'saw the Revelation . . . at the close of Domitian's reign'.[3] It is unlikely that John intends us to interpret 11 : 1f. in a literal fashion, for contrary to many of his apocalyptically minded Jewish contemporaries he did not regard the temple of Jerusalem as impregnable. The little oracle in 11 : 1f. is best understood as originally produced by a Jewish prophet during the siege of Jerusalem, but applied by John to the spiritual security of the Church in her time of trial; just as 11 : 3ff. is most plausibly to be viewed as a Jewish oracle relating to the ministry of Moses and

---

[1] *Commentary*, p. xxxvi.
[2] *Introduction to the New Testament*, London, 1965, p. 331.
[3] *Haer.* v. 30. 3.

Elijah in the last times in Jerusalem, adapted by John to relate to
the Church's task of bearing witness in the world. The seven emperors of chapter 17 are themselves a secondary interpretation of
the seven heads of the monster. The number was not determined by
the actual succession of Roman emperors but by the Babylonian
myth, which was older than Rome itself. In any case John's concern is not with the line of Roman emperors to his day, but with
the reigning emperor and his successor as the predecessors of the
Antichrist. The number of rulers who have already come on the
scene have to be accommodated to the symbolism, and so it represents the whole group prior to the contemporary sovereign.

One of the few significant factors bearing on the date of the
Revelation is John's banishment as a Christian preacher. That
reflects a policy of active hostility on the part of the state towards
the Church. It cannot be shown that such legal measures were
taken by the state against Christians prior to the later years of
Domitian. The Revelation reflects a situation in which the cult of
the emperor was a contemporary force and was bidding to become
world-wide. Nero's persecution had nothing to do with this issue.
It was under Domitian, who claimed and frequently used the
title *Dominus et Deus noster* ('our Lord and God'), that the cult was
taken seriously enough to become a threat to the Church's
existence. Christian tradition unanimously represents Domitian to
be the first persecutor of Christians after Nero. The later date also
suits the portrayal of the Antichrist as a Nero raised from the dead,
for that expectation could arise only at a time sufficiently removed
from the end of Nero's reign for it to be acknowledged that Nero
was certainly dead, and when imposters could no longer claim to
be Nero in exile.

The evidence encourages us to regard the traditional date of the
composition of the Revelation as the most likely one, namely
towards the end of Domitian's reign, *c.* AD 95.

4. THE ABIDING SIGNIFICANCE OF THE REVELATION

The Revelation calls on Christian people to take seriously the
teaching delivered to the Church on the kingdom of God in
history. For John that means the witness borne by Jesus to the
kingdom of God as handed down by apostolic teachers and interpreted through the Holy Spirit in the Church.

Is it possible to trace a connection between the teaching of
Jesus and that of the Revelation? If we keep to the fundamental
elements of eschatology, yes.

The centrality of the kingdom of God to the proclamation of
Jesus is apparent from Mark's summary of his preaching, Mark
1 : 15. That this relates primarily to a kingdom coming in the
future is evident from the beatitudes (Mt. 5 : 3ff.), which describe
various aspects of the blessedness of the future kingdom, and the
Lord's Prayer, the burden of which is, 'Thy kingdom come'
(Mt. 6 : 10). The little parable of the fig tree, which by its blossom
heralds the summer (Mk 13 : 28), illustrates the importance
attached by our Lord to signs that herald the kingdom's coming,
and indicates an affinity with the apocalyptic view of history. On
the other hand it is equally evident that Jesus viewed the promise
of the kingdom as in process of fulfilment through his word and
action. He tells the messengers of John that the miraculous events
which accompany the day of redemption are already happening
through him (Mt. 11 : 5). He declares that the era of law and
prophets came to an end with John, and that since his time the
kingdom of heaven 'has suffered violence' (Mt. 11 : 12f.)—whether
by opponents or by friends of the kingdom is of secondary importance, since the kingdom is there to be 'violated'. The same
conviction is probably to be seen in Luke 17 : 20f., and indubitably
in Matthew 12 : 28: 'If it is by the Spirit of God that I cast out
demons, then the kingdom of God has come upon you.' In Jesus
the Christ the kingdom of God has come with redemptive power
out of its futurity into the present. This is the 'secret of the kingdom'
(Mk 4 : 11). It is the crucial element in our Lord's eschatological
teaching.

Towards the end of his ministry Jesus uttered sayings indicating
that the redemptive action through which the kingdom comes
among men includes his death and resurrection (see Lk. 12 : 49f.,
13 : 32, Mk 10 : 45, and the sayings at the Supper, Mk 14 : 24f.,
cf. Lk. 22 : 28ff.) and culminates in his parousia (so Mk 8 : 38,
Mt. 10 : 23, Lk. 17 : 22ff., and especially the confession made to
the high priest on oath, Mk 14 : 62, and the parable of the burglar,
Mt. 24 : 42f.)[1] According to Jesus, therefore, it is through his total

---

[1] From time to time attempts are made to eliminate the reference of all such
sayings to the parousia, in an endeavour to prove that Jesus did not teach such
a doctrine. See, e.g., T. F. Glasson, *The Second Advent*, London, 1945, J. A. T.

activity as the Christ—his ministry, death, and resurrection, and his parousia—that the ancient promise of the kingdom finds its complete fulfilment.

This 'testimony of Jesus' lies at the heart of the apostolic preaching as it may be gleaned from the Acts of the Apostles and from citations of it in the epistles,[1] and is the presupposition of the apostolic theology as reflected in the whole New Testament. For the primitive Church it was axiomatic that the kingdom of God came through the redemptive work of Christ, i.e., in his life, death, and resurrection, and gift of the Holy Spirit. But the conviction is constantly expressed that while salvation has come through Jesus, we have not yet received the gift as we are to have it. We are justified, but we await the gift of righteousness (Gal. 5 : 5); we are raised with Christ, but we look for the resurrection of the body (1 C. 15); life is Christ, but in comparison with his future 'presence' (parousia) he is absent (2 C. 5 : 6); we have tasted the powers of the age to come and have been transferred into the kingdom of God's beloved Son, but we look for a time when God will be all in all and the yearning of creation will be satisfied (1 C. 15 : 24ff., Rom. 8 : 19ff.). These cardinal features of 'the testimony of Jesus' in the gospels and epistles are the staple of the Revelation, and outweigh all differences which may be discerned between it and the other New Testament writings.

Nevertheless there are emphases in the Revelation which lend the book its peculiar flavour, and which manifest a development of earlier stages of eschatological teaching. These particularly relate to its teaching concerning the Antichrist, the Church's vocation to suffer, and the nature of the future kingdom.

In considering John's teaching on the Antichrist we may, if we wish, take our point of departure with Bousset, whose book *The Antichrist Legend* bears the subtitle, *A Chapter in Christian and Jewish Folklore*, and concentrate on the history of the Babylonian Dragon

---

Robinson, *Jesus and his Coming*, London, 1957. These attempts are doomed to failure in view of the authenticity of the dominical sayings relating to the future coming of the kingdom and the significance of Jesus himself for the coming of the kingdom. For a convenient and persuasive treatment of the subject see W. G. Kümmel, *Promise and Fulfilment*, London, 1957, and more briefly, Cullmann's essay 'The Return of Christ', in *The Early Church*, London, 1956.

[1] See C. H. Dodd's *The Apostolic Preaching and its Developments*, London, 2nd edn, 1944.

myth. Or we may begin with analogous elements in the teaching of Jesus about the powers of evil in relation to the kingdom of God. Without doubt John was acquainted with both, but if his eschatology was as Christ-determined as we believe it to have been, it will be more just to him to begin with Jesus rather than the dragon.

Here we cannot fail to notice that the most characteristic utterances of Jesus relating to the kingdom of God describe its coming in terms of his conquest of the demonic powers. This is evident in the parable of Mark 3 : 27 and the saying in Matthew 12 : 28 (= Lk. 11 : 20), which together may be viewed as a kind of double corner-stone of Jesus' teaching on the kingdom of God. In the first passage the domain of the 'strong man', the Devil, is said to be coming to an end because one equipped with the power of heaven has appeared on the scene and defeated him. The latter complements the former through its explanation of how the victory has come about: the exorcisms of Jesus are performed by 'the finger of God', i.e., by the might of the Spirit of God in Jesus. Since the overthrow of the Devil is a feature of the last times, and the Spirit is essentially the Spirit of the kingdom, the deeds of Jesus are shown to be eschatological—harbingers of the kingdom of God which brings the downfall of all evil powers.[1]

Accordingly it should occasion no surprise that a species of Antichrist-doctrine is reflected in the teaching of Jesus, namely, in Mark 13 : 14ff. In reference to the Lord's prophecy of the fall of Jerusalem it is recorded, 'When you see the desolating sacrilege (lit. "abomination of desolation") set up where it ought not to be . . . then let those who are in Judea flee . . .' There is no just cause for assuming that Jesus would not have cited the Danielic phrase 'abomination of desolation' (Dan. 9 : 27, 11 : 31, 12 : 11), as though Jesus regarded Daniel as sub-canonical, when that book supplied him with his chief messianic designation, Son of Man (Dan. 7 : 13). In Daniel the phrase refers to a desecration of the temple at Jerusalem, whereby the temple is transformed into a heathen shrine for carrying out heathen rites ordained by an antigod emperor (an 'antichrist'). On the lips of Jesus the phrase appears to denote a desecration of the temple by a destructive heathen power, namely, the Romans, but by its associations it

[1] For the significance of these sayings, see my article 'Jesus and the Spirit' in *Mélanges Bibliques en hommage au R. P. Béda Rigaux*, Gembloux, 1970, pp. 468ff.

characterizes the event as a deed of an 'antichristian' power.[1] If this is not a doctrine of the Antichrist on the conventional lines, it certainly gives expression to the basic concept which lies behind it, for it relates to an evil power which oppresses the people of God in the last times.

It is a reasonable hypothesis that Paul's teaching relating to the Antichrist in 2 Thessalonians 2 presupposes a knowledge of the tradition conveyed in Mark 13 : 14, in part because of the likelihood that the eschatological discourse embodied in Mark 13 circulated before the gospel, and also because echoes of Mark 13 appear to be present in 1 Thessalonians 4 : 15–5 : 10 and throughout 2 Thessalonians, chapters 1–2.[2] This is important, for it suggests that while the 'antichrist' tradition of Daniel was influential within the early Church, it was itself modified by the tradition of the teaching of Jesus.

Such a conclusion finds confirmation from the Revelation. On the one hand, there is sufficient parallelism between Mark 13 and the seals judgments in Revelation 6 to warrant the belief that John used the eschatological discourse at this point (just as he reproduces the Egyptian plagues in the trumpets and bowl-cup series). On the other hand, the view of the Antichrist in the Revelation is fundamentally related to that in Mark 13 : 14. In both cases the antichristian power at enmity with God's people is Rome. If in Mark 13 : 14ff. it is the temple of Jerusalem which is desecrated and then devastated, in the Revelation it is the Church of Christ in the world which is ravaged. Significantly in Revelation 11 : 1f. the desolation of the temple is used as a symbol to represent the Church, persecuted by her enemies but preserved by God.

The figure of the Antichrist in the Revelation is undoubtedly developed, as compared with the representations in Daniel and in earlier Christian teaching, and this is due to varied influences. Chief of these is the ancient myth of the sea monster Tiamat, with which has been combined the contemporary myth of a demonic Nero returned from the dead. These in turn were modified by current tendencies to defy the state and worship the emperor. It is doubtful, however, whether we are justified in viewing any of these factors as *originating* the figure of the Antichrist. The Roman

[1] For a detailed exposition of Mark 13:14 see the writer's *A Commentary on Mark Thirteen*, London, 1957, pp. 54ff.

[2] See the author's *Jesus and the Future*, London, 1954, pp. 232ff.

emperors, with their blasphemous claims to deity, did not create an Antichrist expectation, but fitted a type. The Nero-*redivivus* myth gave a convenient and powerful expression to the expectation, for the coming Antichrist would be another Nero, yet more devilish than the first. The sea-monster of the Babylonian creation myth provided a yet richer and more evocative expression of the Antichrist, for it identified the latest appearance of rebellion against God with the evil power which inspired the tyrannies of former ages. Contrary to the supporters of the history-of-religions school, however, it is no more likely that the watery Tiamat gave rise to the Antichrist than the Babylonian hero-god Marduk created the concept of the Christ and his kingdom. Back of the Antichrist stands the Devil, who for John as for Job never rises beyond being an instrument of God; and back of the Christ stands the almighty God who promises redemption to his people. The cartoon of Tiamat and her host provides a means of expressing convictions whose sources lie in very different origins.

The teaching that an Antichrist precedes the coming of Christ and his kingdom highlights a doctrine which is as integral to the gospels as it is to the Revelation: namely, that a power of evil beyond the sinful wills of men and women is at work in the processes of history, that its effect is destructive of all that is good in this world, and that it exceeds the wit or strength of man to overcome it. As in the gospels, so in the Revelation the work of Christ is set in relation to the ruinous effects of this power in the world. Just as the Christ by his redemptive deeds delivers from sin and brings the powers of the age to come into this world, so the Christ in his parousia alone can bring to its final issue the sovereignty of holiness and life. It is ironical that the century which has witnessed the death of the Devil and the Antichrist in theology has experienced the most appalling manifestations of demonic statecraft, the most terrible desolations of war, and the most widespread oppressions of the Christian faith in all history. Those who think that Christian eschatology means that the works of God in Christ were ended in AD 30 should ponder that the destructive power of sin in the world is on a greater scale today than in the generation of Jesus and the first Easter and Pentecost, and that there is no indication of its diminution in the future. Paul Althaus resolutely set his face against dogmatic and cheap applications of the doctrine of the Antichrist, but he believed it to be an essential feature of the Christian theology of history. He went on to affirm, 'The concept of Antichrist is the loud "No" to all secularized chiliasm, and to the optimistic faith in a progressive coming of the kingdom of God on earth.'[1] In history the sovereignty of Christ is perpetually engaged in struggle, and that can be resolved alone by the returning Christ. The Book of Revelation sounds a clamant call to take seriously the reality and the power of evil in this world that has been redeemed by Christ, and so to recognize that only he who inaugurated God's saving sovereignty can bring it to victory.

This leads to a consideration of the role of the Church as portrayed in the Revelation. The calm meditative exposition of this theme in the letter to the Ephesians is far removed from the dramatic scenes of the Revelation, but no more than it is from the passionate references to the Church's mission in the two letters to the Corinthians (e.g., 1 C. 9, 2 C. 5). John's exposition is controlled by his view of God's people as 'the embattled Church',[2] hence his supreme concern is to strengthen the faith of Christian people and their will to persist in obedience to God. There is accordingly less emphasis on the Church's responsibility for the world, which is seen as implacably hostile, than on the worth of the Church to God and its destiny in history and in the eternal ages. Nevertheless there are intimations in the Revelation that the Church of Christ has a greater duty than simply to survive, even in the time of the Antichrist. These appear especially in chapters 11 and 14, wherein the Church's function as the light of the world and the bearer of witness to Jesus is plainly set forth. But it is precisely in the context of the Church's witness to the world that her vocation to suffer is most startlingly set forth. The beast from the abyss makes war on the witnesses of Christ, and they perish in the city's streets (11 : 7ff.; cf. 12 : 11). It is these passages above all wherein expositors have found ground for the belief that John anticipates a universal martyrdom for the Church, and that all Christ's people perish in the time of the Antichrist. This interpretation the present writer believes to be a mistake, since there are other statements in the Revelation which assume that the Church survives to the parousia (e.g., 2 : 25, 16 : 15, 22 : 7, 11, and cf. 3 : 10). Nevertheless, there is no doubt that John viewed the coming tribulation as

1 *Die Letzten Dinge*, Gütersloh, 5th edn, 1949, p. 286.
2 M. Rissi, *Time and History*, Richmond, Va., 1966, p. 109.

a kind of passion which the Church must suffer with its Lord, that it may share with him the glory of his resurrection. If his book was written in order to encourage Christians to hold on to their belief in the testimony of Jesus, it was also written to inspire them to confess that testimony before men.

In this again John, whether consciously or no, echoes the thought of the eschatological discourse in Mark 13; for in its central section, verses 9ff., the earliest intimation of the Church's duty to preach the good news to the whole world is set in the context of persecution in synagogues and before heathen tribunals. It is all too easy for the Church to associate its commission to evangelise the world with the glory of the resurrection (Mt. 28: 18ff.), and to forget that the risen Lord is the Crucified, who sends his disciples to herald the gospel of a reconciliation achieved through suffering and to embody it in a suffering of a like order (observe that the setting of 2 C. 5: 19 is in 5: 14ff., the meaning of which is expounded in 4: 1–12, 6: 1–10). Significantly most of the sermons in Acts are preached in hostile surroundings (e.g., Peter and John before the Sanhedrin, Acts 4 and 5; Stephen before a mob, ch. 7; Paul, in like circumstances, ch. 22, before the Sanhedrin, ch. 23, before Felix, ch. 24, before Festus, ch. 25, before Agrippa, ch. 26, and as a prisoner in Rome, ch. 28). The early Church understood well that suffering in the world is the reverse side of its fellowship with Christ in glory (cf. Rom. 8: 17, 2 Tim. 2: 11f.). To expound the implications of that conviction—the suffering of this present time *and* the glory that is to follow—is a major concern of John's. A Church which takes note of his exposition will not be overtaken by surprise when it meets stern opposition in carrying out its mission to the nations. Nor will it be brought to despair through its sufferings, for the end of the story is the descent of the city of God from heaven to earth.

The assurance of that triumph is the supreme contribution of the Revelation to the Church of Christ. There are strangely contrary anticipations of the future in our time. Those who are impressed by the achievements of man in his early space travels see a marvellous future for man in the coming ages. Others, who are depressed by the increasing accessibility of nuclear weapons and the record of man's inability to live at peace with his kind, join forces with the prophets of doom among the ecologists and with those who see no solution to the problems of the population-

explosion. Christians accustomed to leave out of reckoning the
eschatological perspective of the New Testament might well join
the company of the alarmed, in view of the catastrophic decrease
in the Church in Europe, its disappearance in China, its perilous
future in India, and its uncertain prospects in Africa. Pessimism is
more common among our contemporaries than optimism, particularly where the flame of faith dies low or flickers out. H. G.
Wells at the end of his life became convinced that the unknown
power which evoked our universe had turned against it, and that
man was heading to a voiceless, limitless darkness. 'Our world will
admit none of that,' he wrote. 'It will perish amidst its evasions
and fatuities . . . Mind near exhaustion still makes its final futile
movement towards that "way out or round or through the im-
passe" . . . There is no way out or round or through.'[1] Thirty
years later more men and women hold kindred views than there
were when Wells so wrote, and it can hardly be claimed that the
Church inspires them to rejoice in hope. For the Church itself has
all too often lost hope.

To all men of little hope or none, and to those whose confidence
is based on uncertain foundations, the book of Revelation offers
strong consolation. It is grounded in the almighty God who made
this universe, and whose will cannot be finally frustrated by any
power in heaven or earth or hell. It is grounded in the God who
has wrought redemption in and through Christ, the power of
which is experienced in the world now, and the end of which is the
subjection of all things to God. And since it is God acting in Christ
for the deliverance of mankind and the establishment of his purpose, the end must be good. It embraces history and the incomprehensible ages beyond history, and it signifies an outpouring of
grace beyond our imagining, for it is the city of God, the vastness
of which includes heaven and earth, yet whose every corner is
filled with the love of God in Christ for man. And the end is
assured, because it has already begun through God's action in
Christ, it is now present, and it will be concluded in God's time.

If the language of the last sentence is in any sense enigmatic, it
nevertheless expresses a conviction which John shares with the
rest of the New Testament writers. The recognition of its importance to John helps us to overcome the stumbling-block of the perspective of the end which runs through his book, from its opening

[1] *Mind at the End of its Tether*, London, 1945, pp. 13ff.

paragraph (1 : 1) to its last (22 : 20): the Revelation concerns
'what must soon take place'.

It is perhaps not sufficiently appreciated that this conviction of
the nearness of the end is by no means exceptional, still less is it
peculiar to John. It is characteristic of all prophets of both Testaments. In particular the judgments of God in history are consistently viewed as precursors of his ultimate intervention for the
establishment of his sovereignty. (Observe how Isaiah sets the
coming of God's promised deliverance and sovereignty in the
context of the overthrow of the Assyrian empire, Isa. 7–9, 10–11;
Habakkuk, as following on the destruction of Babylon, Hab.
2 : 2f.; Jeremiah, Ezekiel, and Deutero-Isaiah, as the concomitant
of the end of the Babylonian exile, Jer. 29 : 31, Ezek. 26, Isa. 49,
51; Haggai as following the building of the temple, Hag. 2; and
the New Testament writers simply as in the near future, Rom.
13 : 11f., 1 C. 7 : 29f., Heb. 10 : 37, 1 Pet. 4 : 7, Jas 5 : 8.) In this
respect our Lord was one with the prophets in his view of the impending doom of Jerusalem (Mk 13, etc.). In face of the perpetual
non-occurrence of the promise of the kingdom many are tempted
to view the promise as a chimera. In view, however, of the centrality of the kingdom to the message of the prophets and of Jesus and
of his apostles, to take such a stance is virtually to question whether
there is any word of God at all in the Bible.

Numerous factors contribute to the phenomenon which older
exegetes used to call the 'prophetic perspective', but the chief
consideration for the Christian (in distinction from the Jew) is the
insistence that John makes, along with the whole apostolic Church,
that the event *has* occurred. The decisive significance of the life,
death, and resurrection of Christ for history and eternity is set
forth by John in the vision of chapter 5, wherein it is made plain,
as we have seen, that the work of Christ for the establishment of
the kingdom of God is unitary. Faith, therefore, may look with
confidence to God for the completion of that work of grace which
God has begun in Christ, and which is the mainspring of the
Christian's life in the present. The Christian of the twentieth
century, like his predecessors in the first, may and should live in
the expectation and hope of the triumph of Christ's kingdom. If he
cannot be so sure as the first-century Christian that it will come
soon, neither can he confidently affirm that its coming is far
off.

Here a comment of Althaus, made in connection with related teaching given by the apostle Paul, is worthy to be pondered:

This end, whether it be temporally 'near' or 'far', is essentially very near to everybody. For it is one with Christ, the Crucified and Risen Lord. It is there, where Christ is. The temporal signifies only the redemption of the essential end, which Christ is, inasmuch as he is the Crucified and Risen One, and as the Risen One heading for his coming is for the world and history the Hidden One. To this extent all of us, all generations of the Church, live at the same hour, in the one last hour, in a world and time which is destined to pass away—thus in the twilight shortly before the sunrise.[1]

To sustain such a faith and such an attitude was the intention of the author of the Revelation. He who reads and receives his testimony will surely find inspiration to keep what is written therein (Rev. 1 : 3).

[1] *Der Brief an die Römer* (*Das Neue Testament Deutsch*) Göttingen, 6th edn, 1949, p. 117.

THE BOOK OF
REVELATION

John's introduction to his book is brief. The first paragraph states the origin of the work, and virtually serves as a title to the whole. The second paragraph conveys a greeting from the writer to his readers, with a doxology and two prophetic sayings.

Short as they are, these paragraphs are deeply significant. They indicate the standpoint from which the book is written. Just as the prologue to the Fourth Gospel puts the reader in a position to understand the story of Jesus which follows, so the prologue to the Revelation supplies a vantage point from which the reader may view with understanding the vision of history which follows.

1. The term **revelation** is capable of expressing a variety of meanings. It can signify the act of unveiling, or the object which is uncovered. The former meaning makes possible the application of the term to the coming of Christ—the occasion when the curtain is torn aside and the Lord is seen by human eyes (e.g., 1 C. 1 : 7). The latter meaning relates to the content of God's disclosure of himself, his ways, and his will—matters which hitherto were hidden from the gaze of man (e.g., Eph. 1 : 17). John gives to the word a specialized application. For him *revelation* describes the process of unveiling and the truth unveiled concerning the issues of history. John may well have been the first to use the term to describe a book of this order, but he must have been fully aware that in issuing a book of visions of the end of history he joined the company of many who similarly wrote on this theme. His work in fact has provided the other comparable writings with their generic name—'revelation', or 'apocalypse' (Greek *apokalypsis*).

If John's title links his work with others written in a style similar to his, it yet makes a claim which sets his book apart from all others of its class. It is not, as many of our early manuscripts describe it, 'the revelation of John', but **the revelation of Jesus Christ.** This implies that Jesus Christ himself has torn back the curtain which hides from human eyes the invisible world and the future of this world, and that what is open to view is a vision of reality granted by him. Further, what Jesus Christ has laid open to John's view is a revelation **which God gave him.** Just as in the Fourth Gospel it is reiterated again and again that the Son speaks only what he has heard from the Father (e.g., Jn 5 : 19ff., 8 : 26ff., 14 : 10), so here it is declared that the risen Lord reveals to his followers what the Father has made known to him (cf. Mk 13 : 32, Ac. 1 : 7).

Characteristically in a book of visions, the content of what is unveiled by God to Jesus Christ is conveyed to John by an **angel**. In the visions of prophets and apocalyptists angel-guides are frequent. It is to be observed however that in his work the revealer is Christ (cf. 1 : 12ff.). The angel has a strictly subordinate place as a recipient and interpreter of what is made known. He takes his place along with the prophets and faithful recipients of the revelation (see 22 : 6–9). Naturally the mention of the angel at this juncture bespeaks his dignity, not his lowliness. The conjunction of God, Christ, and the angel, as the source of the revelation has the effect of according an unheard-of authority to the content of John's prophecy.

There is, however, a feature of the title which calls for modesty in assessing John's claims for his book. He states that the risen Christ **made known** the revelation to him by the hand of the angel. The verb so rendered in the *RSV* (*sēmainō*) undoubtedly can have that meaning, as in Acts 25 : 27. But as it comes from the root *sēmeion*, a sign, it was used of less direct ways of prophesying the future, and so to give vague indications of coming events. In reference to the Delphic oracle Heraclitus said, 'it neither states nor hides but merely *indicates*.' Accordingly we find this term used in the Fourth Gospel in parabolic sayings of Jesus regarding his coming death (Jn 12 : 33, 18 : 32), as also in the obscure prophecy about Peter's martyrdom (Jn 21 : 19). In all these passages the Authorized Version uses the term 'signify', which is an excellent rendering, especially if its connection with 'sign' be observed. The occurrence of the term in the title of John's prophecy is almost certainly deliberate. The prophet wishes to make clear that he does not provide photographs of heaven, nor do his descriptions of coming events constitute history written in advance. He uses 'sign language' to portray the invisible realities of the present and the future of man and his history. Even when speaking of the past John prefers picture-language to plain description (as in Rev. 12, which relates the birth and redemption of Jesus to his future victory). By employing this terminology in the title of his book, John in his own way expresses a reserve about the nature of prophetic language similar to that of Paul, who applied a like reserve not only to prophecy but to all speech about God (1 C. 13 : 8–12).

In the Revelation of John we are given 'intimations' of that which God unveiled in fullness to the Son.

2. The revelation to John is further characterized as **the word of God** and **the testimony of Jesus Christ.** That is, it conveys a message from God and witness borne by Jesus Christ. As with the term 'revelation' these phrases can describe the content of the Bible as a whole (in 1 : 9 and 6 : 9 they together denote the Christian gospel in its fullness). In this passage they relate to the content of this book.

3. **Blessed:** the beatitude is the first of seven scattered through the book (see further, 14 : 13, 16 : 15, 19 : 9, 20 : 6, 22 : 7, 14). This first one, occurring at the beginning of the work, is repeated by way of emphasis in the closing chapter (22 : 7). It is invoked on him **who reads** the revelation to an assembled congregation and on those **who hear** and respond in obedience to the message. The latter are a single group. It is presumed that the hearing of the prophecy will be attended with faith. The blessing is not an indication of the piety of those over whom it is pronounced, but an assurance of their participation in the salvation made known in the visions of the book. The beatitudes of the Revelation accordingly should be compared with those in the sermon on the mount, which also proclaim the blessedness of those who look to God for redemption. A 'revelation' of the end of history is given not for the satisfaction of curiosity, but to inspire living in accordance with the reality unveiled.

The time is near, i.e., the time of the fulfilment of the vision disclosed in the revelation. Such is the conviction of all living prophecy, as Bousset observed, and not least of all New Testament prophecy (e.g., Rom. 13 : 11f., 1 C. 7 : 29f., Heb. 10 : 37, 1 Pet. 4 : 7). A number of factors flow together in this foreshortening— one might call it telescopic—view of history. Above all the intensity of conviction, common to the Old Testament prophets, that God will fulfil his promise of deliverance and life is intensified in the faith of the New Testament writers that God has acted decisively in judgment and in the bestowal of life in his kingdom through the redemptive action of Christ. This conviction is at the heart of John's faith and of his vision. But he sees not only the redeeming powers of Christ at work in the world. The elements of ultimate rebellion against God are also at work in the world. John's presence in Patmos is evidence of that. Accordingly 'measuring human affairs with divine measures' (Arethas, cited by Lohmeyer), he sets his day in the context of the last day, and so interprets the issues of his day in the light of the last day. In reality the human measures of time demand that the temporal relationship of John's day to the last day be corrected. Nevertheless John's readers in all times are under the obligation of letting the light of the last day fall on *theirs*, and of relating the issues of their day to the kingdom of God. It is in carrying out that difficult exercise that John's vision ceases to be of archaeological interest and becomes word of God to contemporary man.

4. The greeting of the author to his readers is instructive for its assumptions. The name **John** apparently requires no further definition. His readers know who he is. How helpful it would have been for his modern readers had he added a phrase to identify himself! (For discussion on his identity, see the Introduction, pp. 32ff.)

The seven churches that are in Asia are addressed as though they were an obvious unit. *Asia*, of course, denotes the Roman proconsular Asia, on the west central coast of Asia Minor extending eastwards. There were other churches in this area (e.g., in Colosse). Did John have responsibility for the seven only? Is the precise number *seven* a mere anticipation of verse 11? Or is the number selected for its associations with sanctity and completeness, so that the seven churches represent all the churches of the area? Or are we intended to take all these ideas as self-evident? The last is not impossible.

More important than these is the assumption, implicit in the greeting, that the Revelation is an epistle. It is addressed by the author to a group of churches for which he had pastoral responsibility, as truly as Galatians was sent by Paul to a group of churches in an area not far from the seven, to meet a situation that had arisen among them. This is surely more than a literary device adopted by the author. He writes out of pastoral concern for his readers and through a divine compunction to convey a message directed to their circumstances. Every line of his book has their situation in view. It is well for this to be remembered in the exposition, for no exegesis can be faithful to John's intention unless the seven churches are kept steadily in view.

In conformity to literary customs of the day, the greeting conveys a blessing on its recipients. The content of the blessing however is far from formal. It had become established among Christians to invoke on one another the characteristic gift of the new age—**grace,** and the characteristic blessing of the old—**peace** (cf. Num. 6 : 26). The latter had become the embodiment of the Old Testament hope, the peace of the age to come, and so a comprehensive term for the salvation of the kingdom of God. In Christian faith these supreme gifts of God were seen as realized in and through the redemption of Christ. The greeting here ascribes them to the activity of the triune God.

The description of God as he **who is and who was and who is to come** is an adaptation of the name of God made known to Moses at the bush, Exodus 3 : 14. The Greek Septuagint translation rendered 'I am who I am' as 'I am he who is'. The Jerusalem Targum expanded this to 'I am he who is and who will be'; but in its comment on Deuteronomy 32 : 29 it is reproduced as 'I am he who is, and who was, and I am who will be'. Similar definitions of God in terms of time were known to the ancient Greek world, but it can hardly be doubted that John had in view the revelation of the Name at the Exodus. Jewish writers used it as one of the periphrases for the sacred name Yahweh, which they would never pronounce. Something of the same reverence is manifest in this passage, where John deliberately perverts Greek grammar rather than modify the divine name. (*Grace . . . from he who was . . .* hardly conveys the jolt contained in the Greek.) John, however, gives a twist to the name which no Jew apparently thought of, and no Greek was capable of imagining. Instead of defining God in simple terms of time, he speaks of him as *he who is and was and is to come.* God not alone transcends the ages, and awaits us from the future. It is of his nature that he 'comes' from the future and works his gracious and powerful will. Accordingly, that God should promise grace and peace for his people and then appear in Christ and act in grace for the establishment of peace, was in accordance with his very nature. That he shall **come** and consummate his gracious action in the universal establishing of peace at the appearing of Christ is equally according to his nature. How God will so come in Christ is the theme of the prophecy.

Grace and peace are invoked from **the seven spirits who are before his throne.** Who are these spirits? Traditionally they have been viewed as the representation of the sevenfold gifts of the Spirit with which the Messiah is endowed in Isaiah 11 : 2 (strictly

speaking six are there enumerated, but from earliest times ways
have been found of making them seven). John's language seems too
specific and personal for this explanation to be likely. It has been
suggested, therefore, that the seven spirits are seven angels who
stand before God (see 8 : 2). The seven angels are traditional
figures in Judaism and are prominently featured in Jewish apocalypses (their names are actually recorded in *Enoch* 20). But if this
is what John meant, why did he not use the term angels here, as in
8 : 2, instead of spirits? And how in a Christian writing should
angels come between God and Christ in a benediction? The
association of the seven spirits with God and Christ in a quasi-
trinitarian context makes it difficult to think that they are not
intended to be a representation of the Holy Spirit. But if that be
admitted, it is fairly certain that such a mode of characterizing the
Holy Spirit has a history, and that it is rooted in pre-Christian
thought.

In the history of this concept the vision of Zechariah 4 will undoubtedly have played a part. Caird has pointed out that in
Zechariah 4 we find brought together the symbol of a lampstand
with seven lamps, the seven eyes of the Lord ranging through the
whole earth, and the crucial utterance, 'Not by might, nor by
power, but by my Spirit'. That John is conscious of this reference
is seen in Revelation 5 : 6. In this passage however the seven
spirits of God are identified with the seven eyes of the Lamb (not
with the eyes of God). The association of the seven spirits with
Christ is foundational to John. In 3 : 1 it is stated that the Christ
has the seven spirits of God. But a complication arises at this point,
for 3 : 1 harks back to 1 : 20. A comparison of 1 : 20 with 3 : 1,
4 : 5, and 5 : 6, suggests the equation seven stars = seven torches
= seven spirits. But the concept of the seven stars in 1 : 20 almost
certainly reflects the astral religion of the ancient near east, in
which the sun, moon, and planets were worshipped as deities. So
this symbolism of seven spirits of God has pagan as well as Jewish
connections.

Such knowledge, however, is largely of archaeological value.
We shall see that in 1 : 20 John may well have known the current
adaptation of planetary worship in the cult of the emperors, but in
the symbolism of the seven spirits of God the Zecharian background will have been determinative for him. He could perhaps
have found in a Jewish writing the conjunction already made of

the seven spirits of God with the name of God in a formula of blessing. If so, he will have adopted the precedent, but added the name of Jesus, so producing a kind of trinitarian formulation which no non-Christian Jew could contrive. If this had happened, it would explain why the name of Jesus has come last in John's formulation. John will then have interpreted the concept of seven spirits of God in accord with his use of seven as the sacred number of completeness. The seven spirits of God represent the Holy Spirit in his fullness of life and blessing. Such a symbolism will have been welcome to John in view of the close association in his theology between the Spirit and the seven churches. The complex origin of the symbol is matched by its complex application in John's vision, but he and his readers were happy to have it so.

5. It is easy to overlook that the name **Jesus Christ,** appearing here for the third time in the prologue, does not occur after this point in John's book. The simple name *Jesus* is enough (in 22 : 20 *Lord Jesus* occurs, but in a prayer offered by John). It is not impossible that the threefold description of Jesus has in view the three tenses of his action: in life he was **the faithful witness,** and has left us his 'testimony'; by his resurrection he has become **the first-born of the dead** and brought life for the children of God; his coming will reveal him as **the ruler of kings on earth,** when he will fulfil the promise of the kingdom for mankind (so Schlatter). The language approximates more closely, however, to the gospel proclamation of Christ's death, resurrection, and ascension. In his passion Jesus was the supreme 'martyr' (the Greek term for a witness), faithful to his Father's commission to the end. The recollection of this was a living tradition in the early Church, and an inspiration to Christians who faced trial for the sake of the name (see 1 Tim. 6 : 13). Its pertinence for churches facing the supreme trial of faith is clear. That the Messiah was **the first-born** was a firm tradition in Judaism. Interestingly, it was based on the passage John has in mind here, namely Psalm 89 : 27: 'I will make him the first-born, the highest of the kings of the earth.' In Judaism the first-born was assigned chief rights in the inheritance. It became natural therefore for the first-born to be associated with the first place in the inheritance of God's kingdom, and so to the thought of sovereignty. This suits the recollection of Psalm 89 : 27 perfectly: Jesus by his resurrection becomes the Christ in power, and as the Lord at God's right hand he exercises his sovereignty

over the kings of earth, including the hostile Roman Caesars. The phrase *first-born of the dead*, however, goes beyond the Jewish background, in that Jesus as the Lord of the dead opens life to the dead. Bestowing life now, he pioneers the path of resurrection to glory. Ruler of the kings of earth now, he anticipates the sovereignty which his people will exercise in the final kingdom.

It was a custom of Jewish writers and teachers to utter a doxology at the mention of the name of God. John does not go to such lengths, but it is natural that after pronouncing a benediction which concludes with the name of Jesus, and which reminds him of the redemption he has accomplished and the destiny he has in store for his own, he should utter a doxology of praise for that redemption and for that destiny. Again death and resurrection to sovereignty are at the heart of his thought.

Praise is given **to him who loves us.** If the love was revealed above all in the death of Jesus, it is remembered that the death reveals an eternal love, which lies ahead of us as well as behind us. Praise is given because he **has freed us from our sins by his blood.** The *AV* has followed the variant reading *washed us* (Greek *elousen*, instead of *elusen*). While Revelation 7:14 can be quoted in its favour, the *RSV* is almost certainly right in preferring the reading *freed us*. Quite apart from the parallel with 5:9, there is little doubt that John has in view here an idea which is basic to his whole prophecy, namely, the conception of redemption as a new exodus of the people of God. The beatitude of verse 4 itself expounds the name of God made known to Moses before the exodus. The doxology celebrates the greater redemption of which the first exodus is an anticipation. The sacrifice of the Lamb of God introduces an emancipation from the slavery of sin such as the sacrifice of the passover-lamb could only foreshadow.

6. From the land of slavery Moses led the Israelites to the mount of God, where they received the covenant which made them 'a kingdom of priests and a holy nation' (Exod. 19:6). John's language, he **made us a kingdom, priests to his God,** closely resembles the rendering of Exodus 19:6 in the Greek translations of Symmachus and Theodotian, but the meaning is the same as that which the Septuagint wished to convey by its expression 'royal priesthood'. The term *kingdom* was understood by Jewish commentators as abstract for concrete; i.e., not 'a kingdom consisting of priests', but 'kings and priests' who made up the holy nation (see Strack-Billerbeck, ad loc.). John's prophecy proceeds on the assumption that he understood the terms of the old covenant in this way, and that what they signified has been transcended in their fulfilment under the new covenant. The Christ in the new exodus has given his people to become kings and priests with him (cf. 2 : 26f., 5 : 9f., 20 : 4ff.; for an interesting suggestion as to the implications of this for the Christian mission, see Caird, ad loc.).

God is here described as **his God and Father.** It is possible that the language has especially, though not exclusively, in view the relation between God and Jesus in his redeeming activity. God is he whom Jesus worshipped and revealed, the Father whom he trusted and obeyed. On the other hand in the Revelation God is spoken of as the Father of Jesus alone, never as the Father of believers (see 2 : 27, 3 : 4, 21, 14 : 1). The title indicates the unique relation of Jesus to God, and so is one of honour, setting him apart from all men. Whether John believed that in a less significant sense men can be described as sons of God, or can share in the sonship of Jesus (as Paul and the Fourth Evangelist believed), we have no means of knowing.

7. This verse may be regarded as providing the motto of the book (Bousset). Its theme is that of the whole prophecy. The statement is formed by the conjunction of two Old Testament passages, which had already been fused in Christian tradition (Dan. 7 : 13, Zech. 12 : 10). In Matthew 24 : 20 the two passages are combined in reverse order, but the same understanding of the Zechariah passage appears. In Zechariah 12 : 10 the Jews mourn, apparently in contrition, for one whom they have pierced (some Jewish writers identify the sufferer with the Messiah ben Joseph—it was unthinkable to view him as Messiah ben David). In our passage and in Matthew the application of the mourning is generalized and extended to all peoples. While **every one who pierced him** may denote the Jews (and/or Romans) who were immediately responsible for the crucifixion, it is more natural to interpret the extended application of the statement to all mankind. **All tribes of the earth will wail on account of him,** for all have been implicated in the rejection and the death of the Christ. This is thoroughly Johannine (e.g., Jn 12 : 31f.), and in keeping with the rest of John's vision. Whether or not the mourning of mankind for the sin against the Christ signifies an acceptable repentance or an unavailing remorse is not easily decided. In the light of such a passage as Revelation 15 : 3-4, which celebrates the turning and the worship of the nations, the former is not impossible.

To the declaration of verse 7 the prophet responds emphatically, **Even so. Amen.** *Even so* translates the simple term 'yes', but it is a permissible equivalent, for it indicates the prophet's affirmation of the divine promise, while *Amen* better relates to the believer's trust in the promise (so Lohmeyer). The same conjunction appears at the end of the prophecy, and in a similar context, namely, the promise of the coming again of Christ (Rev. 22 : 20). In both passages the declaration of the promise calls for a like affirmation and faith from the reader.

8. The prologue concludes with a prophetic utterance from God couched in the first person. **Alpha** and **omega** are the first and last letters of the Greek alphabet (= a and long o). *I am the Alpha and the Omega* in English parlance would be represented by 'I am the A and the Z'. The immediate application of the saying is given in Revelation 22 : 13, where the A and the Z are expounded as 'the first and the last, the beginning and the end'. This use of letters of the alphabet was typical of the ancients, and it was adopted by the Jews, whose first and last letters were *aleph* (virtually = a) and *tau* (= t). It was common for Jews to talk about keeping the law 'from *aleph* to *tau*', by which they meant the keeping of the law in its entirety—its first commandment and its last and all that lie between. If that idea were present in John's mind, then the assertion 'I am A and Z' would signify 'I am the beginning of history and the end of history, and the lord of all that lies between'. God is the sovereign lord of all times and all ages. This goes beyond the meaning of Isaiah 44 : 6, which will doubtless have been in John's mind. Its pertinence in this book is its encouragement to believe that the Lord God maintains his sovereign control over the world at all times, even when the powers of this world resist the Christ and his Church and give place to the raging of the Antichrist. God reigns during the storm as well as in the peace and glory of his kingdom, and he has power to fulfil his promise and bring that kingdom to victory.

As though to underline this, John reproduces the full Old Testament name of God, **the Lord God . . . the Almighty.** It is the Septuagintal rendering of the name *Lord God of Hosts.* No other writer in the New Testament uses it (its only other appearance is in

2 C. 6:18, an Old Testament citation), but it is a favourite designation of John's. It is perhaps less an indication of John's 'Jewishness' than his appreciation of the prophetic teaching of the Old Testament that God is the Lord of all nations. The Revelation is a book concerned with the purpose of God not solely for believers, nor even for the Church alone, but for the nations and for history in its broadest sweep, indeed for the universe as a whole. The choice of name, *the Lord God ... the Almighty*, is eminently suitable to John's theme.

ADDITIONAL NOTE ON ALPHA AND OMEGA IN THE REVELATION

The idea of God as the first and last in history and creation is rooted in the Old Testament prophets, notably in the writings ascribed to Deutero-Isaiah. The use of letters of the alphabet to express theoretical concepts is in keeping with the spirit of the ancient world. How early the use of *aleph-tau* was established among Jews to represent the entirety of a thing it is difficult to say. In recent years attention has been drawn to the *Sator-Rotas* word square as possibly throwing light on the appearance of *alpha-omega* in the Revelation.[1]

The square of which we speak is known in two forms:

```
ROTAS          SATOR
OPERA          AREPO
TENET          TENET
AREPO          OPERA
SATOR          ROTAS
```

It will be observed that the same form of words appears from whichever corner of the square one begins. Its five words yield the innocent sentence, 'Arepo the reaper holds the wheels with care'. The second (and later?) form of the square became the more

---

[1] The discussion has become very complicated, and this is not the place in which to pursue an extended enquiry into the origin and history of the word-square. An excellent summary of the history of investigation into the word-square is given in the article by Donald Atkinson, 'The Origin and Date of the "Sator" Word Square', *Journal of Ecclesiastical History*, 2 (1951) pp. 1–18. A briefer statement of the discussions appears in an article by H. Last, 'The Rotas-Sator Square: Present Position and Future Prospects', *Journal of Theological Studies*, ns 3 (1952) pp. 92–7.

popular, and has been traced from early centuries to modern times in many parts of the world, from Europe to Africa and South America. In 1868 a copy was found on a Roman wall-plaster in Cirencester. In 1933 four copies were discovered in Dura-Europos. A partial copy was unearthed in Pompeii in 1925, and in 1936 a complete one was discovered in the same city in a building near the amphitheatre.

The significance of the word-square is disputed. F. Cumont made the suggestion that the square was inspired by the visions of Ezekiel, and that it originated among Latin-speaking Jews. The opening vision of Ezekiel describes the chariot of glory, which bears the Lord from the Temple in Jerusalem to Ezekiel in exile. Emphasis is given in the vision to the chariot-wheels, in which the spirit of the living creatures resides (the wheels virtually = the cherubim). Ezekiel further tells of a man with an ink-horn, who goes through Jerusalem, marking with a *tau* the foreheads of the righteous to preserve them from the impending judgment on the city. Cumont thought that the word-square conveys alike a veiled warning to the wicked and comfort to the righteous, the latter receiving the consolation that the divine Reaper has marked them out for salvation.

This interpretation is ingenious, but its plausibility rests wholly on its connection with the term *rotas*, wheels. A different line of interpretation goes back to an observation, made independently by two scholars, C. Frank and F. Grosser, that the letters of the square spell out the opening phrase of the Lord's Prayer, *Pater Noster*, provided that the N be used twice. The double use of the N however demands that the phrase be spelled out in the form of a cross. When this is done four letters are left over—two As and two Os. This invites the diagram on p. 62.

With this clue in mind it was noticed by the French scholar J. Carcopino that the central letter in each side of the square is the letter T. In ancient times the T was written as a cross. Christians early became conscious of this—it is referred to in the *Letter of Barnabas* (9:8), and early Christian writers could not resist the conclusion that the man with the ink-horn in Ezekiel's vision, in marking the pious in Jerusalem with a *tau*, made the sign of the cross on their foreheads. That apart, Carcopino also observed that in the square the T is flanked on all sides with the letters A and O. These of course are the ways of representing *alpha* and *omega* in

```
                    A

                    P
                    A
                    T
                    E
                    R
        A  PATERNOSTER  O
                    O
                    S
                    T
                    E
                    R

                    O
```

Latin. This could be represented by saying that on each side of the square the central cross is flanked by *alpha* and *omega*.

In the judgment of many scholars it is extremely difficult to believe that these phenomena are coincidental. To prove otherwise appeal has been made to scholars to try to produce word-squares of their own in Latin, manifesting similar phenomena. If the relation of the square to *alpha* and *omega* is accepted as proven, then the Christian origin of the square naturally follows. The significance of the square lies in its embodiment of the faith that he who is the *alpha* and *omega* of all things has been revealed as 'our Father' in the Christ who died on the cross.

The chief ground of hesitation in accepting this solution is the early date of the appearance of the word square in Pompeii. The city was destroyed in the eruption of Vesuvius in AD 79. It is asked whether it is likely that the Christian faith could have been planted in Pompeii before this date; whether the cross had been adopted by Christians as a symbol so early as this; and whether Roman Christians used Latin at this early date in their liturgy of prayer. While some find it difficult to give an affirmative answer to these questions, others think the propositions perfectly possible, particularly since a cross has been found in a first-century house in Pompeian style in nearby Herculaneum.[1]

For the student of the Revelation the Christian origin of the

---

[1] The house and the room in which the cross was found is described in detail by Atkinson in his article, pp. 16f.

word-square has some interesting implications, notably the realization that the application of *alpha-omega* to the belief in God's self-
revelation in Jesus Christ was made a generation earlier than the
commonly assigned date of the composition of the book of Revelation. This suggests either that some elements of the prophecy were
composed at a time well anterior to the publication of the book as
a whole, or that the author of the Revelation adopted the Christian
confession of God in Christ as *alpha* and *omega*, and applied it first
to the prophetic declaration of God as the lord of history, and
secondly to the Christ who has appeared for salvation and is to
appear to complete the divine purpose in history and creation (see
Rev. 22 : 12–13). The latter alternative is surely to be preferred to
the former, and is perfectly comprehensible in a book which
freely appropriates apocalyptic symbols of the Jewish and
Christian traditions.

THE CALL OF JOHN TO PROPHESY 1 : 9-20

9. The vision which John now relates reminds one of the experiences of the Old Testament prophets in which they received
their call to minister to their people (see especially Isa. 6, Jer. 1,
Ezek. 1–3). Whether John's vision actually marked the beginning
of his prophetic activity we are not told. The least we can infer is
that it initiated the experiences which led to the writing of this
book. It is characteristic of the order introduced by the new
covenant that the object of a prophet's vision is not God but the
risen Christ, and equally characteristic that the prophetic commission does not set the prophet at a remove from other Christians
but binds him to them—**I John, your brother . . . share with
you in Jesus.**

In Jesus John shares with other believers **the tribulation and
the kingdom and the patient endurance.** The phrase *in Jesus*
reminds us of Paul's favourite expression 'in Christ', and has a not
dissimilar meaning, viz., fellowship with the Lord who suffered
and rose from death for mankind, and so fellowship with all who
belong to him. In that fellowship *tribulation* and *kingdom* and *patient
endurance* inhere. There is no need to ask whether the first two
members of the trio refer to the present or to the last times. For
John, as for the New Testament writers generally, the last times

have arrived. They were introduced by the redemptive action of Jesus, and will shortly come to their climax in the unveiled kingdom of Jesus. As tribulation is the lot of Christians in this age (Jn 16: 33) and will give place to its intensification under the Antichrist (Rev. 11–13), so sovereignty with Christ marks their present existence (Rev. 1 : 6) and is to find its perfect expression in the kingdom of Christ (Rev. 2 : 26ff., 5 : 10, 20 : 4ff.). Tribulation and kingdom belong to the messianic pattern (Lk. 24 : 26). To be *in Jesus*, therefore, is to experience the reality of both, and it enables that patient endurance of tribulation which ensures participation in the kingdom.

John records, **I ... was on the island called Patmos.** The past tense indicates that at the time of writing he is no longer there. Patmos is off the west coast of Asia Minor, and like other nearby islands was used as a penal settlement for persons deemed by the Roman authorities to be dangerous to the community. John was in Patmos **on account of the word of God and the testimony of Jesus.** The relatedness of the language to verse 2 has led some to consider that John was there not as a prisoner, but 'in the interests of' the word of God and testimony of Jesus, i.e., either to make it known through preaching or to receive it in vision. This is unlikely. Such passages as 6 : 9 and 20 : 4 strengthen the natural presumption that John had been despatched to Patmos because of his ministry of the word of God and the testimony of Jesus. The banishment of a Christian leader indicates hostility to the Church, but not necessarily the existence of widespread persecution. John could have been viewed as a ringleader of the Christian sect, and could have been taken into 'protective custody' to avoid the possibility of his creating a disturbance. As often in Christian history, the measures against the gospel proved to be for the furtherance of the gospel (Phil. 1 : 12). John's banishment gave opportunity to receive the word of God and testimony of Jesus Christ which came to him in Patmos and subsequently to publish it.

10. John's vision took place **on the Lord's day.** This is not to be interpreted as implying a removal of the author to the 'day of the Lord' to witness the events of that day. The term *Lord's* in the phrase *the Lord's day* is an adjective, *kuriakos*, from the noun *kurios*, lord, and it means 'belonging to the lord'. Paul uses it in the well known phrase 'the Lord's Supper', i.e. the supper which is for the

Lord and in his honour. Such is the meaning in the phrase *the Lord's day*. Deissmann has given many illustrations of the use of the term *kuriakos* in official state circles to denote what belongs to Caesar, who claimed the title *kurios*, lord. We read of 'the lord's treasury' (= the imperial treasury), 'the lord's service' (the imperial service), 'the lord's finances' (the imperial finances). Is there any relationship between this use and the Christian 'Lord's day'? Probably yes. In Egypt, in the time of Ptolemy Euergetes, the twenty-fifth day of each month was called 'the king's day', in honour of his ascending the throne of his father on the twenty-fifth day of Dios. This custom spread, so that in various parts of the nearer Orient (in Asia Minor as well as Egypt) a day in the month came to be known as Sebaste, i.e., 'Augustus' day' (virtually 'Caesar's day'). Some scholars think that Sebaste may have been the name of a day of the week in some areas. Whether a day of the week or of the month, the precedent was sufficient for an unknown Christian to claim Sunday as the day when the true and only *kurios* rose from death to the sovereignty of the universe. The Lord's day accordingly is the day set apart in celebration of the accession of Jesus the Lord to the throne of God. As a title it speedily established itself among Christians, and among early Christian writings it appears in the *Didache* (14:1) and in the *Letter of Ignatius to the Magnesians* (9:1).[1]

The trumpet-like **voice** which John heard will be that of the risen Lord, rather than of an angel (observe the repetition of the command **Write what you see** in verse 19, where the speaker is Christ).

11. The enumeration of the **seven churches** is that of their occurrence on the road which led from **Ephesus** northwards through **Smyrna** to **Pergamum** and then wound southwards through **Thyatira, Sardis, Philadelphia,** and **Laodicea.** W. M. Ramsay considered that these seven cities were centres alike for postal delivery and for judicial administration, with Ephesus as their great administrative centre. It is conceivable that for John the social significance of these seven cities and the religious significance of the number seven conveniently coincided. Lohmeyer followed up Ramsay's political interest in the seven cities with a religious

[1] For a discussion of inscriptions relating to the Lord's day, see Deissmann, *Light from the Ancient East*, London, 1910, pp. 361ff, and his article 'Lord's Day' in *Encyclopaedia Biblica*, III, cols. 2813ff.

application. The seven churches were clearly individual congregations. But they also formed the natural centres of groups of churches in Roman Asia, with Ephesus as the leading church of the province. They further represented the Church of Christ in the whole world (see 2 : 7, etc.). Lohmeyer went on to suggest the peculiar fitness of the seven churches under Ephesus to represent the whole Church, for at the time of John's writing the centre of the Christian world had shifted from Palestine to Asia Minor. Roman Asia had become the most strongly christianized area in the whole world, and Ephesus had now succeeded Jerusalem, both in its privilege and in its duty to the Church and the world (see Lohmeyer, pp. 42f.). This is an interesting viewpoint, not least in consideration of the amount of Christian literature connected with the area, e.g., the epistles to the Ephesians, Colossians, the Pastoral Epistles, and the whole group of Johannine writings.

12. In John's vision of the Son of man his first impression is the sight of **seven golden lampstands.** The risen Lord is in the midst of his people and his congregations are gathered about their risen Head. The imagery of lampstands for churches goes back to Zechariah 4 : 2ff., but while the one people of God is there represented by the seven-branched lampstand of the temple, the seven congregations here appear as single lampstands clustered about the Lord. This hints at their nature as each representing the reality of the whole Church, which is the new Israel, yet in their diversity forming one people of the risen Lord. Whether or not John had the saying in mind, his picture inevitably recalls Matthew 5 : 14.

13-16. The portrayal of the risen Christ is especially indebted to the description of the Ancient of Days in Daniel 7 : 9 and of the angel in Daniel 10 : 5f. It is intended to convey the impression of one who possesses the glory of heaven and who shares the likeness of God himself. Significantly John employs the precise Danielic phrase **one like a son of man** (i.e., like a man), not the title which appears in the Synoptic Gospels, the Son of man. It is a direct reminiscence of Daniel 7 : 13, in which the 'dominion and glory and kingdom' of the whole world is given by God to the representative of the saints of the Most High. In this context, therefore, John intends the title to convey the notion of glory, not humility. The **long robe** is often identified with that which the high priest wore in Israel (Exod. 28 : 4). While it is true that the high priest wore such a robe, it was also worn by men of rank generally, and there is no need to bring in the high priest here. The **golden girdle** was worn high **round his breast,** in contrast to the lower position round the waist, as a workman who tucked his robe about it when at work. The ascended Lord has completed *his* work. The fulsome language about the **white hair** echoes Daniel 7 : 9f., and is intended to associate Christ with the God of the ages, the Judge of the world. **Eyes . . . like a flame of fire** recall Daniel 10 : 6, and comport well with the representation of Christ as judge, for his eyes penetrate the hidden depths of the heart. **Feet . . . like burnished bronze** again are reminiscent of Daniel 10 : 6, but also of the cherubim in Ezek. 1 : 4ff.; except that John's word for *bronze* denotes a very precious metal, compounded of gold and silver, beloved of the ancients for its flashing qualities. The voice of the Christ, **like the sound of many waters,** is as the voice of God, described in Ezekiel 43 : 2. It connotes awe-inspiring power and majesty. **From his mouth issued a two-edged sword,** for the word of the risen Christ, overwhelming in its power and majesty, is a word of judgment. In this connection we instinctively think of the role of Christ as judge of the world (as in Dan. 7 the Ancient of Days is judge of the nations), but we must not forget that the vision of the risen Lord introduces the letters addressed to the seven churches. The Christ is the judge of his people (cf. 2 : 16). Yet even in judgment his purpose is beneficent: **in his right hand he held** the **seven stars.** The Lord holds his churches in order to uphold them and protect them (for the significance of the seven stars, see on v. 20).

17, 18. John's reaction to the vision of the glorified Christ is typical of all who have known any comparable experience (see Dan. 10 : 7ff., which is especially in mind, but also Jos. 5 : 14, Isa. 6 : 5, Ezek. 1 : 28, 3 : 23, Lk. 5 : 8). Equally characteristic are the reassuring words of the Lord to the prophet, but in this case the declaration of Christ actually forms the climax of the vision. **I am the first and the last, and the living one** is virtually an exposition of the title *Alpha and Omega* (attributed to God in 1 : 8), and combines Isaiah 44 : 6 with the divine name revealed at the bush, Exodus 3 : 14. As the initiator of all things and the finisher of God's purpose for his creation, the Christ is above the limitations of time to which man is subject. He is the eternally *living one*—a favourite title among the rabbis for God. But the eternal one accomplished the incomprehensible: **I died.** Yet further: **Behold**

I am alive for evermore. The new exodus which the redeemer came to achieve entailed both death and resurrection, and by this twin event he brought about an emancipation which included liberation from guilt and participation in the eternal kingdom. Its significance as an event for others is implied in the affirmation, **I have the keys of Death and Hades.** To the risen Lord has been given power over death as the last enemy of man and the realm of death into which all men pass. Again, this is an assertion of authority such as God alone possesses. The Jerusalem Targum on Deuteronomy 28 : 12 has the comment, 'Four keys are delivered into the hand of the Lord of the world which he has given to no ruler: the key of life, the key of the graves, the key of food, the key of rain.' Death and the grave, therefore, hold no terrors for Christ's people, nor need they fear those who have the power to inflict death and send them to the grave—an important reminder in the context of this book. It is even possible that *Death* and *Hades* in this passage are personified, as in Revelation 6 : 8. That would picture Christ as having wrested the keys from the powers of death and the realm of the dead. He is the conqueror of life and death, as he is the lord of the living and the dead (cf. Rom. 14 : 8–9). Such a view would undoubtedly suit the doctrine of the *descensus ad inferos* (cf. 1 Pet. 3 : 18ff.), but whether this language demands it, as many commentators have suggested, is doubtful (for a discussion on this see Charles, ad loc.).

19. The command **write what you see, what is and what is to take place hereafter** is generally viewed as indicating the author's analysis of the book of Revelation: *what you see* = the vision of chapter 1; *what is* = the letters to the churches, chapters 2–3; *what is to take place hereafter* = the visions from chapter 4 to the end. It accords more with the actual contents of the prophecy to recognize that *what is and what is to take place hereafter* applies to the entire book, for there is a perpetual movement between past, present, and future in the visions. The belief that *what is to take place hereafter* rightly describes chapters 4–22 has been a cause of frequent misunderstanding of the visions through their supposed exclusive reference to the future.

20. The interpretation of **the mystery** (= secret) **of the seven stars** as **the angels of the seven churches** has itself led to a multiplicity of interpretations. The simplest is to view the *angels* as guardian angels, responsible for the welfare of each congregation.

The idea has nothing intrinsically improbable about it, for it has a close analogy in the Danielic doctrine of each nation having a kind of guardian- or patron-angel (see Dan. 10:13f., 20f.). Nevertheless, it seems a difficult idea to think of John as commissioned to write letters to angels, with instructions how to carry out their tasks better. Moreover, the letters which follow clearly have in view the congregations themselves, and even at times individuals within the congregations (e.g., 2:24, 3:20). *Angel* literally means *messenger*, and in the Old Testament the term is freely applied to human as well as to heavenly messengers. From early times therefore it has been common to interpret the angels of the churches as men of responsibility within the churches, whether elders or bishops or teachers, or even literally messengers sent to John from the churches. Billerbeck revived an early conjecture that 'angel of the church' is a precise translation of the Hebrew phrase *shaliach zibbor* = one authorized by the congregation. In the synagogue the name was given to one appointed to lead in the prayers of the congregation, but no office was involved—anyone could be so appointed for a single occasion. On the other hand, the term *shaliach* was widely used for 'authorized person', and the equivalent terms for this are apostle (*apostolos* = Greek for 'one sent') and angel (*malak* = Hebrew for 'one sent'). Billerbeck, therefore, concludes that in John's time and circles 'angel of the churches' could have been the name for the presiding officer of a congregation (see Strack-Billerbeck, ad loc.). Again, while the interpretation is attractive, it faces the same difficulty earlier mentioned, that the seven letters, although addressed to the angels of the churches, have in view the congregations themselves, not simply their leaders.

The most plausible solution of the problem recognizes the Danielic background of angels assigned to nations, but sees them as akin to the Persian *fravashis*, i.e., heavenly counterparts of earthly individuals and communities. The angels of the churches are then heavenly counterparts of the earthly congregations. The idea is not to be literalized, as though John thought of congregations seated in heaven above, answering to their equivalents on earth below. We help ourselves if we think of them as existentially in heaven though living on earth. John writes to people who form very earthly communities, whose life is characterized by the failures and weakness to which any human organization is prone. But these communities have one feature which marks them off

from all others on earth: they are *in Jesus* (v. 9), and so saints of
the Most High, priests and kings with Christ to God, lights in the
world through whom the Light of the world shines. It is because
their determinative life is in Jesus that John writes to the 'angels'
of the churches. Their earthly conduct is the reflection of their
heavenly relationship.

The present writer is encouraged to hold this view, not only by
its plausibility, but through the significance of *the seven stars* in
Christ's right hand, of which the angels are a secondary representation. We know that the seven planets were a common symbol
in the ancient world for sovereignty. Even in John's day there were
many who believed that the planets were gods, exercising a powerful and even fearful influence over the lives of men. From this it
was an easy transition to make of them a symbol of the political
power exercised by the Roman Caesars over the world, and in this
sense the seven stars often occur on imperial coins. When John
declares that the seven stars are in Christ's right hand, he is claiming that the sovereignty over this world resides not in the Caesars of
Rome but in the Lord of the Church. These seven stars he then
defines as the angels of the churches. The purpose of John's prophecy, from its first page to its last, is to assure the saints of God
that they are kings and priests to God through the redemptive
grace of Christ. The purport of the symbolism of *the seven stars =
the angels of the churches* is therefore plain: it declares that the
sovereignty of this world belongs not to those who proudly claim
to be the saviours and lords of men and who seek to crush the
Church of Jesus. It belongs to the Christ of God and his people.
Lohmeyer affirms that in this feature John's opening vision contains the heart and kernel of the whole of the Revelation. The rest
of the prophecy unfolds the significance of this vision of Christ and
how the destiny of his people finds it fulfilment.

THE LETTERS TO THE SEVEN CHURCHES 2:1-3:22

The seven letters of chapters 2–3 comprise the best known and
most frequently expounded section of the book of Revelation. Not
surprisingly the idea has been mooted that the letters had an
existence prior to the composition of the main book. Charles held
that they were composed about twenty years earlier, in the reign

of Vespasian, and that they were sent to the individual churches. He sees a difference of viewpoint between the letters and the main prophecy, in that no reference to the cult of the Caesars appears in the letters, nor is there in them a hint of the impending martyrdom of the entire Church, which he finds in the prophecy itself. On the contrary, the letters reflect the usual Christian belief in the survival of the Church to the coming of Christ. Charles, therefore, suggested that the original letters were amplified by John in the light of the changing attitude of Rome to the Church. The promises to the conquerors (directed to the future martyrs) were added at the close of the letters, 3 : 10 was inserted as a reflection of the coming world-wide persecution of the Church, and an introductory announcement of the risen Lord, in terms drawn from the vision of chapter 1, formed the opening of each letter.[1]

There is nothing objectionable in the idea of a writer incorporating earlier materials in his writings, and it could be so with the seven letters. Charles' hypothesis, however, is not a plausible one. Apart from the consideration that the letters, when shorn of their supposed amplifications, become very short (so short as to make it difficult to envisage their being sent in isolation), the differences of viewpoint between the letters and the rest of the prophecy are not so sharp as Charles believed. For example, the conviction that the Church will survive to the parousia is not confined to chapters 2-3; it appears elsewhere in the book (e.g., in 16 : 15, and especially in the epilogue, 22 : 7, 11ff.). Nor are the victors, to whom promises relating to the kingdom are given, necessarily martyrs (see below on 2 : 7). But the idea of a victor or conqueror entails the concept of the Christian as a warrior for Christ, and this is eminently suitable to a situation already experienced as hostile and which threatens to worsen at any time by the strengthening of forces opposed to God. In view, therefore, of the close relation of the letters with the opening and closing visions of the Revelation, it seems right to assume that the prophecy as a whole provides the context in which the letters are to be understood.[2]

[1] See Charles' commentary, pp. 43-6.

[2] The clear reflections of the closing vision in the promises to the conquerors proves not that the letters were written after the rest of the prophecy, but that the letters were written after the vision in its entirety had been received. It may be assumed as self-evident, however, that the doctrines embodied in the closing vision of the kingdom had been espoused by John before the experiences which led him to write chapters 20-2.

The unity of the letters in the main prophecy is strengthened by the observation, frequently made, that they are more like pro-phetic oracles than formal epistles. The likeness extends to form and content. Lohse aptly cites the parallel of the first two chapters of Amos, which contain seven prophetic declarations of judgment, six directed to states which surrounded Israel and the last to Israel itself (he further notes that there is no likelihood that the seven oracles of Amos were sent separately to the nations con-cerned). Each of the seven letters begins with the formula *tade legei*, rendered in the *RSV* by the phrase *the words of*, but which is a Greek equivalent of the Old Testament prophetic declaration, *Thus saith (the Lord)*. The sole appearance of John's phrase in the New Testament outside the seven letters occurs in Acts 21 : 11, in a prophetic utterance of the Jewish Christian prophet Agabus. Significantly Agabus, the Christian prophet, declares 'Thus saith the Holy Spirit', while John writes, 'Thus saith the Christ', though John concludes each letter with a call to hear what the Holy Spirit says to the churches. The content of the letters is char-acteristic of biblical prophecy in their constant appeal for works which can stand the test of the Lord's judgment and which will not disqualify the hearers from participation in the inheritance of the kingdom. Each letter is adapted to the needs of the individual congregations, but by the generalization that concludes each one the message is driven home to all the churches.

The structure of the letters is uniform, with deviations due chiefly to the individual circumstances of the congregations. Each letter begins with an introductory statement from the risen Lord, citing elements of the opening vision, which are usually pertinent to the message that follows. The message itself conveys praise for the commendable qualities of the church and criticism of its deficiencies (the letters to Sardis and Laodicea have no com-mendations, and those to Smyrna and Philadelphia no censures). The conclusion is marked by a promise to the victor, relating to blessings which are to be bestowed in the kingdom of Christ, and an exhortation for all to heed what the Spirit is saying to the churches.

THE LETTER TO THE CHURCH AT EPHESUS **2 : 1-7**

From every point of view—of travel and trade, of politics and religion—the city of Ephesus was one of the great cities of the

ancient world, and certainly the greatest in Asia Minor. Its position on the coast as the western limit of the Roman system of
roads and as a great seaport ensured that. It was world famous for
its temple of Artemis, a Greek female deity whose worship had
coalesced with that of the mother-goddess of the middle east. The
enthusiasm with which the reputation of Ephesus as the temple-
warden of Artemis was maintained is reflected in Luke's report of
the riot, occasioned by the success of the Christian preaching in
that city (Ac. 19:23ff.). The Ephesians' interest in works of
magic, their religious syncretism, and crass superstition, are exemplified in Luke's account of the growth of the church there (Ac.
19:13-20). For John's generation it was even more significant that
the city prided itself on being warden of two temples devoted to
the worship of the emperor.

As the city, so the church in Ephesus was the most important in
Asia Minor, and possibly the most influential church in the world
at the end of the first century AD. From the letters of Paul and the
book of Acts it is evident that the apostle had the most notable
ministry of his missionary career in this city. Later tradition associated not only Paul's colleague Timothy and John the apostle with
the Ephesian church, but also Mary the Lord's mother, who was
believed to be buried there. It is comprehensible that teachers of
many kinds and of every shade of doctrine were drawn to Ephesus,
to seek the patronage of the church and to influence its ways.

1. The Lord is announced as he **who holds the seven stars
in his right hand, who walks among the seven golden
lampstands.** This serves as a reminder that the churches, whose
life derives from their fellowship in Jesus, are upheld by him and
subject to his power, and their conduct falls beneath his searching
scrutiny as he moves among them on earth. Both elements of the
description are in place in a message which stresses the disciplinary
judgment of Christ upon his people.

2, 3. I know your works. Each message to the churches commences with these words, or their equivalent. Generally, as here,
they express an assurance of the Lord's understanding of the
struggles and achievements of his followers, though they can (as in
3:1 and 15) indicate his knowledge of their failings. In a book
written to strengthen faith, the emphasis in these letters on *works* is
noteworthy. Works are the criterion of the genuineness of faith,
alike in the last judgment and in this time of judgment, hence the

persistent demand for works worthy of faith. **Works . . . toil and
. . . patient endurance** are a traditional Christian triad (cf.
1 Th. 1 : 3), but in this context the works in question especially
relate to *toil* in maintaining true faith, where false teachers are
attempting to win the Ephesians to a different gospel (cf. Gal.
1 : 6f.), and *endurance* for Christ's name in face of temptations to
quit the field.

Who are **those who call themselves apostles but are not**?
From evidence within the New Testament letters generally,
especially 1 and 2 Corinthians, the Pastorals, and the General
Epistles, and from verse 6 and other passages in the seven letters,
we may fairly conclude that they were Gnostics. Such teachers
characteristically made appeal to the heavenly Christ over
against the earthly Jesus, and to the inspiration of the Spirit over
against the apostolic traditions. Their description as **evil men** is
called forth not so much by their unorthodox doctrinal opinions
as by the moral evil which resulted from their doctrine. The
gnostic tenet that matter is evil and only spirit is good led to the
two extremes of asceticism, which abhorred the flesh, and licence,
which regarded it of no account. It lies to hand that the *evil men*
are *the Nicolaitans* of verse 6, whose *works* were hateful not only to
the Ephesian believers but also to Christ. It would appear that
these teachers engaged in immoral conduct and advocated
'Christian' freedom for all believers so to act. Religious sanction
for the permissive society is a very ancient phenomenon. It is
difficult to know whether later statements about the Nicolaitans
were based on actual knowledge of them or on John's references to
them in these letters. They were viewed in the next century as a
society which shared wives as well as their goods, much in the
style of some modern hippy communes. The churches of Pergamum and Thyatira were plagued by people who advocated this
kind of religion (see 3 : 14ff., 20ff.). Anyone who has confronted
teachers of this sort will understand that the Ephesians had to
'toil' to resist them, for such advocates are persistent in their arguments, difficult to rebut, and loth to depart. The Ephesians subsequently gained a reputation for refusal to listen to heretical
teaching and imperviousness to heretical sects (Ignatius alludes to
it in his *Letter to the Ephesians*, 6 : 2 and 9 : 1). This should not be
despised by us, for whom religion tends to be a mild hobby. The
Ephesians in all probability were taught by bitter experience.

4-6. It is right to hate evil in all its forms. The enthusiasm which hates, however, has to be on guard lest it be extended to doers as well as deeds. It is possible that the Ephesians had not watched carefully enough, and that their virtue produced a related vice. The charge is levelled against them: **you have abandoned the love you had at first.** The context suggests that the love which had abated was primarily love for fellow men. This is confirmed by the intimation which follows, that the loss of the early love was accompanied by the cessation of early works of love. Nevertheless the conjunction of love to God and love to man, stressed by our Lord (Mk 12 : 29ff.), is basic to Christian experience. Where love for God wanes, love for man diminishes, and where love for man is soured, love for God degenerates into religious formalism, and both constitute a denial of the revelation of God in Christ. If the price paid by the Ephesians for the preservation of true Christianity was the loss of love, the price was too high, for Christianity without love is a perverted faith. The gravity of the situation is indicated in a warning. Unless there is effective repentance and a return to the early love, **I will come to you and remove your lampstand from its place.** The bluntness of the words must be allowed full force. Christ will come to the Ephesian church for judgment, as one day he will come to the world in judgment to sweep away its evil. (This is more natural to the context than to interpret the words as a threat of judgment upon the Ephesian church at the parousia of Christ.) If the Lord so comes to the church of Ephesus for judgment, that will mean the end of its existence as a church of Christ. Whatever outward appearances may suggest, the congregation will be as devoid of Christ as the temple of Jerusalem was of the presence of God's glory when his judgment fell upon it (see Ezek. 11 : 22f.), and it will lose its place in the fellowship of Christ's congregations. The prospect is a fearful one, but as yet it is only a possibility. The point of no return has not been reached. The Ephesian believers were not wholly without love. It was their early love which had faded, and the early love must be recovered. How is the lost love of a church to be recovered? **Remember then from what you have fallen, repent, and do the works you did at first.** The Ephesians must, to cite the parable of C. S. Lewis, embark on a 'pilgrim's regress'. They must go back to the cross and empty tomb of Christ, where love was kindled at the first. Or rather, return to the Christ who died and rose again, at his feet renounce their self-righteousness, and there let love be born again. (On **Nicolaitans,** see notes on verse 3.)

7. The Lord whose voice is as a trumpet (1 : 10) calls on all the churches to give heed to what he says to the church of Ephesus. Yet not the Lord, but **the Spirit** addresses the churches. This is surprising. There is no suggestion that to this point Christ has been the speaker, and now the Spirit closes with an utterance of special importance. In all cases the speaker who figures in the promises to the conquerors is the risen Lord (see especially 2 : 26f., 3 : 5f., 11f., 21), and in the last four letters the Spirit's word rounds off the whole communication. We are therefore compelled to recognize that throughout the letters the word of Christ is the word of the Spirit. Christ is not identical with the Spirit (cf. 1 : 4–5), but he speaks to the churches through the Spirit. This understanding of the relation of Christ to the Spirit is virtually identical with the concept of the Paraclete in the upper room discourses of John 14–16 (see especially Jn 16 : 12–15)—an interesting datum for the relationship of the Fourth Gospel to the Revelation.

What does the Spirit say to the churches? Not, surely, the promise to the conqueror alone. The Spirit's message to the churches is the content of the whole letter, as is suggested by the position of the appeal in the last four letters. By adding such a call, the message to a single congregation is broadened in application to all the churches of Asia, and so to the Church throughout the world. The message to the church at Ephesus is indeed of significance to all Christ's congregations, for they are composed of men and women of common clay, with common frailty in face of temptations, common need of repentance and grace, and having the same Lord as their head. The Spirit calls on every congregation to show vigilance towards evil men and their evil deeds, and at the same time to keep ablaze an ardent love which expresses itself in loving deeds, for without such love the church of Christ is spurious. John may not repeat his point often in the later chapters of his book but it must be owned that he makes it very plain in this, the opening letter to the greatest of all churches. If the greatest must take heed lest it fall, how much more the rest?

To him who conquers a promise of life is given. Who is the *conqueror*, to whom promises are directed at the end of each letter? The most commonly adopted view is tersely stated by Kiddle: 'In two of the promises—those to Laodicea and Thyatira—the conqueror can be only the martyr: if in two, then in all.'[1] Let the reader consult the passages referred to, and judge the correctness of the observation. The idea that 2 : 26ff. has martyrs exclusively in view arises not from the text but from its relation to 20 : 4ff., interpreted without regard to the implications of the doxology of 1 : 5f., the song of exultation in 5 : 9f., and the nuptial imagery relating to the Church in 19 : 8ff. The restriction of 3 : 21 to martyrs is based on the notion that since the victory of the conqueror is likened to the victory of Christ, and Christ's victory entailed his death, only he conquers who dies for his faith as Christ did. In any other book this would be regarded as an extraordinary interpretation, but neither does it fit its context here. The previous verse (3 : 20) declares that if any man opens his life to Christ, the Lord will enter and eat with him—i.e., the Lord and the believer will together enjoy a foretaste of the messianic feast. The promise follows that he who conquers will sit with Christ on his throne— naturally in the messianic kingdom, when he with Christ will enjoy the messianic feast (cf. 19 : 8ff.). Is it really intended that we should distinguish between the believer and the martyr here— that the foretaste of the kingdom is given to him who shares life with Christ now, but that which answers to it is reserved for him who is martyred for Christ?

The issue is sharpened in the promise to the Smyrnaean church. Here the conqueror is assured that he shall not be hurt by the second death (2 : 11), i.e., he will not be condemned with the wicked (20 : 14f.). This is the reverse aspect of the declaration in the preceding verse, *Be faithful unto death, and I will give you the crown of life* (v. 10). It is to be observed on the one hand that the promise of verse 11 conveys more than the general notion that there is a worse fate than physical death. It is an apocalyptic expression of the doctrine of justification in a negative form— Romans 8 : 1 gives the same idea in a non-apocalyptic manner. This promise cannot be restricted to martyrs. It is part of the gospel proclaimed to the world and assured to all who believe. On the other hand, if verse 10 is framed for the encouragement of Christians facing suffering which could lead to martyrdom, the

[1] Op. cit., pp. 62f.

letter makes it plain that only some of the church at Smyrna will
be called on to make the supreme sacrifice (vv. 9f.). The promise
to the conqueror at Smyrna is for the encouragement of the whole
church, all the members of which are to experience tribulation, all
of whom are called to be faithful to death, some of whom may lay
down their lives. But its assurance of vindication in the judgment
is extended to every faithful believer.

That this interpretation applies to all the promises to the conquerors may be confirmed by a glance at their contents. They
offer the following prospects:

2 : 7: Eating the fruit of the tree of life in the paradise of God.

2 : 10: Escape from the second death.

2 : 17: The gift of hidden manna, and a white stone with a
new name.

2 : 26ff.: Rule with Christ over the nations, and the morning
star.

3 : 5: White garments, the name included in the roll of the
living, and acknowledgement by Christ in the judgment.

3 : 12: Becoming a pillar in God's temple, and bearing the
name of God and the city of God and Christ's new name.

3 : 21: A place with Christ on his throne.

All these symbols relate to participation in the kingdom of God,
as described in the closing vision of the Revelation. They include
acquittal at the judgment (2 : 10, 3 : 5), the gift of eternal life
(2 : 7, 16, 27, 3 : 5), a share in Christ's rule (2 : 26ff., 3 : 21), and a
place in the city of God (3 : 12). This suggests that the promises to
the conquerors are fundamentally assurances to the faithful of the
benefits of Christ's redemption, expressed in the language of
apocalyptic. In the nature of the case the promises afford inspiration for faith and fortitude in all who may be called to lay down
their lives for Christ, and they are intended to do so. But the whole
Church faces a period of severe testing, and the letters themselves
allow neither the view that all who belong to the Church must die,
nor that participation in the redemption of Christ is restricted to a
group of believers within the Church.

Possibly our attention has been fixed too exclusively on the
victor instead of being directed to the Victor who makes victory
possible. Lohmeyer pointed out that the idea of conquering has its
background in the history of religions, in which God is the sole

conqueror and the believer his warrior who conquers through the
divine aid.[1] Such a concept is peculiarly appropriate for the
Christian faith, since the Christ is the redeemer who has overcome the world and all evil powers, and he gives his followers to
share in his victory. While this is implied rather than stated in
3:21, the Christian's dependence on Christ's victory is made
abundantly clear in 12:11. The latter statement makes a crucial
addition to the vision of the woman and the dragon, for by it we
understand that the conquest of the dragon is not by Michael and
his hosts, but by the Christ who has died and ascended to the
throne of God. By their confession of faith in the Victor, and per-
sistence in the confession till death, the followers of the Lamb also
conquer the evil powers that tyrannize this world. The essential
characteristic of the conqueror, therefore, is that he participates in
Christ's conquest by faith, and through persistance in faith he
continues to share in Christ's victory to the end—whether the end
be death or the parousia of Christ. The end may well be martyrdom for some, but that is not the chief point of the concept. Its
essential feature is participation in Christ's victory to the limit. It
is likely that John would have been ready to confess, with the
author of the first epistle of John, that the believer has already
conquered the world through Christ, and is a continuous victor
now as he maintains faith in Christ. (1 Jn. 5:4; the tenses
should be observed: 'Whatever is born of God overcomes the
world; and this is the victory that overcomes the world, our
faith.')

To the conqueror the promise is given **I will grant to eat of
the tree of life, which is in the paradise of God.** The mind is
inevitably carried to the opening chapters of Genesis and the
closing chapters of the Revelation. It was the merit of Gunkel that
he called attention to the importance of the eschatological
principle, enshrined in the maxim quoted in *Barnabas* 6:13, 'The
Lord says, Behold I make the last things as the first.'[2] The first
creation provides the pattern for the new creation. Paradise lost
gives the clue to paradise regained. The term *paradise* here employed occurs in the Septuagint at Genesis 2:8, 15, 3:23f., to
render the term *garden* (i.e., the garden of Eden), and correctly so,
for paradise is a Persian loan word (*pairi-daiza*), meaning a walling

---

[1] Commentary, p. 23.
[2] Gunkel's *Schöpfung und Chaos* is virtually an exposition of this axiom.

round, and so a park surrounded by a wall.[1] At the other end of
the scale, *garden of Eden* and *paradise* become interchangeable terms
in Jewish writings for the abode of the blessed in the future life.
Jewish teachers distinguished between the paradise of Adam, the
paradise of the blessed in heaven (cf. 2 C. 12 : 1ff.), and the
paradise of the righteous in the future kingdom of God. In their
anticipations of the paradise to come the tree of life features
prominently, and its fruits (note the plural, and cf. Rev. 22 : 2)
are said to be freely available to the righteous. John had no
hesitation in appropriating this imagery to represent eternal life in
the coming kingdom, since it is through the risen Christ that the
ancient promise of the kingdom is to find its fulfilment, and it is to
him who persists in faith in the redeemer Christ that participation
in the kingdom is assured. John would doubtless have concurred
with Jewish writers as to the suitability of fruits of the tree of life as
a symbol of eternal life,[2] since the kingdom of Christ is characterized above all by the delights of fellowship with God and the
Lamb (cf. 22 : 1–5).

THE LETTER TO THE CHURCH AT SMYRNA 2 : 8–11

The city of Smyrna, thanks to its situation on the coast and at the
end of a trade route to the east, has been a prosperous city from
pre-Christian times to the present day. Its loyalty to Rome went
back to the period before Rome achieved its position as the leading
world-power. The city erected a temple to the goddess of Rome in
195 BC, and in AD 26 it was honoured with the permission to build
a temple to Tiberius, Livia, and the Senate. The founding of the
church in Smyrna is not recorded, but we may assume that it took
place in the period of Paul's two years' ministry in Ephesus, when
'all the residents of Asia heard the word of the Lord' (Ac. 19 : 10).
It is possible that one of the best known Christians of early times
was a member of this church at the time of John's writing his letter
to it. About twenty years after the sending of this letter (AD 115),
Ignatius wrote to the church at Smyrna and to its bishop Polycarp.
Precisely forty years later the church at Smyrna wrote a detailed

---

[1] The Greek term *paradeisos* was used by Xenophon of the parks of Persian
kings and their nobility. See the lexicon of Arndt and Gingrich.

[2] For Jewish thought on the tree of life and the garden of God, see Strack-
Billerbeck, IV, part 2, *Excursus on Sheol*, etc., pp. 1118ff.

account of the martyrdom of Polycarp, who had become a venerable figure. At his trial he confessed that he had served the Lord for eighty-six years and therefore could not forswear him. It is well possible, therefore, that when John wrote to the church at Smyrna, Polycarp was already actively engaged in its service, even if he had not yet become its leader. The message sent to the church had a poignant application to this saint of God, who was to glorify Christ by a notable martyrdom.

8. The title of Christ as **the first and the last, who died and came to life,** echoes 1 : 17f. and anticipates verses 10f. To a congregation, faced with the prospect of renewed persecution and the death of some of its members, the reminder that Jesus is the lord of Easter serves as a welcome consolation.

9. The message begins with an assurance of the Lord's knowledge of the Smyrnaeans' difficulties—their **tribulation, poverty** and the **slander** to which they are subject from the Jews. Unlike some of the other churches, notably that in Laodicea, *tribulation* and *poverty* are the continuing lot of the Smyrnaean Christians. If the poverty is not the consequence of the tribulation, it will certainly have been aggravated by it, in view of the habit of persecutors to plunder their unfortunate victims (see Heb. 10 : 34). The Lord knows about this situation, but he refrains from intervening. He does not remove the poverty, he does not vindicate his followers in face of the Jewish slanders, nor does he frustrate the Devil's machinations which will bring about the imprisonment and death of some. He simply encourages them to endure. Why no more than this? The author of the book of Job wrestled with the problem, and so have the saints of God ever since. John provides no answer, but his whole book is written in the conviction that the Church of Christ has the vocation of suffering with its Lord, that it may share his glory in the kingdom he has won for mankind. In this he follows in the footsteps of Jesus and is one with his fellow prophets and apostles in the New Testament (cf. Mk 8 : 34ff., 13 : 9ff., Jn 15–16, 2 C. 1 : 3ff., 4 : 7–18, Col. 1 : 24f., 1 Pet. 2–4, etc.). If the phrase in verse 10 *that you may be tested* relates to the divine intention of the suffering, and not simply the desire of the Devil, that would indicate that the suffering is permitted to ensure the approvedness of those for whom the kingdom is prepared.

The opposition of the Jews at Smyrna to Christians was not untypical. Acts and the epistles of Paul provide many illustrations of

Jewish violence against the Church, and Christian writers in the
next century attest the continuance of their active hostility. Never
was opposition so extreme as at Smyrna, when Polycarp was
accused as a Christian. The letter from the church of Smyrna
relates that Jews joined forces with the pagans in denouncing
Polycarp as one who resisted the state religion, and that they
cried, 'This is the teacher of Asia, the father of the Christians, the
puller down of our gods, who teaches numbers not to sacrifice nor
to worship.' They were one with the pagans in demanding his
death, and they diligently assisted in gathering timber for his burning, although it took place on a sabbath day.

Jews who strenuously resist the people of Christ are declared to
have forfeited their very name, for *Jews* signify the true people of
God (cf. Rom. 2:28f.); but here men who should form the
'synagogue of the Lord' (Num. 16:3, as rendered in the Septuagint) have become **a synagogue of Satan.** No longer the
Israel of God (Gal. 6:16), they have degenerated to become tools
of the accuser.[1] Naturally, this is not to be generalized, as though
John believed that the whole Jewish nation had become the people
of Satan. His description applies to a synagogue which implacably
opposed the people of Christ (as the synagogue in Philadelphia,
3:8ff.), and so perverted its nature. The first of the seven letters
was written to give warning that a church of Christ can also become perverted and forfeit its character (2:4-5).

10. Yet more difficult times are ahead of the church at Smyrna.
**The devil is about to throw some of you into prison ...
and ... you will have tribulation.** The reference to prison does
not imply that the Roman authorities are now to turn against the
church. The Devil will presumably use his same agents, 'the
synagogue of Satan', to stir up further trouble. By their accusations they will cause Christians to be committed to prison—not
with a view to prolonged incarceration, but there to await trial
which shall determine whether they are to live or die. This
tribulation will last **for ten days,** i.e., an indefinite but short time
(cf. Gen. 24:55, Dan. 1:12ff.), yet long enough to entail the
ultimate sacrifice for some.

To the believer who remains **faithful to death ... I will give
the crown of life.** It is natural to interpret the crown of the
laurel wreath which is given to the victor in the games, as clearly

[1] For Satan as Accuser, cf. 12:9-10.

is the case in 2 Timothy 2 : 5 (cf. 1 C. 9 : 24f., Phil. 3 : 14, Jas
1 : 12, 1 Pet. 5 : 4). It is not impossible, however, that the symbol
in this instance may have in view the representations applied in
the ancient world, alike to divine beings and to blessed mortals, of
a crown of light surrounding the head, to indicate the glory of the
one on whom it rests. If such were in view it would mean, 'Be
faithful unto death, and I will crown you with glory in the life of
the age to come.'

**11. He who conquers shall not be hurt by the second
death.** The meaning is indicated in 20 : 14f. The *second death* was a
familiar concept to the Jews, though the precise term is not
attested till late. To them it implied a contrast between the death
which all must suffer and the fate of those who are doomed never
to escape its power, whether because they do not qualify for
resurrection, or because they suffer judgment in the world to
come.[1] To suffer the latter fate is to die twice. The pertinence of the
thought in verse 11 is clear: the church of Smyrna faces a period of
trial in which some shall surely die. But to die under the wrath of
man is small compared with the prospect of suffering the judgment
of God. The conqueror cannot be hurt by the second death—
naturally, for he is to receive the crown of life. The negative presumes the positive gift. But the negative is not unimportant. The
second death is as real a prospect as the crown of life. It is unthinkable to allow the latter to slip from one's possession and to
fall victim to the former. **He who has an ear, let him hear ...**
We must overcome!

THE LETTER TO THE CHURCH OF PERGAMUM **2 : 12–17**

The importance of Pergamum dates back to the third century BC,
when it became the centre of the Attalid kingdom. When by the

---

[1] The two aspects were quite distinct to the Jews. Resurrection was limited
to the holy land. The prophecy against Pashhur (Jer. 20:6) tells him, 'To
Babylon you shall go, and there shall you die, and there you shall be buried.'
The rabbis interpreted this to mean that he would die there, but being buried
in Babylon he would remain there for ever. This led to the statement in
pKeth. 12:35f., 21: 'He who dies there (in Babylon) and is buried there suffers
two things (death and remaining in the grave); he who dies and is buried here
(in the Holy Land) suffers one thing (death, but not remaining in the grave, for
the dead of the land of Israel rise in the days of the Messiah).' The thought of
judgment after death is different from this, Psalm 15:5, 'He will not die in the

will of Attalus III (d. 133 BC) his kingdom was handed over to Rome, and it became the Roman province of Asia, Pergamum automatically assumed the position of capital of the province. The city was dominated by its great acropolis, a hill eight hundred feet high on which many temples clustered. The most celebrated of these was devoted to Asclepios, the god of healing. The popularity of this cult caused Pergamum to become, as Charles expressed it, the Lourdes of its day. Most significant of all, from the point of view of the Christian Church, Pergamum was the first city in Asia Minor to have a temple dedicated to Augustus and Rome. As capital of the province it became the centre of the imperial cult in the whole region.

12. The Lord addresses the church as he **who has the sharp two-edged sword.** This element of the vision of Christ (1 : 16) anticipates verse 16, and denotes the Lord as the administrator of the divine justice, with almighty power to execute judgment (cf. 19 : 15, 21).

13. Pergamum is the place where **Satan's throne** is. The expression could describe an enormous altar of Zeus, which stood on a platform on the hill overlooking the city. Erected to commemorate a military victory, John could well have regarded it as a symbol of the idolatry that held sway in Pergamum (so Deissmann, Lohmeyer, etc.). Or the hill itself, with its temples, could have suggested the imagery, in deliberate contrast to the biblical 'mountain of God' (Ezek. 28 : 14, 16), which was sometimes called the throne of God (*Enoch* 25 : 3). The hill would then epitomize that false worship of God which found its supreme expression in the cult of the emperor, which Satan was using to draw mankind away from its rightful Lord and through which he sought the annihilation of the Christian Church (so Charles).

The recognition **you hold fast my name and you did not deny my faith** (i.e., faith in me) suggests that already the Pergamene Christians had experienced difficulties in maintaining their Christian profession by reason of the idolatry of Pergamum and its enthusiasm for the imperial cult. They held firm **even in**

future world', i.e. he will not suffer condemnation. Deuteronomy 33:6 was similarly interpreted: 'Let Reuben live and not die' was understood as, 'May Reuben live in this world and not die in the future world.' So *Sanh.* 92a:11. In the Jerusalem Targum this is paraphrased, 'May Reuben live in this world and not die the second death.' See Strack-Billerbeck, III, pp. 830f.

the days of Antipas my witness. The pressure was upon all,
but one alone suffered martyrdom. Such a circumstance would
better fit the upsurge of mob violence than the initiation of an
official persecution in Pergamum (there would be no reason to
stop at one execution if a policy against the Christians had been
adopted at Pergamum). It is considered by some that the description of Antipas as *my witness* (Greek *martys*) is the first instance of
the use of the term to denote martyr. There is little doubt that
John's employment of the term did much to encourage its use in
this sense, though whether he intended it so is uncertain (cf. 17 : 6,
where *RSV*, following *RV*, adopts the rendering martyr; *NEB*
keeps to the non-technical sense).

14, 15. The Pergamene church is faithful to Christ in its witness to the world. In contrast to the Ephesian church, it is lax to
those who introduce sub-Christian doctrines and practices into its
midst. The **few things** that the Lord has against this church
reduce themselves to one: **you have some there who hold the
teaching of Balaam.** These unnamed people are described as
some who hold the teaching of the Nicolaitans. As Balaam
by his instruction caused the Israelites to stumble, so the Nicolaitans by their teaching ensnare Christians. The stumbling-block
of Balaam consisted in persuading Israelites to **eat food sacrificed
to idols and practise immorality.** The incident is described in
Numbers 25 : 1ff. After the vain attempt of Balak king of Moab
to persuade Balaam to curse Israel (Num. 22–24), the record
describes how the Israelites 'began to play the harlot with the
daughters of Moab', to eat their sacrifices and worship their gods.
While in Numbers 25 : 1ff. this is not directly linked with Balaam's
activity, in Numbers 31 : 16 it is stated that the Moabite women
acted 'by the counsel of Balaam'. Jewish exposition understood
this to mean that Balaam counselled Balak to use Moabite harlots
to persuade the Israelite men to commit idolatry in their (the
harlots') tents.[1] John sees in the Nicolaitans a counterpart to the
havoc wrought by Balaam among the Jews. They persuade
Christians *to eat food sacrificed to idols and practise immorality.* What
precisely is meant by that? In the Old Testament record the eating
of sacrifices was part of idolatrous worship. In the New Testament
writings eating food sacrificed to idols does not necessarily connote entering into sacrificial worship. The meat of beasts so

[1] Strack-Billerbeck, III, p. 793.

slaughtered could be eaten at home or in temple precincts. It
became a problem for Christians whether it was right ever to eat
such food (see Paul's lengthy discussion in 1 C. 8–10). From the
argument in 1 Corinthians 8 : 1ff. it is plain that some Christians
did not hesitate to eat idol meats at any time and in any place,
including heathen temples, and we may presume that the
Nicolaitans advocated this policy.

Did they also engage in immorality and encourage others to do
the same? Some answer, No. The Old Testament prophets
frequently represent idolatry under the figure of immorality
(Israel viewed as a faithless wife forsaking the Lord for other gods),
and John could have done the same (he has done so in chs. 17–18).
It is observed that the letter to Thyatira depicts the activity of a
prophetess symbolically named Jezebel, under the same terms as
those used of the Nicolaitans. But the sin of Jezebel the queen was
that of leading Israel into idolatry, and such was the sin of this
new Jezebel—and of the Nicolaitans in general. If this interpretation be adopted, the Nicolaitans are to be viewed as liberals
who took a broad view of the Christian's place in pagan society,
like their counterparts in the Corinthian church. They will have
maintained that idols are nothing, hence there is no need to fear
idol meats, or places where they are eaten (cf. 1 C. 8 : 1ff.). Therefore Christians need not hesitate to take part in pagan feasts,
whether among trade guilds or in temples. Nor need they be over-
scrupulous about acknowledging the divinity of Caesar, for they
can do it in the same spirit as many pagans did—as a gesture of
loyalty to Rome, without religious significance (Caesar's deity was
a joke to many Romans). In that case John responded to the
Nicolaitans in a similar manner to Paul in his dealing with the
Corinthian liberals. As Paul urged abstention from idol meats,
through the possibility of 'weak' Christians relapsing into idolatry
(1 C. 8 : 7ff.) and 'strong' Christians entering into demonic fellowship (1 C. 10 : 19ff.), so John rejects all eating of sacrificial foods
and all recognition of Caesar's divinity as incompatible with the
confession of Jesus as Lord.

While this is all very reasonable, it should be remembered that
the Nicolaitans were evidently Gnostics (see especially v. 24), and
antinomianism among Gnostics was a menace to the Christian
Church (see the letter of Jude). The Old Testament record of
Israel's apostasy at Baal-peor describes idolatry and immorality.

Current Jewish exegesis so understood it, and John's citation of
the record seems to warrant no different understanding: the
Nicolaitans, like Balaam, encouraged people to eat sacrificed
foods and engage in immoral sexual relations. Among pagans immorality was notoriously a peccadillo—and even less when it concerned prostitutes. To converts from paganism it would not be
difficult to represent it as harmonious with Christian morality and
its practice as a sign of Christian freedom. There was good reason
for the inclusion of abstention from idol-meats and immoral
sexual relations in the so called 'apostolic decrees' (Ac. 15 : 29)
addressed to churches among the Gentiles. To gnostic libertines,
rejoicing in the freedom of the Spirit from rules imposed by men,
the rejection of such scruples would appear as obvious as the refusal
to abstain from things strangled and from blood. It would seem
best, therefore, to understand John's language in its natural sense
and not import into it a symbolic meaning.

16. The whole Pergamene church is called on to **repent**—not
only they who hold the doctrine of the Nicolaitans, but the rest
who tolerate them. The church's integrity is endangered by the
presence of people who advocate such views and practices. Indeed, the toleration of sub-Christian faith and morals within its
fellowship implies a culpable indifference of the church to the
very things which distinguish it from paganism. Failure to repent,
therefore, will entail a coming of Christ in judgment to the church
of Pergamum, like that of which the Ephesian church was warned
(2 : 5). In contrast to the church at Ephesus, however, the coming
is for judgment directed chiefly to the offending Nicolaitans: **I
will . . . war against them with the sword of my mouth.** The
nature of the judgment is not described, but verses 22f. suggest
that it may be comparable with what is threatened against the
followers of Jezebel.

17. The promise to the victor is a double one. **I will give some
of the hidden manna** recalls the manna which the Israelites ate
in the desert—in Balaam's time—and which the Jews expected to
be provided again in the time of the kingdom. That the manna is
hidden may allude to the tradition that the golden pot of manna
(Exod. 16 : 32ff.) was hidden by Jeremiah with other temple
treasures at the destruction of the temple, and that they are to be
restored in the messianic age (2 Mac. 2 : 4ff.). This, however, will
account only for the expression, not for the expectation of the gift

of manna, which was linked rather with the belief that the works of the 'first redeemer' (Moses) will be repeated by the 'second redeemer' (the Messiah).[1] For John the notion is to be treated like other expectations of the Jews—shadows of the realities which the Christ will bring in the day of his kingdom. As the fruits of the tree of life (2 : 7), so the manna is a symbol of the eternal life which the Lord will give in his kingdom. It is hidden from the Jews, and can be received only through the confession of Jesus as Lord. John's thought appears to be closely related to the discourse on the bread of life in John 6 : 26ff. There it is said that the manna which Moses gave in the desert was not the true bread from heaven, for the fathers died in the desert. But the bread of God, which is Jesus, gives life to the world, and he who eats it will live for ever (Jn 6 : 31ff., 58). The inclusion of this symbol in the letter to Pergamum is in calculated contrast to the teaching of the Nicolaitans: they eat food sacrificed to idols and are doomed to judgment by the sword of the Lord. The conqueror will eat the bread of heaven and be sustained in the kingdom by the power of the Lord.

The victor will also receive **a white stone.** The significance of this is uncertain, since stones were given in ancient times for a variety of reasons. Of the many uses adduced to illuminate this passage, three call for consideration. Jurors used to give a stone to a man at the close of his trial, a white one indicating acquittal, a black one guilt. If this were in mind, the promise would be essentially the same in content as that to the conqueror in Smyrna, for he is told that he will receive a crown of life (cf. the gift of manna) and that he will not be exposed to the second death (i.e., condemned in the judgment). There is evidence that a stone could serve as a kind of ticket of admission to public festivals and royal assemblies. On this basis the white stone would admit the recipient to the messianic feast, and the symbolism would extend the idea of eating the hidden manna.

The **new name** will either be that of the believer, who by resurrection has entered on a new status (cf. the change of name of Jacob to Israel, Abram to Abraham) with a unique relation to the Lord (hence **no one knows it**), or it will be that of Christ, again signifying a unique relation of the Lord to his follower. A third interpretation, widely favoured by recent commentators,

1 Strack-Billerbeck, II, p. 481.

takes its rise from the ancient belief in the power of a name, which found expression in the widespread use of amulets in the world of John's day. The Jews naturally associated this power with the name of Yahweh, as is reflected in the story of David's quelling the waters of the deep, when they threatened to overwhelm the world, by throwing into it a potsherd inscribed with the divine name.[1] If this be the background of ideas in our passage, we should interpret it by contrast as well as comparison, for John clearly uses current ideas in a manner all his own (compare the literalness of Jewish speculations about the tree of life, the manna, and all like elements of eschatological hope, with John's use of them as symbols of spiritual realities). It is completely out of context to view the stone as a charm that will see the victor through all unknown perils in the next world (as Lohmeyer suggested). Rather the stone, with the name of Christ or God, will symbolize 'the transcendent powers now placed in the hand of him that has been faithful unto death' (Charles), and the unknown nature of the name will represent the unique role that each has to play in the age to come.

We have to confess our inability to determine with certainty the intention of the author, in view of the many-sided meanings of the symbol he has chosen. The second interpretation given above provides the closest link with the context and allows a consistent flow of thought, but the third allows more room for the significance of the name.

THE LETTER TO THE CHURCH AT THYATIRA 2:18–29

Thyatira was a comparatively unimportant city. It had neither military significance nor administrative importance. Its sole claim to fame was its trade. If Pergamum was a city of civil servants and priests, Thyatira was a town of merchants and craftsmen (Lohmeyer). We recall that Lydia, the dealer in purple cloth, came from Thyatira (Ac. 16:14). In this setting it would not be expected that the church would be unduly troubled by zealous promoters of the imperial cult. Its problems arose from the many trades' and craftsmen's guilds in the city. Every craftsman and trader naturally belonged to his appropriate guild. The meetings of these

---

[1] The story is reproduced in Strack-Billerbeck, III, p. 749.

societies included a common meal, dedicated to a pagan deity, and frequently ended in sheer debauchery and licentiousness. The embarrassment for Christians was obvious. How could they join in such social occasions and maintain faith and conscience unsullied? The Nicolaitans had a ready answer—and thereby they provided the pitfall for the Church at Thyatira.

18. The address is drawn from 1 : 14f. The **eyes like a flame of fire** seeing into the hidden depths of the heart, anticipate verse 23, the terrible **feet . . . like burnished bronze** have in view the destructive judgment of verses 26f. Here alone the Lord is called **the Son of God** (though his unique relation to the Father is frequently mentioned; see on 1 : 6). The title is also probably due to the thought of verses 26f., since the psalm which the passage cites declares the divine decree that the king is the Son of God, and the promise to the conqueror is that of sharing the sovereign power of the Messiah-Son.

19. Praise is given to the church for its **works.** It may be assumed that the terms which follow represent the kind of works which are acceptable to Christ. In the list **love** takes first place. **Faith** is directed towards God, **service** towards fellow men, **patient endurance** the obstacles provided by the world. In view of the precedence of *love*, it is important to note that **the latter works** of the Thyatirans **exceed the first**—i.e., in quality rather than quantity. This in direct contrast to the Ephesian believers, whose early love had waned and whose works had diminished (2 : 4f.).

20. The church, however, has a failing similar to that of the church of Pergamum: **you tolerate the woman Jezebel.** The reason for the symbolic name is clear. The prophetess was no queen, and Jezebel was no prophetess, but both women constituted a threat to the continuance of true religion among the people of God. In the prophetic revolution under Jehu, which brought about the destruction of Jezebel and her house, Jezebel was accused of 'harlotries and sorceries' (2 Kg. 9 : 22), presumably in reference to the licentious cult of Baal which she championed in Israel. That was a close enough parallel to warrant the application of her name to the prophetess, who encouraged Christians **to practise immorality and to eat food sacrificed to idols.** This was the doctrine of the Nicolaitans (2 : 15), and it had considerable acceptance in Thyatira. When it is said, *you tolerate the* *woman*, it is implied that the church did not itself accept her teaching, nor adopt her life-style. But the mention of her paramours and her children in verse 22 shows that a number in the community did so. These would have formed a distinct group within the church, and the church as a whole was content for them to remain. For the craftsmen and traders of Thyatira it would have been a relief to learn on the authority of the Spirit (for 'Jezebel' was a prophetess) that Christians need not separate themselves from the ways of the world, least of all in matters related to business, and that they could take their place in the town's guilds and participate in the celebrations which they organized. They were assured that immorality and sacrificial meals were not to be feared, for men and women in whom the Spirit dwells know that the flesh cannot defile the spirit, and patron-gods of guilds are of no account. This is not an 'eat, drink, and be merry, for tomorrow we die' attitude, but an early form of the 'beyond morality' concept.

21. I gave her time to repent. The Lord—through John or some other Christian voice—has already warned the prophetess of the error of her ways and called for their renunciation, but to no avail. Accordingly the Lord is to come in judgment upon the impenitent group.

22, 23. I will throw her on a sickbed, and those who commit adultery with her I will throw into great tribulation are clearly parallel statements, having synonymous meaning. To fall on a bed is a Hebraistic expression for becoming ill. To throw on a bed is to inflict illness. Both elements of the couplet *throw on a sickbed, throw into great tribulation* denote the infliction of suffering. The following clause has yet another parallel expression: **I will strike her children dead.** That paraphrases John's language. Literally it reads, 'I will kill her children with death.' The statement *I will kill with death* occurs in the Septuagint of Ezekiel 33:27 to render, *I will kill with pestilence.* The same use of 'death' for 'pestilence' is found in Revelation 6:8. We, therefore, have a third line for the threatened punishment of the followers of Jezebel. It is doubtful that we are intended to distinguish the persons mentioned, as though the 'adulterers' were somehow less culpable than the 'children'. John employs typical prophetic language to denote that the entire group of the followers of Jezebel will be brought to an end, both those who participate in her sins (*commit adultery with her*) and those who embrace her teaching and ways (*her children*).

Such judgment will teach all the churches the lesson, which they already know in theory, but whose power they have not yet experienced: **I am he who searches mind and heart.** Curiously the terms *mind* and *heart* could well be reversed here, for *mind* is literally *kidneys*, and in Jewish thought they were associated with the emotions, whereas *heart* was rather associated with the intellect, and the term 'mind' is our closest equivalent to it.

24. On the rest of the church in Thyatira no other **burden** is laid. None, that is, besides the traditions they received in their baptismal instruction (cf. Rom. 6 : 17, 1 Th. 4 : 1, 2 Th. 3 : 6ff., and the common tradition reflected in the New Testament letters). The instruction of Jezebel they can forget, for she taught **the deep things of Satan.** This is often viewed as an ironic description by John of the teaching of the prophetess. She claimed to have access, by the Spirit, to 'the deep things of God' (cf. 1 C. 2 : 10), but John retorts that her notions are *the deep things of Satan.* Her teaching has its inspiration not in heaven but in hell. While this interpretation is possible, it would accord with what we know of trends in Gnosticism, and with the context of this letter, to take John's statement at its face value. Jezebel and her friends entered into the deep things of Satan. This was their boast. In their view the timid Christians who stayed by the elementary instruction of the apostles, who feared to join in the activities of the trade guilds and kept themselves apart from the world, were poor creatures. They on the contrary rejoiced in the freedom of the Spirit to explore the sphere of Satan's rule, to associate with the evil as well as the good, and to demonstrate their superiority over the so-called sins of the flesh. This need not imply that these people were Satan-worshippers, as some groups known to the Church in later times. It indicates rather their consciousness of emancipation from traditional ethics and their boldness in religious expression. The order of Jezebel claimed the freedom of the spiritual world, of hell as well as of heaven.

25-27. In contrast to such attitudes the church is commanded **hold fast what you have.** For the teaching delivered to the church of Thyatira is the teaching of the apostles, and its ultimate source is in Jesus. The conqueror therefore is defined as he **who**

keeps my works until the end. The works of the Christian are the works of Christ. He knows what they are who has learned of Jesus. He does them who adheres to the words and the works of Jesus, for the Spirit sent by the risen Lord expounds the meaning of all that he was and taught (Jn 16 : 12–15). This is the nearest we have in the seven letters to a definition of the conqueror. He *holds fast* the traditions of faith and life delivered to the Church till the coming of Christ (v. 25), and he *keeps* Christ's works till the end (v. 26)—whether that 'end' be the Lord's parousia or his own death.

The conqueror is to receive **power over the nations,** such as Christ received from his Father, power, that is, in the sense of authority (*exousia*). Charles is almost certainly correct in his contention that John attached two distinct meanings to the Greek term *poimainein*, corresponding to the two meanings of the Hebrew word it translates in Psalm 2 : 8, namely, *shepherd* (= rule) and *destroy*. If that be so, the meaning of the promise to the conqueror is remarkably close to that of the psalmist. The king who is the divine Son is promised the nations as his inheritance, and that he will shatter all opposition within them. So the conqueror is promised authority over the nations, and power to crush the opposing forces of paganism and all resistance to the will of God in the world. For John, of course, the opposition and resistance are those of the Antichrist and his allies. As is explicitly stated (v. 27*b*), this is a promise to share in Christ's sovereignty and his judicial rule— an incomprehensible privilege, reiterated again and again in this book, and controlling the final vision of the kingdom.

28. This thought of sharing in Christ's rule is perhaps the leading feature in the final words of the promise, **I will give him the morning star.** While it is tempting to be guided by the utterance of 22 : 16, 'I am . . . the bright morning star', and view this as a promise that Christ will be the believer's, it is more likely that the saying is to be understood along the lines of 1 : 20, where the seven stars in Christ's hand are a polemical representation of the sovereignty over the world which Christ has bestowed on his churches (see the note on 1 : 20). The *morning star* is Venus. Lohmeyer has shown that from Babylonian times Venus was the symbol of sovereignty. In Roman times it was more specifically the symbol of victory and sovereignty, for which reason Roman generals owned their loyalty to Venus by erecting temples in her

honour (e.g., Sulla, Pompey, Caesar), and Caesar's legions carried
her sign on their standards. If then the morning star was the sign
of conquest and rule over the nations, this element in the promise
to the conqueror strengthens the statement that has gone before.
It embodies in symbol the prophecy already cited from the
psalmist. The conqueror is therefore doubly assured of his participation with Christ in the glory of his kingdom.

THE LETTER TO THE CHURCH OF SARDIS 3:1-6

Sardis was a city of past glories. Once the capital of the ancient
Lydian kingdom, it reached its pinnacle of fame under Croesus
in the sixth century BC, flourished under its Persian conquerors,
but then went into an unceasing decline to obscurity. An earthquake in AD 17 called forth the generous assistance of the emperor
Tiberias, which enabled the city to rebuild and recover some of its
lost prestige. Nevertheless 'no city in Asia presented a more de-
plorable contrast of past splendour and present unresting decline'
(Charles). The history of the city was unhappily repeated in the
church in its midst. The judgment uttered in verse 1b could as
well apply to both.

Two further elements in the city's life seem to find echoes in
the letter. Sardis was built on a mountain, and an acropolis was
constructed on a spur of this mountain, which was all but impregnable. Yet twice in the city's history it had been taken una-
wares and captured by enemies. The parallel with the church's
lack of vigilance, and its need to wake up lest it fall under judgment
(v. 3) is striking. Sardis was also the great commercial centre for
woollen goods, and claimed to be first in the field in the art of
dyeing wool. This, too, appears to be reflected in verses 4-5 and
may well have inspired the imagery there employed.

1. The Christ is announced as he **who has the seven spirits
of God and the seven stars.** The *NEB* omits the conjunction
and, indicating agreement with the view that the stars are the
spirits. John undoubtedly fluctuates in his use of imagery, but
since the remaining letters in their address to the churches cite
elements from chapter 1 in the sense there adopted, it would seem
best to make no exception here. The *seven spirits* represent the
Holy Spirit sent in his fullness to the seven churches. The two
chief works of the Spirit singled out by contemporary Judaism

were the inspiration of prophecy and the quickening of the dead.
Both are in keeping here. The message to the church of Sardis is
graver than any so far given. This church in a living death needs
to give special heed to the prophetic warning and to seek the
quickening power of the Spirit that it may live again. In the address of the Ephesian letter a reminder is given, as here, that the
seven stars are in Christ's hand (2:1), suggesting that the churches
are in his grasp to hold and to judge. The like may apply in this
passage.

The Ephesian letter also begins with the words, **I know your
works.** There the statement indicates the Lord's understanding
and approval of their ways; here it denotes disapproval. The works
of the Sardis church show that the community is dead. More
precisely they show the Lord the condition of this church. The
appearance of the Sardis church conveys no such impression.
Observers of this fellowship see all the signs of a prosperous
community: **you have the name of being alive.** But the
appearance is that of a beautifully adorned corpse in a funeral-
parlour, and the Lord is not deceived.

2, 3. The **death** of a church is primarily a matter of relation
to the Lord by the Spirit—a lack of response to the life-giving
presence in its midst. What are the **works** which betray the
cessation of this relation in Sardis? First, that they are not **perfect
in the sight of my God.** The meaning is better rendered in the
NEB: 'I have not found any works of yours completed in the
eyes of my God.' A glance at the list of works which find approval
in the eyes of the Lord (2:19) will illustrate this. They are love,
faith, service, patient endurance. All these could conceivably have
been in evidence in Sardis—but in an unsatisfactory manner.
Their acts of love, worship, endeavours after service, endurance
of temptations and difficulties in the world, were all characterized
by half-heartedness, by lack of zeal, by beginnings that never
came to anything of worth. They were the works of a church
which had become the incarnation of mediocrity.[1] Moreover the
majority of this church come under the judgment of verse 4: they

---

[1] The Germans have a term, currently in vogue, *Halbstärke*, literally 'half
strong', used contemptuously (especially by the older generation of the younger)
to denote wishy-washy individuals who have insufficient motivation to achieve
anything worth while. It is a contemporary expression for the inertia which
John saw in Sardis. The church in this place was a church of the *Halbstärke*.

have **soiled their garments,** for only a few have escaped this condition. The dye of their wool has coloured their souls as well as their hands. If it be right to read in these words an allusion to Sardis's trade, it lies to hand that this community had fallen prey to the same influences as the churches in Ephesus and Thyatira, namely, the teaching of Balaam and the Nicolaitans. No mention is made of any leaders, as in Thyatira, nor of a heretical group within the larger fellowship, as in Ephesus, but the church as a whole could have taken the line of least resistance in its relations with the paganism around it, and silently accommodated to it.

Urgent appeals, therefore, are addressed to the church. **Awake!** The dead who sleep in their graves must arise (cf. Eph. 5:14). **Strengthen what remains**, both of individual Christian character and experience and whatever is of worth in the life of the church. **Remember ... what you received and heard,** i.e., of the apostolic instruction concerning the Christian life and the nature and service of the Church (see on 2:25); **keep that**—in a 'complete' sense (cf. v. 2b)—**and repent.** The believers at Sardis must go back to their baptism, and 'turn' with a humble and contrite heart to him who has power to deliver them.

If the church does not respond to the Lord's appeal, and awake out of its spiritual torpor, **I will come like a thief.** The parable of the burglar at night is clearly in mind (Mt. 24:43f., Lk. 12:39f.; cf. 1 Th. 5:2ff., 2 Pet. 3:10). It is echoed again in 16:15 in a manner extraordinarily in keeping with this passage. Some scholars, therefore, have maintained that 16:15 has been transferred from its original context in this letter to its present position by a later scribe. Charles suggested that the statement of 16:15 should follow the first sentence of verse 3, and so be followed by the second sentence. This is a feasible conjecture, and it may be correct. It is not easy to see, however, why an isolated sentence, so closely related to its context, should fall out of the text and find its way into its present position. Whilst recognizing the possibilities, we do better to leave the text as it is. In the teaching of Jesus the parable relates to his parousia,[1] and it was so understood by the evangelist, by Paul and the author of 2 Peter. It is often presumed without question that the same meaning is intended here. The church of Sardis will be caught off its guard by the Lord at

[1] *Pace* Dodd, *Parables of the Kingdom*, pp. 167ff., and Jeremias, *The Parables of Jesus*, revised edn, pp. 48ff.

his advent, *and so suffer loss in that day*. We cannot however overlook that in the similar commands to repent, addressed to the churches of Ephesus and Pergamum, language traditionally associated with the second advent of Christ is adapted to the Lord's visitation of the churches for judgment (see 2:5, 16). Similarly an application of the parousia-idea to present experience of fellowship with the Lord—in anticipation of the messianic feast—is made in 3:20, and a visitation in judgment, without parousia-language, is described in 2:22f. Accordingly it is most suitable to the context to view the warning of 3:3 as an application of language properly relating to the final advent to the judicial action of the Lord in the present.

4. Sardis has **a few names ... people who have not soiled their garments.** These have not besmirched their Christian profession in the manner of their fellows. They are alive and awake, and their works are approved by the Lord (cf. vv. 1–2). To such, a fitting reward is promised: **they shall walk with me in white.** Followed by the eschatological promise of verse 5, this plainly refers to the believer's presence with the Lord in the day of his kingdom. Charles, taking his cue from 2 Corinthians 5:4 and related passages in apocalyptic writings, considered that the white garments denote the heavenly bodies of glory, to be bestowed on believers at the end. In his view all the occurrences of the figure in the Revelation (3:2, 6:11, 7:9, 13, 14, 19:8) have the same sense. Unfortunately this entails that 19:8b ('for the fine linen is the righteous deeds of the saints') be eliminated as an intrusion into the text, since it does not tally with this interpretation. Even if 19:8b were to be excised (on different grounds), Charles' conclusion does not necessarily follow. John's symbolism is not invariably applied, and the context of 4b must be taken into account. The contrast between soiled garments of sinful believers and unsoiled garments of faithful Christians suggests that the white garments have to do with purity or holiness. If this idea continues into verse 5 the latter part of the promise develops the same thought, first negatively and then positively: the conqueror will appear in garments of holiness, and he will be vindicated in the judgment—his name will not be erased from the roll of the kingdom, and he will be owned as Christ's before the tribunal of heaven. This understanding of the passage would afford a further parallel with the promise to the conqueror in 2:11 (see notes on

2:11 and 17), it would agree with the natural application of the figure in 7:14, and harmonize (though not be identical) with the alleged gloss of 19:8. Accordingly it may be commended as most agreeable to the text in its setting.[1]

5. It will not be overlooked that verse 4 gives the same promise as verse 5a. Since it speaks of accompanying the Lord in his kingdom, the rest of verse 5 must similarly apply to the unbesmirched believer. Yet verse 5 is a promise to the conqueror. It is a further indication that the promises to the conquerors relate to all faithful believers, not to a single group within the Church, the martyrs. Only he could be excepted from the application of verse 5 who had become sundered from Christ (cf. 1 C. 9:27).

The idea of **the book of life** is an ancient one, and is derived from the custom of keeping a register of citizens. Its simplest application appears in Exodus 32:32, where the book which the Lord has written is that of the members of his people in their earthly pilgrimage. To have one's name blotted out from the book is to die. The usage in Psalm 139:16 reflects a thought, early adopted (perhaps from the Babylonian concept of tablets of destiny), that the Lord wrote his book in former ages, and so the symbol included the ideas of election and predestination. Extension into final destiny is made when the register of the citizens is understood as that of the eternal kingdom of God. To have one's name enrolled in the book of life is to be destined to participate in that kingdom (election from eternity for the eternal kingdom appears in Rev. 13:8). In this sense the figure is used by Jesus to denote the supreme blessing of God to men (Lk. 10:20), it was taken up into the Church's teaching (Phil. 4:3, Heb. 12:23) and appears frequently in this book (13:8, 17:8, 20:12, 15, 21:27). If the exalted Lord has power to strike out names from the book of life, this is because the book is his—presumably he wrote it (13:8, 21:27). The symbol thus conveys the notion that alike election

[1] It is to be freely admitted that a symbol capable of conveying a plurality of ideas can have overtones, even when one meaning is predominant. The white robe was associated with festivities and with victory, as appears in chapter 19, as well as in other apocalyptic literature, and these would be appropriate to the present context. Swete would include all the familiar associations in the scope of this saying: 'The promise is that of a life free from pollution, bright with celestial gladness, crowned with final victory', with a possible allusion to the glory of the resurrection body.

and redemption are in Christ and through Christ. From first to
last the believer is dependent on his Lord.

The authority of Christ in the judgment is similarly implied in
his confession of the believer **before my Father and before his
angels.** The saying cites the words of Jesus (Mt. 10:32, Lk. 12:8)
gaining additional force from the fact that in the Revelation
Jesus alone is seen as Son of the Father. In the judgment of God
(20:11) the confession or denial by the Son is decisive.

THE LETTER TO THE CHURCH OF PHILADELPHIA 3:7–13

Philadelphia was a smaller and more recent city than the others
in which the seven churches were set. It was founded in the second
century BC by Attalus II, who was also called Philadelphos, and
so gave the city its name. Situated only thirty miles south-east of
Sardis, it suffered from earthquakes like its neighbour, and shared
in the destruction wrought by the earthquake of AD 17. Though the
city was rebuilt by the help of the emperor, many of its citizens
were afraid to return to live in it, and they settled in the surrounding countryside. The impermanence of life in Philadelphia conceivably is contrasted in verse 12 with the prospect of a permanent
dwelling in the city of God.

While pagan cults flourished in Philadelphia, the letter indicates
that the church was troubled by hostile Jews, as was the case in
Smyrna (the language used to describe the Jews in 3:9 is remarkably like that in 2:9). The nature of this opposition appears to
have determined the form of the letter. If we may deduce from
John's writing that the Jews in this city taunted the Christians of
having no part in the Messiah and his kingdom, the purport of
the letter becomes luminously clear. It is a sustained assurance of
participation in the kingdom of Christ.

7. The risen Lord announces himself as **the holy one, the
true one.** *The Holy One* is a common title for God (cf. Isa. 40:25,
etc.), and the two attributes, 'holy and true', are combined in
6:10 in relation to God. The phrase **The words of the holy one,
the true one,** therefore, conveys the notion that Christ's declarations carry divine authority. He shares the holiness and self-
consistency of God, therefore he cannot lie, nor can his promise
fail.

The Lord has **the key of David,** an echo of 1:18, where the

Christ is said to possess the keys of Death and Hades. The *key of David* must be the key that opens the door into the kingdom of God, and so to the eternal life which characterises that kingdom. The phrase, with its qualifying clauses, adapts the promise to Eliakim in Isaiah 22:22 (also in mind in the related passage Mt. 16:19). This man is to replace the worthless steward Shebna, and will exercise indisputable authority over the house of David. In like manner authority over the kingdom of God has been vested in the risen Christ. When he opens to his followers the door of the kingdom, no one can shut them out, and when he shuts the door on those who oppose his cause none can reverse his decision. Verse 9 indicates that the opponents here in mind are especially the Jews who harass the church of Philadelphia.

8. The metaphor of **an open door** is used by Paul on several occasions to represent opportunities for missionary service (1 C. 16:9, 2 C. 2:12, Col. 4:3, cf. Ac. 14:27). It is accordingly often considered that the Lord rewards the Philadelphians, who have little power but great faithfulness, with the privilege of embarking on a great missionary task embracing the very Jews who oppose them (v. 9). The context appears to be against this interpretation. The description of Christ in verse 7 indicates that he has used the key of David to set before them a door which opens into the eternal kingdom. Despite the asseverations of local Jews that the kingdom belongs to Israel and not to the followers of Jesus of Nazareth, none can shut the door which the Christ himself has opened for his people. The Philadelphians have already shown their loyalty to Christ in suffering for his name—they **have kept my word and have not denied my name.** Consequently the holy one, the true one, will equally keep his word and not deny them in the last day (cf. v. 5).

9. By contrast, the members of **the synagogue of Satan,** who claim that the kingdom has been promised to Jews alone, will suffer an unexpected reversal of an Old Testament prophecy. They will have to render to the Christians—Gentiles though most of them may be—the respect and homage which they as Jews anticipate that the Gentiles will pay to them in the time when the kingdom appears (cf. Isa. 60:14). 'They should play the role of the heathen and acknowledge the Christians to be the true Israel' (Charles). Contrary to what is commonly held (on the basis of interpreting the 'open door' of verse 8 as a missionary oppor-

tunity) this is not intended to convey a promise that the Jewish
opponents of the church will be converted. It is a declaration that
the Jews concerned will have to acknowledge their mistake in
denying the Christians a place in the kingdom and recognize them
to be the beloved of the Lord, the true Israel. This is more akin
to an eschatological judgment than an anticipation of blessing.
Whether John's language further implies a repentance on the part
of the *synagogue of Satan*, and so their incorporation into the true
Israel, is not said; at least the thought is not excluded.

10. The faithful community of Smyrna was warned of an
impending trial which they would have to endure 'for ten days'
(2:10). The Philadelphians, on the contrary, are promised
preservation **from the hour of trial which is coming on the
whole world.** This is the first mention made by John of the
messianic judgments, which take up a large part of his book. It is
improbable, though admittedly possible, that an identical period
of trial is referred to in both 2:10 and 3:10. The *hour of trial* is
not a period of time but a designation of the trial itself (cf. Mk
14:35). The 'tribulation' of which the Smyrnaeans are warned is
to test the church. The hour of trial is **to try** (= test, the same
word is used) **those who dwell upon the earth,** i.e., the non-
Christian world (for the phrase, cf. 11:10). Whereas the Devil
prompts the opponents of the church to persecute the Smyrnaeans
(2:10), it is God who 'tests' the inhabitants of the world during the
hour of trial by his judgments. The preservation of the Church
from the effects of these judgments is set forth under a variety of
images in John's book (e.g., the sealing of the saints, 7:1ff., the
measuring of the altar and its worshippers, 11:1, the hiding of
the woman in the wilderness, 12:6). Undoubtedly the Church
as a whole is depicted as destined to suffer at the hands of its
opponents, above all through the hostility of the Antichrist, but
that is not in question here. Assurance is at this point given that
the Lord will preserve his own from judgments to come for the
kingdom he has prepared (cf. Jn 17:15, which expresses a closely
related idea).

11, 12. States negatively the possibility which the promise to
Smyrna puts positively (2:10). The promise to the Philadelphians,
however, develops the idea which dominates its whole letter, and
entails a coincidence of thought with the oracle of Isaiah 22:15-25
which can hardly be unintended. In the latter passage Eliakim

is told that he will not only bear the key of David, but that he will become 'a peg in a sure place ... a throne of honour to his father's house' (Isa. 22:23). On this 'peg' the whole weight of his father's house will rest, but alas 'the peg that was not fastened in a sure place will give way', and all who depended on it fall (Isa. 22:25). The Philadelphians knew by unhappy experience the insecurity of structures built by men. To the believer the promise is now given that he will be not a mere peg in a wall, but **a pillar in the temple of my God.** Among both Jews[1] and Christians[2] the symbol of a man as a sturdy pillar was familiar. It is thoroughly in harmony with John's employment of symbolism that he declares there will be no temple in the new Jerusalem (21:22), for the city itself is, as it were, a vast sanctuary (21:16). But the meaning of the promise is plain. The conqueror is to have a sure place in the city of God. Moreover it is emphasized, **never shall he go out of it.** In contrast to the fate of Eliakim, who was like a peg that gave way, and the buildings that perished in Philadelphia's earthquakes, the victor is assured that his place in the city which comes down out of heaven is eternally secured.

As in ancient times pillars frequently bore the names of people honoured by them,[3] so the conqueror will be inscribed with **the name of my God, and the name of the city of my God ... and my own new name.** The honour implied in these inscriptions, however, lies not in the deeds performed by the conqueror but in the attestation they provide that the man so inscribed belongs to God, and to the city of God, and to the Son of God.

[1] See Strack-Billerbeck on Galatians 2:9 (III, p. 537), especially the description of Abraham as the pillar on which the world rests.

[2] Cf. Galatians 2:9, 1 Timothy 3:15. Clement of Rome calls Peter and Paul 'those greatest and most righteous pillars' (1 *Clem.* 5:2).

[3] 1 Mac. 14:26ff. affords an instructive parallel. In gratitude for the deeds of Simon and his sons, the Jews recorded on brass tablets their acts of service to the nation and set them on pillars 'within the precinct of the sanctuary in a conspicuous place'. Bousset drew attention to a custom whereby the provincial priest of the emperor-cult at the end of his year of office set up his own statue in the temple, and had inscribed on the statue his name and that of his father, his year of birth and of office. If such a custom were in view, it would well accord with the representation in the Revelation that believers are to be the kingly priests of God in the eternal city. But to read this thought into the symbolism would involve too marked a dependence on this particular custom as against other related examples.

This is illustrated by the saying, ascribed to Rabbi Jonathan
(*c.* AD 220): 'Three are named after the name of God, and these
are the righteous, and the Messiah, and Jerusalem' (affirmed on
the basis of Isa. 43:7, Jer. 23:6, Ezek. 48:35).[1] The new name of
the Christ, which the victor is to bear, is not stated. John could
have had in view the thought later expressed in the description
of the coming of the Lord in 19:13: the Christ to come will
manifest himself to the world as 'the Word of God'.

THE LETTER TO THE CHURCH OF LAODICEA 3:14–22

Laodicea's position at an intersection of three imperial trade
roads favoured its development as a commercial and administrative
centre. In Roman times it became the wealthiest city in Phrygia,
so that when it suffered all but total destruction by earthquake in
AD 60–1 it refused the offer of imperial aid, which other similarly
afflicted cities were glad to accept. Various indications in the
seven letters reflect John's awareness of the circumstances which
conditioned life in the cities of the seven churches, but no letter
shows it so clearly as that to the Laodiceans. For this city was
known throughout the Roman world of its time for three things:
its banks, which even Cicero recommended for exchanging money;
its linen and wool industry, which produced cloth and carpets,
especially from the glossy black wool of sheep reared in the area;
its medical school and widely famed medicines, notable among
which was an eye-ointment made from a powder produced in
Phrygia. These three factors of the city's life seem clearly to be in
view in verses 17–18—first in terms of condemnation (v. 17), and
then as a basis of positive exhortation (v. 18).

Not a word of commendation appears in this letter. On the
contrary its condemnation of the church is the severest in the
seven letters. Yet characteristically the love of Christ for this
church, which has become a by-word in history, is emphasized,
and the promise held out to it forms the climax of all those contained in the letters to the churches.

14. The first two elements in the address give complementary
expression to a single idea—Jesus as the embodiment and expression of the truth of God. The description of the risen Lord as **the**

[1] See Strack-Billerbeck, III, pp. 795f., where other examples of similar identifications are given.

Amen involves the transference to him of the divine title in Isaiah 65:16. In the *RSV* this is rendered as 'the God of truth', but in the *NEB* it reads 'the God whose name is Amen'.[1] As surely as God's own character stands behind his word, so Jesus is the guarantee of the truth of his message. The expression **the faithful and true witness** reproduces the same thought without the use of metaphor. This element in the character of Christ contrasts strongly with the faithlessness and inconsistency of the Laodiceans in relation to the faith they professed.

The beginning of God's creation, while echoing Proverbs 8:22, does so in the sense of the developed Christology which appears in the hymn of Colossians 1:15–20. There Christ is described as 'the first-born of all creation . . . the beginning, the first-born from the dead . . . He is before all things, and in him all things hold together'. When John speaks of Christ as *the beginning of God's creation,* he means not the first of God's creatures but, as the *NEB* renders the phrase, 'the prime source of all God's creation'. The concept is the same as 'alpha' in the title 'alpha and omega'. In 22:13 this is paraphrased by John in relation to Christ as 'the first and the last, the beginning and the end'. Since Colosse was but ten miles from Laodicea, and instructions were given in the letter to the Colossians that that letter and the letter to the Laodiceans be exchanged by the churches (Col. 4:16), it is likely that Paul's doctrine of Christ remained a living tradition in Laodicea, and that it was known among the seven churches generally. The naming of Christ as the prime source of creation in the introduction to the message to the Laodiceans is perhaps intended to emphasize his supreme authority and power to execute the word of which he is the guarantor and the faithful and true witness.

15. No charge is laid against the Laodiceans of evils such as find mention in the other letters. This presumably relates to the nature of their faith. The Laodiceans do not reject the gospel of Christ, nor do they affirm it with joy. They maintain it without conviction, without enthusiasm, without reflection on its implications for life. Paul's language about the world being crucified to

---

[1] The change of rendering involves a difference of vocalization of the Hebrew word. The Septuagint read it as *omen* (= truth), and translated the phrase 'the true God'. Symmachus evidently had the same text as John and understood it in the same way, for he rendered the phrase, 'the God Amen'.

him and he to the world (Gal. 6:14), or of his being dominated by the one aim of pressing forward to win God's prize of life in his kingdom (Phil. 3:12f.) would have sounded to the Laodiceans like another religion, which indeed it was. So alien to the spirit of Christ is the religious profession of the Laodiceans, John declares that the Lord would prefer them to be outright pagans. **Would that you were cold or hot!** To have enough religion to disguise one's need of a living faith is to be in a worse condition than having no faith at all. An honest atheist is more acceptable to the Lord than a self-satisfied religious man, for such a man's religion has blunted his conscience and blinded him to his need for repentance. The road to the cross has always been easier for the publican than for the Pharisee.

16. Accordingly a stern word of rejection is uttered through the prophet: **I will spew you out of my mouth.** It is a violent metaphor, even a shocking one, but it would have produced an instant, if horrified, response of comprehension in the Laodiceans. For six miles away, in nearby Hierapolis, there were well known springs of hot water. As the water made its way over the plateau it lost its heat, and finally poured over a cliff right opposite Laodicea. Owing to the white incrustation of lime, left by the waters, the cliff was perpetually visible in Laodicea, and so its citizens could hardly forget the lukewarm water which would make a man sick if he drank it. Now they learn the dreadful news that they are like that to Christ. The metaphor signifies abhorrent rejection, and puts in picture form the adverse verdict in judgment such as we find in Matthew 7:23. It is nevertheless to be observed that the judgment has not yet been carried out. Verse 16 does not express an irremediable present rejection, but a threat of what will take place if there is no change of heart on the part of the Laodiceans. The burden of the rest of the letter therefore constitutes an urgent appeal for repentance, that the Laodiceans may not suffer this fate but have part in the inheritance of God's kingdom.

17. The complacency of the Laodiceans reminds us of the parable of Jesus about the rich farmer (Lk. 12:16ff.), but the exclamation **I am rich, I have prospered** cites Hosea's expression of self-congratulation made by Ephraim (the Jews of the northern kingdom), to which the prophet responds, 'All his riches can never offset the guilt he has incurred' (Hos. 12:8).

The irony of the Laodiceans' situation is brought home, however, that they are not really rich. With respect to the true riches they are mere beggars. Despite their overflowing banks they are **poor;** despite their physicians and medicaments they are **blind;** despite their clothing factories, they are **naked.** They are in truth **wretched** and **pitiable.**

18. Accordingly these Christians are urged to 'buy' from the Lord **gold refined by fire,** i.e., genuine wealth, such as God alone can give: **white garments** to cover their **nakedness,** that they be not ashamed in the judgment as men guilty before God (for *nakedness* as a symbol of judgment, cf. Ezek. 16:35ff., Nah. 3:5f., 2 C. 5:3); and **salve,** which will cure them of their blindness. The spiritual realities answering to these metaphors are clear in principle, if not in detail. The wealth of faith is often mentioned in the New Testament (Lk. 12:21, Jas 2:5, 1 Pet. 1:7), but since the 'purchase' of these desirable possessions itself represents the exercise of faith in God (see Isa. 55:1—the purchase is 'without money and without price'), the symbolism points rather to the riches bestowed by God to men of faith, above all the new life by the Spirit, which entails participation in the kingdom of God. The holiness which enables a man to face God in the judgment is God's gift through Christ, appropriated by the believer's response in a holy life (7:14, 19:8). Opened eyes enable a man to see God, and so to attain the bliss of fellowship with him in his eternal kingdom (22:3ff.).

19. Christ's call to the Laodiceans to receive the gifts he freely gives prepares us for the otherwise unexpected declaration **Those whom I love, I reprove and chasten.** The harsh words which have preceded flow from a love which would awaken them to their pitiable condition and goad them to seek the riches they are in danger of forfeiting. The principle enunciated is already found in Proverbs 3:12, but it is enriched with the tradition of such words of Christ as John 14:23, 15:12ff., 16:26f. In the light of so great a love, it is fitting that the Laodiceans respond with a zeal such as they have not yet manifested (**be zealous**—a continuous present) and repentance for their lack of love (**repent**—a single act of turning).

20. In harmony with this call the Lord invited the Laodiceans to a new relationship with him. The act of repentance is now viewed as an opening of life to the Lord who waits for entry, followed by a sharing of life with him. The thought is closely parallel to that of John 14:23 (cf. 14:2-3), but the picture itself may have been inspired by Canticles 5:2, messianically interpreted. The ultimate source of the symbolism is the concept of the kingdom of God as a participation in the feast provided by him (see Isa. 25:6ff.). Jesus used the picture frequently, in terms of which this verse is reminiscent (e.g., Mt. 8:11, 22:1-14, Lk. 12:34ff., 22:28ff., Mk 13:29, cf. Jas 5:9). This background of the saying, together with the marked emphasis in the seven letters on life in the future kingdom of God and the context of the passage (cf. 4:21), has led a number of expositors to believe that these words relate to the Church's part in the future kingdom: 'The opening of the door is the joyful response of the Church to the last call; cf. Lk. 12:36' (Swete). This, however, is not a natural interpretation of the words. The individualized appeal **if any one hears my voice and opens the door, I will come in to him** strongly suggests that it is made to individual believers, and that with those who respond to it the Lord will hold fellowship, such as will anticipate that which will be experienced in the final kingdom (much as Jn 14:23 anticipates what is promised in Jn 14:2-3). The similarity of thought and language to that which is used in connection with the Lord's Supper (cf. Jn 6:35ff., 53ff.) is due less to direct reminiscence of the Supper than to the event to which the Supper itself looks forward (Mk 14:25, Lk. 22:28ff.).

21. In contrast to the present application of eschatological hope in verse 20, the promise of verse 21 relates exclusively to the future. To the conqueror the promise is given, **I will grant him to sit with me on my throne.** The language is as pictorial as that of verse 20, but whereas the earlier statement relates to Christ's coming to the believer, to share life with him now, this speaks of the believer's sharing sovereignty with Christ in his triumphant kingdom. Its fulfilment is portrayed in 20:4ff., the millennial rule of Christ, but also in 22:5, the eternal kingdom of the new creation. Related ideas are found in Matthew 19:28, Luke 22:30, 1 Corinthians 6:2, 2 Timothy 2:11f. Here the privilege of sovereignty with Christ is correlated with Christ's exercising rule with the Father. As the Lord's conquest of the world (Jn 16:33) in his obedience to death was rewarded with exaltation to the Father's side, to rule with and for him (Phil. 2:9ff., 1 Pet. 3:18, 22, etc.), so the Christ honours him who

" SIT ON 12 THRONES, JUDGING THE 12 TRIBES OF ISRAEL " — MT 19:28

maintains faith in him with fellowship with him in his kingly rule. No higher honour than this can be imagined. But it is promised to the Laodiceans. The sincerity of the love expressed in verse 19 is matched by the height of its expression here. Lohmeyer justly comments, 'This saying promises the last and final privilege; it concludes equally effectively the crown of the seven promises to the conquerors and the seven letters themselves.'

THE VISION OF HEAVEN 4:1-5:14

It is evident that a fresh beginning in the book of Revelation is made at 4:1. A door in heaven is opened to enable the prophet to enter its portals and see what transpires in heaven, that he may understand what takes place on earth. It is, however, a new beginning and not the commencement of the Revelation. The Lord's day vision of the exalted Christ in chapter 1 is itself a prophecy as well as a vision, and it provides more than a hint of the outcome of history. Chapters 4–5 may be viewed as the fulcrum of the Revelation. In relation to what has gone before they provide a fuller understanding of him who dominates the letters to the churches. In relation to the rest of the book they serve the double purpose of initiating the series of judgments which lead to the final advent and descent of the city of God to earth, and of supplying the form for the series of messianic judgments (the seven seals) which immediately follow. In this respect these chapters constitute the pivot of the structure which holds the book together, for the rest of the visions dovetail into this main structure. Yet the vision of chapters 4–5 is also a self-contained whole, serving a highly important function regarding the message of the book. It reveals the ground of assurance that God's gracious purpose for the universe will come to pass, and so it is dominated by praise and adoration.

A single motif binds together the double vision of chapters 4–5, namely, that the God of creation is the God of redemption, accomplishing his gracious will through the crucified and risen Christ. The impact made by John's presentation of this theme is the more powerful through his extending it into two scenes instead of confining it to one. He could have let it be known at the outset of chapter 4 that the Lamb is seated on the throne with the

Almighty, and then have described the ineffable glory of the
Creator and the wonder of redemption. By delaying the description of the Redeemer and the proclamation of his mighty acts,
he has enabled his readers the better to grasp the significance of
Christ's redemption, and brought home to them the marvel of
the gospel. No part of the Scripture is more calculated to evoke
worship than these two chapters of John's prophecy.

In chapter 4 the attention of the prophet—and the reader—is
wholly directed to the Creator. As Lord of the universe, exalted
in his holiness and splendour, he is far removed from the storms of
history, whether they arise from the efforts of puny antichristian
emperors and armies to resist his will, or from attempts to disrupt
the peace and holiness of the churches. It is not a deist view of
God which is presented, as though the Creator had no concern
about earth's affairs. Rather there is a concentration upon the
glory of the Creator, who cannot be deflected by any power from
his purpose of good for his creatures. The existence of this purpose,
and the divine intention to bring it to pass, is hinted in the terms
of adoration given by the living creatures. The thrice-holy God
'was and is and is to come'. His exaltation over creation is celebrated in the final song of chapter 4:

> *Worthy art thou, our Lord and God,*
> *to receive glory and honour and power,*
> *for thou didst create all things,*
> *and by thy will they existed and were created.*

The creation exists for God, and he will 'come' and fulfil his
intentions concerning it.

In chapter 5 the focus of attention is no longer the Creator but
the Redeemer. He has 'conquered', and so gained the right to
open God's book of destiny for the world and to carry out what
is written in it. We now understand that the 'coming' of God to
fulfil his purpose for the world takes place in and through the
Lamb. Accordingly the worship of heaven from this point is
dominated by the cry, 'Worthy is the Lamb!' He is worthy to
execute God's purpose because he ransomed men for God by his
blood, made them a kingdom of priests, and gave them the right to
reign on earth (vv. 9f.), and he is worthy to receive all sovereignty
and universal acknowledgement (v. 12). Significantly the elements of the doxology of 5:12 appear in 7:12 in a song of

adoration addressed to God. Their application to Christ in 5:12 shows that he is recognized as the divine Redeemer. Chapter 4, therefore, depicts the adoration of God the Creator, chapter 5 the glory of God the Redeemer. The final song of the vision is fittingly addressed to God and the Lamb (v. 13), and it is uttered not alone by the mysterious creatures in the neighbourhood of the throne, but by every living thing in heaven and earth and hell.

It has been frequently recognized that the vision of chapter 5 gives us a Christian prophet's version of the enthronement ceremony known to the ancient world, when its potentates ascended their thrones.[1] Here the king is the Christ, his domain the universe, and his throne the throne of God. When does this assumption of authority take place? When does he ascend the throne of the universe? Similar questions arise in relation to the passage most closely related to this in the New Testament, namely Philippians 2:6–11, which describes the exaltation of the Christ over all powers and the universal acclamation of his sovereignty. One answer alone is possible. Despite the declaration of 4:1, that John is now to view 'what must take place after this', it is evident that the victory of Christ has already taken place in his cross and resurrection, that he has ascended the throne of God, and that his reign has begun. The steps of the ancient enthronement are commonly described as exaltation, presentation, enthronement.[2] If we apply these to chapter 5, the exaltation must be seen in the conquest of the Lamb referred to in 5:5, the presentation in verse 6, and the bestowal of authority in verse 7. It is the acclamation which extends beyond the past and present into the future. Whereas the vision records in an unbroken series the recognition of the Lamb's sovereignty, first by the angelic beings near the throne (vv. 8ff.), then by the myriads of angels (vv. 11f.), and finally by the whole creation (vv. 13f.), the acknowledgment by the hosts of heaven alone lies in the past. The response of the whole creation lies in the

[1] The criticism of this view by W. C. van Unnik (in his article, 'Worthy is the Lamb' in *Mélanges Bibliques en hommage au R. P. Béda Rigaux*, Gembloux, 1970, pp. 447ff.) is inadequate. His contention that the text does not speak of the Lamb receiving a new and higher status, or of his taking his place on the throne, signally fails to take into account the terms of the worship offered in verses 9f. and verse 12, and also the relation of the vision to 3:21.

[2] See notes on chapter 5.

future. This discontinuity in time of the continuous vision accords
with the eschatological teaching of the New Testament generally.
With the life, death, and resurrection of Jesus the kingdom of God
decisively came into the world, but its presence is hidden to all
but those with eyes of faith. Its manifestation awaits the day of the
unveiling. So in this vision it is heaven alone which understands
the nature of Christ's redemption. That a special exercise of the
sovereignty of the Lamb must take place before the subjugation
of all rebellion and the universal acclamation is the subject of the
following chapters of the Revelation. But this will be the outworking
of the central action of the vision. The messianic judgments and
the parousia are the closing acts of the Easter drama. The concentration on the great redemptive acts in chapter 5 enables us
to see that the victory of God in Christ is one, and that it has been
won. This is the chief lesson from the prophet who views earth
from the standpoint of heaven. This it is which compels him to
telescope the work of Christ for the deliverance of the world into
a single sentence, and which evokes the Church on earth to join
the company of heaven in the adoration of the Lamb.

THE VISION OF THE CREATOR GOD 4:1-11

1. The clause **After this I looked** occurs frequently in the
Revelation at the commencement of a new vision (e.g., 7:1, 18:1,
19:1). At this point it harks back to what the prophet saw in the
opening vision (1:12). As the first vision of Christ issued in the
letters to the churches, so a second vision of the Lord now begins,
which shall issue in an account of events leading to the coming of
Christ and his kingdom. John, therefore, is about to witness **what
must take place after this**—a description of chapters 6ff. rather
than of chapters 4ff., since the time reference in chapters 4–5
is a complex of past, present, and future.

The prophet sees **in heaven an open door**—a not unnatural
sight for a visionary (cf. 3 Mac. 6:18, 1 *Enoch* 14:15, *Test. Levi*
5:1). He is invited to ascend and enter by **the first voice which
I had heard speaking to me.** Since the speaker on the first
occasion was the risen Lord (see note in 1:10f.), presumably he is
the speaker now. Objection has been made to this, since the central
figure in chapter 5 is none other than the Christ. Can he be conceived of as inviting the prophet to ascend and see him in heaven?

The answer to this could be, Why not? Reflection, however, will suggest that such questions should not be asked. A seer who invites us to see a woman and then shows us a city (21:9f.), and who adapts biblical images as freely as he has in this chapter should not be expected to preserve an undeviating consistency in his pictures. They are for kindling the imagination, not for transference to the drawing board.

2. For this reason we should not be too surprised to read **At once I was in the Spirit.** Why does this not precede verse 1, since the vision of the open door in heaven presupposes a condition of ecstasy? Charles thinks that we have here an indication that the author has woven earlier written materials to form this chapter, and that in combining them the author did not perceive his inconsistencies. While this is not impossible, the impression given by chapters 4–5 is of a carefully composed progression. It is more likely that verse 1 indicates the beginning of a new section in the Revelation and verse 2 emphasizes the Spirit's inspiration of the prophet. Further, since John immediately records his sight of the throne in heaven, it is possible that he wishes to convey the notion that in the Spirit he was transported in his ecstasy through the open door into heaven (hence the *NEB* rendering: 'I was caught up by the Spirit').

3. Significantly the first impression of heaven received by the prophet was the sight of **a throne ... with one seated on the throne.** To discuss whether the heaven which John describes is conceived of in terms of a palace or temple, and the position of the throne in relation to other features of the building, is pointless. Not walls, but an awe-inspiring throne dominates John's vision, hence all idea of limiting surroundings fades in the vision of countless myriads of heaven and earth surrounding the throne and worshipping the Lord (5:11ff.). As in the last day heaven and earth flee away to leave the throne of God as the only reality for mankind to see, so now it fills John's vision as he steps away from earth into heaven. As Schlatter observed, 'The sign of God's sovereign power is the throne; for we are about to view God's work, and God's work consists in the fact that he reigns.'[1] While John's description at this point is inspired by Ezekiel's overwhelming vision of the Lord on his throne, borne by the cherubim

---

[1] *Briefe und Offenbarung des Johannes*, ad loc.

to the land of exile (Ezek. 1:26f.), unlike Ezekiel he makes no attempt to describe the form of God. He contents himself with conveying an impression of colours like those which emanate from precious stones, flashing through a strange rainbow-cloud. The appearance of God was as **jasper and carnelian.** The former could vary in appearance from a dull yellow to red or green, or even translucent like glass (as apparently in 21:11). In view of the later passage we may take the last to be in view. *Carnelian*, or sardius (originating from Sardis), was red. The divine appearance, therefore, was as it were transparent 'white' and red. Round the throne was **a rainbow that looked like an emerald.** The rendering *emerald* is an interpretation of the term *smaragd*, which varied in colour from green to a colourless state. John may wish to indicate that about the Lord on the throne was a halo, green in colour, which served alike to suggest and conceal his glory from his creatures. The comparison of the rainbow to the *smaragd*, however, has suggested to some that the latter was a rock crystal, which served as a prism and so yielded the rainbow colours. In that case the primary reference in this passage is to the rainbow as a reminder of the covenant of God with humanity, made after the flood, that the waters would never again be permitted to destroy his creatures (Gen. 9:8ff.). The throne, symbol of the Creator's omnipotence, is surrounded with the sign of the divine mercy—a significant feature in the vision preliminary to descriptions of the judgments of God.

4. Round the throne John sees **twenty-four elders** seated on **thrones.** In Daniel's vision of the judgment of the antigod empire the throne of the Ancient of Days is set alongside other thrones, which presumably are for the angelic assessors in the judgment about to be executed. John's portrayal of heaven, however, is not a judgment scene. His imagery has more in common with the oracle in Isaiah 24:23:

> The moon will be confounded, and the sun ashamed;
> for the Lord of hosts will reign on Mount Zion and in Jerusalem
> and before his elders he will manifest his glory.

In the Targum these elders are interpreted as leaders of the Jewish people. Conformably with this a favourite early interpretation of the *elders* in John's vision viewed them as representatives of Israel and the Church—more specifically the twelve patriarchs from

whom the nation sprang and the twelve apostles who founded the
Church. This interpretation finds support in John's description
of the new Jerusalem, for on its twelve gates the names of the
twelve patriarchs are inscribed, and on its twelve foundations the
names of the twelve apostles (21:12ff.). Others have believed it
significant that there are twenty-four priestly orders enumerated
in 1 Chronicles 24:4ff., and that these were under the authority
of the 'heads of fathers' houses'. There were also twenty-four
orders of Levites, whose duty it was to 'prophesy with lyres, with
harps, and with cymbals' (1 Chr. 25:1). The twenty-four elders
in the Revelation appear to have quasi-priestly functions, as is
especially seen in their worship of God and their presentation of
the prayers of God's people, and in 5:8 where it is stated that each
elder has a harp. On the other hand the fact that the elders present
the prayers of the people of God makes it unlikely that they are to
be viewed as individual men, risen to an exalted life in heaven.
The position of these elders in a vision of the Creator, with a
function related to that of the four living creatures (vv. 6ff.),
suggests that they, like the living creatures themselves, are to be
interpreted as an exalted angelic order. Whether we should further
view the elders as representatives of the old and new Israel in
heaven is uncertain, indeed doubtful. This would involve a quite
different understanding of 'angels' than that in chapters 1–3,
where the angels of the churches appear to be the churches themselves, under the aspect as citizens of heaven as well as earth
through their being 'in Jesus'. Even allowing for the possibility
of a different concept of anglic representation here, the scheme
of chapters 4–5 seems to indicate that in chapter 4 (in distinction
from ch. 5) humanity does not come into view in any way. God
is exalted in his universe, far removed from the turmoil of earth.
It is more plausible to see the number twenty-four as relating to
the twenty-four priestly and twenty-four Levitical orders, thereby
suggesting the function of the twenty-four elders as that of adoring
and serving the Lord of the universe.[1]

[1] So Charles. But he, as most modern commentators, accepts the view of
Zimmern (*Keilinschriften und d.alte Testament*, p. 633) and Gunkel (*Schöpfung
und Chaos*, pp. 302ff.) that the twenty-four elders have their origin not in the
Christian tradition nor in the Old Testament but in Jewish apocalyptic, which
in turn was indebted to the Babylonian astrological religion. This last recognized twenty-four star-gods, twelve to the north of the zodiac, twelve to the

5. The **flashes of lightning, and voices and peals of thunder** which issue from the throne (*voices* and *peals* are virtually synonymous and alike refer to the thunder) are reminiscent of the theophany at Sinai (Exod. 19:16ff.). This may have influenced Ezekiel's description of the divine glory (Ezek. 1:13), and certainly was a powerful element in the thought of the Jews (and Christians) of the first century (see Heb. 12:18ff.). A passage like Psalm 18:9ff. illustrates the connection in the mind of the Jew between the storm and the fearful power and glory of Yahweh. Such would be the prime thought in John's mind here. He would have been aware that in the Old Testament the revelation of God in the storm is commonly for judgment (e.g., 1 Sam. 2:10) or salvation (Ps. 18:16ff.; Job 37:12 includes both). So in the Revelation the lightning and thunder appear with earthquake at the conclusion of each series of judgments, when God is about to be disclosed in glory (8:1ff., 11:15ff., 16:17ff.). Their presence in chapter 4 suggests that the power of holiness for wrath and redemption is inherent in the God of creation.

Is the mention of **seven torches of fire** due to Ezekiel 1:13? There the torches move among the cherubim. For John it would be natural to identify the torches as **the seven spirits of God,** for they were in the midst of the cherubim, even as the sevenfold Spirit of God (1:4) is in the midst of the churches.

---

south. Gunkel further thinks that these entered the Jewish apocalyptic tradition via the Persian concept of the twenty-four *Yazata*. As in Judaism generally, these astral divinities became relegated to the status of angels. John saw the happy coincidence of twenty-four angels with twenty-four orders of priests and Levites, and so combined the two unrelated concepts. It is an attractive theory, and there are those who think that John would have been happy had he learned of the origin of the 'elders', since he was concerned to set forth by symbols the glory of the Creator, not the nature of angels. Nevertheless itshould be observed that there is no evidence at all that Jewish apocalyptic knew of an angelic order of twenty-four in heaven. References to angels in charge of the stars and planets and the whole phenomena of the skies (including winds, waters, hail, thunder, etc.,) abound, especially in 1 *Enoch* and *Jubilees*. 2 *Enoch* 4:1f. explicitly mentions the elders and rulers of the stellar orders, and the 200 angels who rule the stars, but never do we find the number twenty-four. In view of the clear OT references to this number, and the pertinence of the twenty-four orders of priests and twenty-four of Levites to John's symbolism it seems wiser to recognize the likelihood of this origin of the number, and therefore the probability that John was responsible for the choice, rather than affirm confidently a connection for which at present we have no evidence.

6. No such precedent from the prophets exists for the **sea of glass, like crystal** before the throne. We probably have here a transformed reminiscence of 'the waters which were above the firmament', which were separated from 'the waters which were under the firmament' (Gen. 1:7). These upper waters are assumed in the Old Testament references to the heavens and earth (e.g., Ps. 148:4). In Psalm 104:3 the throne of God is depicted as set upon them. In 2 *Enoch* 3:3 they are described as 'a very great sea, greater than the earthly sea'. A whole mythology exists about them in ancient religions (e.g., in Assyrian myths the gods were produced from a union of the masculine waters in heaven with the feminine waters on earth). John's conception is wholly different. He does not actually state that there is a sea in heaven. He says that there is something which looks like one (**as it were ...**), having the appearance of glass or crystal. It is vast, precious, glorious, awesome. Is this not intended to heighten the impression of God's holiness, removing him to a distance from his creatures? The next mention of this sea is in 15:2, where the sea of glass is mingled with fire, eloquent of impending judgment. The conquerors stand by it, and like the Israelites at the Red Sea they sing the song of Moses and the song of the Lamb. Another exodus is about to be enacted, with plagues like those of Egypt. The waters of holiness therefore betoken wrath against unholiness. Kiddle is perhaps justified in regarding the sea as 'a symbol of God's separateness ... and a threat against those who dishonour his creation and persecute his servants'.

John sees a second group of angels near the throne, forming a closer circle round it than the twenty-four elders. The **four living creatures** are described in terms drawn from the visions of Ezekiel (ch. 1) and Isaiah (ch. 6), though freely modified—a reminder, if such were needed, that John presents us with a parabolic portrayal of the glory of God, not a photographic reproduction of heaven. The living creatures stand **round the throne, on each side of the throne** (or as the *NEB* more accurately renders, though reversing the phrases: 'in the centre, round the throne itself'). They do not, like the cherubim of Ezekiel 1, bear the throne, but stand as sentinels round it. Accordingly, the wheels of the throne-chariot, described by Ezekiel, do not feature in John, but the representation of the many eyes in the rims of the wheels, as a symbol of all knowledge, is retained. As the wheels were said

to be 'full of eyes round about', so the living creatures themselves
are said to be full of eyes in front and behind—an impossible
visual image, but comprehensible as a symbol.

7. The creatures have but one face, unlike those in Ezekiel,
which have four each, but the four likenesses are the same, namely,
lion, ox, man, eagle. What is the significance of these appearances, and why were they chosen? It is widely believed that the
reason lies far back in the history of religion. We recall that
Ezekiel, living in Babylon, would have been familiar with the
enormous winged ox- and lion-figures with human heads which
stood at the entrance of temples. He might also have seen representations of the sacred tree flanked by winged creatures having
human bodies and eagles' heads. These figures are thought to have
been derived from stellar constellations. Zimmern identified them
with the four chief signs of the zodiac, namely the Ox, the Lion,
the Scorpion, and Aquarius. By reason of their position these
represented the four quarters of the heavens, and so the four
directions of the winds, and the four seasons.[1] The Ox and Lion
clearly correspond. The Scorpion is often represented as a man.
It is suggested that Aquarius was replaced by the eagle constellation, because the former had fewer bright stars. The theory is
attractive, though it remains uncertain how the eagle got into
the picture.[2] It would be interesting to know whether the rabbinic
exposition of the four cherubim of Ezekiel was in circulation in
John's time. Rabbi Abahu (*c.* AD 300) taught: 'There are four
mighty creatures. The mightiest among the birds is the eagle, the
mightiest among domestic animals is the ox, the mightiest among
wild animals is the lion, the mightiest of them all is man; and
God has taken all these and secured them to his throne.'[3] Such a
tradition would be harmonious with an interpretation, known from
ancient times, that the four creatures, in their ceaseless worship
of God, represent the entire animate creation.[4] The fact that the

---

[1] Op. cit., pp. 631ff.

[2] Farrer identified the Man as the Waterer, and considered that the Eagle
replaced the Scorpion, since the latter was a sign of ill-omen and the Eagle
comes over the horizon at the same time as the Scorpion.

[3] Strack-Billerbeck, III, p. 799, who cite other parallels and add that the
exposition is based on a saying of R. Simeon b.Laqish, *c.* AD 250.

[4] This interpretation is already found in the commentary of Andreas, and
is supported by many moderns, including Swete, Kiddle, Farrer, Caird.

interpretation is of long standing is no reason for its rejection by
moderns. It is in harmony with the spirit of this chapter and with
the evidence we have reviewed. It would be strengthened rather
than diminished by the possibility that the link between the forms
of the cherubim and the constellations was known still in John's
day.[1]

8. The worship of the cherubim modifies the Isaianic chant in
one important particular. The second line, 'the whole earth is
full of his glory', is replaced by **who was and is and is to come.**
The Lord of creation is also Lord of the ages. The future is characterized by his 'coming'. The nature of that coming, and its consequences for the world, form the subject of the rest of the book.
Its mention at this point suggests that it is the inner necessity
of his own faithfulness which prompts the God of creation
to take all needful steps to fulfil his purpose of good for his
creatures.

9, 10. This feature within the character of the eternal God is the
presupposition of the final paragraph of the chapter. At first sight
the picture seems incongruous. Verse 8 has already described the
ceaseless worship offered by the living creatures. We now read
**whenever the living creatures give glory . . . the twenty-four
elders fall down . . . they cast their crowns before the
throne.** This implies that the elders are perpetually prostrating
themselves before God and laying down their crowns as a sign
of their homage—a difficult but admittedly not impossible idea
in a book which contains some strange pictures. It is more consistent with the language, however, to interpret *whenever* as a

[1] Charles contests the above interpretation, on the grounds that it conflicts
with the angelology of Jewish apocalyptic. The latter distinguished two groups
of angels, the angels of the presence and angels of sanctification on the one
hand, and the angels of service on the other. The former worship God and keep
sabbath with Israel; the latter are set over the works of nature and so cannot
keep sabbath for they operate continually. Charles insisted that since the
cherubim must be classified with the former group, they cannot represent
nature. But this is not a compelling argument. It presumes that John must be
confined within the limits of the angelology of Jewish apocalyptic, though
in other respects he manifests a sovereign freedom in his treatment of
Jewish apocalyptic sources. Moreover the angels of service were many and
inferior, and therefore could not represent the higher orders. Only the highest
order of angels could represent all other living creatures, and such were the
cherubim.

simple 'when', indicating not an unbroken process but notable
occasions when the Creator 'comes' and manifests his sovereignty
in judgment and redemption. The occasions which are in mind
will be above all those represented in chapter 5 and in chapters
11 and 19, namely, on the achievement of redemption through the
redeemer's incarnation, death, and resurrection, and his coming
to his kingdom.

11. The ascription by the twenty-four elders of **glory and
honour and power** expresses and brings to a climax the tone of
the whole chapter, every sentence of which is calculated to set
forth the glory of the Creator. If the living creatures celebrate
the holiness and majesty of God in his character, the elders acknowledge the glory and power of his works. He alone is responsible
for the coming into existence of the created order, and by his will
it exists. It should not go unnoticed that there is an ambiguity
in the last line of the song: **by thy will** literally should read 'because of thy will', which can denote either the operating cause
or the intention of creation ('for the sake of thy will'). The *RSV*
interprets the phrase in the former sense, Charles opts for the latter.
He contrasts with it the idea, frequently encountered in apocalyptic writings, that the world was created for man, more specifically
for the sake of Israel, or for the righteous in Israel (e.g., Ezra
6:55ff., *Ass. Mos.* 1:22, 2 *Bar.* 14:19). Clearly that thought is out
of harmony with John's vision. God alone is exalted on his throne.
The universe came into being through him and everything should
subserve his holy purpose—a sentiment basic to the monotheistic
Jewish-Christian tradition taught to pagans (1 C. 8:6). It is
precisely because the will of God is the ultimate power in this
universe that the rest of the Revelation can be penned. The
Creator's purpose will be accomplished, despite the resistance to
it from the evil powers of this world. In this respect two points
are worthy of note. The precise phrase **our Lord and God** does
not occur in the Greek translation of the Old Testament, but it
is the exact rendering of the title, blasphemously claimed by the
emperor Domitian, *Dominus et Deus noster*. Further, the term
receive is not in the present tense but the aorist, most naturally
(though not necessarily) indicating a single action: 'Our Lord and
God, to whom such names belong, is worthy to receive the glory
and honour and power which the universe will one day render to
him.' In this sense the doxology of verse 11 is the presupposition

of the remaining doxologies in this book, and an implicit promise that they will surely follow.

THE BOOK WITH THE SEVEN SEALS 5:1-14

The vision in chapter 4 of the Lord exalted in majesty above the strife of earth gives way to an animated scene in chapter 5. One has the impression of mounting excitement over the victory of the Lamb, which reaches a great crescendo in the burst of praise offered by the universe of living things to God and the Lamb. True the reader has to wait for the revelation of the Victor and his conquest. The description of the scroll, the inability of any man to open it, the prophet's tears, and the elder's consolation, all serve to hold up the narrative. But the delay has the dramatic effect of focussing attention on the action of the Lamb, and its significance for the world and the kingdom of God.

1. Few features of the Revelation have been so widely discussed as the nature of the **scroll ... sealed with seven seals.** The *RSV* is probably right in describing the writing as a scroll, rather than a book. A codex sealed with seven seals is an unlikely phenomenon. It has been common to interpret the scroll as a book-roll, for its description echoes Ezekiel 2:9, and it is a characteristic of Jewish apocalyptic writing for prophecies of the end to be represented as sealed from human eyes until the time of fulfilment (e.g., Dan. 8:26, 12:9). The scroll could be viewed as such a prophecy. Nevertheless it is more likely that the scroll is intended to be understood as some form of legal document relating to the destiny of mankind. In recent years claims have been advanced for two types of document that John could have had in view, the one a doubly inscribed contract-deed, the other a testament.

The former is a type of contract known all over the middle east in ancient times.[1] It goes back to early Babylonian custom of inscribing the content of a deed or contract on a clay tablet and wrapping it round with clay, on the outside of which the nature of the contract was briefly stated. This procedure excluded the possibility of subsequent alterations being made in the terms of

---

[1] A full account of the history and nature of the doubly written contract is given by O. Roller in a posthumous article, 'Das Buch mit sieben Siegeln' *Zeitschrift für neutestamentliche Wissenschaft*, 26 (1937) pp. 98ff.

the deed or contract. When papyrus and parchment were used (among Egyptians and other nations) the deed was commonly written on the top of a page, which was folded and sealed with seven seals, and the contract statement repeated on the lower half of the page. The document was usually preserved in a small jar (the process is perfectly illustrated in the story of Jeremiah's purchase of a field, Jer. 32:9ff.). As the Romans used wax sheets for these contracts, they wrote the deed or contract in inner pages, sewed them together and sealed them, and indicated the content of the deed on the outer sheet. Whereas by the first century AD this custom had died out in much of the middle east, through the increased use of notaries, it was developed by the Romans from the time of Nero on, and was particularly employed in relation to the rights of soldiers. This kind of document would admirably suit John's description of the scroll. Of itself, of course, this does not inform us as to the nature of the deed or contract, for, as Roller pointed out, every conceivable kind of legal transaction was concluded in this way, including marriage-contracts, renting and leasing houses, releasing slaves, bills of contracts, debentures; but not apparently a testament, since the contents of a testament were always kept secret.

This last observation is of interest, for since Zahn it has been a popular interpretation among commentators to view the scroll as a testament. Zahn expressed his understanding of the matter as follows: 'The word *biblion* itself permits of many interpretations, but for the readers of that time it was designated by the seven seals on its back beyond possibility of mistake. Just as in Germany before the introduction of money-orders everybody knew that a letter sealed with five seals contained money, so the most simple member of the Asiatic churches knew that a *biblion* made fast with seven seals was a testament. When a testator dies the testament is brought forward, and when possible opened in the presence of the seven witnesses who sealed it; i.e., it was unsealed, read aloud, and executed ... The document with seven seals is the symbol of the promise of a future kingdom. The disposition long ago occurred and was documented and sealed, but it was not yet carried out ... As to the opening of the seals, the point of comparison is not so much that no one knows the contents of God's will as that they still await realization. No one is authorized to open the will except the Lamb; the returning Christ will open the testament of God and execute it.'[1] The idea is attractive and in harmony with the theology of the Old and New Testaments. God has covenanted to establish among men a new order of life in peace and righteousness, and the Christ is his executor. The objection that the progressive carrying out of God's judgments as the seals are opened does not fit the symbol of a testament, which is not executed till the whole is read out, is not serious, since a symbol does not have to fit at all points. The same difficulty arises if the document is viewed as a doubly written deed. The important element in the picture is God's will to bestow the kingdom. The judgments which precede the kingdom are secondary to the gift of the kingdom itself.

But what of Roller's objection that a testament never had the form of a doubly written deed? If John placed the scroll within this category, it would be decisive against his viewing it as a testament.[2] It is, however, of importance to observe that the crucial phrase which determines the identification of the document **(written within and on the back)** is cited from Ezekiel 2:9, and that in Ezekiel this does not describe a doubly written deed, for it has no seals. Roller freely admits this and excludes Ezekiel 2:9f. from the list of biblical examples of the document in question. The point to be determined, therefore, is whether in conjoining the phrase from Ezekiel with the seven seals John consciously modifies Ezekiel's document to make it a contract-deed, or whether he changes Ezekiel's prophecy of overflowing judgments to a testament of the kingdom preceded by judgments. In the latter case the use of Ezekiel's language would be to establish rapport with the prophet's message of judgment, but would have no significance for the form of the document. Regretfully I submit that we have no means of determining which change John had in mind, and that both Zahn and Roller used stronger language in stating their respective interpretations than the evidence warrants. Nevertheless, they have pointed us in the right direction, and in the end the difference between the two symbols is small.

It will be recalled that a doubly written document covered a variety of contracts and deeds. Roller himself concluded that in

---

[1] *Introduction to the New Testament*, III, pp. 393f.

[2] Roller emphatically declares that no example of a testament in the form of a doubly inscribed contract has come to light in all ancient middle east studies, op. cit., p. 106.

our passage the document was a debenture. It affirmed the debt
of sin owed by mankind to God and the judgment to which the
debtors were liable. The vision tells of joy because the Lamb has
paid the debt, releasing those who own their guilt, but confirming
the judgment of the impenitent. Chapter 5 is therefore a judgment
scene. Now this is surely an impossible interpretation. Chapter
5 is not a judgment scene. It describes the tumultuous joy of an
enthronement which initiates the new era of salvation, the age of
God's long promised kingdom. The exultant tone of chapter 5
confirms the interpretation on which this commentary is based,
namely that the three series of judgments are fundamentally
three pictorial presentations of one reality, i.e., the messianic
judgments that precede the kingdom of God. The important feature of the sealed document is not the judgments which accompany
the opening of the seals, but the supreme event to which they lead.
If, therefore, the scroll written within and on the back is a doubly
inscribed deed, it must signify a deed which conveys the promise
of the kingdom of God to mankind. Its conditions none can fulfil
until there appears on the scene the Christ who is Lion and Lamb,
King and Redeemer, and heaven rejoices at his achievement on
behalf of man and his assumption of the throne with God as judge
and king. If the scroll is a testament, it views the bestowal of the
kingdom as God's covenant promise, the fulfilment of which has
been made possible through the death of the Lamb of God and
his exaltation to the throne of God. The chief difference between
the symbols is that one employs a concept of a deed of promise,
the other a covenant, but the thing symbolized is one.

2-4. From the language of **no one was able to open the
scroll,** Charles concludes that **Who is worthy** = 'Who is able',
and with good reason, since the vision assumes that he who
opens the scroll has power to execute what is written therein.
Nevertheless, if the scroll represents God's disposition of the
kingdom to man, the question of moral worth and dignity is in
place here, and it is not surprising that **no one in heaven or on
earth or under the earth** (= Hades) could rise to the height of
excellence required for the task.

5-6. The weeping of the prophet is restrained by an elder, for
one has proved his worth, **the Lion of the tribe of Judah, the
Root of David.** The former title is derived from the song of
Jacob, Genesis 49:9: 'Judah is a lion's whelp ... He stooped

down, he couched as a lion', the latter from Isaiah 11:1, and especially verse 10, 'In that day the root of Jesse shall stand as an ensign to the peoples, him shall the nations seek . . .'. Both passages were interpreted by the Jews as messianic, and it is wholly in keeping with the content of the messianic prophecies for the elder to say that the Lion of Judah, the Root of David **has conquered.** But how has he **conquered, so that he can open the scroll and its seven seals?** The answer is given in the next paragraph where, as in the rest of the vision, the Christ appears as the Lamb, of whom it is immediately said that it looks **as though it had been slain** and whose worth is celebrated precisely because it had been *slain* (vv. 9, 12). How the Lamb conquers through being slaughtered is not immediately evident, any more than the rationale of identifying the Lion of Judah with the Lamb. But these things lie at the heart of John's theology and must be clarified.

The first thing to be noted is that the Lamb which appears to have had its throat cut ('slain') *stands*. The slain Lamb is the risen Lamb. Secondly, even apart from the slit throat, this is no ordinary lamb. It has **seven horns** and **seven eyes.** In the Old Testament horns symbolize power (e.g., Dt. 33:17), and at times royalty (e.g., Dan. 7:7; cf. Rev. 17:3, 12). *Seven horns* then signify fullness of strength. The Lamb of God is immensely powerful. The *seven eyes* signify fullness of knowledge, i.e., omniscience. The language here used is drawn from Zechariah 4:10, where we read of 'seven . . . eyes of the Lord, which range through the whole earth'. Our passage not only ascribes to the Lamb that which belongs to God, but it identifies the seven eyes with the seven spirits of God. In 4:5 the seven spirits are seen before the throne of God. John here would seem to say that the energies of the sevenfold Spirit are loosed into the world through the slain and risen Lamb (Caird). Now this collocation of Lion of Judah, Root of David, Lamb, slaughter, resurrection, seven horns, seven eyes which are seven Spirits of God sent by the Christ into the world, and conquest through death and resurrection, is comprehensible only on the recognition that we have here a unique blend of Jewish and Christian traditions. The Lion and the Root of David is the Messiah of the Old Testament; that is clear, Who is the seven-horned Lamb? Despite protestations to the contrary,[1]

[1] Notably by Traugott Holtz, *Die Christologie der Apokalypse des Johannes*, 1971, p. 41.

there seems to be no doubt that this figure is derived from Jewish
apocalyptic imagery, which represented the people of God as the
flock of God out of which arises a deliverer who rescues them from
their foes. He is a lamb because he is young. He has seven horns
and so is strong and able to destroy the beasts which terrorize the
flock. This symbolism is employed in the *Testament of Joseph* 19:8f.,
where a lion and a lamb appear together, the former the Messiah
from Judah, the latter the Messiah from Aaron: 'And all the
beasts rushed against him (the lamb), and the lamb overcame
them, and destroyed them and trod them underfoot. And because
of him the angels and men rejoiced, and all the land ... His
kingdom is an everlasting kingdom, which shall not pass away.'
The last sentence presumably relates to the kingdom of God,
rather than a kingdom of the Lamb. But the deliverance which
leads to the coming of the kingdom is wrought by the lamb. Now
this figure of the conquering lamb has nothing to do with sacrifice,
nor has his victory any connection with death. He is the champion
of God's flock and conquers the wicked by his superior strength,
so making way for the age of righteousness. In the vision of the
Testaments, therefore, the Lion and the Lamb are not contrasting
figures. They are variant symbols of one idea, the all prevailing
Messiah. The present writer has no doubt that this was the Messiah whom John the Baptist proclaimed (Jn 1:29). But John the
Seer beholds a *slain* Messiah. Why not a dead Lion, instead of a
slain Lamb? Clearly because the symbolism would not fit. The
Messiah has been slain as a sacrifice. In this book, which is full of
the exodus typology, it is virtually certain that the prophet has
in view the Christ as the passover-lamb (hence in v. 9 the Lamb
has 'ransomed' men for God—freed them through his death, as
in the doxology of 1:5).[1] The warrior-Lamb then has conquered
through accepting the role of the passover-Lamb. And this
unheard-of notion is complemented by another. He is the risen
redeemer, and he shares the divine attributes and has sent into
the world the seven Spirits of God. Here the Christ of the old
covenant promise and apocalyptic hope stands revealed in terms
of the new covenant fulfilment. Naturally he is the Root of David,
the Lion of Judah, and the Lamb who leads God's flock. But he is

[1] The same reinterpretation of the warrior-Lamb as the passover-Lamb is
made by the Fourth Evangelist, whose understanding of John 1:29 is made
evident in John 19:14, 31–6.

also the crucified and risen Redeemer, the Lord, the Bringer of
the new age, the Giver of the Spirit. Indeed, he is one with God.
If this section of the vision represents the first step of the enthronement ceremony of the Messiah, namely, the presentation, then
the awesomeness of the revelation must be recognized, for never
has the Christ been so introduced.

7. He went and took the scroll. Did he then move from a
position of distance from God towards God **on his throne?** The
interpretation of John's language in the *RSV* of verse 6 would so
suggest. The Lamb was standing away from the throne 'among
the elders', and he here advances towards God on the throne. The
NEB interprets verse 6 differently (the Lamb is 'in the very middle
of the throne, inside the circle of living creatures and the circle
of elders'), but not verse 7. The important feature on any understanding of the picture is that the Lamb *took* the scroll. This it is
which causes the acclamation of the living creatures and elders in
verses 8f. The Christ is authorized to execute the judgments which
will conclude this age (cf. 6:1–8:5) and to initiate the kingdom
which belongs to the new age (cf. 19:11–22:5). This element of
the vision represents the exaltation of the Christ, expressed in other
terms in Matthew 28:18, Philippians 2:9ff., etc.

8. The response of the supreme angelic powers of heaven is
noteworthy: they **fell down before the Lamb.** In 4:10f. the
twenty-four elders fall down before the Lord on his throne and
worship him in song. Here the elders and living creatures fall
down in adoration of the Lamb, ascribing a similar doxology of
praise to him as they do to God. We are evidently expected to
understand that on receiving the scroll the Lamb took his seat on
the throne with God (cf. 3:21). The enthronement-ceremony,
therefore, now reaches its climax. Having taken his place on the
throne with God, the Lamb receives the worship of heaven. The
living creatures and elders accompany their song with harps, and
they offer with their own praise **incense ... the prayers of the
saints.** The impression is thereby conveyed that the prayers so
offered are presented to the Lamb as to God, but perhaps this
is an unintended accompaniment of John's symbolism which
should not be pressed.

9, 10. The angelic leaders now take up **a new song.** This is a
well-known expression in the psalms, relating to songs sung on
festal occasions and celebrating new mercies from God, especially

his deliverances from distress (e.g., Ps. 40:1, 98:1). It receives a deeper meaning in Isaiah 42:10, where the new song relates to the new and greater deliverance which the Lord is about to make in the earth. Such is its implication here. A new song is raised in thanksgiving for the accomplishment of the promised redemption and the advent of the new age. It is repeated in 14:3 (and 15:3f.), and anticipates the new heaven and new earth, in which all things are made new by God (21:1ff.).

The words with which the song begins, **Worthy art thou,** are identical with those which open the ascription of praise to God in 4:11. He who has taken the scroll and undertakes to put into effect its decrees carries out the divine functions of judgment and sovereignty, and so is to be acknowledged as divine. **For thou . . . by thy blood didst ransom men for God.** As the passover-lambs were slain for Israel's release from sin, and thereby made possible the nation's emancipation from the Egyptian slavery to become the covenant people of God in the promised land, so the death of the Lamb of God, coupled with his resurrection, brought to men emancipation from sin's slavery, that they might become members in the race drawn from all nations, a company of kings and priests to God in the new age.[1] It is in keeping with the passover-theology of John that the sacrifice of the Lamb led not simply to a general emancipation of men, but to the creation of a people for God. The redeemed become a kingdom and priests to our God (cf. Exod. 19:6; and see the note on 1:6).[2] Inasmuch as the exaltation of the Lamb initiates the new age, the privilege of being kingly priests for God belongs to the emancipated people

[1] This is closely related to the interpretation of the passover current in Judaism during John's time. See Jeremias, *The Eucharistic Words of Jesus*, E.T., pp. 225f., and note especially the saying of R. Eliezer: 'For the merit of the covenant blood of the circumcision and of the passover blood I have redeemed you out of Egypt, and for their merit you will be redeemed at the end of the fourth world empire (= Rome; i.e., in the days of the Messiah)', cited by Jeremias, p. 225, n. 4.

[2] See Holtz, op. cit., pp. 48ff., to whom I am indebted for his exposition of Revelation 5. He considers that the real ground for the enthronement of the Lamb is indicated in the closing stanza of the new song, 'and hast made them a kingdom and priests to our God'; i.e., the creation of the Church is the presupposition of the Lord's assumption of the throne. This is perhaps an overstatement, for it is the death of the Lamb which makes possible the redemption which creates the Church, and which brings the cosmos under the sway of the Lamb.

even now. Nevertheless, as the revelation of Christ in his kingdom takes place at his parousia, so the full exercise of their royal priesthood belongs to the time of his triumph. Hence the song ends with the words, **they shall reign on earth** (cf. 20:4ff.).[1]

11, 12. The living creatures and the elders are joined by the countless throngs of **angels** in adoration of the Lamb (**myriads** is the highest number known to Greeks). As in the two previous doxologies (4:11, 5:9), the first word is **Worthy.** The opening formula is changed so as to make it a doxology in the third person, as in 7:12, and strangely it brings together all but one of the elements of worship offered to God in 7:12 (in the latter **wealth** is replaced by 'thanksgiving'). It would suit the context of the doxology here if its first four elements were to be viewed as expressive of the sovereignty exercised by Christ on behalf of God, and the last three of the recognition accorded by the universe to the newly enthroned Lord. This cannot be pressed, but it would be in harmony with the dynamic conception of the kingdom which is characteristic of the New Testament (e.g., Mt. 6:33, 11:5, 12:28, Rom. 14:17, 1 C. 4:20) and of this book also (cf. especially 12:10). It should be observed, however, that the sovereignty of the Lamb is redemptive. The worship offered to God in 4:11 is to the Creator for whom all things exist, and who intends to fulfil his gracious purpose in the creation he has made. The worship offered to the Lamb in 5:12 is to the Redeemer who has accomplished God's purpose (the outworking of which is unfolded in the rest of the book).

13. The triumph of the Lamb reaches its fitting climax in the acknowledgment of his worth by **every creature** in the universe, not only by the 'living' but by those in the realm of the dead. Here, however, the worship is offered conjointly to God and to the Lamb. While it is not explicitly stated, it is assumed that the Lamb is seated **on the throne** with God. In vision the end of history has been reached, the doxology anticipates the rule and the glory of God and the Lamb in the city which descends from heaven (see 21:22ff., 22:1-5). Indirectly the song throws light on the nature of the Messiah who initiates the new order. He is the one through whom God accomplishes his will in creation, at its end as at its beginning (cf. 3:14) and through all the ages

[1] Some MSS read a present tense ('they reign . . .'), but the future is better attested.

between (cf. 22:13), and this he does because he is one with God, to be worshipped and adored with him **for ever and ever.**

14. The final word is with **the four living creatures,** as they utter their **Amen** to the song of adoration given by the whole universe. As representatives of creation in their ceaseless adoration of God (see 4:8 and note), they fittingly conclude the worship offered to God and the Lamb by the whole creation at the close of history.

THE JUDGMENTS OF THE SEVEN SEALS 6:1–8:5

The opening of the seven seals of the scroll by the Lamb provides the occasion for John's first representation of the messianic judgments, which are so characteristic a feature of the Revelation. Despite the concentration of attention on the judgments, to which the opening of each seal leads, it is not to be doubted that John steadily bears in mind the nature of the book to which the seals are affixed, namely God's disposition of the kingdom to man. The judgments of the seals are but the precursors of the salvation of the world. Admittedly this is only briefly hinted at after the opening of the seventh seal (8:1ff.), but it is jubilantly sung after the sounding of the seventh trumpet (11:15f.), and plainly indicated after the outpouring of the seventh cup (16:17ff.). Nevertheless the description of the kingdom is held back till the fate of the antichristian empire, city, and ruler is made known, i.e., till chapters 20–2.

The conviction that judgments must fall prior to the coming of the kingdom of God is rooted in the teaching of the Old Testament prophets concerning the day of the Lord (for typical references see Am. 5:18ff., Isa. 2:12ff., Zech. 1:2ff.). This teaching was developed by the Jewish apocalyptists and it finds many echoes in the New Testament writings. No passage in the New Testament is more closely related to this element within the Book of Revelation than the eschatological discourse of the gospels, Mark 13 and its parallels (Mt. 24, Lk. 21). For this there are the best of reasons, since there is ground for believing that the content of the seven seals, as distinct from their form, reproduces the essential features of that discourse. The parallels between Revelation 6 and Mark 13, etc., have frequently been observed by expositors. Charles set them out in detail, and summarized them as follows:

Mark 13:7ff., 24f.	Revelation 6
1. Wars	1. Wars
2. International strife	2. International strife
3. Earthquakes	3. Famine
4. Famines	4. Pestilence (=Death and Hades)
5. Persecutions	5. Persecutions
6. Eclipses of the sun and moon, falling of the stars, shaking of the powers of heaven	6. Earthquakes, eclipse of the sun, ensanguining of the moon, falling of the stars, men calling on the rocks to fall on them, shaking of the powers of heaven

From the Marcan list the passage relating to the fall of Jerusalem has been omitted by John (vv. 14ff.), as also the references to the false prophets expected to appear (vv. 21ff.). Since the fall of Jerusalem lies in the past, it is understandable that John should omit mention of it at this point. But he subsequently develops in a different manner the hints about the Antichrist contained in Mark 13:14 and the warnings about false prophets (cf. chs. 13 and 17). The transference of earthquakes from the middle of the list to the end is not merely for the purpose of combining it with the cosmic signs, but still more to preserve it as one of the signs which immediately herald the conclusion of this age (cf. 11:19, 16:18ff.). The one item in Revelation 6 missing from Mark 13 is the pestilence (if we are right in so interpreting John in v. 8). This, however, is found in Luke's version of the discourse (Lk. 21:11). Luke's account of the concluding signs is also closer to John's description, notably in its mention of the perplexity of men and their dire fear at the prospect of the end (Lk. 21:25f.). This is not to suggest that John knew Luke's gospel and valued it more highly than the other gospels. Rather it is likely that the eschatological discourse circulated before the gospels were written and continued to do so after their publication, and that John knew such an independent version of it.[1]

If the contents of the seven seals reflect the substance of the eschatological discourse, the images in which it is presented come

[1] As apparently Paul did, for a knowledge of the discourse seems to be presupposed in 1 and 2 Thessalonians. For a discussion of the issue see G. R. Beasley-Murray, *Jesus and the Future*, chapter 5.

from elsewhere. The events following the opening of the first four seals are portrayed by symbols adapted from the visions of Zechariah. In Zechariah 1:8ff., 6:1ff. we read of four chariots drawn by four groups of horses of different colours. They go out 'to the four winds of heaven', i.e., to the four quarters of the earth, patrol it and bring back a report to the Lord of all the earth. In John the chariots have disappeared. There are simply four riders on horses, and they ride, not to view the world but to bring judgments upon it. Whereas in Zechariah the colours of the horses appear to be those traditionally associated with the four winds, in John they correspond with the nature of the disasters which their riders bring. The figures of riders on horses to represent instruments of disaster will have been natural to John and to his readers, for in ancient times horses were primarily used in connection with war.

1, 2. In agreement with the vision of chapter 5, it is **the Lamb** who **opened one of the seven seals.** The language is Hebraistic and should read '. . . the Lamb opened the first of the seven seals, and I heard the first of the four living creatures . . .' Here, as later, the call of one of the living creatures **'Come!'** is addressed to a rider, who obeys the command forthwith. It is extraordinary how frequent and persistent is the identification of the first rider with Christ, due to his possessing **a white horse** (cf. Rev. 19:11), being given **a crown,** and being victorious in mission **(conquering and to conquer).** But this is to play havoc with the whole scheme of John's vision. The Lamb on the throne of God opens the seals, and as he does so horsemen come forth one by one. It is a strange notion to make the Lamb one of the riders. The parallels between the seals and the eschatological discourse on the one hand and the later series of judgments in the Revelation on the other shows that all four riders initiate judgments—the first no less than the other three. The first rider has a *bow*, the second a *sword*, and both are for inflicting death. For this reason the alternative suggestion that the first rider represents the triumphant progress of the gospel in the world (cf. Mk 13:10) is equally to be excluded as alien to the context. The rider with the bow, crowned and conquering, represents an overwhelming power in warfare. Whether on this basis one should advance to an identification of the rider with an individual nation is doubtful. The idea is frequently canvassed that the Parthian empire, on Rome's eastern borders, is in mind, since the Parthians used the bow, and

by their defeat of the Romans in AD 62 encouraged the belief
that Rome would be overthrown by an eastern power. Yet there
are enough references in the Old Testament prophets to the bow
as an instrument of slaughter in time of judgment to account for
John's symbolism, as a glance at the concordance will show. That
the rider went out *conquering* described not victories of the past
but instant successes; *and to conquer* relates to future victories.[1]

3, 4. The rider on **another horse, bright red** goes forth **to
take peace from the earth,** and so is **given a great sword.**
In what respect does his activity add to that of the first one? The
language suggests that the first rider represents an army invading
other countries from without (the rider 'conquers'), the second a
general confusion of strife including hostilities between countries,
and perhaps civil war **(that men should slay one another).**
The two signs follow the pattern of the eschatological discourse,
where we read of 'wars and rumours of wars' (= wars near and
far), and then that 'nation will rise against nation, and kingdom
against kingdom' (Mk 13:7f.). The second seal extends and intensifies the strife, so that all peace is taken from the earth.

5, 6. The third rider's horse is appropriately **black,** for he
introduces famine. The **balance** implies that food will have to be
weighed out and rationed with care (cf. Lev. 26:26, Ezek. 4:16).
The prices quoted in verse 16 indicate both the scarcity of food
and its high cost. **A quart of wheat** was currently regarded as
the amount required by a man for food for one day; **a denarius**
was the standard wage for a day's work. Accordingly a man's
entire earnings are required to buy bread for himself alone. But
what of his family? They can feed only if he buys inferior **barley.**

---

[1] It is often suggested that while the judgments of the seals are admittedly
traditional, John intends a contemporary application of each one; e.g. the
conquest of the Romans by the Parthians is in view in the first seal, the progress
of Rome's armies in the second, the famine of AD 62 in the third, the pestilences
following on recent wars in the fourth, the persecution of Nero in the fifth.
These secondary applications are held to underscore John's conviction that the
sixth seal will be opened shortly, leading to a speedy consummation. While the
theory is attractive, its weakness is apparent in all but the first seal. It is, for
example, arbitrary to claim that the sword given to the second rider indicates
Rome's conquests, equally so to identify a famine in verse 6, a pestilence in
verse 8, and a single persecution in verse 9. John is portraying by the seals,
trumpets, and bowls the messianic judgments of the last days. The commentators' lust for identifications must be resisted.

Even so three quarts of barley represent a very low subsistence for a whole family, and the price for such a starvation diet is exhorbitant (it is eleven to sixteen times the prices cited by Cicero for wheat sold in Sicily; see *Verr.* III. 81). The command **do not harm oil and wine** has caused some perplexity. It has been suggested that it reflects an ancient tradition that in the year that stands under the sign of the constellation 'the Scales' (once every twelve years) the grain harvest will be bad but the olive and vine will yield plentifully.[1] Lohmeyer thought it expressed a concern for the availability of oil and wine for Christian use (cf. Jas 5:14 and the requirement of wine for the Lord's Supper). It is more plausible to view it as reflecting a concern for these commodities in time of famine, whether for the sake of the wealthy, who are less likely to be affected by shortage of food than by the poor, or simply for the more reckless of men. There is a lengthy description in the Mishnah (*Sotah* 49a) of the evils that will come on earth in the days prior to the Messiah's coming, which includes the following: 'Insolence will increase and honour dwindle; the vine will yield its fruit abundantly but wine will be dear; the government will turn to heresy (= Christianity) and there will be none to offer them reproof.' The same sentiment appears in *Sanhedrin* 97a, and in both passages the editors of the Soncino Talmud interpret the second clause as implying that despite the plentiful grape harvest, wine will be dear because of the prevalence of drunkenness. Its sole pertinence here is the illustration provided that there are those who will not be denied the right to self-indulgence, even in time of famine.

7, 8. The fourth rider is on **a pale horse,** appropriate for his significance as a harbinger of death. In this context it is fairly certain that John uses the term **Death** with deliberate ambiguity. He is fully aware that in the Greek translation of the Old Testament 'death' can translate the Hebrew term for pestilence. Ezek. 14:21 provides a significant example. After recounting one by one the effects of God's judgments on the land the prophet concludes, 'How much more (will Noah, Daniel, and Job deliver none but themselves) when I send upon Jerusalem my four sore acts of judgment, sword, famine, evil beasts, and pestilence'.

---

[1] So Boll, *Aus der Offenbarung Johannes* (cited by Lohmeyer, ad loc.), who elaborates the point and identifies the rider on the black horse with the divinity of the Scales in the zodiac.

The Septuagint renders the last by 'death'. John himself appears
to use 'death' for pestilence in 2:23, and certainly in 18:8, where
RSV renders 'death' by pestilence. The rider on the pale horse,
then, represents pestilence. But **Hades followed him.** On
another horse? or sitting behind on the same horse? Either picture
would destroy the symbolism of the four horsemen. Hades surely
follows on foot, grimly gathering in the victims of pestilence. In
view however of John's linking of Death and Hades together
elsewhere (1:18, 20:13f.) it is likely that in this passage Death
stands first for pestilence (as in Lk. 21:11) and secondly for death
in its general meaning. For this reason the passage goes on to
extend the scope of the activity of Death and Hades to embrace
the 'four sore acts of judgment' enumerated in Ezekiel 14:21,
namely **to kill with sword and with famine and with
pestilence and by wild beasts of the earth.** The last rider,
with his accomplice stalking behind him, gathers the results of the
work of the previous three, and for John's readers that would be
comprehensible, not only because of Ezekiel's prophecy, but
because war was commonly followed by famine, pestilence, and
wild beasts, which multiplied without check.

9. The fifth seal introduces a very different scene, a vision of the
souls of the martyrs crying out for judgment. The passage is
steeped in Jewish thought, yet it is central to the author's purpose.
The theme of the martyrs crying for vengeance (cf. Gen. 4:10),
with the assurance that God has set a definite limit on the number
so to be slain and at the set time will answer the martyrs' prayers
by the revelation of the kingdom is well known in Jewish apocalyptic writings.[1] Nevertheless it has an important expression in the

[1] Its expression in 1 *Enoch* 47 is so instructive as to warrant quoting:
In those days shall have ascended the prayer of the righteous,
And the blood of the righteous from the earth before the Lord of Spirits.
In those days the holy ones who dwell above the heavens
Shall unite with one voice
And supplicate and pray . . .
On behalf of the blood of the righteous which has been shed,
And that the prayer of the righteous may not be in vain before the Lord of
Spirits,
That judgment may be done unto them,
And that they may not have to suffer for ever.
In those days I saw the Head of Days when He seated himself upon the throne
of his glory . . .

gospels. Its place in our chapter is due to the prominent part in the eschatological discourse of the theme of persecution for Christian testimony (see Mk 13:9ff.), but it finds a closer parallel in the address of Matthew 23:29ff.: 'You witness against yourselves that you are sons of those who murdered the prophets. Fill up, then, the measure of your fathers . . . that upon you may come all the righteous blood shed on earth, from the blood of innocent Abel to the blood of Zechariah the son of Barachiah.' This last passage encourages the belief that **the souls of those who had been slain for the word of God and for the witness they had borne** includes the martyrs of all ages, although this description naturally has immediate application to those who die for 'the word of God and the testimony of Jesus' (cf. 1:9).

But why are the souls of the martyrs **under the altar?** It is possible that several streams of thought merge here. The concept of death for Christ's sake as a sacrifice to God appears in Philippians 2:7, 2 Timothy 4:6 (and in later Christian writings, Ignatius *Rom.* 2:2). In Jewish circles it was simple to draw the parallel that as the blood of beasts sacrificed on the altar of the temple of Jerusalem is poured out at the base of the altar (Lev. 4:7, etc.), so the souls of the martyrs sacrificed on God's altar in heaven rest beneath it in repose. Another line of thought finds expression in Rabbi Akiba. He said, 'He who is buried in the other countries (other than Babylonia and Palestine) is as if he were buried in Babylon; and he who is buried in Babylon is as if he were buried in the land of Israel; and he who is buried in the land of Israel is as if he were buried beneath the altar, for the whole land of Israel is appropriated for the altar; he who is buried beneath the altar is as if he were buried beneath the throne of glory.'[1] How far Akiba himself was prepared to go in applying this thought is doubtful, but later R. Eliezer was prepared to affirm, 'The souls of the righteous are hidden under the Throne of Glory, as it is said, "Yet the souls of my Lord shall be bound up in the bundle of life (with the Lord thy God)"' (*Shabbath* 152b). Here to be under the throne of glory is to be in the presence of him who sits on the

And the hearts of the holy were filled with joy,
Because the number of the righteous had been offered,
And the prayer of the righteous had been heard,
And the blood of the righteous been required before the Lord of Spirits.
[1] *Aboth* RN, in Strack-Billerbeck, III, p. 803.

throne. So, too, John sees the martyrs in a place of honour, under the watchful eye of God.

10, 11. The prayer, **how long before thou wilt judge and avenge our blood?** is a plea by the martyrs not for personal revenge, but for the vindication of the right and truth of the cause for which they gave their lives, which is Christ's cause. The martyrs had been condemned by those who dwell upon the earth, i.e., by the opponents of Christ and the Church (cf. 13:8). They had been put to death as propagators of lies and enemies of mankind. Their prayer that God will put them in the right and reverse the judgment of the world can be answered finally only by the revelation of Christ in his kingdom, when it will be seen that Christ is no deceiver but the Lord of truth and the Lord of the universe, and that they are his true servants. In that event they will be vindicated, and those who put them to death be judged.[1] Their cry is heard, but their request is not immediately granted. Instead they are given **a white robe and told to rest a little longer.** The white robe can hardly signify the garment of resurrection (as Charles and Lohmeyer maintain), since the martyrs' rest is to last till the tally of those destined for martyrdom is completed, at which point they will all participate in the first resurrection (20:4ff.). The application of the symbol in 7:13 is pertinent for its significance here. As they who came out of the great tribulation 'washed their robes and made them white in the blood of the Lamb', so the martyrs are here given the sign of their justification through Christ (in contrast to their condemnation by the world), which is itself a sign and a pledge of the final glory to be bestowed upon them (cf. Rom. 8:30).

For the modern reader in the western world this passage may well appear like an antiquarian's cameo—a vision from remote days, to be viewed with interest and curiosity. For the Christian

---

[1] If this be a correct understanding of the martyrs' cry it is misleading to contrast it with the prayer of Jesus (Lk. 23:34) and Stephen (Ac. 7:60) for the forgiveness of their murderers. It is not the individual perpetrators of the crime but the world's judgment which is in view. The real parallel to this passage is another Lukan pericope, namely the parable of the widow's cry for vengeance, reluctantly answered by the judge, with the lesson 'How much more will not God vindicate his elect, who cry to him day and night?' (Lk. 18:1–8). Here too it is the reversal of the world's judgment which is in the mind of Jesus, and for which he looks from God. See the illuminating discussion on verses 9ff. by Caird, ad loc.

of John's day, facing pagan pressures which at times erupted into fearful persecution, and which now threatened to escalate into the ultimate war on the Church, it was otherwise. The *how long* ascended from earth, as well as from beneath the altar. To a Church facing a struggle with powers able to inflict the worst at will, it is consolation to know that there is a limit to the activities of those who shed blood on the earth, and that the sacrifice of Christ's slain witnesses is not in vain, but is part of the process by which the kingdom finally comes and is to be vindicated in the day when their prayer is answered. From this viewpoint the events of the fifth seal, as those of the other six, constitute a judgment on **those who dwell upon the earth.**

12–17. The opening of the sixth seal leads to cataclysmic events of cosmic proportions: a great earthquake, in which every mountain and island is removed from its place, the darkening of sun, reddening of moon, falling of stars, vanishing of the sky, and terror of men at the arrival of the great day of wrath. This description has puzzled some of the most notable expositors of the Revelation, for whereas it should immediately lead to the end of history, the end does not yet come—indeed, the worst is yet to be. Charles, therefore, following a hint from Bousset, views verses 16f. as expressing the alarm of the conscience-stricken inhabitants of the earth, but not the author's own understanding, for the author knows that there is more to follow. Lohmeyer considers that the events of the sixth seal simply herald the beginning of the eschatological struggle which precedes the end of the age. Bousset himself accepted a suggestion of Spitta to account for so unsuitable a passage as this, occurring in the middle of an apocalypse. The paragraph originally concluded an earlier apocalypse, which by this description of cosmic portents actually portrayed the end of the age, and John was content to let the passage stand without modification. These suggestions do less than justice to John's intelligence and artistic sense. Certainly Bousset is right in thinking that an earlier apocalypse lies behind chapter 6, but as we have earlier said, this happens to be an 'apocalypse' of Jesus, preserved for us in Mark 13 and its synoptic parallels, and in all the versions of the eschatological discourse these portents immediately herald the parousia (see Mk 13:24ff., etc.). That is what John intended his readers to understand from this paragraph. His conclusion of the seven trumpets series has a different form from this, but John makes it plain beyond doubt that after the sounding of the seventh trumpet the kingdom arrives (11:15ff.). The outpouring of the seventh bowl repeats the form of the sixth sealjudgment and is described in a manner closely related to it. Here, too, a great earthquake occurs, the islands flee away, every mountain disappears, and Babylon drains the cup of the fury of God's wrath. Yet chapter 16 is followed by an account of the splendour of Mother Babylon. This threefold attainment of the brink of the last day, without the day itself being described, is John's way of letting us know that his representations of the messianic judgments depict the last times from different vantage points. Admittedly he must have been aware that his language in 6:12ff. is hyperbolic, for he as well as any would have recognized that if verses 12ff. were taken literally, the inhabitants of earth would be hard put to it to find a mountain to fall on them and hide them from the wrath of heaven. And how could the rocks hide from God, anyway? The entire passage in every clause utilizes well known prophetic anticipations of the day of the Lord, and by his use of these images John identifies the day for his readers. One may check this by consulting the chief scriptures John employs, notably Joel 2:10, 30f., Isaiah 13:9ff., 2:10ff., 34:4, Ezekiel 32:7f., Hosea 10:8. These passages depict the concomitants of the day of the Lord and supply John with all his pictures.

The earthquake is a constant feature of representations of the end (Am. 8:8, Ezek. 38:19, Jl. 2:10, etc.). As was pointed out above, John transfers it from its earlier place in the eschatological discourse to this position to identify the occasion as the end of the age (cf. 11:19, 16:18). In the description of the heavenly portents, Joel 2:31 and Isaiah 34:4 fill out the language of Mark 13:24f. The observation of Charles as to its significance is worthy of note: 'The world and its well-being depend on the faithfulness with which the luminaries of heaven fulfil their parts. The unvarying order and loyalty with which they do so was a favourite theme with apocalyptic writers . . . When, then, the sun and moon and stars forsook this order, the end of the world was at hand.' The enumeration in verse 25 of the people who seek to flee from the coming wrath is characteristic of John's writings. It is a sevenfold classification of mankind, ranging from the emperor of Rome (among **the kings**), through the nobility and soldiers, the powerful and the ordinary citizens, down to the slaves. Their cry in verse 16 in

part answers the cry of the martyrs (v. 10). Again its relation to
Isaiah 2:10ff. and Hosea 10:8 identifies the occasion, which
nevertheless contains a feature not in the Old Testament prophets.
The day of the Lord is the revelation of the wrath **of him who is
seated on the throne** and **of the Lamb.** The world of John's
day was dominated by the rule of an emperor-god, seated on his
throne in Rome and despising the 'superstition' of the Lamb. The
day of the Lord unveils the only throne which has power over the
world, who he is who sits upon it, and the possession by the slain
Lamb of the omnipotence represented by that throne. When his
wrath is revealed, **who can stand?**[1]

THE SEALING OF THE 144,000 AND THE TRIUMPH OF THE COUNTLESS
MULTITUDE **7:1–17**

The sixth seal has brought us to the dawn of the last day. We now
await the opening of the seventh seal and a description of the day
itself. Instead John interposes one of several interludes in his book
which hold up the narrative. 'Those who dwell upon the earth'
are in terror of the last day. How will the people of God fare then?
And what happens to them when the calamities initiated by the
opening of the seals fall on earth? John here gives the first of
several answers to these questions. His chief concern at this point
is to show that the followers of the Lamb have no cause to be in
terror of the great day of wrath, any more than they have of the
judgments which precede it. God himself will set his mark on
them, to preserve them for his kingdom (v. 8), and for their encouragement he shows the outcome of this measure—a vision of
the redeemed standing in the presence of God, rejoicing in the
blessings of the new age (vv. 9–17).

So much is clear. But how are we to relate the two groups in
the two visions of chapter 7? It is understandable that many
readers of the Revelation have concluded that the 144,000 'out of
every tribe of the sons of Israel' are either Jews or Jewish Christians, and that the 'multitude which no man could number' con-
sist of Gentile believers. Nevertheless that simple identification
will not do. It would imply that Jews alone receive the seal of

---

[1] In view of the description of the Lamb in 5:6, and his assumption of authority as portrayed in that chapter, the phrase 'the wrath of the Lamb' is not
the paradox it is often represented to be; see the note on 5:6.

God, and that Gentile Christians have to get along without it.
In view of the significance of the seal—the preservation of the
people of God from the dangers of the last times for their participation in the kingdom of God—that idea is hardly feasible. As
Charles pointed out, the sealing must be coextensive with the
peril, and must therefore embrace the entire Christian community.[1]
Moreover in 9:4 it is assumed that the Church as a whole has
been sealed against the assaults of the demonic powers, and
13:16ff. tells of an effort to compel all to receive the mark of the
Beast. John evidently anticipates that a time will come when mankind is divided under two allegiances. Those who have received
the seal of God and those who have received the seal of the
Antichrist. Accordingly we must take it that 'the sons of Israel'
(7:4) represent 'the servants of our God' (7:3) without limitation
of race, in accordance with the meaning of the latter phrase
elsewhere in this book (2:20, 11:18, 19:2, 5, 22:3, 6). They are
the Church viewed as the new Israel, a concept which again
recurs throughout this book from its earliest paragraphs (1:5f.)
to its latest visions (21:10ff.).

If the identity of the two groups is admitted, the special aspect
under which they are viewed is also to be recognized. It is not a
timeless picture of the Church which is here given, but a representation of the Church in the climax of history. The fact that the
multitude in the second vision is said to be innumerable (v. 9)
and their happy condition described in terms which properly
relate to the blessedness of all God's people (vv. 15ff.) has led
many to assume that the Church of all ages is depicted here. This
is not so. So far as John is concerned the Church of his day is the
Church of the last day. He writes in expectation that the four
winds are shortly to blast the earth, and his object in writing is
to assure his fellow believers that neither these destructive winds
nor any other power in heaven or earth or hell can rob them of
their part in the promised kingdom. Admittedly verses 15ff. give
a characteristic anticipation of the felicity of all the people of
God in the time to come. John's inclusion of the vision at this point
serves to inspire his contemporaries with faith and courage. When
that day comes, they will be there. Naturally the like applies to
God's people of all ages.

It is freely to be admitted that the contrast between the repre-

[1] Commentary, p. 200.

sentations of the Church in verses 1–8 and 9–14 is unexpected, not
to say violent. For it is hardly a natural procedure to list with such
precision the members of a defined company of people, consisting
of the component tribes of a single nation, and then go on to
identify them with an innumerable host drawn from every nation
under heaven. And even when we grant the obvious symbolism
in the number 144,000—made up of twelve tribes, each characterized by twelve multiplied by 1,000—it remains that verses
4–8 provide an unusual description of the Church. Indeed, it is
hard to resist the conclusion that in the first instance it was never
meant to apply to the Church. It is much more likely that the
passage was composed as part of a Jewish prophetic oracle, affirming Israel's part in the kingdom of God. The twelve tribes had
long ceased to exist as an entity, and we know that Jews cherished
with great longing those prophecies in the Old Testament which
spoke of the reuniting of the tribes in the coming kingdom (e.g.,
Ezek. 47–8). The passage before us could well have been originally
an emphatic expression of that hope, and John could unhesitatingly have adopted it as a symbol of the Church, since its ideal
comes to perfect realization in the Church. But verses 4b–8 are
more than a mere list of tribes. They provide a list of those
which have been sealed for the kingdom. If verse 4a is an integral
part of verses 4b–8, it is strongly possible that the entire paragraph
verses 1–8 constituted an original unity, a Jewish apocalyptic
prophecy which John adopted and freshly applied since it fitted
his purpose well.[1] This is far more credible an account of chapter 7
than the idea that John deliberately composed the passage verses
1–8 to represent the Church as the new Israel and then followed
it in verses 9–17 by a picture of the Church of all nations victorious
in the kingdom. We shall find other evidences in the later chapters
of this book of John's employment of earlier apocalyptic writings.

THE SEALING OF THE 144,000 7:1–8

1. The vision opens with **four angels standing at the four
corners of the earth, holding back the four winds.** Why do

---

[1] Charles considers that verses 1–3 were derived from a separate source, so
that in verses 1–8 we have two distinct Jewish prophecies taken over by John and
modified to bear a Christian meaning. This is possible. But the connection between the two parts of the paragraph is good enough for it to have been original.

they restrain the winds in this manner? To produce a calm? Only in the sense of a calm before the storm. For destruction by the four winds is almost as common an element in expectations of the end as the earthquake, etc.[1] It is a plausible suggestion that the four winds are viewed by John as an alternative symbol for the four riders of chapter 6, for in Zechariah this is precisely what they represent (6:5). If then the four destructive winds have replaced the four destructive riders, it is unlikely that in verses 1ff. John wishes to convey the impression that a fresh series of plagues is to be launched after the restraint of the angels has been removed. The scene in verses 1-3 is retrospective, and relates to the events described in 6:1-8. In that case the opening words of the paragraph, **After this I saw,** relate to succession in order of John's apprehension, not chronological succession in order of occurrence. The same thing applies to the opening words of verse 9, which also state what John next sees, not what immediately takes place. In reality verses 1ff. take us to a point in time prior to the opening of the seals, whereas verses 9ff. look forward to the age which succeeds the tribulation and the advent of Christ, so anticipating the vision of chapters 21-2.

2, 3. The four angels are addressed by **another angel ... from the rising of the sun.** The direction of his coming is appropriate, for in Jewish thought God's gracious manifestations are especially connected with the east. Paradise was set in the east (Gen. 2:8),[2] the glory of God comes to the temple from the east (Ezek. 43:2), and the Messiah is expected from the east.[3] He comes **with the seal of the living God.** Possibly this is intended to be understood as a signet ring, which a ruler can hand to another for use in his name. The symbolism goes back to Ezekiel's vision of the man with an ink-horn, who is told to go through Jerusalem and put a mark on the foreheads of the righteous, that they be

[1] Jeremiah 49:36 is an early example of this. Its development became possible through apocalyptic speculation, such as appears in 1 *Enoch* 76: there we read of twelve portals through which the winds pass, three in each direction; through four of these portals winds of blessing and prosperity blow, through eight come harmful winds. 'When they are sent they bring destruction on all the earth and on the water upon it, and on all who dwell thereon, and on everything which is in the water and on the land.'

[2] And still is, according to 1 *Enoch* 32:3f.

[3] *Sibylline Oracles* 3:652: 'From the sunrise God shall send a king, who shall give every land relief from the bane of war ...'

spared by the agents of destruction (Ezek. 9:1ff.). So here **the servants of our God** are to have a seal **upon their foreheads,** that they should not be harmed by the destructive winds. The idea is purely pictorial and has no reference to any sacramental action in the Church, e.g., baptism. The action is set strictly in the last time, immediately prior to the impending tribulation.[1] An early parallel to what is in view in our passage is provided by the tradition that at the time of the flood the angels of the waters were commanded to hold the waters in check while Noah was completing the ark (1 *Enoch* 66:1f.). As the angels of the waters had to restrain the waters until Noah had entered the ark, so the angels of the winds have to restrain their destructive powers until the servants of God are made secure.

4-8. The enumeration of the twelve tribes which comprise the 144,000 is unusual on two counts. The first is the placing of Judah at the beginning of the list instead of Reuben, who was the first-born son of Jacob (e.g., Gen. 35:22ff., Num. 13:4ff., Dt. 33:6ff.). This doubtless was due to Judah being the tribe from which the Messiah comes. The second is the omission from the list of the tribe of Dan, whose place is taken by Manasseh, which was actually a section of the tribe of Joseph. This could not be accidental. The rabbis persistently associated Dan with idolatry. Dan's dwelling in Israel was in the north (Num. 2:25), it was held, since darkness comes from the north, and through his idolatry Dan had brought darkness into the world. From 1 Kings 12:28f. it was deduced that Jeroboam went round all the Israelites trying to persuade them to take up his golden calf, but only Dan was willing to do this.[2] In the *Testaments of the Twelve Patriarchs* (*Test. Dan*

---

[1] The interpretation of the seal as referring to baptism became inevitable in view of Paul's teaching on the relation of baptism to the seal of the Spirit; see 2 Corinthians 1:22, Ephesians 1:13, 4:30. In these passages the seal of the Spirit is not baptism, but the Spirit himself, whose gift to the believer is associated with the declaring and confessing of the name of Jesus in baptism. The Spirit seals the believer as God's, with a view to his participating in the coming kingdom. Later writers tended to apply the term 'seal' to baptism itself (e.g., Hermas, *Sim.* 9, xvi. 3f.), though in time the seal was viewed as the laying on of hand, and/or charism, and/or the sign of the cross which took place at baptism. This sign of the cross was especially significant, since the mark inscribed by the man with the ink-horn in Ezekiel 9:4 was the Hebrew letter T (*tau*), which in early times was written in a cruciform shape. That the sign of the cross at baptism was thereby prefigured was an inevitable conclusion.

[2] So *Numbers R.* 2, 137*b*; *Pesiq. R.* 46, 188*ab*; see Strack-Billerbeck, III, p. 805.

5:6) Dan is told, 'Your prince is Satan.' From Irenaeus on, it was maintained among Christians that Dan's name was omitted from the list of tribes because his was the tribe from which the Antichrist should come.[1] It is hardly likely that that tradition was due to Christian speculation. It is in harmony with its Jewish origin that the list before us presumably stems from a Jewish source. We may take it then that the list reflects the view that as Judah was the tribe of Christ, so Dan was the tribe of the Antichrist. We should observe, however, that John himself makes no reference to this tradition, either in this chapter or elsewhere. His own doctrine of the Antichrist would be difficult to harmonize with it.[2]

THE TRIUMPH OF THE COUNTLESS MULTITUDE 7:9–17

9. The 144,000 sons of Israel are replaced in vision by **a great multitude which no man could number, from every nation.** Farrer observes that this contrast of the numbered tribes and the innumerable host gives expression to two antithetical themes of the Scriptures. First, God knows the number of his elect; secondly, those who inherit the blessing of Abraham are numberless as the stars (Gen. 15:5). Whether that contrast was present to John's mind is uncertain, even though it agrees with his theology. Whereas the previous vision originally reflected a particularistic viewpoint, John employed it solely to illustrate God's concern for his people in the last time, and the second vision shows the effectiveness of that concern. But the observation

[1] For details, see Charles, ad loc.

[2] The reason for the order of enumeration of the tribes in our passage has been widely discussed. G. B. Gray (Enc. Bib. IV, col. 5209) pointed out that the order would be much improved if verses 5c–6 be transposed after verse 8. The order then assumes a remarkable appearance. First come the sons of the first wife Leah—Judah, Reuben, Simeon, Levi, Issachar, Zebulun; then the sons of the second wife Rachel—Joseph and Benjamin; then the sons of Leah's handmaid Zilpah—Gad and Asher; and finally the sons of Rachel's handmaid Bilhah, which should be Naphtali and Dan, but Dan has been replaced by Manasseh. If this was original, the present order would be due to a simple mistake in transmission by an early copyist. It has to be recognized that this is no more than a guess, for Gray admitted that more than twenty different ways of reproducing the list of the twelve tribes occur in the Bible, and we cannot insist that the original compiler of this one was concerned to be logical. Nevertheless the guess is a brilliant one, and may well be right.

brings out the point that the promise to Abraham, that his seed should be as countless as the stars in the sky, is fulfilled in the Christian Church. Observe, however: in the Church, not in a group within the Church. It is a puzzling feature to the present writer that the majority of commentators on the Revelation in this century identify the *great multitude* with the martyrs. Of this there is not a hint in the text. We have seen that in the previous vision John affirms that the entire Church of the last days, not a section of it, is sealed for the kingdom. This vision shows the result of that act in the triumph of the entire Church of the last days. Certainly the whole multitude have come out of *the great tribulation* (v. 14). But the whole Church faces the tribulation, and this book is written to inspire the whole Church to endure it with courage and unswerving obedience to Christ. Accordingly, it is the Church as such[1] which is seen **standing before the throne and before the Lamb**, i.e., in the presence of God in his kingdom,[2] **clothed in white robes** that denote victory and holiness

---

[1] It undoubtedly gives cause for thought that the uncountable throng in verses 9ff. represents the Church of one generation only—the last. For the immediate impression conveyed by verses 9ff., followed by the praise of the angelic host in verses 11f., is that the Church in its entirety is in view. Yet verse 14 is explicit on this point: the multitude has emerged from the great tribulation of the last days. Charles accounted for this by suggesting that John has employed an earlier vision of his own, which originally had no limitation of time or number, but portrayed the redeemed people of God in the kingdom. The vision has been adapted so as to apply to the triumph of the Church of the last generation. There is no *a priori* reason why this should not have been so. If John adapted an earlier vision of a Jewish apocalyptist in verses 1–8, there is no reason why he should not do the like with a vision of his own. I am, however, tempted to consider that in verses 9ff. John has described the whole Church, but that he especially has the Church of his own generation in view. After all, very many of the second generation Church were still alive at the time of writing. The old men of that time were all alive when Jesus ministered in Palestine. (Cf. the significant words in the opening sentence of Hebrews: 'In these last days (God) has spoken to us by a Son.' The second-generation Church still lived in the days of Jesus.) It was not difficult to think of the Church in terms of the present generation, and in John's view the present was the last. Accordingly, the reference to the generation of the tribulation in verse 14 is comprehensible, if they were especially rather than exclusively in mind.

[2] Possibly as his appointed servant (cf. v. 15); 'to stand before' often = to attend upon, to be the servant of; cf. 1 Kings 17:1 with 2 Kings 3:14, Luke 1:19.

and glory, **with palm branches in their hands** that signify the joy of victory.[1]

10. The cry of the redeemed is significant. Faithful and self-sacrificing they may have been, some to the limit of life as they defied the Antichrist in the great distress. But **Salvation belongs to our God ... and to the Lamb!** The deliverance they have experienced is from the enemies of God and man, from weakness of the flesh and from sin and death, and it is for the blessedness of the kingdom of glory. Only God and the Lamb can achieve that. The cry is paralleled by the shout which is uttered after the ejection of Satan from heaven, consequent on the victory of the Lamb in his death and resurrection (12:10), and again by that which follows the overthrow of the antigod city Babylon (19:1). In both cases *salvation* is filled out with such expressions as 'the power and the kingdom of our God and the authority of his Christ' (12:10), and 'glory and power' (19:1). The salvation of God and the Lamb has been made possible by the death and resurrection of Christ, his exaltation to power and his coming again in the victory of his kingdom, and therefore it includes participation in the sovereignty which those events signify for Christ.

11, 12. The numberless host of *angels* (cf. 5:11) join in the adoration offered by the countless host of the redeemed, and their first word is one of confirmation of the agreement with the song of triumph: **Amen!** They give to God the sevenfold ascription of praise which earlier they had offered to the Lamb at his enthronement (5:12, see note). To reinforce it they add yet another **Amen!**

13, 14. The dialogue between John and the elder serves to emphasize the sheer miracle of the deliverance which has been celebrated by the saints in heaven and the angels. The victors are the kind of people John knows and serves, humble men and women whom the powers of this world despise, and against whom they will shortly turn their might. **These are they who have come out of the great tribulation.** The definite article employed with

---

[1] Cf. the description of Simon's entry into Jerusalem, in response to the plea of its citizens: 'He entered into it on the 23rd day of the 2nd month, in the 171st year, with praise and palm branches and with harps and cymbals and with viols and with hymns and with songs, because a great enemy had been destroyed out of Israel.' John 12:13 reflects a similar complex of ideas.

tribulation is significant. It refers not to the trials to which Christians are always subject (Jn 16:33), but the tribulation which forms the climax of history prior to the revelation of the kingdom (cf. Dan. 12:1, Mk 13:19), and to which reference was earlier made in 3:10. Strictly speaking the main verb is in the present tense: they 'come' out of the tribulations. Some expositors, therefore, have interpreted this of martyrdoms, present and to come in the future. The *RSV* and *NEB* are almost certainly right, however, in viewing the verb as having a past reference, just as the next verb has **(they have washed . . .)**; for the vision is written from the standpoint of the future, after the conclusion of the tribulation, in the happy estate of the kingdom.

The victors have overcome because **they have washed their robes and made them white in the blood of the Lamb.** The emphasis is the same as in the doxology of verse 10: the victors are in the kingdom in virtue of the sacrifice of the Lamb. The imagery of washing robes white in the blood of the Lamb is strange to our thought, and highly paradoxical (*white* in the *blood* . . .), but it was not so to one who, as John, was conditioned in thought and in speech by the Old Testament. The symbolism of dirty clothes for an unclean life is frequent in the Old Testament (e.g., Isa. 64:6, Zech. 3:3) as also the corresponding idea of clean clothes for a pure life (Zech. 3:4), and even of washing one's clothes when approaching God (cf. Exod. 19:10ff.). The idea of washing in blood already occurs in the song of Genesis 49 (it is said of Judah, 'he washes his garments in wine and his vesture in the blood of grapes'). A prophet had spoken of God's forgiveness making sins that are as red as crimson to become white as wool (Isa. 1:18). Remembering that the phrase *the blood of the Lamb* is a shorthand expression for the death of Christ viewed as a sacrifice for sins, it is easy to see how the imagery of verse 14 can express the effectiveness of Christ's redemption in the lives of his people. Before God they are conscious of being arrayed in filthy clothes. But the Lamb has died and risen for their forgiveness, they have become renewed in character, and have maintained faith in him, not soiling their garments even when severely tempted (3:4), for the Lamb who forgives is the Lamb who enables his followers to share his victory (12:11). The white robes of Christ's innocence also includes the glow of his glory (cf. Mk 9:3); for the crucified and risen Lord has returned for their vindication.

15. The lyrical description of the happy condition of the victorious Church is full of echoes of prophetic anticipations of the salvation which God will bring about. It indicates that the victors have now attained to the fulfilment of the ancient hopes and promises cherished by the people of God through the ages. To be **before the throne of God** implies the possession of direct access to God himself, and so to dwell with him. His people **serve him day and night.** Therefore they share with the most exalted of angelic beings, the cherubim and the elders, the privilege of attendance upon him and of offering him their worship (see 4:8ff.). It is noteworthy that existence in the consummated kingdom is here said to include the service of God **within his temple**; for 21:22 states that there will be no temple in the perfected kingdom. It is a doubtful expedient to resolve the difficulty by relating verse 15 to the condition of the Church before the new age, in distinction from the new order in which they will serve God apart from a temple. The whole idea of verses 9ff. is its glimpse of the Church vindicated and victorious in the kingdom of God (as the parallels with the description of life in the new Jerusalem, 21:9ff., show). John probably desired simply to embody the idea that the vocation of God's people to be a kingdom of priests now reaches fulfilment (cf. 1:6). In the perfected existence of the new age they serve the Lord as the priests on earth and the angels in heaven. In that time God **will shelter them with his presence.** The phrase *shelter* . . . is a paraphrase for a verb associated with God's glory (the *Shekinah*) resting upon his people as a sign of his presence. It recalled for the Jews the overshadowing of God's people with the glory visibly expressed in the pillar of cloud and fire in the desert wanderings (Exod. 13:21f.), the glory which filled the tabernacle at its dedication (Exod. 40:34ff.) and the temple in like manner (1 Kg. 8:10), and the promise of its manifestation again as the sign of God's presence with his people in the future kingdom (Isa. 4:5f.). This presence of God in manifest glory among men was held by the Fourth Evangelist to be the distinguishing feature of the incarnate life of Christ on earth (Jn 1:14). John the prophet looks for it to be the characteristic experience of his people when the kingdom comes in its fullness (cf. 21:3).

16, 17. The beautiful picture of the return of the exiles to their homeland in the time of redemption (Isa. 49:10) now finds its

complete fulfilment, when all **hunger** and **thirst** which plague
the human heart are satisfied and met, and the tormenting conditions known on earth come to their end. There is one feature in
this picture, however, which neither the prophet of the exile nor
any other prophet of the Old Covenant could have included:
the Lamb in the midst of the throne will be their shepherd.
The figure is not so incongruous as may appear to western towns-
men. Even tourists in Europe have seen a herd of cattle, led by a
cow with a large bell round its neck to their place of rest and feed-
ing. So Palestinians were familiar with the picture of a sheep that
went ahead as leader of the flock. The Lamb who delivers the
flock by his sacrificial dying and his rising to sovereignty (5:6ff.)
goes ahead of God's flock. He fulfils the prophetic promise of
God's appearing as shepherd of his sheep, caring for those who are
lost, wounded and hungry (Ezek. 34:11ff.). He is indeed the good
shepherd, calling his sheep by name and leading them out, giving
them life to the full (Jn 10:3ff., 10ff.). The **springs of living
water** to which he guides, as sung by the shepherd psalmist
(Ps. 23:2f.), in the fuller vision turn out to be a river of water of
life (Rev. 22:1f.)—more than enough for the needs of all. So
shall grief be swallowed up in the eternal gladness of the new creation, **and God will wipe away every tear from their eyes,**
for the former things have passed away for ever (21:4).

THE SEVENTH SEAL **8:1-5**

1-5. In view of the consequences of the opening of the sixth
seal (6:12ff.) it is reasonable to expect that the seventh seal will
lead to 'the great day of wrath' (6:17) and the appearance of the
kingdom of Christ. But the immediate consequence of the seventh
seal is a prolonged **silence in heaven.** What is the significance
of this silence? Some consider it no more than a dramatic pause:
heaven waits in breathless expectancy for the judgment to fall
and the kingdom to come. Swete can offer no better suggestion
than to regard it as 'a temporary suspense of revelation'. M. Rissi
has persuasively argued that it represents a return to the total
stillness which existed at creation, the expectation of which is
attested in various apocalyptic writings, notably 2 Esdras 7:29ff.
In this book it is said that when the messianic kingdom comes to its
end, 'the world shall be turned back to primeval silence for seven

days, as it was at the first beginnings, so that no one shall be
left. And after seven days the world, which is not yet awake, shall
be roused, and that which is corruptible shall perish.' The **half
an hour,** for which the silence lasts, is then explained as the
first dark half of God's great eschatological hour, to be followed
by the other half, the bright new creation.[1] It is an attractive
interpretation, and it fits the view that the seventh seal introduces
the end. But had this really been John's purpose one would have
thought that he would have given a clearer indication of the
significance of the silence, since there is no suggestion in the context
that a relapse of the world into primeval silence had taken place.
This idea would be more in place at the end of chapter 20, after
the end of the messianic kingdom and so at the conclusion of
earth's story, when the new creation is about to be revealed. But
in that case the whole creation is involved in the silence, not
heaven alone.

In reality the context does supply a reason for the silence in
heaven. The rest of the paragraph after verse 2 is dominated by
the theme of prayer and its relation to God's kingdom. We are
indebted to the erudition of Charles for drawing our attention to
the parallel to John's symbolism in the Talmudic tractate *Hagigah*
(12b). There we read that Resh Lakish distinguished seven heavens
and their functions. The fifth, *Maon* (= dwelling) 'is that in which
there are companies of ministering angels, who utter (divine)
song by night, and are silent by day for the sake of Israel's glory,
for it is said, By day the Lord doth command his lovingkindness,
and in the night his song is with me.' Here the idea is that God
silences the angels by day, that he may hear the prayers of Israel
and so show them his loving kindness. Its application to John's
portrayal of heaven is striking, for he tells of the continuous
worship of God by the highest angelic beings (ch. 4), and describes
the tumultuous worship accorded to God and the Lamb for their
redemption (ch. 5). Here all heaven is silenced, and the prayers
of all the saints are to be presented by an angel to God. That the
silence is for the solemn hearing of the prayers is thoroughly
plausible. The mingling of **incense** with the **prayers** is either
a symbolic representation of the prayers themselves, offered to
God by the angel (cf. 5:8, where the incense = the prayers of
the saints), or it is regarded as a sacrificial accompaniment of the

[1] *Time and History*, Richmond, Virginia, 1966, pp. 4–6.

prayers, that they may be acceptable to God in virtue of the sacrifice of Christ. The motif of the incense is important to the context, for after the rising of its smoke before God, **the angel took the censer and filled it with fire from the altar and threw it on the earth.** It is difficult to resist the conclusion that this portrays an action expressive of judgment in response to the prayers of the saints (cf. 6:10). The falling of fire on the earth from the altar is followed by the accompaniments of the end, such as John describes after the sounding of the seventh trumpet (11:19) and the outpouring of the seventh bowl (16:18ff.). The prayers of the saints are answered in a final manifestation of judgment and by the coming of the kingdom.

The significance of this picture can hardly be overestimated. No one was more aware than John of the limitations to what individual men and women can do to change the course of history and to bring in the kingdom of heaven, particularly in face of the cosmic forces against them and the transcendent character of the kingdom itself (none of us can raise the dead). But we can pray to him who has almighty power, and it would seem that God has willed that the prayers of his people should be part of the process by which the kingdom comes. The interaction between the sovereignty of God and the prayers of the saints is part of the ultimate mystery of existence. Faith is called on to take both seriously.[1]

If the seventh seal brings the kingdom in response to the prayers of the saints, what is the significance of the **seven angels** with the **seven trumpets** appearing at this point? The juxtaposition of their appearance with the opening of the seventh seal has led many to believe that the series of events initiated by the sounding of the seven trumpets in 8:6–11:19 denote the contents of the message made known by the removal of this seal. That, however,

[1] On this Schlatter has given a typical utterance in his comment on this passage: 'In depicting to us the power of our prayer John has imprinted on our minds, with the same seriousness as he has with regard to the relation between God and the Lamb, the supremacy of God; and in representing prayer as incense kindled by the angel he tells us two things: first that prayer does not take place in vain, and die away unheard, but reaches God and moves the powers of heaven; and secondly that it is not the request of the Church which impels God to righteousness and gives him his grace, but God's will is in his own hands, and he accomplishes his work as he has written it in his book' (*Erläuterungen zum N.T., Briefe und Offenbarung d. Johannes*, p. 211).

is irreconcilable with the significance of the rest of the paragraph, and indeed with our understanding of the structure of the Revelation as a whole. The seventh seal, as we have seen, leads to silence for the hearing of the prayers of the saints, and to the divine answer in judgment and the gift of the kingdom. The statement concerning the seven angels, therefore, should be viewed as a parenthesis, preparing the way for the next description of the messianic judgments, since it interrupts the sequence of events described by John, and finds its true connection with verse 6, to which it forms an introduction.[1]

THE JUDGMENTS OF THE SEVEN TRUMPETS
8:6–11:19

A fresh presentation of the judgments which precede the kingdom of Christ is now given, employing a different imagery from that which has gone before. The symbolism of breaking seven seals which enclose the divine disposition of the kingdom to man is a highly original concept, and is bound up with John's recognition of Christ as the mediator of redemption. The symbolism of trumpets heralding the end of the age, on the contrary, is traditional, with roots deep in the history of Israel, and powerfully evocative of a variety of associated concepts.

Trumpets are especially associated with war, declaring a state of emergency and summoning men to battle (e.g., Jg. 3:27ff., 7:8ff., Neh. 4:18). It was natural for the prophets to use the symbolism of sounding the trumpet when warning men of the approach of divine judgment. Ezekiel's picture of the watchman is a perfect illustration of this. As the watchman is set to blow the trumpet when he sees the enemy at hand, so Ezekiel is appointed

---

[1] Charles has no hesitation in removing verse 2 after verse 5, considering that it has been misplaced by the editor of the book. Without doubt the paragraph reads better if the verse is so transposed, but one has to admit to perplexity to find a reason for an editor's removing back a statement, introductory to the following section, to so unsuitable a position as that between verses 1 and 3. It is not impossible that John himself was responsible for the present order, being dominated in his thinking by the sequence 'seventh seal, silence in heaven, trumpet series', and that having so written he then proceeded to explain the significance of the silence and rounded off properly the seventh seal episode.

to warn the people of the coming judgment of God. They who ignore his call are as truly responsible for their doom as they who ignore the sound of the trumpet (Ezek. 33:1ff.). Zephaniah's lengthy description of the day of the Lord culminates in likening it to the onset of battle. It is 'a day of trumpet blast and battle cry against the fortified cities and against the lofty battlements' (Zeph. 1:15). Joel similarly warns of the approach of the day of the Lord in the locust plague: 'Blow the trumpet in Zion; sound the alarm on my holy mountain! Let all the inhabitants of the land tremble, for the day of the Lord is coming' (Jl 2:1).

If the day of the Lord brings judgment for the wicked, it also brings the kingdom of God for the righteous. Accordingly the trumpet which sounds the alarm for some heralds a day of gladness for others. It is probably true to say that for many Israelites trumpets were associated with joy rather than with terror, by reason of their use in the worship of Israel. Numbers 10:10 is instructive in this respect: 'On the day of your gladness also, and at your appointed feasts, and at the beginning of your months, you shall blow the trumpets over your burnt offerings and over the sacrifices of your peace offerings; they shall serve you for remembrance before your God'; i.e., they will call Israel to God's mind and so bring his blessing upon them. The first day of the seventh month is of particular interest in this connection, for in rabbinic times it marked both the beginning of the season of repentance, with its climax in the Day of Atonement, and the beginning of the new year. *Tishri* 1, proclaimed with trumpets as a day of holy convocation (Lev. 23:24), was in fact viewed as an anticipation of the Day of Judgment.[1] This linking of judgment, new beginning and call for repentance is frequently found in prophetic proclamations of the last day that conjoin it with the trumpet sound. In a beautiful and moving passage Joel 2:12ff. exploits this association, with a plea to return to the Lord with all the heart that he may turn to his people in mercy instead of judgment. Here too the trumpet call is mentioned: 'Blow the trumpet in Zion; sanctify a fast; call a solemn assembly ... Let the priests, the ministers of the Lord, weep and say, "Spare thy people, O Lord".' And the

[1] Caird, ad loc., who cites the saying in the Mishnah that God judges the world at Passover in respect of produce, at Pentecost in respect of fruit, and at Tabernacles in respect of rain, but *Tishri* 1 is the day when he judges mankind (*Rosh H.* 16a).

prophet goes on to speak of the day of the Lord in terms of deliverance and blessing for his people.

Accordingly, there are contexts in which the trumpet which sounds in the last day is explicitly thought of as proclaiming salvation in the new age about to begin. In particular it heralds the deliverance of Israel, and calls the exiles to return from the lands of their banishment to enjoy the peace and consolation and glory of the kingdom (e.g., Zech. 9:14ff., *Ps. Sol.* 11:1). This aspect of the day of the Lord as a gathering of God's scattered people for salvation leads to the idea of the trumpet as a summons to resurrection, since it calls the living from afar and the dead from the land of shadows for life in the kingdom of light—see Matthew 24:31, 1 Thessalonians 4:16, 1 Corinthians 15:52.

Judgment, repentance, deliverance, salvation, new age heralded by the trumpet sound, call to mind the use of the trumpet in ancient Israel to proclaim the accession of a king to the throne (e.g., 1 Kg. 1:39). This feature was taken up in the coronation psalms to celebrate the kingship of God (e.g., Ps. 47:5; 98:6). So in the last day the trumpet proclaims to the universe the commencement of the new era in which the Lord is king in undisputed sway.

To all these varied associations must be added the recollection of the theophany which had deepest significance to Jewish thought, namely, the manifestation of the Lord in the fearful splendour of Sinai at the giving of the Law, when the trumpet-blast proclaimed his presence and summoned the people to the mountain (Exod. 19:11ff.). The record of the revelation of the Lord in that day naturally gave rise to the conviction that the revelation of the Lord in the last day would be attended by similar phenomena. This association of the trumpet with Sinai and the last day is peculiarly fitting for the trumpet-series of John's vision, since they herald the approach of a new exodus by plagues which are reminiscent of those which attended the first.

Indeed, the pertinence of all the foregoing to the trumpet-series in Revelation 8:6–11:19 is clear. The trumpets herald judgments, that is obvious. More clearly than in the seal-judgments it is stated that they are directed against 'the destroyers of the earth' (11:18). The first four trumpets affect primarily the elements (land, sea, rivers, sky) but with devastating effects on men also. The last three are directed against 'those who dwell on the earth' i.e., the rebellious of mankind (cf. 9:4). Here is expressed the belief that those who reject the Creator and seek to ruin his work are themselves destroyed in judgment. Kiddle believes that in this respect this section of the Revelation is John's equivalent to Paul's indictment of the world in Romans 1:18–32. On the other hand the trumpet-series, in contrast to the seal-series, explictly balances the judgments with the salvation of the new age. The seventh trumpet leads to a scene closely akin to that of chapter 5 and which virtually signifies the coronation of God and the Lamb. The trumpets, therefore, end in joy.

In both respects the exodus typology is fitting, i.e., with regard both to the judgments and to the deliverance which follows them. The parallel to the exodus narrative in the Old Testament is not accidental but conscious and deliberate, and in the case of the first four trumpet-judgments it is spelled out in detail. For example, the account of the effects of the first trumpet-blast is modelled on the description of the Egyptian plague of thunder, hail, and fire, which brought destruction on man and beast, and on 'every plant of the field . . . every tree of the field' (Exod. 9:23ff.). The second and third trumpets extend and divide the account in Exodus 7:20ff. of the turning of the Nile waters into blood, so making them undrinkable. John distinguishes between a judgment which affects the sea and another which affects the rivers, in part because he has in view the world itself and not simply one country, and in part because he wishes to make up the number of the initial plagues to four, to match the first four seal-judgments introduced by the four riders. The fourth trumpet parallels the Egyptian plague of darkness (Exod. 10:21ff.). In each case the plagues which have served as models for John are reproduced on a vaster scale, for they are universalized in scope and given a cosmic setting. This corresponds with the change of situation, in that an Egyptian ruler oppressing the Jews has been replaced by a world emperor who persecutes the Church throughout the world, and the conflict is seen as one between the powers of hell and the Lord of heaven. As in the original Old Testament narrative the plagues were succeeded by a notable deliverance from the tyrant who defied God and his people, and subsequently by the entry into the promised land, so the sounding of the seventh trumpet is succeeded by the deliverance into the kingdom of God. But the development of the exodus typology to describe the salvation itself is reserved to a later part of the Revelation (see especially 15:2ff.).

The motif of repentance is not explicitly stated, but it is present in the trumpet-judgments in a manner not true of the others. It is likely that the emphasis in the first four trumpet-judgments on the limitation of their effects—to a third of the earth, a third of the sea, a third of the rivers, a third of the sun, moon and stars— reflects a conviction that God restrains the extent of these judgments to give men opportunity to turn from their evil ways and so end the necessity for further judgments to fall. This is more than hinted at after the description of the sixth-trumpet plague. The rest of mankind who survived the plagues 'did not repent on the works of their hands, nor give up worshipping demons and idols of gold . . . nor did they repent of their murders or their sorceries or their immorality or their thefts' (9:20f.). The very mention of the failure of such men to turn from their evil and to seek the living God indicates John's belief that these judgments ought to have led men to repentance. He would have concurred with Paul, that if the kindness of God is meant to lead men to repentance, so is his judgment; and the maintenance of a 'hard and impenitent heart', alike in face of the kindness of God and his resistance to evil, means that men are 'storing up wrath . . . on the day of wrath when God's righteous judgment will be revealed' (see Rom. 2:4f.). Despite such hardness, the apostle continued to preach his gospel, and John to write his warnings, that men may yet avert the limit of God's righteous judgment.

THE FIRST FOUR TRUMPET-CALLS 8:6–13

6. It is to be observed that **the seven angels who had the seven trumpets** were *seven* in number not merely to suit seven trumpets, nor because John was enamoured by the number seven, but by reason of the tradition of the seven archangels, of whom Michael was one (cf. v. 2, which refers to them as 'the seven angels who stand before God', i.e., who wait instantly on his bidding, in distinction from those who perform more lowly tasks in the world and in nature). Characteristically, the author of 1 *Enoch* 20 is able to inform us of the names of those seven and the duties assigned to each of them.

7. The trumpet blast of the first angel corresponds to the seventh

Egyptian plague (Exod. 9:23ff.). There we read of **hail and fire**
(= lightning) which causes destruction to man and beast, and to
trees and plants. But there is no mention of **blood** mingled with
hail and fire. Does this, like the hail and fire, relate to a known
natural phenomenon? Swete points out that blood-red rain is
not unknown, and he recalls accounts of it falling in Italy and
south Europe in 1901 due to the air being full of particles of fine
red sand from the Sahara. Such could have been in John's mind,
but it is the sort of thing which kindles the imagination to formu-
late apocalyptic portents. Possibly Joel 2:30 is influential here, as
it certainly is in the *Sibylline Oracles* (v. 377ff.): 'Fire shall rain
on mortal men from the fields of heaven, fire and blood, water,
meteor, darkness, heaven's night. . . .'

There is no need to be perturbed that whereas **a third of the
earth was burnt up,** and **a third of the trees, all** (not a third)
green grass was burnt up, yet in 9:4 the locusts are told not to
harm the grass of the earth. It is the intent of the prophecies, not
their detail that is important. Total scorching of grass is regular
enough in hot climates, and this occasion is specially hot. That
a third of earth, not the whole, was burned is important to John,
for these judgments are tempered to give opportunity for repentance. A different point is being made in 9:4; not vegetation but
man is the target of the locusts. There are more glaring oppositions
in John's imagery than this one, and he doubtless was not disturbed
by any of them.

8, 9. The blast of the second trumpeter led to **a third of the
sea** becoming **blood,** so that **a third of the living creatures
in the sea died** and **a third of the ships were destroyed.**
The first Egyptian plague is in view (Exod. 7:20ff.), for when
the waters of the Nile were turned to blood the fish in the river
died 'and there was blood throughout the land of Egypt'. Unlike
the Nile plague, however, this was caused by **something like a
great mountain, burning with fire** being **thrown into the
sea.** It is unlikely that we are meant to recall Jeremiah 51:25 at
this point. The burning mass is characteristic of apocalyptic
imagery. It has a close parallel in the *Sibylline Oracles* (v. 158ff.):
'Then shall come a great star from heaven into the divine sea, and
shall burn up the deep sea and Babylon itself, and the land of
Italy on whose account many faithful saints of the Hebrews
have perished, and the true people.' Here also the mountain in

the sea affects especially the wicked who persecute the righteous.

10, 11. The third trumpet-judgment continues the reminiscence of the first Egyptian plague, for a blazing **star** falls on **a third of the rivers and on the fountains of water.** As the Nile 'became foul, so that the Egyptians could not drink water from the Nile', so the waters are here **made bitter.** But John has in view other Old Testament motifs. The waters smitten by the star **Wormwood** (so called because of its effects on the water) tasted as bitter as wormwood. We recall that twice in the prophecies of Jeremiah the word of the Lord is recorded: 'I will feed this people with wormwood, and give them poisonous water to drink' (i.e., on account of their sins, see Jer. 9:15, 23:15, in context). Wormwood is not in fact a poisonous plant, but its bitterness was proverbial, and in the vision the effect of the star Wormwood upon the fresh waters was similar to that of the mountain in the sea: **many men died of the water.** Observe: *many men*, not a third of men. Contrary to Charles' contention, it is unlikely that John originally wrote 'one third', and that this was replaced by the term many, for it is not until the fifth and sixth trumpet-judgments that mankind as a whole is seriously affected (see 9:18—one third of mankind is then killed).

12. The fourth trumpet-judgment recalls the Egyptian plague of darkness (Exod. 10:21ff.). But John gives it some characteristic modifications, partly in accordance with apocalyptic style and partly to keep to the principle that in the will of God these plagues have a limited effect on the world. In contrast to the total darkness of Egypt, the effect of this plague is that **a third of the day was kept from shining, and likewise a third of the night.** Admittedly an unusual twist is given to the astronomical data to achieve this end, for one would imagine that the striking of a third of the sun, moon, and stars would result in their light being reduced in intensity by that amount, rather than a reduction of the length of their shining. But as in other respects, the astronomy is less important than the thing signified. John wishes to affirm that men experience darkness in the day and intensified darkness in the night by reason of their sins. But the Lord is merciful in sparing them light both by day and by night—that they may forsake their moral darkness for life in the unending light of his presence.

13. Following on the fourth trumpet **an eagle** is seen by John flying **in midheaven,** i.e., the zenith of the sun, so that the entire world may hear his cry: **Woe, woe, woe to those who dwell on the earth!** The threefold woe corresponds to the three trumpets yet to sound. Their effects upon the unbelieving world will be far more drastic than those that have preceded, since they are directed no longer to the elements, as in the first four trumpet-judgments, but against rebellious mankind.

The phenomenon of an eagle sounding out a warning to the world is unparalleled in Jewish apocalyptic writings. Lohmeyer has been able to unearth from the Mandaean *Book of John* some mournful utterances of an eagle which visited the 'world of darkness', but these are hardly to the point (besides being very late). In 2 *Baruch* a final long address is written out by the prophet and tied round the neck of an eagle, which is solemnly addressed and told to take it to the nine and a half tribes. The eagle, however, only delivers the message, he does not preach it. In this book of lively imagery we should not be surprised at any symbol used by John—certainly not when we have read chapter 9. Nevertheless, it is worth pondering Caird's suggestion that in this passage *eagle* may = *vulture*, as in the enigmatic saying, recalled by some expositors at this point, Luke 17:37. In that case the messenger which cries out the threefold woe is a bird of prey, and an Old Testament passage of extraordinary pertinence is called to mind: 'Set the trumpet to your lips, for a vulture is over the house of the Lord' (Hos. 8:1). In John admittedly the vulture warns about the trumpeters instead of the other way round. That makes the future even more ominous: the vulture will not go hungry.

THE FIFTH AND SIXTH TRUMPET CALLS 9:1-21

The exodus-typology appears to be in mind as the trumpets continue to summon the judgments of the Lord, but the adherence to this typology is less apparent than in the first group of four trumpets. The fifth-trumpet episode clearly offers a parallel to the Egyptian plague of locusts (Exod. 10:1-20), but its elaboration owes more to Joel's description of a locust-judgment which heralds the day of the Lord than it does to Exodus 10. The judgment following the sixth trumpet is conceivably intended to correspond with the slaying of the first-born in Egypt, for as the latter forms the climax of the Egyptian plagues, so does the event to which the sixth trumpet leads. In contrast to the locust-army which inflicts pain only, the demonic horsemen cause widespread death, but there is no noticeable dependence on the exodus-narrative in John's account. The imagery used by John in these two episodes reaches the height of fantasy, above all in the second one. Nevertheless it is, so to speak, controlled fantasy, for John does not give his imagination free reign but employs well known images in his pictures. Neither the locusts nor the horses have any reality in the phenomenal world, but locust-swarms and Parthian cavalry were very real and greatly feared by many of John's contemporaries. These two kinds of visitation, the one natural and the other historical, provide the basis for John's highly imaginative descriptions of divine judgments. The nature of these judgments will perhaps become clearer after the details of the chapter have been considered.

THE FIFTH TRUMPET-CALL 9:1-12

1-4. The **star fallen from heaven to earth** is evidently an angel. That he 'falls' may represent no more than that he descends from heaven to earth. If, however, an evil angel is in mind (as the fallen stars of 1 *Enoch* 86:1ff., 88:1) he yet remains an instrument of the divine will, for **he was given the key** which opens the abyss; i.e., he received it by divine authority. The term **bottomless pit,** or abyss, originally denoted the chaos of waters which covered the earth, and which were confined not only by the shores but below the earth (cf. Ps. 33:7). In the creation-myth the chaos waters are personified by Tiamat, the dragon-like monster and enemy of God, and this link in thought between the 'deep' and evil persisted in many forms (e.g., the dragon continues to remain in the deep, Isa. 27:1, Am. 9:3). It was, therefore, natural in the development of ideas about the spiritual world for the term to denote the place where demons and fallen angels are kept (in 1 *Enoch* chs. 18-21 it is described as 'a place which had no firmament of the heaven above, and no firmly founded earth beneath ... the end of heaven and earth ... a place chaotic and horrible'; in one section of the abyss 'a great fire burned and blazed ... being full of great descending columns of fire'). Accordingly, when the shaft of the pit was unlocked there came

smoke like the smoke of a great furnace. The reference to the darkening of the sun and air in verse 2 harks back to Joel 2:10, but there the darkness is due to the cloud of locusts, whereas in this passage the cloud is made by the smoke from the abyss. It is out of that smoke that there came **locusts on the earth.** Their demonic character is immediately suggested by their origin, as also their task. For ordinary locusts eat vegetation but do no harm to men. These ignore vegetation and attack men. For this reason **they were given power like the power of scorpions of the earth.** Their object was to harm **those of mankind who have not the seal of God upon their foreheads.** We later learn not only that such men are devoted to idolatry and reject the fundamental bases of morality (vv. 20f.), but that they bear on hand or forehead a different mark, namely, the name or number of the beast (13:16). Ironically it is creatures from the abyss, the abode of evil, which attack the followers of the Antichrist.

5. The 'locusts' **torture** their victims (an appropriate verb for the intense pain caused by scorpions) **for five months.** The duration of the plague is worthy of note. The life of a locust is about five months, and therefore the season during which swarms of locusts cause devastation is about the same length of time (from early spring to the end of summer). But naturally swarms normally move on from place to place. Lohmeyer's observation therefore is to the point, viz., that five months is a traditional round number to denote a long period of time (cf. Gen. 7:24, and consider the use of the number in Mt. 25:15, Lk. 14:19, 16:26, 1 C. 14:19). Its occurrence here carries the suggestion that this is an abnormally long time for a locust-plague. As Rissi observed, 'While natural swarms of locusts last only a few days, these demonic swarms bring their torments throughout the whole "time of locusts".'[1]

6. In such circumstances of relentless torment **men will seek death and will not find it,** for these 'locusts' inflict only agony, not death. This preference of men to die rather than to endure the burden of living has many echoes in pagan literature. Alford, however, observes a parallel which has at the same time the strongest contrast, viz., Philippians 1:23, where death is welcomed in prospect, not as an escape but for the riches of fellowship with Christ which it brings, but where life is embraced for the opportunities of service it provides. To faith both life and death are full.

[1] Rissi, op. cit., p. 26.

7-12. The description of the locusts reads like a verbal picture, besides which Picasso pales. In reality it follows Joel's example (in Jl 1:6, 2:4f.) and heightens features of the ordinary locust on which comment has often been made by people of the east. Two centuries ago (1772) Carsten Niebuhr reported that an Arab from the desert, in the neighbourhood of Basra, spoke to him about the locust: 'He compared the head of a locust with the head of a horse, its breast with the breast of a lion, its feet with the feet of a camel, its body with the body of a snake, its tail with the tail of a scorpion, its antennae with the hair of a maiden.' On which Niebuhr commented, 'In short this comparison seems to explain Revelation 9:7ff.'[1] John's description, therefore, takes popular similitudes relating to locusts and adds to them Joel's point that in flight they were 'like a powerful army drawn up for battle' (Jl 2:5). In naming their leader, however, John differs from his sources. Proverbs 30:27 states that locusts have no king. John declares that these **have as king over them ... Abaddon,** whose name in Greek is **Apollyon.** The former name represents a personification of a Hebrew word meaning 'destruction'. Its use in the Old Testament is confined to the Wisdom Literature, where it is a synonym for Sheol, the realm of the departed (see especially Job 26:6 where the two terms are in parallelism, and Job 28:22, where Abaddon and Death are personified together). For John, therefore, Abaddon will mean precisely what Hades means in 1:18, 6:8. Apollyon is not an exact rendering of Abaddon, as John perfectly well knew (the usual term is *apoleia*, which John himself uses in 17:8, where it is translated 'perdition'). Apollyon comes close to the verb *apollumi*, to destroy, and it may well be intended to reproduce the name Apollo, which some Greek writers (e.g., Aeschylus, *Agam.* 1082) derived from *apollumi*. Not only did the cult of Apollo use the symbol of the locust (along with the mouse and lizard), but more importantly both Caligula and Nero aped the deity of Apollo, and Domitian gave himself out to be an incarnation of Apollo. If John had this in view, his last word about the fifth trumpet was a master stroke of

[1] See Lohmeyer, appendix 6, p. 205, who also reproduces an Arabic poem from the Middle Ages which reproduces similar comparisons: 'They (the locusts) have the two haunches of a young camel and the two legs of an ostrich, the two wings of an eagle and the breast of a lion, the belly of a viper and the head and mouth of a horse.'

irony: the destructive host of hell had as its king the emperor of Rome!

THE SIXTH TRUMPET-CALL 9:13-21

The first woe is passed, and the second one now comes (v. 12). Its severity is such that both the first woe and the first four trumpets may be viewed as its prelude. Yet despite its fearful nature, the theme of restraint in judgment that men may come to repentance, which is apparent in the previous trumpet scenes, recurs here also. Behm speaks of this episode as 'a last, but admittedly vain appeal for repentance to mankind sunk in heathenism' (cf. vv. 20f.).

13. Immediately after the sounding of the sixth trumpet **a voice** is heard **from the four horns of the golden altar before God,** and this voice is responsible for unleashing the woe which follows. *The golden altar* in heaven corresponds to that which stood in the tabernacle and the temple in the holy place (Exod. 27:2). We have already learned of prayers being offered at the altar, first by the martyrs (6:9f.) and then by the Church as a whole (8:3ff.), and we have seen that such prayers have the powerful effect of bringing on the judgments of God which lead to the revelation of the kingdom (see notes on these passages). It would appear that the same thought is in mind here. The voice from the altar will not be that of an individual believer but the voice of God (cf. 19:5), or possibly of an angel, in response to the prayers offered on the altar. If we may take it that the prayers are for the deliverance of the Church and the coming of the kingdom, the immediate answer may appear to be a strange one, but it is in harmony with the entire character of this book, which affirms that the kingdom comes with judgment. In reality the joy is not long in following (11:15ff.).

14. The four angels ... at the great river Euphrates have been compared with the four angels at the four corners of the earth, which hold back the destructive winds from the earth (7:1). There is, however, no other relation between them than their number and their destructive function. The four angels of chapter 7 hold back the winds. These in our passage are themselves held down. The former stand at the limits of the world, these at the Euphrates. But why at *the Euphrates*? Without doubt because this river formed the eastern boundary of the Roman empire. Beyond it lay the Parthian empire, whose hordes were to the first-century Roman world what the Huns were in later times. The Roman armies had been defeated by the Parthians in the first century BC (at Carrhae 53 BC and again a century later, in the famous victory of Vologeses AD 62). Here if anywhere in the world was the area to which Romans looked apprehensively, and Jews hopefully, for possible future disasters. The Jews themselves had experienced grim visitation in earlier years from Assyrian, Babylonian, and Persian invaders from beyond the river. Moreover the Scriptures themselves have warnings concerning terrible armies from the north (i.e., of Palestine) which one day should be unleashed against the south and west (the warnings are especially frequent in Jeremiah; e.g., 1:14f., 6:1, 25:26, 46:24, 47:2, the last two including invasions of other nations than Israel), and it is to this expectation that the prophecies against Gog are related, since he and his armies come from the north (Ezek. 38:1ff., 39:1f.). This last prophecy was especially pondered by apocalyptic writers, and the *Book of Enoch* interprets it in a manner which is significant for our passage:

> In those days the angels shall return
> And hurl themselves to the east upon the Parthians and Medes:
> They shall stir up the kings, so that a spirit of unrest
>   shall come upon them,
> And they shall rouse them from their throne,
> That they may break forth from their lairs,
> And as hungry wolves among their flocks.

The sequel shows that the writer is utilizing the Gog prophecy, and looks for its fulfilment from the Parthians and Medes beyond the Euphrates. John looses it from its connection with the Jews and the Holy Land, and extends the invasion to the whole world. But he also breaks the connection with the Parthians themselves. For the army he awaits is more terrible by far than any human army. It is a supernatural, indeed an infernal, host.

15-19. The release of the four angels takes place at a time most precisely prepared. It is therefore most precisely defined—'in a definite hour of a definite day, in a definite month of a definite year' (Charles). Strangely enough the release of the four angels alone is mentioned, not that of the army which they command. It is not even said from where the multitude comes. In 16:12 we read of an army marching across the dried-up bed of the Euphrates, but our passage assumes something very different from that. Possibly we are to think of the army issuing, like the locusts, from the abyss (9:1). The object of this force is **to kill a third of mankind.** And there are enough of them to do it—**twice ten thousand times ten thousand,** i.e., 200 million. It is curious that this, and other computations like it, stem from Psalm 68:17, which gives the number of the chariots of God as he came from Sinai to the holy place, and Daniel 7:10, which tells of the number of angels who stand before God to serve him. This unimaginable host is 'an army straight from the jaws of hell' (Caird). But it too serves God, though in a different way from the heavenly host. It is an odd feature of this demonic host, however, that the horses seem to be more important than the riders. The language John uses to describe them is ambiguous. *RSV* renders verse 17, **This is how I saw the horses ... the riders wore breastplates ...** How is it that the *riders* are depicted in a sentence that tells how the *horses* looked? In the Greek text the description of the breastplates could relate to either, though it seems more natural to refer it to the horses than the riders. The *NEB* resolves the ambiguity in a manner which perhaps corresponds to what John wished to say: 'This was how I saw the horses and their riders in my vision: They wore breastplates ...' It was indeed a feature of Parthian cavalry that both riders and horses carried bright plate-armour. If, as Gunkel[1] and others have suspected, John was reproducing two different traditions, one which depicted squadrons of cavalry clothed in fiery red, smoky blue and sulphurous yellow armour, and another telling of mythological creatures which spit out fire, smoke, and brimstone, John himself is surely clear enough: these riders and horses have virtually melted into a unity, so that their deadly weapons are precisely the **fire and smoke and sulphur issuing from their mouths.** It was by these three plagues that the objectives of the army were achieved and **a third of mankind was killed.** The additional feature of **the power of the horses** lying **in their tails,** like serpents, as well as **in their mouths** which spit fire, etc., is but another fantastic detail in an already inconceivable picture. The picture is meant to be inconceivable, horrifying, and even revolting. For these creatures are

[1] *Zum religionsgeschichtlichen Verständnis des N.T.*, pp. 52ff.

not of the earth. Fire and sulphur belong to hell (19:20, 21:8), just as the smoke is characteristic of the pit (9:2). Only monsters from beneath belch out such things (cf. Job 41:20f.—an echo of the chaos-monster's ways).

20, 21. For any with eyes to see and a mind to comprehend, these judgments should lead to a forsaking of the works which call them forth. All through the trumpet series the motif of repentance sounds, and this one is no exception. Is it unreasonable to expect that the experience of judgment will humble the proud and sinful will? The whole Bible proceeds on the assumption that speech is not enough to deliver man from his plight and bring him into the divine kingdom—not even the speech of God. God reveals himself through action, alike in judgment and salvation. Both come to their climax in his action in Christ. So sure as the love of God can be comprehended finally only in the loving acts of God, to which man responds in love, in such ways alone can his power, righteousness, and holiness be expressed, the fitting response to which is repentance and faith. The revelation of righteousness, however, like that of love in the cross, can prove abortive: **the rest of mankind ... did not repent.** As with Pharaoh in ancient Egypt, the plagues did not soften their hearts. They remained obdurate, and continued **worshipping demons and idols,** as in their **murders, sorceries, immorality,** and **thefts.** (For the worship of demons, here distinguished from idolatry, see Dt. 32:17, Ps. 106:37, 1 C. 10:20.) The *murders, immorality, thefts* relate to three of the ten commandments, and occur in this order in Exodus 20:13ff. *Sorceries* are commonly linked with demon worship, and all too often entailed the other prohibitions, notably murder and immorality. Like Paul before him, John found it impossible to look with tolerance on the varied forms of pagan worship. He saw them as springs of moral and spiritual corruption, and a prime reason for the wrath of God on mankind (cf. Rom. 1:18ff.).

One question remains. We have read in this chapter two highly coloured accounts of God's judgments on impenitent men. What are we to make of them? And how did John expect us to understand them? One thing is surely clear: he did not expect his descriptions to be interpreted literally. He would have been astonished, and possibly amused, to learn for example that some later readers assumed that his picture of the riders and horses in verses 16ff. was to be taken with solemn realism. In discussing whether such creatures were ever or should be expected to stalk the earth, Schlatter answered: 'Just as the heavenly things seen by John, the trumpets, the altar, the throne, and everything he describes are parables, so the figures which he sees going over the earth will never be seen in reality.' If that be true, what then is signified by the 'parables'? It is hardly good enough to say, with Swete, that the locusts of the abyss 'represent to us memories of the past brought home at times of divine visitation, which hurt by recalling forgotten sins' (p. 118). Schlatter contented himself with laying down a broad principle: 'These visions fulfil an important purpose; for they impress on the Christian world the holy necessity and the strength of the divine execution of justice . . . For God's grace and kingdom do not appear without judgment on fallen man, but through it.' The observation is helpful, but it does not carry us far in interpreting the detail of the visions.

Caird deals with the issue more fully. He sees in the abyss from which the locust-army pours out an indication that in God's universe there are elements still recalcitant to the divine will. It is a reservoir of evil from which human wickedness is constantly reinforced, and which in turn is fed from the springs of human vices. It may even be viewed as 'the collective bad conscience of the race, from which come the haunting and avenging furies' (p. 119). Similarly in the monstrous army from the Euphrates he sees a symbol of the immense reserves of the powers of evil, which imperil the security of every earthly order. They are a grim reminder that in a world like ours it is unrealistic to expect that the progress of the gospel will suffice to dispel Satan's power. On the contrary we may expect a constant and even increased resistance to it till the last great battle.

This comes close to John's outlook. He himself would wish to affirm the existence of objective powers of evil that press on man and oppose the will of God. But the forms of those powers he is content to depict by way of symbol—locusts and monstrous horses. Just how they were to plague human beings he possibly never asked. It was sufficient to indicate that the almighty God will use them as his instruments of judgment, and to warn men to be led by them to repentance. For there is something worse than pain and death. To avert that is worth enduring both.

INTERLUDE: THE LITTLE SCROLL AND THE TWO WITNESSES
10:1-11:13

It will be recalled that after John had described the events ushered in by the opening of the sixth seal, which seemed to bring us to the end of tribulations and the advent of the kingdom, he held up the narrative by an intermission, the purpose of which was to give the Church an assurance of its spiritual security through all the trials which precede the end (ch. 7). That pause was made up of two visions, the first anticipating the trials as though they were future (although the story had almost reached its end), the second looking back on them as concluded. The second advanced on the first, not only from the temporal viewpoint, but in hinting that the preservation of the Church, of which the first vision spoke, did not mean the immunity of the Church from suffering. The victors clad in white robes had 'come out of the great tribulation' (7:14); i.e., they had passed through it and endured it.

John now follows the same procedure. Seven angels had been given seven trumpets. Six have sounded them, and of these the last two have brought mankind to a chaotic situation. Only the seventh remains, but John holds up his account of what takes place when the seventh announces the end of the age. He wishes to make two points unambiguously plain. The one answers the perennial question of the saints of God, 'How long?' With the most emphatic declaration possible it is affirmed that when the last trumpet sounds the last day comes, and God's purpose for the world and its history comes to its fulfilment (10:7). The second answers a question which so far has not been raised in John's visions of the end: 'What is the task of the Church in these troublous times?' John replies that it must bear witness to the last breath. For the first time it is made plain that many of Christ's followers are going to be demanded precisely that: their last breath, for Christ's sake. But their faithful testimony will be accompanied by an unleashing of extraordinary spiritual power, as the contest between the Antichrist and the Church becomes the dominant issue before mankind. The end of their witness will be the vindication of the Church and the conversion of many (11:1-13).

The temporal standpoint of the author has confused not a few readers, for it changes in the interlude, as apparently the prophet's spatial standpoint also. The vision of the angel declaring the imminence of the end unmistakably relates to the time after the

events of the sixth trumpet have taken place and immediately
before the seventh trumpet sounds. For this vision it would appear
that John has come down to earth to view the scene. That impression is confirmed by John's hearing a voice 'from heaven'
(v. 4), his taking the scroll from the angel bestriding land and
sea (vv. 8–11), and by the command given him in 11:1 to rise
and measure the temple of God in Jerusalem. The receiving of the
scroll from the angel, however, seems to relate to John's position
as a prophet in Patmos, in his situation prior to the whole story
which he is recounting. It is indeed intimately related to the opening vision of chapter 1, for the essential meaning of verses 8–11 is
its reaffirmation of John's commission to prophesy. The standpoint
of chapter 11, however, is the same as that of the first vision of
chapter 7, immediately prior to the onset of the trials which
conclude this age and usher in the next.

The first two verses of chapter 11 constitute a little oracle, the
significance of which is identical with that of the opening vision
of chapter 7. As the new Israel is sealed for protection from the
judgments of the end, so the sanctuary of God is measured off
and secured from the devastations that take place around it. And
'power to prophesy' through the period of tribulation, the last
half of the last week of history, as Daniel had characterized it, is
given to the witnesses (11:3). The oracle of 11:3–13 therefore
relates not to the time of the last trumpet, as many have held, but
to the entire period of the seven trumpets, and so to the entire
period with which this book is concerned. For the time of the end
is an era in which mankind's rebellion against God reaches its
climax. In all ages the Church of Christ is expected to fulfil its
vocation of witnessing to the gospel before men, cost what it may,
but in that time above all others its members are called on to
endure a passion like that of its Lord. As they face that prospect
they are assured that in the midst of their passion they will experience the power of Christ's resurrection.

THE ANGEL AND THE LITTLE SCROLL 10:1–11

A reading of the closing vision of the book of Daniel will show how
indebted John is to his predecessor. The vision begins with a
description of a majestic angel (Dan. 10:4ff.), which John echoes
in his own writing. After receiving a lengthy account of the fortunes

of the nations, the prophet asked the angel how long it would
be to the end of the wonders of which he has heard. Standing above
the waters of the stream where they were, the angel raised his
hands towards heaven and swore by him who lives for ever that it
would be for 'a time, two times and half a time', and that 'when
the shattering of the power of the holy people comes to an end'
all would be accomplished (12:6f.). This passage illuminates not
only the language and imagery employed in John's vision, but
gives an insight into the reason for the emphatic declaration that
there would be no more delay. In his vision John stands near the
close of the period of messianic judgments—six trumpets have
already sounded. But that period is the same as Daniel's three and
a half 'times' (= years), the season of tribulation. And it is to be
characterized by two vastly different phenomena. Christ's witnesses
will prophesy with power sent down from heaven (ch. 11) and the
'beast that ascends from the bottomless pit' will exercise his ferocious rule (11:7). Consequently two very significant situations
will come about. The evil of men will reach its limit as they give
their allegiance to the Antichrist, and the roll of the martyrs will
attain its completion in the 'shattering of the power of the holy
people' (cf. 6:11). History thus reaches its appointed hour of
climax, and the seventh trumpet sounds out the end of the story.

1. The majesty of the angelic figure has led some to identify
him with Christ, especially since **his face was like the sun** (see
1:16), and he towers over the earth, with one foot on land and the
other on the sea. The identification is mistaken, however, for
John refers to him as **another mighty angel,** harking back to the
first mighty angel of 5:2 ('strong' in 5:2 = 'mighty'; the same
word is used). That the angel's face shines as the sun suggests
that he shares the glory of Christ, like other heavenly beings (cf.
1 Jn 3:2), and his vast size befits the awesome nature of his message. The remaining features of his description echo Daniel
10:5f., which, it should be observed, tells of the appearance of the
angel who takes the oath in Daniel 12:6f. Since the prophet's
angel-guide in his two previous visions was Gabriel (8:16, 9:21),
it is likely that he is envisaged as the medium of revelation in
Daniel 10–12. John would not be ignorant of that. He could conceivably have intended a play on the name Gabriel in the term
mighty angel, since Gabriel is related to the Hebrew word *gibbōr* =
mighty man. It has often been noticed that this verse has echoes

of Exodus 14:19, 24, where we read of the angel of God who accompanied the Israelites in the pillar of fire and cloud—observe the **pillars of fire** here. This, however, is a coincidence of language rather than a suggestion that the angel of the presence accompanies God's servants in this age as he did Israel in the desert.[1]

2. The angel had **a little scroll open in his hand.** This is the second scroll of which we have read in the Revelation. The scroll with the seven seals in chapter 5 was a highly important document, containing God's disposition of the kingdom. What does this one enclose? The answer commonly given proceeds in the following manner. John describes it as *a little scroll*. The scroll of chapter 5 extends only from 6:1 to 8:5. A little scroll must be a good deal shorter than that. Its bitter-sweet contents will suit chapter 11, which tells of the suffering and triumph of the Church. The little scroll accordingly is 11:1–13. That is about as wooden an exegesis of a vision of this book as one can hope to find, and one is surprised that so many distinguished scholars support it.[2] In reality it is misleading to say that the scroll of chapter 5 covers 6:1–8:5. It represents God's promise of the kingdom, and therefore anticipates chapters 20–2. Further it enables John to present the judgments of the end under the imagery of the opening of a sealed document, but this does not mean that the scroll = two and a quarter chapters of John's writing. Nor should emphasis be placed on the shortness of the scroll in 10:2ff., on the ground that the term is a diminutive (*biblaridion* is a diminutive of *biblarion*). The term for scroll in chapter 5 is also a diminutive (*biblion* = a little book), and in 10:8 it is applied to the little scroll handed to John. Moreover the scroll in chapter 5 is not a book roll, as in chapter 10, but a document. But one feels that this is toying with words. The subject of this vision is not the scroll, but the time of the end. When, however, that question is dealt with, the scroll itself comes to the fore. It then appears the scroll has not a small

---

[1] Farrer's extraordinary imagination makes the suggestion almost acceptable: 'When the prophets describe the God of Exodus coming up from the wilderness of Sinai, they see the theophany embodied in a marching storm. St John's angel may be seen as a strongly conventionalized figure of the sort: the sun in the rain cloud makes the bow, and projects rods or pillars of light from the skirts of vapour down on shore and sea; the voice of thunder breaks like the roar of a lion' (p. 124).

[2] The argument outlined above is that of Charles, who is followed by Lohmeyer, Behm, Lohse, Kiddle, Rissi, etc.

but a large significance. For the handing of the scroll to John is not the passing on of a note for communication to the churches, but the imparting to him of a prophetic commission, like that which Ezekiel had when he became a prophet (Ezek., ch. 3). As if to underline this, John is told, like Jeremiah in his call to be a prophet (Jer. 1:10), that he must prophesy 'about many peoples and nations and tongues and kings'. That clearly has to do not with 11:1-13 but with the later visions of the Revelation, notably with those in chapters 13, 17, 19. The little scroll therefore signifies the re-affirmation of John's prophetic ministry as a whole.

3, 4. The angel astride the sea and land made proclamation **like a lion roaring** (cf. Am. 4:8, Hos. 11:10). His shouts were echoed by **the seven thunders.** These communicated an intelligible message to John (cf. Jn 12:28), but when he was about to write it down he was forbidden to do so (**Seal up** should mean, 'Don't make known what you have written', but in this context = 'Don't reveal what you have heard'). In telling us that *the seven thunders* spoke, yet withholding their message from us, John set us a pretty puzzle. Naturally everybody wants to know what the thunder said, and why they should not be told of it. It is a fair guess that *the seven thunders* are connected with the seven effects of the Lord's thunders in Psalm 29. This led critics, in the days when a commentator's job on the Book of Revelations was to dissect its constituent sources, to the view that the seven thunders were a well-known series of messianic portents, akin to those of the seven seals, seven trumpets, and seven bowls, and that John was of a mind to include them in his book, but decided on reflection that he should not, and this is his apologia for leaving them out (so Bousset, Holtzmann, Moffatt, etc.). Needless to say, that kind of solution does not appeal to scholars today, who have a greater appreciation of John's literary and artistic ability. Could it be that the prohibition to make known a further series of possible judgments is an apocalyptist's way of expressing the idea that God has shortened the days for the sake of his elect? So thought Farrer, and Caird developed this idea, with the suggestion that the days have been shortened because God has cancelled the doom which the seven thunders symbolized. This is difficult to reconcile with the fact that later John is to give us a further series of seven judgments which 'complete the wrath of God' (15-16).

Not unreasonably Paul's experience of being raptured to paradise and hearing 'things that cannot be told, which man may not utter' (2 C. 12:3) is often recalled at this point. Could the like apply to the seven thunders? Hardly, unless the seven thunders spoke revelations more sacred than those of the rest of John's book. It was Swete's view that this was one of those experiences which John could neither recall nor express, and that he rightly interpreted the fact as a prohibition to write it down.[1] That is questionable, but his further observation is more cogent: 'The Seer's enforced reticence witnesses to the fragmentary character of even apocalyptic discourses' (p. 128). The same point is made by Schlatter, who viewed this as an encouragement to the little groups of Christians to whom the Revelation was addressed, since the non-communication of the angel's words is a sign that the will of God is far greater than that which prophecy is able to express: 'It (God's will) remains along with the prophecy a secret, because God's work is greater and mightier than that which the prophetic view shows.' That may not be precise exegesis, but it is a not unworthy lesson to draw from the scene.

5-7. The angel ... lifted up his right hand to heaven. The lifting up of the hand is a typical gesture when taking an oath (cf. Deut. 32:40). Indeed in Hebrew the phrase 'raise the hand' is synonymous with 'swear', as e.g., appears in Exodus 6:8, Ezekiel 20:5ff., etc. The angel swears **by him who lives for ever and ever, who created heaven ... the earth ... the sea.** No higher power than this could be invoked when making an oath. The angel swears by the eternal Creator, since his oath affects all creation, and the Creator has power to carry out its content. Its object is that **there should be no more delay.** This rendering of the *RSV* is correct, as against the well known *AV*, 'there should be time no longer'. There is no question of time being suspended to give way to an eternal and timeless order, but rather an end being made to the all but intolerable waiting for the fulfilment of the divine promise. This is confirmed by the source which provided the form for John's vision. The prophet had asked the question, 'How long shall it be till the end of these wonders?', and he was given an enigmatic answer (Dan. 12:6f.). John is now given an unambiguous answer: 'There shall be no more delay.' For as chapter 11 will show, wickedness has reached its limit and

[1] Op. cit., p. 223.

the number of the martyrs is complete (see introduction to chs. 10–11). Consequently **in the days of the trumpet call ... by the seventh angel, the mystery of God should be fulfilled.** *The mystery of God* is not to be limited to the appearance of the Antichrist and the beginning of tribulation, as Charles inferred from chapters 11 and 13. Rather it is the completion of God's purpose in creation, and in the history of man in particular, which is to be fulfilled when the seventh angel sounds his trumpet. This is shown beyond cavil in 11:15ff., which portrays the joyful scene when the last trumpet is sounded. The kingdom of the world becomes the kingdom of God and of his Christ, and the Lord God Almighty has a new name—no longer 'He who is and who was and is to come', but simply 'He who is and who was'. He has 'come', and has ascended his throne (11:17, 'Thou hast ... begun to reign').

8–10. The voice which bids John **Go, take the scroll** is said to be the one which earlier forbade him to make known the message of the seven thunders (v. 4). Presumably it is the voice of Christ, from whom the whole Revelation comes (1:1). Having denied John one message, he now gives him a fresh commission to proclaim other messages. The passage invites comparison with Ezekiel 2:8–3:3. As Ezekiel, John is commanded to take the scroll and eat it; i.e., he has to make the message his own. Ezekiel relates how he ate the scroll, and writes, 'It was in my mouth as sweet as honey' (3:3). John is told, **It will be bitter to your stomach, but sweet as honey in your mouth.** The bitterness is strangely mentioned before the sweetness, perhaps because of its unexpectedness. So it happened when John ate the scroll: it was sweet to the mouth and made his stomach bitter. This goes beyond that which Ezekiel records, though we could infer a similar experience for him, in that his scroll was overflowing with 'words of lamentation and mourning and woe' (2:10). Jeremiah offers a closer parallel. In one of his dejected outpourings of prayer he states, 'Thy words were found and I ate them, and thy words became to me a joy and a delight of my heart.' But the words of the Lord to him were hard words, consequently he adds, 'I sat alone, because thy hand was upon me, for thou hadst filled me with indignation' (Jer. 15:16ff.). Here and in Ezekiel the impression is given that the word of God was a delight to receive, but it caused pain when its grim nature was grasped and declared.

It is doubtful, however, that the same applies to John's use of the figure. Both Jeremiah and Ezekiel had messages to proclaim which were suitably characterized by the phrase 'lamentation and mourning and woe'. Prophecy after prophecy in their books announce unrelieved disaster—terrible to read in Ezekiel, and in Jeremiah's case continuing through a generation and more. Some glimpses of hope admittedly appear in Jeremiah's early chapters, but generally speaking the message did not change to one of hope till the fearful judgments fell. (This is even more true of Ezekiel.) This is not the case, however, with John's book. He balances warning and encouragement through all its parts, and significantly the Apocalypse itself begins and ends with rejoicing (chs. 4–5, 21–2). Accordingly it is more suitable to view the vision of the scroll as illustrating the mixture of joy and pain which the word of God by its varied contents conveys, rather than the joy of receiving it followed by the pain of understanding and declaring it. The duality of joy and pain applies equally to the word for the Church as it does to the word for the world. For the Church must learn the weight of the cross before she participates in the glory of the kingdom, and the world must learn the reality of judgment before it experiences the grace of the kingdom.

11. The final word to John indicates the real meaning of the little scroll given to him by the angel: **You must again prophesy about many peoples and nations and tongues and kings.** Observe *again*: this is not the first time John has been commissioned to prophesy, as the opening vision of the book and the Revelation to this point testifies. Nevertheless it should not be overlooked that John's record of his earlier call to prophesy states only that he is to write what he sees in a book and send it to the seven churches (1:11). It will certainly have been assumed that the scope of the book for the churches will extend beyond the confines of the churches themselves, but no reference was made to that. The implications of the earlier call are explicitly spelled out at this juncture, and understandably so, for from henceforth John will have much to say about *peoples and nations and tongues and kings*. Moreover it should not be overlooked that prophets and preachers, like all other Christians, need encouragement for their tasks, and John on Patmos was no exception. He was about to receive and make known yet more burdensome messages than those he had so far received and declared. But here was grace and consolation for him. The

Lord Christ by the hand of his mighty angel sends him on his way again.

THE TWO WITNESSES 11:1-13

The style and content of the second part of John's interlude between the sixth and seventh trumpets differ markedly from those of the first. Chapter 10 recounts a vision which, despite its dependence on Old Testament precedents, is obviously John's original composition. We cannot be sure that the same applies to 11:1-13. To an unusual degree it reflects the imagery and thought of contemporary Jewish apocalyptic writers. Indeed, many features of this section are best explained on the assumption that it was originally a Jewish prophecy, which John adapted in a similar manner as he did the oracle concerning the sealing of the twelve tribes (7:1ff.; see introduction to that chapter).

Since Wellhausen[1] it has been common to view verses 1-2 as derived from a Zealot prophet in the siege of Jerusalem. It is suggested that when the Jews were being pressed by the Romans, a prophet affirmed that, although the outer court of the temple and the city itself were given over to the Romans, God would not allow the temple and its inner court to fall, but would protect them and the faithful who had taken refuge in them. John saw in this prophecy, discredited though it was, a means of setting forth a real concern of God, as well as of rectifying false ideas. For God's real temple is made up of people rather than stones, and he undertakes to provide for those who are one with him through the Spirit of the Messiah. Accordingly John took up the little oracle and made it a vehicle for conveying these thoughts and set it as the introduction to the prophecy of verses 3-13.

This is an attractive view, and it has much in its favour. Despite the denials of some, it is comprehensible that an oracle as short as this should survive in apocalyptic circles, whether orally or as one of many brief oracles written and circulated during the Jewish war, when eschatological expectations ran at their highest. It has been objected, however, that verses 1-2 ought not to be isolated from the rest of the passage (a sentiment with which the RSV translators evidently concurred). No obvious break occurs between the two parts of the narrative, and they can be made to

[1] *Skizzen und Vorarbeiten*, VI, pp. 221ff.

harmonize. Moreover, as Lohmeyer observed, there is no need to invoke the Zealot prophet for the idea that Jerusalem will be trampled by heathen invaders. Belief in the inviolability of the temple was almost as old as the temple itself, and it was never more keenly held than in the first century of our era, when multitudes assumed that Herod's temple would be the temple of the new age. There is, however, a difficulty about the idea that verses 1–13 are an original unity which seems to be generally overlooked. In Daniel 9:26f., 11:31ff., 12:11f., it is stated that the temple will be profaned by the antigod tyrant during the middle of the last week (= seven years) of history, and that the abomination of desolation will be set up in the temple for the rest of that week, i.e., for the three and a half years or forty-two months of tribulation. Verses 3–13 describe the prophetic ministry of the two forerunners during that period, and give a picture in harmony with the teaching of Daniel. But verse 2 bluntly says that the Antichrist will not be allowed to take over the temple in that time. He can trample down the city itself, but the temple and its court and altar will be inaccessible to him. Now it is one thing for men in the stress of siege to believe that the Lord will do his 'strange work' and intervene in unexpected ways, but it is another thing for a prophet deliberately to contradict the teaching of the Scriptures. The connection of the Antichrist with the temple was a living tradition in the first century AD, as Mark 13:14ff., 2 Thessalonians 2:4 illustrate. Accordingly the present writer joins those who see in verses 1–2 an originally independent oracle which John (or a predecessor) took over and made it form an introduction to verses 3–13.

The second and longer oracle (vv. 3–13) seems also to have been Jewish in origin and in thought. That the city of Jerusalem is presupposed as its setting is indicated by verses 8 and 13. The phrase 'where their Lord was crucified' was doubtless John's addition, but it shows how he interpreted the oracle. There were Jews before Jesus who believed that their fellow countrymen, and Jerusalem in particular, were as wicked as Sodom and resistant to God as Egypt (cf. Isa. 1:9f., Ezek. 16:46ff.). That seven thousand people were killed when a tenth of the city fell in an earthquake (v. 13), is commensurate with Jerusalem's population (in contrast, e.g., with Rome's). The two witnesses of verses 3ff. are described in terms which suggest that the writer viewed them

as Moses and Elijah, the two forerunners of the Messiah expected
by the Jews (see notes on vv. 3–6). In their prophesying they are
resisted by the beast from the bottomless pit (v. 7), known from
Daniel's prophecies (cf. Dan. 7), and they are slain by him. That
the forerunners of the Messiah will meet a fate of this kind accords
with the enigmatic saying in Mark 9:13. In answer to an enquiry
about the awaited ministry of Elijah, Jesus said, 'I tell you that
Elijah has come, and they did to him whatever they pleased, as
it is written of him.' That is, John the Baptist perished in agreement with what was written about Elijah's ministry in the end of
the times. The vindication of the witnesses by resurrection and
rapture to heaven is inspired by the traditions concerning the
taking of Moses and Elijah to heaven and the vision of Ezekiel 37
(see notes on vv. 12f.). We observe in passing that no reference
is made to the parousia of Christ, which one would expect in a
Christian description of resurrection at the end of the times. The
whole conception is Jewish, as is also the representation of the
earthquake in Jerusalem and the repentance of its survivors (v. 13).

The detail of John's reinterpretation of this prophecy belongs
to the exegesis which follows, but its outline can be traced at once.
The significance attaching to lampstands in the Revelation indicates how John understood the two witnesses. They represent
the churches fulfilling their vocation to bear witness to Christ in
the final time of tribulation. Whether the whole Church is so
imaged, or only a part of it, is contested. A number of commentators hold that John has in view the Jewish-Christian Church in
Jerusalem.[1] Rissi, while agreeing generally with this position,
wonders whether the two witnesses may not be the Jewish and
Gentile Christian churches in their joint witness to the Jewish
people in Jerusalem.[2] Yet others consider that the restriction of the
lampstands to two in number, as against seven, which earlier
represented the whole Church, indicates that a part only of the
Church is in mind (corresponding to the two faithful churches of
the seven, Smyrna and Philadelphia?), and so that the two witnesses symbolize the martyrs of the Church. They are Christ's
'witnesses' (*martyres*) *par excellence*, and their resurrection to heaven

---

[1] So Schlatter, Lohmeyer, Lohse. Charles also thinks that Jerusalem is the
scene of the witnesses' prophesying, but he holds to their continued identification with Moses and Elijah.

[2] Op. cit., pp. 97ff.

after death comports with teaching elsewhere given in this work as to the reign of the martyrs (e.g., 20:4ff.).[1] On such a view the conflict with the Antichrist is world-wide, not confined to Jerusalem. The holy city is then to be understood as representing the city of the world in its opposition to God, what Bunyan called the City of Destruction, or Vanity Fair.

This last identification is probably right, even if the restriction of the witness to the martyrs is doubtful (see notes on 3ff.). From the general standpoint, if John has taken one Jewish oracle which concerned the faithful in the temple of Jerusalem and made them symbolize the whole Church of God (i.e., vv. 1–2), it is likely that the oracle to which it forms an introduction also mirrors the whole Church, and not a section of it. It is doubtful that the book of Revelation teaches that the whole Church is called to martyrdom, and there is no evidence at all to suggest that a section only of the Church is called to bear witness to the world.

But is the Church called to witness? This has been called in question of late by the Japanese scholar Akira Satake. A detailed examination of this passage[2] led him to believe that John had no interest in the idea of the Church bearing witness to the world. In the period which John had in view in chapter 11 the world is the object of the judgment of God, not of proclamation from God, and so this oracle portrays the two witnesses in deadly combat with the world, rather than bearing testimony to it. Killing opponents who resist the gospel is hardly the conduct of evangelists who are trying to win the world. Accordingly Satake believes that the intention of the prophecy in chapter 11 lies in a different direction altogether from that of witness-bearing. It was written to demonstrate that in the time of tribulation the Church stands under the mighty protection of God.

Despite the forcefulness with which this case is argued, it is surely mistaken. In order to maintain it, Satake has to maximize the powers given to the prophet-figures to inflict punishment and minimize those given to enable them to function as witnesses. This is to overlook that John here puts to Christian use an earlier oracle which emanates from Jewish circles, in which there would naturally not be the same recognition of obligation to witness to

[1] So Kiddle, Caird.
[2] *Die Gemeindeordnung in der Johannesapokalypse*, Neukirchen-Vluyn, 1966, pp. 119–33.

the world, as was current in the primitive Christian Church. The miracles of Moses and Elijah are represented in a striking, even highly mythological manner (cf. fire from the mouth), but these are not the central features for John. Verse 3 shows where he placed the emphasis in this description. These figures in whom the Church is symbolized are called *witnesses*. They are given power to prophesy ('I will grant my two witnesses power to prophesy' virtually = 'I will commission my two witnesses to prophesy'). This is their vocation, hence they are called witnesses, not warriors, and their primary work is to prophesy rather than fight. For this reason they are clothed in sackcloth (v. 3). This indicates both their calling as prophets (Isa. 20:2 suggests that sackcloth was a prophet's dress) and the nature of their message as a call for repentance in face of judgment.[1] In accordance with this verse 7 reads: 'When they have finished their testimony the beast . . . will kill them.' Testimony is their task, and not till it is completed are their foes permitted to slay them.

All this is in harmony with the general understanding of the anticipated ministry of Elijah current among Jews. Malachi 4:5 encouraged the thought of Elijah as a great restorer, and therefore as a preacher of repentance. One rabbi left it on record, 'Without repentance Israel will not be redeemed . . . They will show great repentance only when Elijah comes.'[2] In Ezra 6:26 it is written, 'The men who have been taken up, who have not tasted death from their birth, shall appear. Then shall the heart of the inhabitants of the world be changed, and be converted to a different spirit.' The reference appears to be to Elijah and Enoch, but the statement is strikingly at one with our passage. The last clause of 11:13 relates that the survivors of the earthquake 'gave glory to the God of heaven'. That is Jewish terminology for saying that they repented. If the first sentence of 11:3–13 stresses the witnessing and prophetic function of the Church, and its last sentence records the repentance of their hearers, that is fair indication as to how John intended the prophecy to be understood. The miracles of verses 5–6, therefore, must not be allowed to minimize this feature of the prophecy. In John's application of it they serve to identify the prototypes of Christian witness in the last days, and to

[1] So Charles, Lohmeyer, ad loc; see also in *TWNT* the article by Jeremias on Elijah, vol. II, p. 933, and that by Stählin on sackcloth, vol. VII, pp. 56–64.
[2] *Pirque R. El.* 43.

symbolize the power of their ministry. Inasmuch as the Church
fulfils the expected ministry of Moses and Elijah, the passage
underscores the importance of the Church's task as witness. God
sends no other agencies to men in the time of earth's distress than
the witnesses of Christ.

This, then, is the purpose of 11:1-13. It commences with an
assuring word about the protecting hand of God upon his people,
but its chief concern is to illustrate the task of the Church in the
time of distress and the consequences of carrying it out. The out-
stretched hand of God over his people does not prevent them from
enduring the cost of bearing witness to Christ before a rebellious
generation. On the contrary they must learn the weight of the
cross before they taste the power of the resurrection. In this respect
11:1-13 afford an explanatory parallel to chapter 7; for if 11:1-2
correspond to 7:1-8 (the sealing of the tribes), 11:3-13 instructs
as to the kind of tribulation it is from which the victors emerge
(7:9-17). The passage shows that the Church has something
more important to do than simply to survive. It is set in the world
to bear witness to men, even when the witness is resisted with
force. The darker the hour, the more need for the Churches to be
what they are: lamps, through which Christ's light shines. Witnesses
may be crushed, and lamps put out, but in the end both witness
and light achieve their desired object: men give glory to God.

1, 2. The imagery of the opening verse of this prophecy is
drawn from Ezekiel 40-48, where an angel guide conducts
Ezekiel in his vision through a new temple and measures its
constituent parts. In that passage the measuring was with a view
to reconstructing the temple (for the old had been destroyed).
In this it is for preserving the measured sections of the temple from
destruction (contrast Isa. 34:11, 2 Kg. 21:13, Am. 7:7ff., wherein
the same action portends destruction). **The temple of God and
the altar** means the temple proper with its inner court. In the
first temple there were two courts, inner and outer, but in the
Herodian temple the inner was divided into three—the courts of
the priests, in which the altar stood, the court of the Israelites, and
the court of the women. Between them and the court of the Gentiles was a low wall with notices regularly spaced, forbidding
Gentiles on pain of death from advancing beyond their court
(= 'the dividing wall of hostility' of Eph. 2:14?). **The temple
of God and the altar and those who worship there**

accordingly represent the area of the temple set apart for Israelites' use, together with the faithful Israelites themselves. In John's use of the oracle it symbolizes the Church of Christ, and approximates to the imagery of the Church as the temple of God (cf. 2 C. 6:16, Eph. 2:19ff., 1 Pet. 2:5). **The court outside the temple** = the court of the Gentiles, and readily lends itself to symbolize the unbelieving world. This is left unmeasured, and therefore during the time of tribulation it is exposed to destructive forces. Strictly speaking the trampling of the holy city signifies its subjugation and profanation (i.e., by Gentiles, who are unclean in the sight of the law). But history had shown that this kind of profanation is generally accompanied by destruction (cf. Mk 13:14ff., Lk. 21:24, *Ps. Sol.* 17:25). **Forty-two months** = three and a half years, the last half of the last week of Daniel's seventy weeks of history, each of which represents seven years (see Dan. 9:24–7, 12:7). In 12:14 John uses the Danielic phrase 'a time, and times, and half a time', but in verse 3 and 12:6 he expresses it by the number of days it represents.

By this oracle John conveys the same notion as is set forth through the vision of the sealing of the twelve tribes, 7:1ff., namely the divine provision for the preservation of the Church during the great distress. In both visions (7:1ff. and 11:1ff.) he has adopted Jewish models to set forth the idea. It is but reasonable to believe that the extent of their application is identical. As the twelve tribes = the whole Church throughout the world, so the temple and its worshippers = the whole Church in all lands. It is arbitrary to restrict verses 1–2, as some expositors do, to the Jewish-Christian church in the city of Jerusalem. This confounds the symbol with the thing signified.

3, 4. Who is the speaker? Since he refers to **my two witnesses** he must be God or Christ (or possibly his angel-representative, cf. v. 1). The witnesses are granted **power to prophesy.** For John prophecy and witness are closely related. He himself wrote his prophecy as 'witness to the word of God and the testimony of Jesus Christ' (1:2). In 19:10 he states, 'The testimony of Jesus is the spirit of prophecy.' The burden of prophecy, therefore, is the testimony which Jesus bore. Whatever the original writer may have had in view in verse 3, John will have interpreted the prophetic task of the two witnesses as that of declaring the testimony of Jesus Christ.

Their ministry lasts for **one thousand two hundred and sixty days,** the period of the great distress (v. 2) and of the work of the Antichrist in the world (v. 7, see especially 13:5). Such a time will call for a stress on that element in the teaching of Jesus which demands decision and repentance in face of the impending judgment and kingdom of God (cf. Mk 1:15, 8:34ff., Mt. 10:28ff. Lk. 13:1–5). Accordingly the witnesses are **clothed in sackcloth,** a garb associated above all with penitence and mourning (cf. Jn 3:5). Thus in the very time when the Antichrist works for the seduction of men, God provides that powerful prophetic witness to Jesus be given, in fulfilment of the word of Jesus concerning the proclamation of the gospel in circumstances of tribulation and distress (Mk 13:10).

But why *two witnesses*, neither more nor less? And who are they? The prophecy appears to develop the promise which closes the Old Testament canon, that God will send Elijah the prophet before the great and terrible day of the Lord (Mal. 4:5f.). It came to be believed that in the last days Elijah would be accompanied by another. An early tradition said that he would be joined by Enoch (so 1 *Enoch* 90:31, 4 *Ezra* 6:26). The view that the two witnesses in our passage were Enoch and Elijah became early established in Christian circles (so Tertullian, *De Anima* 50, and see Bousset, *Antichrist Legend*, p. xlv). It seems clear however that verses 5–6 presume that Elijah is accompanied by Moses, since the plagues inflicted by the witnesses are reminiscent of the deeds of Elijah and of Moses. A first-century Jewish teacher, Jochanan ben Zakkai, declared that God said to Moses, 'If I send the prophet Elijah, you must both come together' (*Debar. R.* 10:1). The composer of the original text of this prophecy gave expression to that expectation. How did John interpret the prophecy? Some think that he shared the contemporary Jewish view and looked for Moses and Elijah to come back in person. This would suit the representation (11:5ff.) that they fulfilled their ministry in Jerusalem (so Schlatter, Charles). An alternative suggestion is that in John's thought they are replaced by the apostles Peter and Paul, who bore testimony and were martyred in Rome (Munck).[1] Verse 4 seems to put all such views out of court. The witnesses are identified with **the two olive trees and the two lampstands.** This is a reinterpretation of Zechariah 4:3ff., where the two olive

[1] *Petrus und Paulus in der Offenbarung Johannis*, Copenhagen, 1950.

trees originally denoted Zerubbabel and Joshua the high priest, who stood on either side of the lampstand and supplied it with oil. John, however, interprets the olive trees as the *two lampstands*. In view of his firm use of lampstands to represent churches, it seems plain that he wishes to indicate that the witnesses are the churches of Christ. As prophetic witnesses they fulfil the role of kings (like Zerubbabel) and priests (as Joshua). Earlier John had symbolized one church with a single lampstand and the whole Church by seven lampstands. He could not introduce the number seven at this point without confusion. Accordingly the single lampstand of Zechariah is made two, so as to correspond with the two witnesses, but the whole Church is thereby represented. The number, moreover, accords with the tradition that valid testimony requires two witnesses (Dt. 19:15). In obedience to this principle the Jewish authorities used to send to the Jews of the Dispersion emissaries in pairs. Jesus did the like when sending his disciples on mission (Mk 6:7, Lk. 10:2), and the primitive Church continued the observance (Ac. 13:2, 15:39f.).

5, 6. The two witnesses experience strong opposition (the Antichrist is abroad), and they retaliate with awesome powers of destruction. Verse 5 recalls Elijah's destruction of the messengers from Ahaziah (2 Kg. 1:10ff.), and verse 6 has in view the drought described in 1 Kings 17:1 and the plagues brought about through Moses in Egypt.[1] Doubtless these plagues were literally expected by the Jewish prophet who produced the original oracle. Was John of the same opinion? Possibly so, in a broad sense. The similarity of these plagues with those of the seventh trumpet have been frequently observed. It may be that just as John saw the messianic judgment falling in response to the prayers of the martyrs and of the Church (6:10, 8:1ff.), so he viewed them as a consequence of the prophetic declarations of the witnesses. It should be observed, however, that John's description is susceptible of interpretation in a symbolic way; e.g., Sirach 48:1 speaks of Elijah as 'a prophet like fire, whose word was like a burning furnace', and similar

[1] Verse 6a has an interesting contact with contemporary Jewish thought about Elijah's famine. 1 Kings 17:1 does not specify the length of time of the drought, only that it would last for 'these years'. In Luke 4:25 and James 5:17 the drought is said to have lasted for three and a half years. This is a clear reminiscence of the three and a half years of Daniel, and suggests that the drought of Elijah's time was akin to the judgments of the great distress of the last days.

metaphorical speech occurs in Jeremiah 5:14. It is likely that
verse 6 was retained by John without a literal application being
intended, beyond its suggestion of the power of faith in Christian
warfare (just as in v. 2 the altar is retained from the original oracle
without any significance for the Christian reader).

7. A limit is set to the period of testimony given by the witnesses.
When they have finished their testimony, the beast . . .
will make war upon them . . . and kill them. The limit is
set by God, and at its conclusion he permits the beast to conquer
them. He permits his people to be overcome by the beast, as he
permitted his Son to be crucified by the Romans. In them the
passion of the Christ is set forth afresh. **The beast that ascends**
from the bottomless pit is referred to as though well known to
the readers. His activities are described at length in chapters 13
and 17. But teaching on the Antichrist was familiar to Jews through
the book of Daniel (7:2–21, 9:27, 11:31ff.), and therefore to
Christians also (though with varied applications of the figure;
e.g., Mk 13:14, 2 Th. 2:3ff., 1 Jn 4:1ff.). The beast makes war
upon the witnesses as Daniel had said ('This horn made war with
the saints', 7:21). The citation is a further indication that the
two witnesses represent the whole people of God and not two
individuals. Does John intend to teach that the entire Church will
be martyred under the Antichrist? Such a conclusion ought not
to be drawn from this passage. In the original document the
two witnesses are killed in a single day and lie in the street of
Jerusalem for three and a half days. That is a clear and comprehensible picture. But in John's application it has to be modified.
It is not true, as this prophecy taken literally and in isolation
would suggest, that the Church is permitted to go through the
tribulation unscathed till its end, suddenly to be destroyed in a
mass carnage of unimaginable proportions. The picture has to be
corrected by John's teaching elsewhere, which indicates that
martyrs will die at various times in the tribulation (cf. 6:9ff.), but
not all are marked out for martyrdom (cf. 3:10f.). The war of
the Antichrist is carried out ruthlessly, but we must take it that
if many are killed, others are merely repressed—driven underground, as we should say.

8–10. Similarly the description of **the great city** has to be
extended. As applied to Jerusalem it characterizes the city as a
place of moral and spiritual degradation (cf. Isa. 1:9f., and

especially Ezek. 16:46, 55), opposition to God's people and rejection of the Lord's Christ. But in so far as the world manifests these characteristics it unites itself in the same condemnation. Jerusalem allegorically interpreted becomes, in the words of a later allegorist, The City of Destruction, Vanity Fair.

Universally in the ancient world to refuse the dead a decent burial represents the limit of outrage and indignity that can be accorded to the dead (for Jewish attitudes, cf. Ps. 79:2f., 1 Kg. 13:22, Tob. 1:18, 2:3ff.). So the bodies of the two witnesses **lie in the street,** with none permitted to bury them. The enemies of the Church **(those who dwell on the earth)** hold parties to celebrate their victory over the Church. They **exchange presents,** i.e., of food prepared for the feasts (for the custom, still known in some parts, cf. Est. 9:22, 2 Esd. 18:10). In this way they fulfil the prediction of Mark 13:13, 'You will be hated by all for my name's sake', and so rejoicing over the apparent defeat of the Church, they associate themselves with the guilty.

The rejoicing of the enemies of the Church however is as short-lived as their triumph. It lasts for **three days and a half**—a deliberate play on the three and a half years of the tribulation. In this case however it contrasts with the three and a half *years,* of the powerful ministry of the witnesses. In comparison with that the Antichrist's victory is ephemeral—it is no victory. The Church rises from death. The language of verse 11 is drawn from Ezekiel's vision of the valley of dry bones. The Jewish nation is like the scattered bones of an army slain in battle. At the bidding of the prophet the bones come together, they are clothed with flesh, and at a further word from the prophet, 'the breath of God came into them, and they lived, and stood upon their feet' (37:10). Ezekiel applied the idea of resurrection from death to the spiritual renewal of the nation. The unknown Jewish prophet applied it to the literal resurrection of the two witnesses, but added that they were taken **up to heaven** again, as had happened to them once before.[1] In view of the Christian tradition of resurrection of the dead and transformation of the living (1 C. 15:51ff., 1 Th. 4:14ff.) we take it that John interpreted this passage in the light

---

[1] In Jewish tradition the unknown grave of Moses was testimony to his translation to heaven, as Enoch and Elijah. Such was related in the *Assumption of Moses,* according to Clement of Alexandria, *Strom.* 6:15, and Origen, *In Josuam hom* 2:1.

of the Christian hope. It is a symbol of the 'first resurrection'
(20:5).

11–13. The resurrection of the witnesses was accompanied by
great fear in those who saw them and **a great earthquake.**
As the resurrection of the witnesses corresponds to the event of
the last trumpet (cf. 1 C. 15:52), so this earthquake corresponds
to that which John consistently associates with the end of the age
(v. 19, cf. 8:5, 16:18ff.). But its accompaniment is related to the
proportions of a severe earthquake in Jerusalem. **Seven thousand
people were killed in the earthquake,** an obviously generalized
figure, but curiously in harmony with the result of a tenth of the
city being destroyed by earthquake.[1] More important, however,
is the effect on the living. **The rest were terrified and gave
glory to the God of heaven.** In Joshua 7:19, Jeremiah 13:16,
to give glory to God means to confess sin and repent of it. So
here it signifies glorifying God by ceasing from apostasy and
returning to the God of heaven. In the original prophecy the
populace of Jerusalem is in mind. For John, who sees in the great
city an image of the world, this glorification of God prefigures the
repentance of multitudes of mankind. The judgments of God have
been revealed, and all nations have come and worshipped (15:4).

THE SEVENTH TRUMPET **11:14–19**

14. The declaration verse **The second woe has passed,
behold the third woe is soon to come** is a further indication
that 11:1–13 is a section complete in itself, which was inserted
into the scheme of the seven trumpet judgments, for v. 14a follows
on 9:13–21 as though nothing had intervened.

The third woe coincides with the events of the seventh trumpet,
yet it is not described. There is no need to invoke speculations
about missing sections of the book, or to identify the third woe
with the seven bowls or the like. In reality no action of any kind
is introduced by the seventh trumpet. We simply hear songs which

[1] Estimates of the population of Jerusalem in ancient writers vary enor-
mously. On the basis of the reported measurements of the city walls, Jeremias
estimates that the population in the first century AD will have numbered
between 55,000 and 95,000, but probably nearer the lower limit. That is
uncommonly close to the presuppositions of the original prophecy worked over
by John. See Jeremias, *Jerusalem in the Time of Jesus*, Eng. Tr. 1967, p. 83, n. 24.

celebrate a series of actions that are not described (note especially vv. 17f.). In so writing John is adhering to the mode of presenting his vision of the end which we have seen in the seven seals and which we shall see again in the seven bowls. The end of the age has been reached with the third woe and the seventh trumpet, but it is not described, for we are not yet in a position fully to grasp its relation to history, and we shall not be in that position till the contents of chapters 12–17 have come before us. We shall not greatly err if we see the third woe reflected in verse 18*a*, referred to more explicitly in 16:19 (the seventh bowl) and in greater fullness in 17:12–18, sung in the dirge of chapter 18 and in the hymns of exultation in 19:1–10, and described in 19:11–16 (especially 19:15). In this passage, as elsewhere in John's book, the day of wrath is subordinated to the joy of the kingdom of God. Or as Caird puts it, *dies irae* is seen as *dies gaudii* (the day of wrath = the day of rejoicing).

15. When the seventh seal is opened, there was silence in heaven (8:1). When the seventh trumpet is blown **there were loud voices in heaven.** The contrast is startling, but comprehensible. Following on the silent listening to the prayers of God's people (8:4), the answer to their prayers in the gift of God's kingdom is celebrated. Comparing the worship of heaven in chapter 4 with that described in this passage, it would appear that *the loud voices* are those of the cherubim (cf. 4:8), after which the elders voice their thanksgiving in verses 16ff. (cf. 4:9ff.).

The thought is clear. The world has become the sphere of the visible reign of God in Christ. The end of mankind's rebellion and of the usurped sovereignty of evil powers has come. The language invites comparison with Matthew 4:8. It should not go unobserved, however, that in Matthew 4:8 'the kingdoms of the world' are concrete, whereas in our passage John may be understood as meaning, 'The sovereignty over the world has now passed to (= become the sovereignty exercised by) our Lord and his Christ'; for the dynamic concept of kingdom as rule or sovereignty, dominant in the New Testament, is evident in John's writing also (cf. especially 12:10).

The kingdom belongs to **our Lord and his Christ.** The phraseology echoes Psalm 2:2, but the theology is an advance on anything in the Old Testament. For whereas the messianic (= millennial) rule is immediately in view, it is called not the

kingdom of Christ but *the kingdom of our Lord and of his Christ,* for
the sovereignty of God and Christ is indivisible. The next line
presumes the same conception. **He shall reign for ever and
ever** directs our gaze to the eternal rule in the new creation. But
who is *he*? Is it *our Lord,* or *his Christ*? For John the question is
immaterial, since for him the Lord and the Christ are an indis-
soluble unity (so Lohmeyer). It is in harmony with this that the
eternal order of the new creation is dominated by the splendour
of the throne of God and of the Lamb (21:22–22:4).[1]

16, 17. The song of the elders addresses the **Lord God
Almighty** with a new name: **who art and who wast.** No
longer can it be said, 'and who is to come' (1:4), for he has come.
As in the preceding song (v. 15) the implication of these words is
unmistakable. In the coming of Christ God comes, for God and
his Christ are one. But God comes to reign, hence the song continues, **thou hast taken thy great power and begun to reign.**
God has ascended the throne. The clause deserves to be pondered.
John knows well that the Lord God Almighty has never set aside
his *great power,* as his vision of God on the throne in chapter 4
illustrates. But the rebellion of man and the evil powers, with the
consequences of death and ruin in the world, is writ large in this
book as in large tracts of the Bible. God alone can deliver man and
his world from the evil and ruin which have overtaken them.
Chapter 5 shows us that he has put forth his great power in order
to reign in grace through Christ the redeemer. The reign began
when the Christ ascended his throne, but the same language is
used in this passage to denote the time when all rebellion is quen-
ched and the sovereignty of God is visibly established in the supremacy of his grace and glory.

18. The succession of clauses has caused some perplexity,
not least by the mention of the last judgment in the second line.
Some commentators (e.g., Charles, Lohmeyer, Lohse) wish to
keep to a chronological order in the lines of the song. Verse 17
is then related to the millennial kingdom, 18*a* to the uprising of
Gog and Magog (20:7ff.), 18*b* to the judgment before the throne
of God (20:11ff.), 18*cd* to the blessedness of the saints in the city

---

[1] This teaching of John raises the question whether Paul's mind regarding
the future kingdom can adequately be assessed by 1 Corinthians 15:28 alone,
or whether he too entertained a conception similar to John's. Ephesians 5:5,
along with the implications of Colossians 1:16, suggests that he did.

of God (chs. 21–2) and 18e to the final destruction of the evil
powers (cf. 20:10). To maintain this order Charles suggests that
the last line has been accidentally transposed from its original
place after 18a. This is certainly possible, but on reflection the
difficulties of this view become apparent. Above all we observe
that 18a is formed from Psalm 2:1 and 5, and is most naturally to
be referred to the raging of the nations prior to the advent of
Christ, rather than to the episode narrated in 20:7ff. The song
then is best viewed as giving joyful expression to the meaning of
Christ's coming to the world. It entails the revelation of God in
Christ in glory, the exercise of his judgment alike in putting down
all rebelliousness of man and setting all generations of history before
the tribunal of God, the reward of God's people in his kingdom
and the destruction of all destroyers of earth. This last item
includes all agencies of evil, from Babylon to Satan, death and
hades. The last things form a plurality of events, and John is at
pains to illustrate their fullness and complexity. In view of John's
utilizing Jewish oracles in verses 1–13, it would not be surprising
if in verses 15–18 he cites Christian songs which celebrate the last
advent of Christ and its consequences for the Church and the
world. They contain features with which John is especially
concerned, but they do not maintain the order of his own prophecies. Since John himself is not too scrupulous in observing
chronological order, he would not be worried by such a minor
consideration here.

The rage of the **nations** has been illustrated already in verses
1–3, but it finds fuller exposition in chapters 13, 17 and 19. The
wrath of God is seen especially in the three series of judgments
(seals, trumpets, and bowls), but also in chapters 17–19. The
judgment of the **dead** is described in 20:11ff., and the destruction
of earth's **destroyers** in all the passages which describe the
putting down of rebellion against God, above all in the judgments
on Babylon and on the evil trinity mentioned in 16:13.

19. God's temple in heaven was opened, not for the revelation of God on his throne (he has come), but for the manifestation
of **the ark of his covenant.** In the earthly temple this stood in
the innermost shrine, the 'holy of holies', and so was seen by the
high priest alone on the annual occasion of his entrance into the
shrine on the day of atonement. The ark of the covenant was the
symbol of God's presence with his people and sign of his promise.

John would have thought more on the latter aspect. The earthly
ark of the covenant had been lost or destroyed in the destruction
of the temple by Nebuchadrezzar (586 BC), and the Jews looked
for its restoration at the coming of the Messiah. John portrays a
better fulfilment of the hope. The heavenly reality of the earthly
ark is visible to men's eyes in the fulfilment of the promise of the
kingdom.

The accompaniments of the concluding acts of this age are again
recounted, signifying that the end has now come (cf. 8:5 and
especially 16:17–21).

THE CONFLICT BETWEEN THE CHURCH
AND THE EVIL POWERS 12:1-14:2

THE DRAGON AND THE LAMB

These chapters constitute the most substantial parenthesis in the
Revelation. Yet they are more than a parenthesis, for they form the
central section of the book. Not only do they come at the mid-
point of the work, they provide an understanding of the nature of
the conflict in which the Church is engaged, and into which John
sees she is to be drawn to the limit. The struggle of the saints
against the Caesars is here portrayed in the context of an age-long
resistance to the God of heaven on the part of evil powers. That
process is about to reach its climax in an all out warfare against the
Church of Christ. The raging of the powers of hell, however,
terrible as it may be, is shown to be in vain, for in the victory of
the crucified and ascended Christ they have been defeated, and
their final overthrow is not far distant. Indeed the sharpness of the
conflict is due precisely to the realisation of the enemy of God and
man that his time is short. The Lord's hand overshadows his
saints, and though their blood may flow, their vindication is sure,
since it has been already achieved in the victory of the Lamb.

The exotic style of apocalypse reaches it height in these chapters,
and in no small measure this is due to the sources on which the
prophet has drawn. It would appear that in chapter 12 he has
utilized traditions known all over the world of his day. In chapter
13 his figures, though originating from this background, have
been stamped by Old Testament associations, while in chapter 14
he has kept more to models familiar to contemporary apocalyptic

writers. Throughout the whole section John has rigorously subordinated the material to his purpose of bearing testimony to Christ, with the result that it is one of the most powerful pieces of his composition.

Chapter 12 has received special attention from scholars of antiquity.[1] Whereas attempts earlier made to demonstrate its derivation from one particular ancient religion are now regarded as implausible, it is widely agreed that the story told in chapter 12 is an adaptation of an ancient myth, known throughout the world of John's day. His use of it is an astonishing example of communicating the Christian faith through an internationally known symbol, comparable in a fashion with the Evangelist's exposition of the incarnate ministry of the Lord in terms of the Logos, also an internationally known symbol in his day.

The closest parallel to the narrative of our passage occurs in the Greek myth of the birth of Apollo from the goddess Leto. The great dragon Python, son of Earth, learned that he would be killed by the (as yet unborn) son of Leto, whereupon he pursued Leto to do away with her. She was carried off to Poseidon, who placed her on the island Ortygia and sank the island beneath the sea. After vain search Python went away to Parnassus, and Leto's island was brought up from the depths. When the infant Apollo was born he immediately attained to full strength, and four days later he went to Parnassus and killed the dragon. A variant form of the myth represents the dragon as raising the waters into such an uproar that Leto could not bear her child, until the earth came to her aid and raised up the island of Delos.

The middle east provides more primitive forms of the story. The Ugaritic Baal cycle for example tells of the battle of Baal, the storm god, with Yam, the prince of the sea. Mot, the god of death, declares to Baal:

> When thou smotest Leviathan, the slippery serpent,
> and madest an end of the wriggling serpent,
> the tyrant with seven heads,
> the heavens wilted and dropped slack as the belt
> of thy robe . . .

[1] A. Dieterich's *Abraxas*, 1891, and H. Gunkel's *Schöpfung und Chaos*, 1894, were epoch-making works in this field. A compendious review of the interpretation of this chapter in Christian history is provided in the work of P. Prigent, *Apocalypse 12, Histoire de l'exégèse*, Tübigen, 1959.

After his defeat of the sea god Baal proclaims his kingship and is given by El the right to build a palace and so exercise his rule. In the Akkadian creation epic Tiamat, the seven headed monster of the deep, threatens war against the gods of heaven; Marduk, the young god of light and also a storm god, slew the dragon and cut her asunder. Marduk's mother Damkina was represented in a manner similar to that of the woman of Revelation 12, and in the war with the gods Tiamat threw down a third of the stars. The Zend religion of Persia also offers parallels to our narrative. Here the brilliant Fire, son of Ahura, fights the evil dragon Azhi Dahaka, the representative of Angra Mainyu, the enemy of Ahura. The prize of the contest is the recovery of the 'great kingly glory', which had fallen into the sea. The counterpart in Revelation 12 to the 'kingly glory' is thought to be the woman crowned with twelve stars, since she represents the theocracy. Her twelve stars correspond to the twelve constellations created by Ahura, while the seven diadems of the dragon appear to reflect the seven planets created by the evil Angra Mainyu. In the Iranian literature also the dragon throws to earth a third of the stars.

Egyptian mythology offers closer parallels to Revelation 12 than either the Babylonian or Persian traditions. Here it is the goddess Hathor (= Isis), wife of Osiris, who gives birth to Horus the sun god. Hathor herself is portrayed with the sun on her head. The dragon Typhon was pictured as red in colour and was also represented as a serpent or crocodile. He slays Osiris and then pursues Hathor, who is about to give birth. In a miraculous manner she bears her child and escapes on a papyrus boat to the island Chemnis. Horus eventually overcomes the dragon, who is imprisoned and subsequently destroyed through fire (cf. Rev. 20:1f., 10). As in the Greek myth, however, the woman escapes to an island, not to the desert, and the child is not taken up to heaven.

The materials of the story reflect these ancient myths, and there is evidence to show that they were adapted in various ways so as to buttress the claims of the Roman emperors to religious adulation. A Jew with a knowledge of Old Testament prophecy would not have found it difficult to link this world wide tradition, embodying as it does the universal desire for salvation, with the messianic prophecies. For the portrayal of the nation, particularly under the figure of Zion, as a woman whose offspring were the individual members of the chosen people was frequent in the prophets. Indeed the language of verse 5 is very close to that of Isaiah 66:7, wherein Mother Zion is described as bringing forth sons for the age of salvation. It has been pointed out[1] that Isaiah 26:16–27:1 forms an impressive parallel to the central thought of Revelation 12, for there we have a representation of the nation as a woman in labour, an exultation in prospect of resurrection, an intimation of the unveiling of God's wrath on the inhabitants of the earth, and a promise that the Lord 'will punish Leviathan the fleeing serpent ... and he will slay the dragon that is in the sea'. The parallel is the more striking in the Septuagint of Isaiah 26:14, where instead of reading 'we have brought forth wind', it has 'we brought forth thy beloved', so intimating that the birth pangs of the nation issued in the birth of the Messiah. There is an extraordinary parallel to this in one of the Qumran thanksgiving hymns (*Hymn E*), where the writer compares himself with a woman in labour. Dupont-Sommer renders it as follows:

> I was confused like the Woman about to bring forth
> at the time of her first child-bearing.
> For terrors and fearful pains have unfurled on its billows
> that She who is with child might bring into the world (her)
>   first-born.
> For the children have reached as far as the billows of Death,
> and She who is big with the Man of distress (?) is in her pains.
> For she shall give birth to a man-child in the billows of Death,
> and in the bonds of Sheol there shall spring from the crucible of
>   the Pregnant one
> a Marvellous Counsellor with his might;
> and he shall deliver every man from the billows
> because of Her who is big with him.[2]

There is no evidence to suggest that this psalm was in the mind of the writer of Revelation 12, but it does illustrate how the Old Testament imagery of Mother Zion bringing forth children for the messianic age became developed to include the idea of Mother Zion bringing forth the messianic Deliverer of God's suffering people. This will have enabled the connection between the Old Testament messianic hope and the pagan religious myth to be more easily made. The motive for the link-up could have been to

[1] Rissi, op. cit., pp. 36f.

[2] See Dupont-Sommer, *The Essene Writings from Qumran*, 1961, p. 208. The whole psalm should be read, with the very illuminating notes by Dupont-Sommer.

show that the hope of the world was to be realized in the Messiah, whom God was to send in fulfilment of the promises made through the Old Testament prophets.

The belief that a Jew first effected the transition from pagan myth to apocalyptic prophecy is strengthened by observing the role of Michael and his angels in verses 7ff. For Michael is the guardian angel of the people of God, and on their behalf he contests the angels of the Gentile nations (Dan. 10:13, 21, 12:1). In the *Testaments of the Twelve Patriarchs* Michael appears to be viewed as the intercessor for the righteous of all nations (*Test. Levi* 5:7). It is easy to see how he could be represented as the champion of the right and good against the powers of darkness, above all against Satan and his forces. To a Jew it would not be strange that the Messiah should be born to rule the nations with a rod of iron (v. 5 echoes Ps. 2:9), but that the conquest of evil prior to the kingdom should be achieved through angelic representatives of God, for broadly speaking the Old Testament Messiah does not bring the kingdom, but rules on God's behalf when it comes. In Revelation 12 the original myth is essentially set forth in verses 1–5, 13–17. It becomes substantially changed into a vehicle of prophetic message through the addition to verse 5, whereby the child is identified as the Old Testament Messiah, and the introduction of Michael and his angels in verses 7f. The dragon is thus overthrown by Michael, not by a heathen god, and the mother of the Messiah is interpreted as Zion, the people for whose deliverance the Messiah has been destined to come. It is conceivable that the story was intended to give consolation to Jews suffering persecution from the Romans. God protects his people from the onslaughts of the bestial empire, which is the tool of the Devil. Deliverance is to come through the champion of their race; and the Messiah, who may well be born and will shortly appear, will soon reign over them in the kingdom of God.

It was such an adaptation of the story which came to John's notice. It needed but little further modification on his part. The fundamental story was suitable for the Christian message. The Christ was born of the messianic people, and from his birth he was persecuted by the dragon, but God raised him to the heights, to his very throne (vv. 1–5). The Devil vents his wrath on the messianic people, but God cares for them during the time of tribulation (v. 6). The conquest of the dragon by Michael is allowed to remain in the text, for the angels represent the forces of God. But a decisive change takes place in the song of triumph, which celebrates the coming of the kingdom. The conquest of the Devil by 'our brethren' has been made possible 'by the blood of the Lamb and by the word of their testimony'. It is the redemptive death and resurrection of the Christ, confessed in the gospel (the 'testimony'), which has conquered the Devil. Accordingly the real cause of the casting out of the dragon from heaven down to earth is not Michael but Christ in his redemptive action. Verses 10-11 transform the story into a confession of the victory of the crucified and risen Lord.[1] By using this vehicle of expression John has at a stroke claimed the fulfilment of pagan hope and Old Testament promise in the Christ of the gospel. There is no other deliverer but Jesus. The Babylonians' Marduk, the Persians' son of Ormuzd, the Egyptians' Horus and the Greeks' Apollo are all mythical expressions of pagan piety and religious yearning, which Jesus alone can fulfil. The Jews need look no longer for the promised Messiah, for he has come and wrought his awaited work of deliverance. 'Jesus only, none beside, He's the Saviour'[2]

---

[1] The limits of John's work in the song of verses 10-12 are difficult to define. Charles, following on many predecessors, restricts John's hand to verse 11, which he considers to interrupt the flow of the context. That verse 11 comes from John there can be no doubt. If we are to judge from the flow of context, however, one could as well make out a case for verses 10-11 forming a unity, interrupting the sequence 7-9, 12, or equally regard verses 10-12 as an original whole, interrupting the sequence 7-9, 13ff. The narrative reads equally well on the omission of verse 11 alone, or verses 10-11, or verses 10-12. The sole reason adduced by Charles for verse 12 not being Johannine in origin is the plural form of 'heaven' in the sentence, for John uses elsewhere the singular form. It so happens that the clause 'rejoice you heavens' occurs in this precise wording in Isaiah 44:23, 49:23 (LXX), but admittedly it is significant that nowhere else in the Revelation does the plural 'heavens' occur. Verse 10 is perfectly possible on the lips of a Jew. It takes on a fuller meaning on the lips of a Christian. Lohmeyer believes that the close-knit rhythm of verses 10-12 forbids viewing it as anything but an original unity. Prigent on different grounds also affirms the unity of verses 10-12. The present writer feels the arguments are indecisive and so prefers to leave the matter open, apart from affirming the undoubtedly Christian origin of verse 11.

[2] William Carey, Jr, caught the mood of Revelation 12 in a hymn he wrote for Indian Christians, which contains among others the following stanzas:

> Who is he who'll rescue me from this great load of sinning?
> Jesus only, none beside, He's the Saviour,
> Jesus only, none beside.

is the message of Revelation 12. He is the fulfilment alike of pagan hope and Old Testament prophecy, but the affectations of messianic powers and divine status by the Roman emperors are lies of the Devil. The dragon's wrath may be great, but 'his time is short'. His raging against the followers of the Lamb will be the sign that deliverance is at hand. Accordingly faith, encouragement, and endurance are the keynotes of the message extracted by John from the ancient cartoon of redemption.

THE WOMAN, THE CHILD, AND THE DRAGON 12:1–17

1. Both **the woman clothed with the sun** and **the great red dragon** (v. 3) are characterized as a **great portent in heaven.** They were marvels in the sky, like 'images projected on a screen where all may see them' (Kiddle). If, as is likely, the woman was originally an astral figure, she should not be thought of as denoting a single constellation (such as Virgo), for her crown of twelve stars would have represented the twelve signs of the zodiac. So impressive a figure as this should be compared with the harlot of chapter 17. Both represent communities, the former possessing a heavenly calling, the latter being an agent of hell (the harlot is an alternative symbol of the beast on which she sits). It would not have been difficult for a Jew to see in the figure of the *woman clothed with the sun* a symbol for the people of God, in view of the Old Testament precedents relating to Zion and contemporary ideas about the heavenly Jerusalem. A vision in the *Testament of Naphtali* v. 1ff. relates that Levi laid hold of the sun, and Judah seized the moon, and they were lifted up with them. The one had the appearance of a sun and the other the brightness of the moon, 'and under their feet were twelve rays'. So the woman crowned with twelve constellations could have been viewed as Mother Zion, God's people viewed from the aspect of their heavenly life

Gods and goddesses throng us with promises,
But they all will guilty fall 'neath their load of sinning.
　Jesus only, none beside, He's the Saviour,
　Jesus only, none beside.

Clasp the feet of Jesus, for 'tis he who frees us,
He has laid on his own head all your load of sinning.
　Jesus only, none beside, He's the Saviour,
　Jesus only, none beside.

and calling, much as the churches in chapters 1–3 are symbolized as stars having an angelic existence through their calling 'in Jesus'.

2. That the woman is pictured **with child** and **she brought forth a male child** (v. 5) led many in the medieval Church to identify her with Mary the mother of Jesus, and this interpretation is still current in the Catholic tradition. Some Catholic exegetes endeavour to do justice to the Old Testament background of Zion as the mother of the faithful by suggesting that in this passage the woman has a double aspect. She is the messianic people of both covenants, but as represented by Mary, in whose person the transition is made from the synagogue to the Christian Church.[1] It is difficult to sustain this interpretation in view of the lack of support for such an estimate of Mary in the rest of the New Testament,[2] and not least because verse 17 represents the Church as the children of the woman. This use of the figure seems clearly to depend on the prophetic symbolism of Jerusalem (= Zion) as the mother of the people of God. In our passage she is viewed by the Christian prophet as including the people of the new covenant as well as of the old. The imagery of the nation as a woman giving birth to the Messiah already appears in Isaiah 26:18 LXX and more strikingly in the Qumran *Thanksgiving Hymn E* (see introduction to this chapter, p. 194).

3. The second **portent ... in heaven** is the seven-headed monster of the chaos waters, Tiamat, the enemy of the powers of heaven. This figure appears in a number of Old Testament contexts under various names. Sometimes it is linked or identified with Leviathan (Ps. 74:12), the dragon in the sea (Isa. 27:1), Behemoth (Job 40:15ff.), Rahab (Ps. 89:9f.), the serpent of the sea (Am. 9:3), and is even pictured as a crocodile (Ezek. 29:3ff.). Frequently the dragon serves as a cartoon of an oppressor nation, above all to represent Egypt as the monster subdued at the Exodus (e.g., Isa. 51:9f.). In Ezekiel 32:3ff. the figure is applied to the tyrant Pharaoh, whose doom is declared to be as sure as that of the watery Tiamat. The image conjures up the idea of evil on earth defiant against God, and at the same time suggests the

[1] See Feuillet, *L'Apocalypse*, p. 97.
[2] The idea that John 19:27 indicates that Jesus committed his *disciples* to the care of his mother, and so gave to Mary a unique place in his Church, is hardly to be considered as in the mind of the evangelist.

inevitability of judgment on the power so symbolized. In Daniel
it is employed to represent the evil political powers that tyrannize
the earth, and above all as a symbol of the last great antigod nation
and ruler that should oppress Israel (Dan. 7:1ff., and especially
v. 7). In the Revelation the dragon represents the Devil who
inspires the evil political powers of history, the empire which
embodies his nature (ch. 13), and the ruler of the empire (ch. 17).
In 17:9ff., **the seven heads and ten horns** are interpreted
in relation to the antichristian kingdom, but when applied to the
Devil the description is merely traditional. The **seven diadems**
will have been viewed by John as blasphemous claims to sovereignty, in imitation of the divine royalty of the Christ (cf. 19:12).

4. That the dragon **swept down a third of the stars of
heaven** may reflect in the original narrative an account of a war
between Satan and the angels of heaven, in which many angels
were thrown down (cf. Dan. 8:10, which independently echoes
the same tradition). Verse 7 could further imply that the myth
went on to relate how the dragon attempted to storm heaven for
a second time, in order to overcome the child of the woman.
However that may be, John has a more limited interest in mind.
For him it would suffice to see in the statement of verse 4a a
pictorial allusion to the dragon's terrible power. **The dragon
stood before the woman** who was about to give birth to her
child, but he is foiled of his purpose to devour it through the
child's being snatched to heaven immediately on birth. The import
of the original story is clear. But how did John understand it?
Not a few expositors maintain that since it was impossible for a
Christian to represent Jesus as exalted to heaven as soon as he
was born, the 'birth' must be interpreted as the death and resurrection of Jesus. This interpretation is held to be confirmed by the
citation of Psalm 2:9 in verse 5, for in the psalm the statement
occurs in a context relating to the enthronement of the king-
Messiah, whose 'birth' or adoption by God takes place when he
becomes king (Ps. 2:7, 'You are my son, today I have begotten
you', follows on the divine declaration, 'I have set my king in
Zion, my holy hill'). Moreover, this interpretation harmonizes
with the early Christian confession of Christ as 'designated Son
of God in power ... by his resurrection from the dead' (Rom.
1:4). Despite the attractiveness of this view, it is doubtful if
John intended the narrative so to be understood. He knew quite

well that the story he was using originated from a background wherein there was not the remotest understanding of redemption through the death and resurrection of the incarnate redeemer. Nevertheless, at this juncture he is content to let the narrative of the deliverer's birth and rapture to heaven stand without modification, for his readers were all aware that Jesus, prior to his ascension, had a life and ministry among men, and experienced a death and resurrection. The chief point that John wishes to make here is the identification of the deliverer of whom the story speaks. It is no divinity of pagan myth but the Messiah of Old Testament prophecy (v. 5a), who has now been exalted as the Christ at God's right hand. The birth and the ascension of the Redeemer are viewed as representing the entire Christ-event, as we term it, and in the totality of that event the turn of the ages took place. John will make clear in the song that later celebrates its happening (vv. 10f.) that the event includes the death of Christ as its cardinal feature. At this point, however, it is sufficient for it to be recognized that the conqueror of the ancient foe is seated at God's right hand.[1]

5, 6. Consequent on the snatching of her child to heaven **the woman fled into the wilderness, where she has a place prepared by God.** Verse 6 anticipates the longer description of verses 13–17, wherein the theme briefly alluded to here is amplified. The parallel is apparent between the people of the new covenant being sheltered and sustained by God in the wilderness, during the last days of the age that precedes the kingdom, and the people of the old covenant marching through the wilderness to the promised land under the providential care of God. The typology is also certainly in mind in verses 13ff. The significance of the picture in verse 6 is fundamentally the same as that in 7:1–8 and 11:1f. During the period of tribulation (the three and a half years of Dan. 9:27) the Lord's people will experience his protecting care. That this assurance has to be balanced with the implications of verse 11 concerning the Church's destiny to suffer is consonant with the juxtaposition of 7:1–8 with 7:13ff. and 11:1f. with 11:3–13. It should further be observed that the

---

[1] It should be observed that the song of 1 Timothy 3:16 passes straight from the birth of Christ ('He was manifested in the flesh') to his ressurrection ('vindicated in the Spirit'). The stanza contains no mention of the life and death of Christ.

conjunction of these passages makes it clear that the three and a half years of tribulation are not to be expanded so as to make them coincide with the whole period of Christian history.[1] Such an interpretation can undoubtedly be extracted from verses 6 and 13ff. taken in isolation, but it does violence to John's intention. The three and a half years are the time of the Antichrist's raging (13:5), and so of the Church's exposure to his attempts to crush it out of existence (11:1f., 3–13). This does not characterize the period of the Church between the ascension and the parousia of Christ.

7, 8. War arose in heaven—precipitated through the advent of the Christ. But surprisingly the heavenly warriors are not led into battle by the Christ. It was **Michael and his angels fighting against the dragon.** This feature of the story can hardly have been instigated by a Christian writer, for whom there is but one mediator between God and man (1 Tim. 2:5). The Jews of John's time however held just such an estimate of Michael. In the *Testament of Dan* 6:2 he is actually described as 'a mediator between God and man', and the writer adds, 'and for the peace of Israel he shall stand up against the kingdom of the enemy'. Whereas in Daniel Michael is viewed as the protagonist of Israel against the angelic leaders of tyrannical Gentile nations which oppress Israel (Dan. 10:13ff., 12:1), in later writings his function is extended to championing the cause of the righteous generally (*Test. Levi* 5:7), hence his task is to resist not the representatives of other nations but the foe of mankind, the Devil himself. So here he resists the onslaughts of the dragon and his angels and throws them out of heaven. Not till then can the messianic rule commence. This is characteristic of Jewish theology generally, wherein the Messiah has a limited function, and his kingdom is of limited duration (see on 20:4ff.).

9. The great dragon is given his full titles—not in his honour, but as an expression of the prophet's exultation that at last the ancient foe has been overthrown. He is **that ancient serpent,** doubtless in a reminiscence of Genesis 3, where (certainly originally) the serpent is but a guise for the Devil, even as the dragon is in this chapter. He is **called the Devil and Satan.** The former translates the latter (*Satan* is Hebrew for accuser, *Devil* is Greek for slanderer, accuser). It is likely that in due time

[1] Rissi takes the contrary view; op. cit., pp. 39f.

the name *Devil* came to be established in its own right, so that
John set it alongside the name *Satan*. The significance of the names
is illustrated in Job 1:6f., Zechariah 3:1ff. **The deceiver of
the whole world** appears to generalize the narrative of Genesis
3 and apply it to the race (cf. Wis. 2:24: 'It was the devil's spite
that brought death into the world, and the experience of it is
reserved for those who take his side'). That Satan **was thrown
down to the earth** is an unusual picture in a Jewish writing. It
would have been more characteristic for him to have been put
out of harm's way completely (cf. ch. 20), but on the contrary
his ejection from heaven leads to an intensification of his activity
on earth. Two things are in mind here. First, that Satan has no
place in heaven represents an important victory won for man,
since Satan is no longer able to accuse man before God, which
suggests that God will no longer listen to accusations against his
people, for they are forgiven. Secondly, Satan's defeat in heaven
signifies that his power has been broken in the affairs of man in
history, so that even if he does intensify his efforts to control the
nations and destroy the work of God, the extent of his influence
is limited (he has for example no power over the Church), and his
days are numbered (vv. 13ff.).

10. A loud voice in heaven (cf. 10:4) declares that the age
of God's redemptive sovereignty has arrived. As uniformly in the
apocalyptic tradition, the overthrow of the Devil signifies the
coming of the kingdom of God (note the conjunction **for,** and
cf. Mk 3:27, Mt. 12:28, 2 Th. 2:8). In this context **salvation** =
victory, as in 7:10, 19:1, and **kingdom** = sovereignty (the
primary meaning of its Greek equivalent *basileia*). We therefore
have an instructive series of synonyms to denote the reign of God:
victory, power, sovereignty, authority. The sovereignty of God and
the authority of his Christ are strictly equivalent, although the
theology of both Old and New Testaments would suggest that the
former is exercised through the latter.

The *loud voice* tells of the downfall of **the accuser of our
brethren.** Who is represented by *our*? Are they members of
redeemed humanity in heaven? Charles strongly affirms that they
must be, since angels are never viewed in apocalyptic literature
as brothers to the people of God, and he assumes that the reference
is to the glorified martyrs in heaven (cf. 6:9–11). The interpretation may be correct, or more simply the Church triumphant may

be in the writer's mind. But it is surely not impossible that the *loud voice in heaven* may come from a member of the angelic orders (cf. 6:1ff., 10:1ff., 18:20, 19:5), for the kinship between angels and the people of God is presumed in 22:9. Both are creatures called to responsive obedience to the Creator and appointed to serve his redemptive purpose.

11. They have conquered him by the blood of the Lamb and by the word of their testimony. This central utterance of the song is the most significant statement in the chapter. It provides the real reason for the overthrow of Satan and the coming of the kingdom of God, as narrated in verse 9, and celebrated in verse 10, and makes clear why there is no possibility of Satan lodging an accusation against the people of God. *The blood of the Lamb* has prevailed. That is a shorthand expression for the redemptive sacrifice of the Lamb of God in his death for the world. He has died as the representative of mankind, and has been vindicated by the resurrection to God's throne. Thereby the new age of divine victory and power over evil, the sovereignty of God, and the authority of the Christ has been initiated. Now we see that the overthrow of Satan has actually taken place not through Michael, but through the power of the sacrifice of Christ and his resurrection to universal sovereignty. Michael and his angels are allowed to remain in the narrative for a similar reason as the dragon's sweeping with his tail a third of the stars of heaven from the sky is retained. It forms a part of the symbolism of a narrative, the real purpose of which is to expound the sole saving might of the Redeemer Son of God. The best commentary on this passage is provided by the remarkably similar John 12:31f.: 'Now is the judgment of this world, now shall the ruler of this world be cast out; and I, when I am lifted up from the earth, will draw all men to myself.' The death of Christ on the cross entails his lifting up to the throne of God. This brings about the judgment of the world, the dethronement of the Devil, and the beginning of the new age of life with Christ in the kingdom.

The redeemed have conquered by the blood of the Lamb **and by the word of their testimony;** i.e., through their receiving the 'word' testified to them and confessing it by faith. By this means the testimony passed on to them becomes the testimony made by them. Essentially the testimony is that which Paul described as 'the word of the cross' (1 C. 1:18), and which becomes of power when received in faith (Rom. 3:25, 10:17). Confessors of Christ participate in the conquest of the Lamb over the Devil, sin, and death, as they own him as Redeemer and confess him as Lord. Moreover, those of whom the hymn sings **loved not their lives even unto death.** This is not to be interpreted as though they assisted in the overthrow of Satan by their martyrdom. Rather it indicates that since their love for Christ was greater than their love of their own lives, they continued in faith and obedience towards him in whose conquest they shared through unity with him. As Caird observes, this is fundamentally the same doctrine as that which Paul expressed by his teaching on Christ as the last Adam, the inclusive representative of men in his redemptive action on their behalf. Whether or not men are called to lay down their lives as martyrs for Christ, they who maintain the word of their testimony and love not their lives even unto death, share in the power of Christ's redemption. He has achieved it; they enter into it. The song therefore transforms the episode of this multiform narrative into a parallel to the enthronement scene of chapter 5:6-13. It invites comparison with the primitive hymns of Philippians 2:6-11 and Colossians 1:15-20, and the theology of 1 Corinthians 2:6-8 and Colossians 2:15. Surprisingly our passage expresses a clearer theology of atonement than any of these just cited.

12. The inhabitants of **heaven** are called on to **rejoice** by reason of the conquest of the Lamb and his followers over the dragon, but **woe** is pronounced over the **earth and sea, for the devil has come down to you in great wrath, because he knows that his time is short!** The time is forty-two months, to be precise (13:5). Its brevity is determined by the final intervention of him through whom the dragon was thrown down to the earth. In comparison with the age which will then be initiated, marked by a reign which will endure 'for ever and ever' (11:15), the time of the dragon's wrath in truth is *short*. The manner in which his wrath is exercised during the three and a half years is the subject of chapters 13 and 17.

13, 14. The narrative now takes up the story broken off at verse 6 concerning the mother of the wonder-child. The child has escaped to heaven, so the dragon pursues the woman who has given him birth. **But the woman was given the two wings of the great eagle.** The language used suggests that the great

eagle must have been a specific creature, and that in the culture
from which the original story came the allusion was self-evident.
There is an obscure statement in the *Assumption of Moses* 10:8,
which may relate to an eagle that bears Israel on high to safety
in the day of the Lord.[1] Lohmeyer thinks that that passage and
the one we are considering are both related to the tradition in the
Mandaean *Book of John*, according to which the eagle is a symbol
of the Redeemer. If this is so we have to confess that our sources
do not enable us to trace the varied stages of the tradition. But so
far as John is concerned we recall that the second exodus-motif,
glimpsed in verse 6, is present in this passage. If it be in mind at
this point we should surely recall Exodus 19:4: 'You have seen
what I did to the Egyptians, and how I bore you on eagles' wings
and brought you to myself.' The Lord who executed his judgments
on Pharaoh and delivered his people from his power will again
rescue them from their great opponent in the final distress of
history (with 14*b* cf. 11:2-3, 12:6, 13:5, Dan. 7:25, 12:7); and
as he provided Israel of old with manna to eat and water to drink
in the desert wanderings, so he will nourish them in the wilderness
in the last days. The typology serves to remind the people of the
new covenant that, like the people of the old covenant on their
journey from Egypt to the promised land, they are pilgrims, having
no settled home in this world, and that they are being prepared for
life in the inheritance of the kingdom.

**15-17. The serpent poured water like a river out of his
mouth.** We recall that the original narrative depicted the sea
monster's pursuit after the mother of the infant redeemer. **But
the earth came to the help of the woman,** presumably
because in the ancient story the earth feels its kinship to the God of
heaven and delights to serve him— an interesting counterpart to
the biblical imagery expressed in Judges 5:20, 'From heaven
fought the stars, from their courses they fought against Sisera.'
For John, however, with the exodus-typology in mind, the story

---

[1] Charles renders the verse:

> Then thou, O Israel, shalt be happy,
> And thou shalt mount upon the necks and wings of the eagle,
> and they shall be ended.

Clemen (in Kautsch, *Die Pseudepigraphen des A.T.*) renders the last line:
> 'And the days of the eagle will be fulfilled.'

Charles would emend the text and relate the statement to judgment on Rome.

could not but be reminiscent of the Israelites being confronted by the waters of the Red Sea, which were dried up to enable them to pass through. God the almighty creator has resources in his creation to meet every crisis brought upon his people through the evil powers, and this they will experience in the last trials. Such is the ground of the Church's confidence as she faces the prospect of the dragon's anger. As surely as the dragon was unable to destroy the Christ of God, even when he seemed to have him in his power (v. 4), so he will be unable to destroy the Church of Christ, despite the apparent helplessness of her children. For **those who keep the commandments of God and bear testimony to Jesus** remain under the protection of the God in whom they trust, and by the blood of Jesus and by the word of their testimony they will conquer as he did (v. 11).

THE ANTICHRIST AND THE FALSE PROPHET 13:1-18

The purpose of this chapter is clear. Satan having been foiled in his attempt to destroy the Church concentrates his efforts on an endeavour to annihilate the Church of Christ, and to this end he calls to his aid two helpers. The first rises from the sea. It is a beast like himself, a monster from the evil abyss. The initial description of this creature identifies it as the culminating empire of Daniel's vision of the end (Dan. 7), but it speedily becomes evident that John has in view the empire as embodied in its ruler. This is the Antichrist, who wins the allegiance of men for the Devil, blasphemes God, makes war on the Church, and claims the worship of mankind (vv. 1-8). A second beast joins in the fray. This arises from the land, rather than the sea, and works as an accomplice of the Antichrist. It has the task of persuading the world to worship the Antichrist and of putting to death those who refuse to do so, and therefore is an instrument of propaganda and of slaughter. John's readers will have recognized it instantly as the priestly agency for promoting the emperor cult.

Unlike chapters 11 and 12 there is no convincing evidence that this chapter had an earlier literary history, although a number of attempts have been made to analyse earlier sources on which it was allegedly based (see Charles, pp. 334-44, who considers that vv. 1-10 and 11-18 were formed from the basis of two earlier Jewish apocalyptic oracles). Certainly traditional symbolism is laid under contribution in this narrative. The beast with seven heads and ten horns is a duplicate of the dragon of chapter 12, and so a variant figure of the chaos monster. John wishes it to be understood that the antichristian empire and emperor are embodiments of the satanic spirit which has animated earlier antigod empires and rulers in history. The beast from the land, representing the priesthood of the imperial cult, comes from the same traditional background. For this, however, John has borrowed the figure of Behemoth rather than Leviathan, but the two are one in the evil which they promote (see note on v. 11). Nevertheless no Jew who had not given his allegiance to Jesus Christ as Lord could have penned chapter 13. It is unique in its presentation of the antichristian movement of the last times in a kind of continuing dialogue of opposition to the Christian teaching on God and his redemptive work in and through Christ. The exposition of the chapter will take note of this motif, but it will be well to point the theme before we embark on it. First, it is to be noted that Satan, the Antichrist and the false prophet form a kind of trinity of evil, demanding the religious allegiance of mankind (the dragon, the beast, and the false prophet are brought together in a single sentence in 16:13). If Satan seeks to be recognized as God, the Antichrist is presented as the Christ of Satan. He has ten diadems (13:1), as the Christ has many diadems (19:12). He has a blasphemous name (13:1), over against the worthy name of the Christ (e.g., 19:11, 12, 16). He causes men to worship Satan (13:4), while the Christ brings men to worship and serve God (1:6, etc.). He has had a wound to death, but lives (13:3, 12, 14) in a monstrous imitation of the Christ who died and rose from death. He has the power and throne and authority of the Devil (13:2), as the Christ shares the power and authority and throne of God (12:5 and 10). The second beast, called by John the false prophet (16:13), is described in terms which are reminiscent of Christ. It has horns like a lamb (cf. 5:6), though it talks like a dragon (v. 11). It is its speech however which especially characterizes its activity, and in this respect it performs the kind of prophetic activity in relation to the Antichrist that the Holy Spirit does in relation to Christ. It is 'the instrument of the revelation of the satanic authority, as the Holy Spirit is the mediator of God's revelation'.[1] The false prophet, in prevailing upon the in-

[1] Rissi, op. cit., p. 66. His exposition of this whole theme (pp. 62-72) is very illuminating and has clarified the issues for the present writer.

habitants of the earth to worship the Antichrist, fashions them into a kind of church of Antichrist. Accordingly it demands that all should be marked on the right hand or the forehead with a mark which conveys the name or representation of the Antichrist (13:16ff.). This is clearly intended as a parody of the seal of God on the forehead of his servants (7:3). As the seal of God marks off its recipients as his people, reserved for his saving sovereignty, so the mark of the beast divides off those who receive it as the servants of the Antichrist, the community of Satan, with corresponding consequences for their destiny. There can be no doubt that this parallelism is deliberate. It is an example of John's taking hold of the prophetic and apocalyptic traditions of the Old Testament and of his contemporaries and reshaping them in the light of the history of his times and the revelation and redemption wrought by God in Christ.

The last short sentence of chapter 12 should be observed. It will be noted that its reading differs from that of the *AV*. **He** (not I) **stood on the sand of the sea.** The textual evidence is strongly in favour of the *RSV* reading. The dragon, seeking to wage war on the offspring of the woman, i.e., Christian believers, stood beside the sea in order to call from it an ally in the battle.

1, 2. The **beast rising out of the sea** is a duplicate of the dragon, sharing his nature. His origin and shape declare him to be a further manifestation of the principle of evil which has been active against God and man through the ages. *The sea* stands for the abyss, the abode of evil. The seven-headed beast reproduces the form of Tiamat, the primeval monster of ancient mythology. Daniel had already used this figure to characterize the empires of earlier centuries. Despite the animal appearances of the beasts of Daniel 7 (lion, bear, leopard, and nameless creature), they all issue from the sea, and so all share the same evil nature. John has employed Daniel's descriptions of the four beasts to portray his single beast, but he combines into one the features of all four, although curiously he mentions the features in reverse order. The fourth beast, indescribable and most terrible of all, possessed **ten horns.** This beast represented the Greek Seleucid kingdom which succeeded Alexander's empire. The third beast was like a **leopard** and represented the Persian empire. The second was like a **bear** and stood for Media. The first was like a **lion** and symbolized Babylon. The heads of the four beasts totalled seven, since

the third one had four heads. This however was probably a
happy coincidence. The chaos monster was depicted as a seven-
headed beast, and that was of major significance to John. That
its mouth was like a lion's mouth was said in order to enable
the first beast to be represented. We are not to ask which head
had the mouth, any more than we are to question how the ten
horns were distributed among the seven heads. It is the pictorial
ideas that are of account, not the visual image. The ten horns of
Daniel's fourth beast stood for ten kings in the Seleucid line which
preceded the antigod-emperor, Antiochus Epiphanes (Dan. 7:24).
John later identifies the ten horns of his beast with ten kings contemporary with the Antichrist (see 17:12), though at this point
it is not necessary for the identification to be in mind. For him
the beast represented the empire of Rome, and the seven heads
were its emperors. The **blasphemous name** on each head alludes
to the titles which were applied to the emperors increasingly
through the first century AD. These included God and Son of God,
and culminated in the desire of Domitian to be addressed as
Dominus et Deus, 'Lord and God'. The beast stands primarily for
the empire, yet the transition is speedily made to the empire as
represented in its ruler. This appears to be so in the last clause of
verse 3, but it is possible that this double meaning may be present
at the outset, for the **ten horns** have **ten diadems,** whereas this
is not so in Daniel, and in 17:12 the horns stand for comparatively
unimportant kings. Here alone are the diadems mentioned, and it
is likely that they are envisaged as pertaining to the individual
Antichrist, who claims a sovereignty comparable with that of the
Christ of God (cf. the many diadems of 19:12). It is the first
instance of the satanic imitation of the true God, his 'Christ', his
rule and his redemption, which dominates the portrayal of evil
powers in this chapter. A further example of this same principle
of imitation of the true by the false occurs almost at once. It is
said **the dragon gave his power and his throne and great
authority** to the beast. But the dragon has been defeated and
thrown out of heaven. Has he any authority to bestow on earth?
Only in so far as the world is content to recognize his authority.
Satan is a usurper among men. If he is called 'the god of this
world' (2 C. 4:4) or 'the prince of this world' (Jn 12:31), it is
because men are blind enough to acknowledge him as such. The
claim in the temptation narrative that to him has been delivered

all the authority and glory of the kingdoms of the world (Mt. 4:8f., Lk. 4:6) is made by the father of lies (Jn 8:44). Significantly the Christ of God spurned the offer of authority over this world at the hands of Satan, and received it instead at the hands of God, whose throne he shares (3:21). The 'Christ' of the Devil accepts the power and authority that the Devil can give and so assumes his throne in the world.

3. The most extraordinary element in the satanic imitation of the Devil's 'Christ' is implied in the immediately following sentence. Here the *RSV* is insufficiently clear. **One of its heads seemed to have a mortal wound** literally should read '(I saw) one of its heads as (though) it had been slaughtered to death'. The term here rendered 'slaughtered' is used elsewhere in the Revelation, meaning plainly to slay or to murder (so 6:4, 9; 18:24). Above all the precise phrase 'as (though) it had been slaughtered', which occurs here, is used in 5:6 of the slaughtered Lamb of God who rose from the dead. This appears to be the thought here. **Its mortal wound was healed** is interpreted in verse 14 as resurrection from death: 'the beast . . . was wounded by the sword and yet lived', where 'lived' means not 'continued to live in spite of the wound', but 'lived again after being smitten by the sword'. This is why the whole earth followed the beast with wonder. He had risen from the dead. The Christ of God has risen, but the world declared it a lie (Mt. 28:13ff.), or madness (Ac. 26:24). The 'Christ' of the Devil comes from death—and the world worships him!

One may ask what on earth John is talking about. He is speaking of a 'head' of the beast, i.e., one of its rulers, which had a mortal wound and was healed. There is one person only whom this description can fit, and that is Nero. After his suicide in AD 68 (presuming that Suetonius (*Nero* 49) is right in his report that Nero so died, and that he was not murdered), Rome went jubilant at the news. But the joy was replaced by unease and fear in the minds of many that the report was false. Impostors made capital out of this ignorance. Edicts were issued in his name, as though he were still alive, and no less than three imposters known to us claimed to be Nero. One in AD 69 led a rebellion against Rome, another was welcomed by the Parthians in AD 80, and a third in AD 88 nearly persuaded the Parthians to march against Rome. Finally the belief that he was alive and would return to take vengeance on Rome was replaced by the belief that he had died, but would return from the dead to lead armies against Rome. This idea is alluded to several times in the *Sibylline Oracles*, most illuminatingly in book III, lines 28ff., written two generations after Nero's death:

> Then he shall be sovereign who has the letter of fifty (= *N* for Nero), a direful serpent causing grievous war, who shall one day put forth his hands on his own family and slay them, and shall throw all into confusion, as athlete, charioteer, murderer, and doer of a thousand extravagant acts. He shall pierce, too, the hill between two seas (= the Isthmus of Corinth), and besprinkle it with blood; yea, even when he disappears, he shall be malignant. Then he shall return, making himself equal to God; but God shall convince him that he is not.

Charles reminds us that so completely did the idea prevail that Nero would return as the Antichrist that in Armenian the word Nero became and remains the equivalent for the Antichrist. When John wrote the Revelation these ideas were vividly present among his contemporaries. The precise significance which they had for him will be considered later, when we contemplate his teaching on the antichristian empire, city, and ruler (pp. 248ff.). At this juncture it may suffice to observe the symbolic nature of the context and the strong element of typology in the presentation of the Antichrist-figure. Provisionally we may adopt Caird's statement of the matter, 'Nero will indeed return, but reincarnated in a new persecuting emperor, an eighth who is one of the seven (17:11).'

4. As **men** (= 'all who dwell on earth', vv. 8, 12, 14) **worshipped the dragon . . . and the beast,** ascribing to them that which rightly belongs to God and his Christ, so they imitate the psalms of praise in which the people of God express their adoration. With **'Who is like the beast . . .?'** cf. Exodus 15:11f., Psalm 89:6ff., Isaiah 40:25f., Micah 7:18f. It was precisely Rome's demand that men render to Caesar and to the state that which belongs to God alone which compelled the early Church to resist Rome to the death. John believed that in making this demand the state became demonic, and he vigorously represented this by drawing on the ancient mythological pictures to caricature the role that the state and its rulers were playing. For this he has been severely criticized, and his position has been constantly contrasted with Paul's teaching on the state in Romans 13:1ff.

Nevertheless it is conceivable that John would have assented to Paul's doctrine of the state, given the simple recognition that a minister of God can, like Judas, apostatize and become the instrument of the Devil. Paul's proposition that there is no authority except from God is at one with the apocalyptic tradition that 'the Most High rules the kingdom of men, and gives it to whom he will' (Dan. 4:25). Daniel teaches that a ruler who does not recognize this axiom of religion becomes a beast, and he illustrates the thesis by the story of a king who sank to bestiality through his pride, but recovered his humanity when he acknowledged the supremacy of the King of heaven (see the whole story in Dan. 4). This same writer gave John the precedent of depicting world powers as embodiments of the spirit of the chaos-monster. John both followed the precedent and anticipated that men would learn the lesson taught to Nebuchadrezzar, for he looked for the repentance and conversion of nations and their rulers (15:4, 21:24). But he does not hesitate to point out the nature of their actions while they deny it. His experience of Rome's claim to dominate the souls of men leads him to declare that such a totalitarianism comes not from the God who bestows authority on men but the Devil, who usurps it to destroy men.[1]

5-7. The language of the opening clause echoes descriptions in Daniel of the **haughty and blasphemous words** (lit. 'great things and blasphemies') uttered by the antigod emperor (see Dan. 7:8, 20, 25; 11:36). But the first word in John's Greek text does not occur in Daniel, and it sets the tone for the paragraph beginning at verses: '(there) **was given** to him **a mouth**'. The same verb is translated in the next clause **it was allowed.** The emphasis is more consistently brought out in the *NEB*, thus: 'The

[1] On this issue, cf. Cullmann: 'If the Roman State had had a loyalty-test in any other form than that emperor worship which was blasphemous for the Christians, the Christians would have been able to meet it in good conscience, and much bloodshed would have been avoided. So long as the State demanded a loyalty-test in the form of submission to emperor worship, there could be no peace between Christianity and the State, however loyal the Christians might be as citizens and however humane individual emperors like Trajan, Hadrian, Antoninus, or Marcus Aurelius. At this point the Roman State remained continuously, up to the time of Constantine, a satanic power. The author of the Johannine Apocalypse saw with astonishing acumen that the satanic element in the Roman Empire lay in this deification. For this reason in his stirring description he concentrates almost exclusively on this aspect.' (*The State in the New Testament*, pp. 79f.)

beast was allowed to mouth bombast and blasphemy, and was
given the right to reign . . . It was also allowed to wage war on
God's people . . . and was granted authority over every tribe and
people . . .' Who *allowed* the beast to mouth bombast and blasphemy, to reign for forty-two months, to wage war on God's
people and conquer them, and to have authority over every tribe
and people? It is insufficient to answer, 'The dragon, for he gave
his authority to the beast' (v. 4). The dragon did not limit the
reign of his agent to forty-two months. That was due to the decree
of the Lord God Almighty. No, we must recognize unequivocally
that it is God who gives the beast his blasphemous mouth, who
accords him the right to reign over earth in apparent defiance
of his will, who permits him to crush his people and take control
of the nations. And why does he permit the Antichrist to do such
things? To bring to pass his own purpose of good and of grace, of
judgment, and of glory. The problems of the existence of evil, of
human freedom, and of divine love and power, come to an extraordinary meeting in the raging of the Antichrist. In that time God
suffers, his saints suffer, evil is rampant, and the world goes mad.
But in it all one has to say with Luther that even when the Devil
works his worst he remains *God's* Devil.[1] At no time in history
does this appear with such clarity as in the hour when the Son of
God died on the cross at the hands of sinful man. There is something fitting in the thought that the other hour in which the nature
of history is laid bare is the season when the Church of God suffers
its passion.

8. **All who dwell on earth will worship** the beast, i.e.,
**every one whose name has not been written . . . in the
book of life of the Lamb that was slain.** The *RSV* relates the
phrase **before the foundation of the world** to the writing in
(or rather omission from) the book of life. It may be safely said
that no group of translators would have come to such a decision
were it not for the statement in 17:8, for the phrase in question
immediately follows *the Lamb that was slain*, and normally one

[1] With this compare the startling words of Stauffer: 'However much the idea
of Satan has developed since the time of the Book of Job, the basic thought of
Job 1:6ff. remains true: Satan is an authorised minister of God' (*New Testament
Theology*, p. 67). Stauffer's point is that Satan cannot burst out of God's order,
but must remain co-ordinated in it, and despite his enmity remain God's servant till he has done his work and departed.

would not question the application of the phrase to that antecedent. Yet there is a clear parallel to the idea of the election of the Lamb of God to redemptive sacrifice in 1 Peter 1:19f., and it accords with the thought of apocalyptic writers concerning God's foreordaining his instruments of redemption. Apart from the teaching on the foreordination in heaven of the Son of Man in the *Similitudes of Enoch* (e.g., 1 *Enoch* 62) there is a striking saying in the *Assumption of Moses* 1:14: 'He designed and devised me, and He prepared me before the foundation of the world, that I should be the mediator of his covenant' (said in reference to Moses, the 'first redeemer'). It would seem most plausible, therefore, to retain in this passage the reference of the predestinating act of God to the slain Lamb. The sacrifice of the Lamb of God lay hidden in the heart of God from all eternity, and expresses the very nature of God.

9, 10 A solemn message is now to be delivered to the Christian reader. The writer, therefore, uses the formula with which he concluded each of the letters to the seven churches: **If any one has an ear, let him hear.**

The address to the reader in verse 10 combines and adapts two passages of Scripture, Jeremiah 15:2 and Matthew 26:52. The former is a burning message of judgment directed to Jerusalem. The people are to depart out of the sight of the Lord, and if they ask 'Where?' the answer is to be given:

> Those who are for pestilence, to pestilence,
> And those who are for the sword, to the sword;
> those who are for famine, to famine,
> and those who are for captivity, to captivity.

It is the last line which is cited by John, but the spirit of the saying is quite different from its use in Jeremiah. The Christian who faces banishment to a place of exile, as John himself has suffered, is not to suffer judgment for his sin, but on the contrary will by his obedience glorify God and vindicate the testimony of Jesus. As this prospect looms before him he is not to think of resort to force of arms. Peter did this in Gethsemane, as he tried to defend Jesus and himself from the aggressors, but was rebuked with the words, 'Put your sword back in its place; for all who take the sword will perish by the sword.' The truth of that saying was appallingly illustrated in the fate of the Jews in Jerusalem during the war with Rome, when the fanaticism of the Zealots brought destruction to

multitudes of their fellow countrymen. The Church of God is
called to take another path when it is faced by the Roman might.
When they tread the Via Dolorosa in the footsteps of their Lord,
they must walk along that way in the same spirit as he did.
Accordingly, **here is a call for the endurance and faith of
the saints.**[1]

11. The **beast which rose out of the earth** has a very different appearance from the beast which rose out of the sea. But
the nature of the two beasts is clearly akin. They both stand in the
service of the dragon. The origin of the second creature is the
same circle of mythology as that of the first.[2] This is plain in 1
Enoch 60:7ff., where we read of two monsters who were parted,
Leviathan to dwell in the abysses of the ocean and Behemoth, who
was cast 'unto the dry land of the wilderness'. 4 *Ezra* 6:49ff. gives
a like account of the two monsters, saying of the second, 'And thou
didst give Behemoth one of the parts which had been dried up
on the third day to dwell in, where are a thousand hills.' The writer
then adds enigmatically, 'and thou hast reserved them to be de-
voured by whom thou wilt and when'. This is explained in 2
Baruch 29:4, where it is said that these two monsters, who were
created on the fifth day of creation, 'shall have been kept until

---

[1] Verse 10 is susceptible of a quite different interpretation. The last clause
is virtually repeated in 14:12, where it follows the prospect of judgment falling
on the worshippers of the beast. It could be given a similar force in 13:10, and
in that case the captives are those who will fall to the judgment of God, and
the slayers themselves are doomed to slaughter. Such an interpretation suits
the context, but it does not seem to be so natural as the one advocated above.

In a different direction from this, some copyists have a variant reading in
the third line of verse 10: 'If any one is to be slain by the sword' (with the sword
must he be slain). This would form another couplet after the first two lines,
and apply to the Christian facing martyrdom. Charles strongly believed that
this was the correct reading. It undoubtedly makes excellent sense, but it is
less well supported by the textual authorities, and in the present state of our
textual knowledge should probably be viewed as secondary.

[2] M. H. Pope in the *Anchor Bible* commentary on Job, pp. 268ff., has a
discussion on the mythological figures in the Ugaritic texts which could have
formed the counterpart of the two creatures described in Job 40–1 as Behemoth
and Leviathan. In particular of the monsters supposedly slain by the goddess
Anat, Leviathan is mentioned and 'the ferocious bullock of El', which seems to
be related to the Behemoth of Job 40:15ff. It is possible that in Job 40–1 the
originally mythological figures of a water-monster and a land-monster have
become rationalized and their descriptions made to suit the crocodile and the
hippopotamus.

that time (viz., of the Messiah), and then they shall be for food for all that are left'. This is a parallel to the tradition that the manna will be restored for the people of God in the kingdom, as is mentioned in 2 *Baruch* 29:8. It is important to observe that both the figures of Leviathan and Behemoth are linked with primeval beginnings and the end of history. This is why it was easy for John to adapt them to political and religious figures of his time, which were allowing themselves to become satanic institutions and to play an antigod role in the end of the times. The description of the *beast out of the earth*, that **it had two horns like a lamb and it spoke like a dragon,** is a stroke of genius. Since the description of the beast from the sea adapts Daniel 7:1ff., it is possible that the fundamental features of the beast from the earth are reminiscent of the ram with two horns in Daniel 8:3ff., but there the likeness ends. Quite certainly the change of picture from a horned ram to a horned *lamb* is in imitation of the Lamb of God (5:6ff.). But whereas the Lamb of God is and speaks the Word of God (19:13, and chs. 2–3), the beast from the land is the 'Lamb' of Satan, and it is and speaks the word of Satan. It looks *like a lamb*, but its speech betrays its origin.

12. This beast **exercises all the authority of the first beast ... and makes the earth and its inhabitants worship the first beast.** This is its chief task, to persuade the earth to give religious veneration to the beast. There can be no doubt that the second beast is thereby identified with the promoters of the cult of the emperor. If it is identified, as most are content, with the priesthood of the emperor-cult, we should recognize nevertheless that this priesthood was set within a wider institutional life. Cullmann interprets the second beast more broadly as 'the religio-ideological propaganda authority of the totalitarian state'.[1] In provincial Asia its spear head was the so-called 'Commune of Asia', a council made up of representatives from the chief cities of the province and whose president was called Asiarch. Historically it was the enthusiasm of this Asiatic league for the cult of Rome and the emperor which popularized this particular form of idolatry in the empire. Augustus had no desire to pose as a god, and Tiberius severely checked the new cult. Their successors were less modest, especially the mad Caligula and Claudius who followed him. None, however, exploited the cult to such a degree

[1] Op. cit., p. 76.

as Domitian, who arrogated to himself the title *Dominus et Deus noster*, 'our Lord and God'.[1] John predicted that this process would come to its climax in the Antichrist. Observe that **the first beast, whose mortal wound was healed** now denotes the Antichrist as the embodiment of the antichristian empire, not the empire itself.

13-15. It works great signs. The expectation that the prophet of the Antichrist will work miracles is in harmony with the apocalyptic teaching of the New Testament and of Judaism. In Mark 13:22 it is said that both false Christs and false prophets will perform signs and portents. In 2 Thessalonians 2:9, *Sibylline Oracles* 3:63ff., *Ascension of Isaiah* 4:10, the Antichrist himself will do these works. John sets them to the account of the false prophet, since it 'exercises all the authority of the first beast' (v. 12). **Making fire come down from heaven to earth** recalls the descent of the fire on Elijah's sacrifice in his contest with the prophets of Baal (1 Kg. 18:38). What the prophets of Baal could not do, the false prophet will do. The making of an **image** to **speak** was wholly in accord with pagan expectation, and not a few reports of such happenings circulated in the ancient world.[2] Sorcery and trickery were part of the stock-in-trade of pagan priesthoods. John's description here may be taken as indicating the likelihood that such proceedings took place in the imperial cult even in his day. Certainly the priests of the emperor-cult set images of the emperor in temples dedicated to Rome and the Caesars throughout Asia Minor. Not only did these images serve to foster the worship of the emperor; they provided an effective means of revealing the opponents of the cult by their refusal to acknowledge the images. In the context of this chapter the

---

[1] Suetonius reports that the imperial edicts under Domitian began, 'The Lord our God commands'. Stauffer tells that Domitian had a predilection for cruel forms of execution, and he liked to preface his condemnation with the words, 'It has pleased the Lord our God in his grace . . .' (see Stauffer, *Christ and the Caesars*, pp. 158ff.).

[2] 'Statues were regarded as the natural means by which gods or demons could have intercourse with their worshippers, and were accredited with the power of working miracles, and of possessing supernatural energies. At Troas a statue of a certain Neryllinus was supposed to utter oracles and to heal the sick, and the statue of Alexander and Proteus at Parium to utter oracles' (Charles, who cites Theophilus *ad Autol.* i, 8 and Athenagorus *Leg.* 18 as sources).

activity of the false prophet is thus seen as a means by which the dragon prosecuted his war against the Church of Christ. The followers of the Christ are brought to light with a view to their destruction by the imperial judicial authorities.

16. This doubtless lies behind the imposition by the false prophet of the mark **on the right hand or the forehead.** The intention is not so much to impose sanctions on the trading activities of those who reject the worship of the Antichrist as to reveal their identity, and so to bring about their downfall.

The attempts to decipher **the mark** of the beast are legion. It is desirable to distinguish the *notion* of the mark from its *identification.* Clearly the idea is to provide a parallel with 'the seal of the living God' (7:2), stamped on the foreheads of God's servants (7:1–8; the connection is explicit in 14:1). The seal of God marks out people as belonging to him, and so for preservation for his kingdom. The mark of the beast similarly identifies men as his servants, and without this mark they cannot live. The idea seems to reflect the practice in ancient society of marking men, by branding or tattooing, as the property of others, whether of slave owners or of gods. This could be reflected as early as Isaiah 44:5, but the closest parallel to our passage is 3 *Maccabees* 2:28–30. There we read that Ptolomy IV Philopator demanded that Jews should offer pagan sacrifices as well as sacrifices to their own God. Those who opposed this were to be put to death. Those who merely refrained from it were to be reduced to the condition of serfs and branded with the sign of the ivy-leaf, the emblem of Dionysus (= Bacchus). Those who were willing to be initiated into the mysteries would have equal rights with the citizens of Alexandria. It is to be observed that this branding with the mark of the god was not necessarily a disgrace, for Ptolemy allowed himself to receive it. The mark indicated that the recipients were the 'slaves', i.e., obedient worshippers of the god. Precisely the same idea is reproduced by Paul in Galatians 5:17, where, however, the 'marks of Jesus', indicating that Paul was his 'slave', are scars due to physical sufferings for Christ's sake.

17, 18. Is the mark of the beast to be understood as visible or invisible? We cannot be sure. God's mark is invisible (cf. 7:1ff., 3:12), indicating a spiritual reality, and so this counterpart could represent a sinister mark of satanic ways as well as worship. The pagan parallels, as well as the trade requirement of verse 17,

would suggest that some outward sign of conformity is in view.[1]
In any case the chief point John wishes to make is that the mark
of the beast represents the climax of that satanic imitation of
Christ which is traced all through chapter 13.

What then is the precise meaning of the mark? In 13:17 it is
described as *the name of the beast or the number of his name*. Verse 18
puts this in another way by stating that this is a *human number*
(i.e., it represents a man's name; so *NEB*), and that the *number is*
666.[2] The identification of a *name* with a *number* is made possible
through the fact that in languages like Hebrew and Greek numbers were indicated by the letters of the alphabet (as though $a = 1$,
$b = 2$, $c = 3$, etc.). This led to the possibility of making play
(sometimes quite literally) with the numerical equivalents of
names, and even to the construction of puns on them. Deissmann
tells of a legend scribbled on a wall in Pompeii, 'I love her whose
name is 545.' He further cites Bücheler's discovery that Suetonius
(*Nero* 39) by this method interprets 'Nero' as 'matricide'.[3] The
writer of the *Sibylline Oracles* (5:12–42) refers to the Roman emperors in succession by mentioning the number of the first letter
in each name (e.g., 'There shall be a king first of all who shall
sum up twice ten with his initial letter', i.e., K for Kaisar =
Julius Caesar).

It is clear that many possibilities arise in trying to determine
which name is intended by 666, and it is no purpose of ours to
review all the conjectures that scholars through the ages have
offered. Of one thing we may be sure. John did not intend to
pose a riddle for his readers; the issue was far too serious for that.
They would have known the secret of the name. That suggests that the
number did not originate with John, but that he adopted it from
his predecessors in the apocalyptic tradition. This is why it had
become widely known. That points to the likelihood that the
relation between the number and the name arose among Jewish
people who used the Jewish language (whether Hebrew or
Aramaic). Now every commentator duly notes that the name Nero
Caesar rendered into Hebrew from Greek yields the number 666.

---

[1] Ramsay thought it represented an official certificate issued on compliance
with the demands of the imperial cult, *Letters to the Seven Churches*, pp. 110ff.
The interpretation certainly fits 13:17, but hardly 13:16.

[2] Some MSS give 616 instead of 666.

[3] *Light from the Ancient East*, pp. 275ff.

Strangely, if it is put into Hebrew from the Latin form it gives 616, the alternative reading in our text. It has, however, seemed to many an impossible identification for two reasons. First, it requires the name Caesar to be slightly shortened in Hebrew (or Aramaic); and secondly, it has seemed ludicrous to expect simple Asiatic Christians to know the Hebrew equivalents of Greek and Latin names. The objections nevertheless are insubstantial. The shorter Semitic form of Nero is attested both in the Talmud and from the Dead Sea Scrolls.[1] And if the characterization of the Antichrist as Nero occurred among Jews before John wrote his book, it would most naturally have taken place in their language and yet could have become known amongst Jewish and Gentile Christians, just as the Aramaic cry *Maranatha* became known among the churches in all countries in the first generation (1 C. 16:22). Naturally we cannot know who first identified Nero with the cipher 666. It could have been a Zealot prophet in Palestine in the lifetime of Nero, as the Jewish war was approaching;[2] or it could have been a Jewish-Christian prophet in the apocalyptic tradition. Nero had given cause to both Jews and Christians to be cast in the role of the Antichrist. The idea that he was assuming that role, or that the future Antichrist would be (another) Nero would have been comprehensible to either group.

But why did John use this symbol at all? Why not use more obvious identifications of the Antichrist? In part, of course, because this suited his general style. But also because of the suitability of the symbol. *It was significant in itself.* Here we may recall that *gematria* (related words and numbers) enabled word-plays or arithmetic puns to be made. It has long been realized that 666 is eminently suitable to characterize the Antichrist, since it implies a consistent falling short of the divine perfection suggested by 777. Now it was early realized among Christians that the name *Jesus* in Greek totals 888.[3] Manifestly the contrast between 666 and 888 strikingly conveys the difference between the Devil's 'Christ' and God's Christ. Whether this contrast was generally understood by John and his contemporaries, and whether it was recalled by the mere use of 666 alone, is beyond our knowledge. It certainly suits the eschatology of Christian apocalyptic,[4] and would

---

[1] See Charles, ad loc., and Rissi, op. cit., p. 76, n. 93.

[2] So Schlatter, ad loc.   [3] It is mentioned in *Sibylline Oracles* 1. 324ff.

[4] The notion of history as a world week was familiar to John. The history of

harmonize with the suggestion more than once hazarded that 666 was recognized as significant even before the equivalence of Nero's name with that number was perceived. If the contrast between 666 and 888 was present to John's mind, the use of 666 in 13:18 crowned in a superb way the theme of satanic imitation that runs throughout chapter 13. The Antichrist of Satan falls as far short of being the true deliverer of mankind as the Christ of God exceeds all the hopes of man for a redeemer.

VINDICATION AND JUDGMENT **14:1-20**

This chapter forms a climax to the visions of the two preceding chapters. Chapter 12 relates the victory of the Redeemer over the dragon, with the consequent persecution by the dragon of the messianic community. Chapter 13 described how the persecution is carried out by the conjoint agency of the beast from the sea and the lamb with a dragon's accent. In face of the threat of total annihilation of the Church, chapter 14 conveys the assurance of vindication for the followers of the Lamb of God and judgment upon the followers of the beast.

The *RSV* divides the chapter into eight paragraphs. The *NEB* by including verse 12 with verses 9-11 reduces them to seven, and this may accord with the author's intention. He then presents us with seven short oracles on the end of the age. These may be summarized as a vision of the outcome of the believers' faithfulness to Christ (1-5); a proclamation of the gospel to all the world during the period of tribulation (6-7); an announcement of Babylon's doom (8); a warning of the consequences of receiving the mark of the beast (9-12); a beatitude upon those who die in the faith of Christ (13); two visions of judgment at the coming of the Son of Man, one under the figure of the grain harvest (14-16) and the other pictured as a grape harvest (17-20).

1, 2. Every feature of the opening sentence of the first oracle stands in contrast to what is written in chapter 13. The persecuted Christians are no longer at the mercy of their enemies but stand triumphant **on Mount Zion,** the place of deliverance and divine glory (Jl 2:32; cf. Isa. 24:21ff., Mic. 4:6f.). They are in the

man = six days, followed by the rule of the Messiah as the sabbath of the world. The eighth day ushers in the age when time is no more and when God and the Lamb are all in all. See the commentary on chapter 20.

presence of **the Lamb** instead of being dragged before his caricature, the 'lamb' of the Devil. They bear on their foreheads the
name of the Lamb **and his Father's name** instead of the mark
(= the name) of the beast.

But where do they stand? On the hill of Jerusalem's temple, or
in heaven? Some, with 21:9ff. in mind, consider that the former
is in view. The saints have returned to earth in the millennium.
Others believe that the Church's impregnable position, at the
end of the times as in all ages, is portrayed, in contrast to the
picture of the Church in the wilderness in 12:13ff. Probably it is
right not to think of a location, though it is the triumph of the
saints in the kingdom of Christ rather than in this age which is
in view. The contrast in the picture of verse 1 is not between the
Church as strong in God though weak in the world, but between
the earthly Jerusalem which has become the symbol for the godless
world (11:8ff.) and the Jerusalem which descends from above,
wherein heaven and earth are brought into a unity (see notes on
21:16). It is not impossible that Psalm 2:6 was in John's mind
at this point. The heathen have raged in vain. God's king stands
on his holy hill victorious.

The 144,000 in this vision are surely to be identified with the
similar company in chapter 7. As there the 144,000 have the seal
of God on their foreheads (7:2), so these have *the name* of the Lamb
and his Father's name written on their foreheads. (For the dual
name of the redeemed in the kingdom, cf. 3:12; in 22:4 only the
Father's name is mentioned.) As in chapter 7 the whole people
of God are included under the image of 12 × 12,000, so here they
are said to be the 'redeemed from the earth' (v. 3), to be 'first
fruits for God and the Lamb' (v. 4). In this passage the symbolic
number, signifying completeness, is even more apposite than in
chapter 7. Despite the raging of the Antichrist, the whole company
of the redeemed will share with the Lamb in his triumph.

3, 4. The deliverance is marked by a song of thanksgiving (for
the **new song** see note on 5:9). Who are the singers and harpists?
The precedent of 5:9 suggests that they are angelic hosts, and in
that case **no one could learn that song** means none but the
redeemed could grasp it. The analogy of 15:2ff., however, favours
the 144,000 as the singers. If that be so, *no one could learn that song* =
none could join in the singing but the redeemed. The declaration
that the 144,000 **have not defiled themselves with women,**

for they are chaste has puzzled many. Charles insisted that the statement is an impossible one, taken literally or metaphorically, for granting that the term *chaste* (literally 'virgins') can be used of men as well as women, the first clause has to cover women as well as men, since it represents the whole church. But the statement cannot apply to women in any way. He therefore regarded the sentence (as far as 'mankind') as an interpolation, perhaps originally being a marginal comment by a man with a monkish prejudice towards marriage. Other writers (e.g., Bousset, Moffatt, Kiddle) take the statement at face value and attribute the prejudice to the prophet himself. In that case the 144,000 must be viewed as an elite group within the Church. To limit the application of the 144,000 in this way, however, is highly implausible (see notes on v. 1). The whole Church is in view. The language must therefore be interpreted symbolically, and this is not unduly difficult. The 144,000 are viewed as male because they are the *soldiers* of the Lamb (so Lohmeyer). Caird suggests on this basis that the Deuteronomic regulations for holy war are in mind, which demanded that soldiers going to war preserve ceremonial purity (Dt. 23:9f., cf. 1 Sam. 21:5, 2 Sam. 11:11). From this it is a short step to view the ceremonial purity of verse 4 as a symbol for abstention from fornication with the prostitute Babylon, which is idolatry (note the explicit reference to this seduction of Babylon in v. 8).

The soldiers of the Lord **follow the Lamb wherever he goes.** As on earth, so in the kingdom. The earliest disciples followed Jesus in Galilee and Judea, serving along with him (Mk. 1:17f.). They were called to follow him in wider fields after Easter (Jn 21:19-21). They and their successors continue in their following and service after his parousia. They have been redeemed to be **first fruits for God and the Lamb.** While it is true that in the Greek *OT* the term here rendered *first fruits* often signifies 'sacrifices', in a general sense, its common *NT* significance of the 'first reaping' offered to God is more likely. The first reaping of the harvest, on being dedicated to God, sanctified the whole harvest. So Jesus in his resurrection was viewed as the first fruits of the harvest of the dead—the forerunner of the resurrection of all mankind (1 C. 15:20ff.). The Holy Spirit sent to Christians is the first fruits of the harvest of the consummated kingdom (Rom. 8:23, Eph. 1:14, etc.). So the Church is the 'first fruits of humanity for

God and the Lamb' (*NEB*, cf. Jas 1:18), an offering to the praise of God which anticipates the greater harvest of humanity which the Lord shall reap.

5. As with their Lord, **in their mouth no lie was found** (cf. 1 Pet. 2:22, echoing Isa. 53:9 and Zeph. 3:13), an eminently suitable expression in this contest for rejection of the lie of the Antichrist. And **they are spotless,** i.e., unblemished offerings for God (as Jesus, 1 Pet. 1:19). They kept the faith to the end (2 Tim. 4:7).

6. I saw another angel, writes John. With which angel is this one compared? The learned point to various angels earlier in the book (note especially 8:13 and 10:1), but the reference here is vague. The same phrase occurs later (in vv. 8, 9, 15, 17f.) where, as Lohmeyer observed, it serves to unite and to distinguish the separate visions of the chapter and their *dramatis personae*.

Flying in midheaven, i.e., at the highest point of heaven to reach the greatest possible number, the angel proclaims **an eternal gospel** to **those who dwell on earth,** i.e., to all in the world who do not believe. That God should call the Gentiles at the end of history to share with his people in the inheritance of his kingdom is a part of the prophetic hope, and it is reflected in the teaching of Jesus.[1] The hour for that call arrived with the exaltation of Jesus in the resurrection to the sovereignty of the world, and the Spirit of the last days was poured out on his people for witness (Mt. 28:18ff., cf. Ac. 1:8).

7. It need not be doubted that John intended the **loud voice** of the angel to represent the tongues of Christ's witnesses in the time of tribulation. In their distress they have the obligation of bearing witness to the gospel (so 11:3ff.). But is the proclamation consonant with the gospel of Jesus and the apostolic Church? Essentially yes, it is. Observe that it is *an eternal* gospel which is proclaimed: i.e., it has reference to the judgment and salvation of the age to come, and it has eternal validity. Such is the essential proclamation of Jesus according to the summary given in Mark 1:15. More closely related in language is Paul's reminder of his preaching to the Thessalonian believers in 1 Thessalonians 1:9f., which is couched in terms reminiscent of the Jewish monotheistic instruction given to Gentiles. This latter passage, like verse 7, contains no mention of the 'word of the cross', but like verse 7 concentrates

[1] This is the burden of J. Jeremias' book, *Jesus' Promise to the Nations*.

on turning from idols to the living God and escaping the wrath
to come. Paul assumes the redemptive work of Christ in that
passage, and so does John in this. He knows the apostolic gospel.
The focal point of this book is an exposition of it in terms of adoring
apocalypse (ch. 5). Here he concentrates on the appeal for repentance (**Fear God and give him glory** = 'Repent', cf. 11:13,
16:9), and that men **worship** the Creator instead of the Beast
and the evil power he represents. To all who heed the eternal
gospel a share will be given in the eternal kingdom. This is not
the whole gospel, but it is good news of God to those who heed it.

8. The opening declaration of the angel cites Isaiah 21:9
(with Dan. 4:27). Its second part brings together the thought and
language of various *OT* scriptures, notably Jeremiah 25:15 and
51:7 (cf. Isa. 51:21ff.). As in ancient times Babylon had exercised
a powerful and ruinous rule over the nations, so Rome fulfilled
a like role in John's day. The prophecies of doom relating to
ancient Babylon were applied to Rome as the new Babylon (so
already in 2 *Bar.* 11:1, *Sib. Or.* 5:143ff., 1 Pet. 5:12). It was not
Rome's violence to which the prophet objected, but the corrupting
effect of her moral and spiritual influence. She was among the
nations like a prostitute, leading her clients to excesses through
the intoxication of her wine.

The phrase **the wine of her impure passion** is ambiguous.
NEB prefers the accent on the impurity: 'the fierce wine of her
fornication'. Literally it should be rendered 'the wine of the wrath
of her fornication', clearly combining the two ideas of wine which
leads to fornication and wine which symbolizes the wrath of God.
That the latter is in view as well as the former appears from verse
10, and 16:19, 19:15. We may therefore paraphrase the clause,
'she made all nations drink the wine which leads to fornication
and the wine of God's wrath'. The acceptance of the former brings
the latter. Babylon's wickedness becomes a means of divine judgment upon the nations, and Babylon herself is judged for her evil.

9–11. The oracle of verses 9–12 has in view 13:11–18. It provides a warning against yielding to the attempts of the false prophet to enforce universal submission to the beast.

Following on the vision of verses 6f., the declaration **If any one
worships the beast and its image . . .** (note the singular)
must mean, 'If any one continues to worship the beast . . .', i.e.,
in spite of the call for repentance recorded in verse 7. The eternal

gospel (v. 6) includes the granting of forgiveness and a place in the kingdom to those who receive the message in repentance and faith, even though they have been worshippers of the beast. The judgment here announced therefore pertains to those who reject God's call and persist in the idolatrous service of the beast. These will have to drink **the wine of God's wrath.** They will learn the implications of the angel's cry in verse 8. God's wine is strong stuff. **Poured unmixed** more naturally is rendered by the paradoxical expression *mixed unmixed*; i.e., mixed with spices to make it powerful but not diluted with water to reduce its strength. The cup of God's anger has dire effects. But a different imagery is employed to describe them, viz. **he shall be tormented with fire and brimstone.** The language reflects the description of the destruction by volcanic eruption of Sodom and Gomorrah in Genesis 19. This became a standing symbol of divine judgment (cf. the fate of Edom in Isa. 34:8ff.). In Revelation 19:3 Babylon's fall, mentioned in 14:8, is referred to in similar terms as those used in verse 11. The immediate thought appears to be that the worshippers of the Beast will share the fate of the city of the beast. Babylon will become as Sodom and Gomorrah, and so will her supporters, wherever they may be.

It is possible that *the holy angels* forms a periphrasis for God (as apparently in Luke 12:8f., cf. Matthew 10:32f., and Luke 15:7). If this be correct, the judgment is represented as executed before God and the Lamb, who pass judgment on all. This is quite different from the pictures in 1 *Enoch* (e.g., 27:3f., 48:9, 90:26f.), cited by various commentators in illustration of this passage, which portray the sufferings of the wicked as an ever present spectacle to the righteous in bliss. John here stresses the inescapability and finality of judgment, not the satisfaction it could afford to those who witness it.

12. Here is a call for the endurance of the saints. It has been suggested that this and the following verse are unmotivated at this point. Charles accordingly would transpose them to follow 13:15. On the contrary, they are thoroughly in place here. Verse 12 forms, as it were, the 'punch line' for the oracle of judgment in verses 9–11. The train of thought runs: If such be the fate of the adherents of the beast, Christ's people must at all costs continue to **keep the commandments of God and the faith of Jesus.** Eternal issues are at stake in the struggle between the Devil's 'lamb' and the followers of God's Lamb. Let them not yield in the final hour of crisis. Accordingly verse 12 is intended not to provide a satisfactory prospect of judgment on the impenitent, but a spur for Christians not to join their number.

13. Blessed. This is the second beatitude of the Revelation, and one of the most frequently quoted sayings of the book. Why are the dead in Christ blessed **henceforth?** It is commonly answered that they are the martyrs who lay down their lives in the tribulation of 13:11–17. Dying for Christ in the final crisis of history, they are immediately glorified with Christ. Hence the prayer of 6:9–11 is answered.[1] This is hardly to be received. Undoubtedly in this context the saying is calculated to strengthen the resolution of Christians facing the supreme trial of strength with the Antichrist. Verse 12 gives a negative encouragement to faith by reminding believers of the judgment which follows the crisis, and this beatitude conveys a positive assurance of the blessedness which awaits them. Death has lost its terror for **the dead who die in the Lord,** for they are united to him who by his death and resurrection conquered death for them (the language is closely similar to that in 1 C. 15:18, the theology to that of 1 C. 15:20ff., the confidence to that of Phil. 1:21). Manifestly all this applies to all who 'die in the Lord'. If any point of time is intended by *henceforth*, it must be the 'now' of Christ's redeeming acts (12:10).[2] Nevertheless it is likely that the term translated *henceforth* (*ap' arti*) should so be punctuated as to produce the word *assuredly* (*aparti*), as in the *NEB* margin. In that case no time-reference is intended at all. The statement is simply emphatic: 'Blessed assuredly are the dead who die in the Lord.'[3]

The blessedness of the dead in Christ consists of their **rest from their labours.** The toilsomeness of earth lies behind them, and their future service of God will be joy, unsullied by pain (cf. the service rendered to God in ch. 4 and the conditions described in chs. 21–22:5). The blessedness is rooted in that **their deeds**

---

[1] So Charles, who paraphrases verse 13, 'Blessed are those who are martyred in the Lord from henceforth.'

[2] So Rissi, op. cit., pp. 29f. Lohmeyer (ad loc.) contends that verse 13, like other sayings prefaced by the command 'write' (1:11, 19; 19:9; 21:5) and other utterances of the Spirit (chs. 2–3, 22:17), relates to the present of John's time, not to the future.

[3] So A. Debrunner, *Conjectanea Neotestamentica*, Lund, 1947, p. 46, following a suggestion of A. Fridrichsen.

follow them. This is a Jewish thought baptized into Christ. An early rabbinic dictum, often cited by later Jewish writers, ran, 'In the hour of a man's decease neither silver, nor gold, nor precious stones, nor pearls accompany him, but his knowledge of the Torah and good works.'[1] More commonly it was said that a man's good works reach heaven before he does, and bear testimony to his merit. This, however, is an expression of the Jewish teaching of salvation by works, which is other than John's. His stress on the redemptive power of Christ (as in ch. 5) indicates that the works which accompany a man to God's throne are the fruit of Christ's redemption in his life. Such works are confessed by Christ as 'perfect in the sight of my God' (3:2), and so outlast this world and are taken up into the eternal kingdom.

14-20. The sixth and seventh oracles (vv. 14-16, 17-20) are closely related. They dramatize Joel's double parable of the judgment (Jl 3:13), and so bring the series of seven oracles to the end of the age. While they imply that the parousia now takes place (v. 14) they do not actually describe it (the same strictly holds good of 19:11ff., which is parallel in thought but employs different imagery).

The precise relation between the two prophecies is disputed. A persistent strain of interpretation views the first as depicting the harvest of the righteous for the kingdom, the second the gathering of the impenitent for judgment.[2] The rooting of the two visions in Joel 3:13 and their parallelism in imagery makes this view difficult of acceptance. Most therefore consider that the two visions depict a single event of judgment executed upon the unrighteous.[3] Caird agrees that the two oracles must be viewed as parallel in meaning as in structure, but maintains that since the former appears to relate to the gathering of the righteous, the latter must have a similar reference. The blood shed must be that of the martyrs, who like their Lord suffer outside the city (cf. Heb. 13:12). Attractive as this interpretation is, it is hardly compelling. If verse 14 relates to the parousia, as it surely does, it is natural to view the reaping as for judgment in the widest sense—for gathering the righteous for the kingdom and the unrighteous for punishment. The grape harvest could have been given a similar double ref-

---

[1] *Aboth* 6:9; see Strack-Billerbeck, ad loc.
[2] So e.g., Swete, Lohmeyer, Behm, Farrer, Rissi (op. cit., pp. 9f.).
[3] So e.g., Bousset, Charles, Kiddle, Lohse.

erence, but the use of the figure in the *OT* (especially Isa. 63:3) made it natural for John to apply it exclusively to the punishment of the rebellious.

14. The vision of verses 14-16 is so toned down in its colours, some scholars have hesitated to recognize in it the parousia of the Christ, the Son of man. Yet the conjunction of **the cloud,** the **one like a son of man,** and the **golden crown,** compel the identification. The language echoes Daniel 7:13, but our passage is unique in the Bible in speaking of the Son of man as seated on a white cloud instead of the traditional storm-cloud of Yahweh (e.g., Ps. 18:9ff.). This must be intended to convey the thought of his coming in light and glory and blessing to a dark world. The crown sets him forth as the King-Messiah, but the sharp sickle indicates his coming for judgment.

15. That **another angel** commands the Christ to commence his work of judgment is at first sight surprising. But this angel **came out of the temple,** the abode of God. He therefore conveyed to the Christ the command of the Father (for a related concept of cf. Mk 13:32, Ac. 1:7). The language is reminiscent not only of the *OT* prophets (with Jl 3:13 see also Isa. 17:5, Jer. 51:33) but also of the parables of Jesus (e.g., Mt. 13:30, Mk 4:29). The Markan parable speaks explicitly of the reaping of grain, but the harvest symbol inevitably connotes the judgment of separation—(as Mt. 13:30, cf. Mt. 3:12). Such is the action of the reaper in verse 16.

17, 18. Another angel came out of the temple—to execute judgment, as the one like a Son of man did. Since his description is more modest than of many angels in the Revelation (e.g., 10:1ff., 15:6, 18:1), we must view him as the agent of the Christ rather than an angel of comparable authority as the Christ (cf. the subordinate position of even Michael and his angels in John's rewriting of his sources in 12:7-11). The angel is commanded by **another angel . . . from the altar.** We are reminded of the angel with a censer, who offered the prayers of the saints on the altar before God's throne, and threw fire from the altar to the earth, to execute judgment (see 8:1-5). Presumably John views the two as one. If the angel has **power over fire,** we may assume that John relates its use especially to divine judgment. This judgment is expressive of the holiness of God, but it is also related to the prayers of the saints for deliverance (see notes on 8:1ff.).

19, 20. When the **vintage of the earth** was thrown into **the great wine press** of God's wrath, it was trodden **outside the city** (v. 20). The city is not named. Is it Babylon, or Jerusalem? In 11:8 the two are identified. The question should not be pressed, still less the view that it is the heavenly Jerusalem, for the picture is general. The same is true of the extraordinary measurement of the flow of 'blood' from the vat **as high as a horse's bridle for 1600 stadia.** Evidence can be produced to identify that as the length of the Holy Land accepted in early times,[1] or even as representing the whole earth[2]—which would entail a tall story, even for John. A more plausible suggestion as to the significance of the figure is that it is the square of forty, the traditional number for punishment (cf. Israel's forty years in the desert, Num. 14:33, forty lashes for a criminal, Dt. 25:3).[3] On any reckoning the imagery is grotesque—as absurd as that of a camel or elephant going through the eye of a needle, and apparently as well known among Jews. 1 *Enoch* 100:1ff. describes the internecine warfare of the last days, when fathers and sons fight one another and brothers fight brothers, 'till the streams flow with their blood . . . and the horse shall walk up to the breast in the blood of sinners, and the chariot shall be submerged to its height'. 2 Esdras 15:35f. more modestly restricts the height of the blood flow to the belly of the horse and the knee of the camel. When the Jews came to describe the carnage wrought by the Romans in Hadrian's time they used no such restraint: 'They murdered people (of Bether) continually, till a horse sank to its nostrils in blood. And the blood . . . poured into the sea to an extent of four miles. If you think, however, that Bether lay near the sea, do you not know that it was 40 miles away?'[4] As a historical description that is as exaggerated as John's prophetic picture, but both reflect the hyperbole characteristic of the Jew. John's prophecy should be recognized as a typical apocalyptic cartoon of the messianic judgment at the parousia, and be interpreted in the light of the nature of apocalypse.

[1] According to the *Itinerary* of Antonius the distance from Tyre to El-Arisch on the borders of Egypt is 1664 stadia.

[2] On the basis of the understanding of the city as the new Jerusalem, 1600 could be thought of as 400 × 4 and so symbolize the four quarters of the earth. Thus Victorinus, and some moderns.   [3] So Farrer, ad loc.

[4] *P.Ta.* 4, 69*a*, 7, and elsewhere in the Talmud. See Strack-Billerbeck, iii, p. 817.

THE JUDGMENTS OF THE SEVEN BOWL-CUPS
15:1–16:21

The great parenthesis of chapters 12–14, inserted to illuminate
the struggle between the Church and the forces of darkness,
concluded with visions of the second advent of Christ. John returns
to his exposition of the messianic judgments of the last times,
already considered under the figures of the seven seals (6:1–8:5)
and the seven trumpets (8:6–11:19). He now sets them forth
under the symbolism of seven bowls of the wrath of God (15–16).
In referring to the seven 'bowls', we do so in deference to the *RSV*
and the general usage of modern commentators. The term however
is misleading, and it has obscured John's symbolism. For it is
not the image of a domestic bowl which John wished to conjure
up in our minds, but the cup of God's wrath, of which the prophets
frequently spoke and to which John himself has already referred
(in 14:8 and 10). The source of the symbolism in all probability
was Isaiah 51:17ff. Jerusalem is bidden to rouse herself:

> You who have drunk at the hand of the Lord
>   the cup of his wrath,
> who have drunk to the dregs
>   the bowl of staggering.

The 'cup of his wrath' and 'the bowl of staggering' (i.e., the bowl
which causes the drinker to stagger) are clearly synonymous. Later
in the paragraph (v. 22) it is stated:

> Behold, I have taken from your hand
>   the cup of staggering;
> the bowl of my wrath
>   you shall drink no more;
> and I will put it into the hand of
>   your tormentors. . . .

Observe that there has been an interchange of terms qualifying
'cup' and 'bowl' in verse 22 as compared with verse 17 which
again underscores the identity of meaning of cup and bowl. The
term in Isaiah 51:17, 22, translated 'bowl' (*qebaath*) is a loan-word
from Assyrian, meaning cup or goblet. It appears only here in
the *OT*, and each time it is defined in the Hebrew text by the
term 'cup' (*kos*) inserted by a later scribe. The Greek word used
by John (*phialē*, *AV* 'vial') denotes various types of vessels, ranging

from a bowl used as a saucepan for cooking to a bowl-shaped cup used for drinking. It passed directly into Hebrew and Aramaic, and interestingly enough was used in the Targum on Isaiah 51:17 to render the term 'cup' in the phrase 'cup of his wrath'. In verse 22, however, it renders 'bowl' in the phrase 'bowl of my wrath'. It is altogether likely that John's language in 15:7, 'seven golden bowls full of the wrath of God', consciously echoes Isaiah 51:17 and 22. Moreover in the concluding vision in the series of seven plagues, Babylon itself is made to drain 'the cup of the fury of his wrath' (16:19). There is hardly room for doubt therefore that the 'bowls' of God's wrath are intended to mean broad goblets containing wine which symbolizes God's wrath. The emptying of these 'bowls' employs a standing symbol used by the prophets to represent God's judgments among men (for further examples, cf. Ps. 75:8, Jer. 25:15ff., 49:12f., Ezek. 23:33, Hab. 2:16). That the contents of the cups are poured on earth, sea, waters, sun, etc., rather than handed to men does not seriously affect the symbolism, since in all cases it is judgments upon men which are in view.

The contents of the bowl-cups we shall consider in the exposition of chapter 16, but one feature of them should be mentioned before chapter 15 is examined. They bear a striking similarity to the plagues of the exodus. This feature already appeared in the first four trumpet-judgments of 8:7–12, whereby an indication was given that the circumstances of the first exodus will be reproduced in another exodus in the last times. This theme comes to full bloom in chapters 15–16. Not only do all seven judgments of chapter 16 repeat in varied ways the plagues of Egypt. Their conclusion in a redemption greater than that from Egypt is celebrated in a song, appropriately entitled 'the song of Moses, the servant of God, and the song of the Lamb', sung beside a heavenly Red Sea (15:2–4), and the counterpart of the tent of witness erected in the desert appears in heaven (15:6), indicating that the holy will of God, embodied in the tablets of the law, is about to be enacted in judgment and redemption. Undoubtedly the intervention of chapters 10–14 between the trumpet-judgments and those of the bowl-cups enables a richer content to be put into this theme. For the cruel oppression by Pharaoh of the Jews adumbrates the tyranny of the Antichrist in the city which is symbolically called Jerusalem, Sodom, and Egypt (11:8). The

magicians of Egypt have a devastating counterpart in the false
prophet (13:13ff.). The sufferings of the Israelites under their
taskmasters foreshadow the more terrible persecution of the Christians at the hands of the Antichrist's agents. On the other hand,
the judgments of the Lord on the land of Egypt are but pale anticipations of the greater judgments which are to fall on the kingdom
of the beast, and the emancipation from Egypt is far surpassed
by the redemption of the Lamb, as the saints rejoice in the resurrection glory and sing of the turning of the nations to God (15:2ff.).
The duality of exodus as judgment and redemption is maintained
in chapters 15–16, and to ensure that this is understood by the
reader, the positive element of redemption is placed first.

THE LAST EXODUS 15:1–8

This introduction to the closing series of messianic judgments
consists of a superscription (v. 1) and two visions. The first depicts
the risen saints, standing beside the celestial sea and singing a
song of deliverance (vv. 2–4). The second introduces the seven
angels who are commissioned to pour out the cups of wrath
(vv. 5–8).

The first vision has a function comparable to that of 7:9ff. An
anticipation of the victory of those who conquer the beast is given
before the onset of the last plagues which will afflict mankind.
John does not intend us to understand that the victors of verses
2ff. have been removed from earth prior to the events of chapter
16, any more than the vision of 7:9–11 is intended to signify that
the multitude which no man can number is rapt to heaven before
the trumpets sound their judgments. On the contrary, 7:13ff.
states that the victors have endured a great distress, of which little
account is given in the seal-judgments. Their song is to be sung
after the distress is concluded when the salvation of God's kingdom
has appeared. The coming of that kingdom is celebrated at the
end of the trumpet-judgments (11:15ff.), as it is after the fall of
Babylon (19:1–10), when the second advent takes place and the
kingdom is revealed (19:11–20:6).

The second vision, describing the seven angels with the seven
bowl-cups of God's wrath (vv. 5–8), reminds us of 8:1–5, following
the vision of the victorious saints in 7:9ff. There the seven angels
of the presence are given seven trumpets with which to herald

the messianic judgments. This structural parallelism between chapters 7–8 and chapters 15–16 corresponds to a parallelism in content, as we have already noted, and to which we must give closer attention in the exposition of chapter 16.

1. John commences chapter 15 by reference to **another portent** (literally 'sign') **in heaven.** It is tempting to view this as a counterpart to the portent of 12:1ff.—the woman and the dragon in the sky (12:1ff.). But this is to press an accident of language. The earlier chapters have related many signs in heaven. The real counterpart to 15:1ff. is 6:1ff. (preceded by chs. 4–5) and 8:2, 6ff. (preceded by ch. 7). The question is often asked how John can say that he **saw** this portent at this juncture, when he declares in verses 5ff. that the angels did not appear till after the temple in heaven was opened. The question is an unreal one. A new section has begun and its chief feature is forthwith declared: **seven angels with seven plagues.** How they came to be seen is narrated subsequently. Bousset aptly views verse 1 as a kind of superscription over all that follows in chapters 15–16.

The *plagues* about to be described are described as the last, **for with them the wrath of God is ended.** Do they then follow chronologically those narrated under the seals and trumpet visions, as well as those of chapter 14? That is impossible, for the sixth seal brought us to the end of the age, the seventh trumpet ushered in the kingdom of God, and chapter 14 concluded with visions of the second advent. The opening sentence of chapter 15 would not have had an essentially different meaning if chapters 6–14 had not stood in John's book. The bowl-visions depict the judgments of the end of the age, when God's wrath on rebellious mankind comes to a finish. Standing at this point in the Revelation, however, they declare how that wrath, revealed in the other portrayals of divine judgments, reaches its goal. In fact we shall see that the first three bowl-visions virtually extend judgments already narrated in the trumpet-series, and in this sense they may be said to appear later than the earlier ones, but the same does not hold good for the rest of the bowl-judgments.

2. When John first saw the likeness of **a sea of glass** in heaven, it appeared to emphasize the majesty and holiness of God, even his remoteness from the restless upheaval of a sinful world (see notes on 4:6). Here two extraordinary changes are to be observed. On the one hand the 'sea' is **mingled with fire**—in this context

quite certainly conveying the notion of wrath about to be revealed
from heaven (cf. 8:5). On the other hand there are people beside
the sea—**those who had conquered the beast** stand there **with
harps of God in their hands,** jubilant in song. The sea of
separation had become a kind of heavenly Red Sea, and the victors over the beast by the miracle of redemption had been brought
over to God's side of it. Delivered from their would-be destroyers
(the **image and the number the number of its name**
covertly refer to the murderous persecution of the second beast,
13:11–18), they now stand in the presence of God. It is a repetition of the vision of 14:1–5, given to emphasize the aspect of
God's judgment and deliverance as a counterpart to the first
exodus. We may accordingly deduce that the fiery aspect of the
sea of glass indicates the overthrow of the beast and his allies, just
as Pharaoh and his host perished in the sea.

3. Accompanied by *harps of God* (= harps for the worship of
God), the conquerors sing **the song of Moses ... and the song
of the Lamb.** Two great songs are ascribed to Moses in the *OT*,
that which Israel sang beside the Red Sea, exulting in the deliverance of the Lord (Exod. 15:1ff.), and another at the end of Moses'
life, recounting God's mercies to his people and his judgments
on their waywardness (Dt. 32). Obviously the former is chiefly
in view here. Nevertheless, while lines 1–2 echo the theme of
Exodus 15, lines 3–4 are distinctly reminiscent of the later song of
Moses (Dt. 32:4).

Is one song meant by *the song of Moses ... and the song of the
Lamb*, or two? Surely one. It would be artificial to divide verses
3–4 into two songs (e.g., v. 3 as from Moses, v. 4 from the Lamb).
Should then John have entitled the composition 'the song of
Moses and of the Lamb'? No, for the duality in the title preserves
a distinction. Moses celebrated a deliverance by the Lord which
adumbrated a greater deliverance to come. The greater redemption eclipsed the former by a similar degree as the second redeemer
transcended the first. Moses and the Lamb are no more to be
bracketed than the promised land of Israel is to be equated with
the kingdom of God. The unity of God's purpose and the con-
tinuity of God's people under both covenants include a dis-
junction of his action in Christ and of his people's experience of
redemption.

The song is a psalm of praise, every word of which echoes the

OT. The **deeds** of God are described as **great** as in Psalm 92: 5, 111 : 2, and **wonderful** as in Psalm 118: 1, 139 : 14, 1 Chronicles 16: 9. The title **Lord God the Almighty** occurs in Amos 4 : 13. God's ways are **just** as in Psalm 145: 17, **true** as in Deuteronomy 32: 4. The fourth and fifth lines cite Jeremiah 10 : 7, with Psalm 86 : 9, 12, Malachi 1 : 11. God is confessed as **holy** as in 1 Samuel 2 : 2, his worship by the nations anticipated as in Psalm 86: 9, and his judgments revealed to the world as in Psalm 98 : 2. Yet while every word of the song stems from the *OT*, the dimensions of what it celebrates are a consummation and not a mere repetition of *OT* psalm and prophecy. The great and wonderful *deeds* of God are his acts of redemption and judgment through Christ, by which the new age was introduced (chs. 5 and 12), and his subjection of the evil powers and raising of the dead at the parousia of Christ (this includes most of chs. 6–20, perhaps 21 : 9–22 : 5 also). All of it is comprehended under the notion of the exodus wrought through Christ. The justice and truth of God's ways are seen precisely in the faithfulness of God, manifest in these judgments and acts of redemption, as in his kingly rule through Christ during the times between the resurrection and parousia. These acts and attributes of God, set forth in verse 3, were truly in evidence under the old covenant (they initiated it); but they received a deeper, broader and higher embodiment under the new covenant.

4. Similarly verse 4 proclaims the imminent fulfilment of a vision cherished by some *OT* prophets (though by no means by all). **Who shall not fear and glorify thy name, O Lord?** demands the answer 'No one; all will fear and glorify the Lord's name.' Is this an anticipation of nations cowering in submission to God as they are overwhelmed by his judgments, like defeated soldiers forced to bow the knee before their execution? Surely not. The statement, **All nations shall come and worship thee** (literally, 'in thy presence') should be taken at face value. It looks forward to the willing subjection of the nations to God in the kingdom of Christ, i.e., in the period alluded to in 20 : 4–6. God's **judgments have been revealed** in the events described in this book, above all in those which relate to the Antichrist and his followers. The rest of the nations have learned the lessons and acknowledged their true Lord. For Christians under the stress of a militant emperor-cult, anticipating a struggle to the death with an idolatry claiming the allegiance of all mankind, this song affords great encouragement. The last word of history is not with Satan and his Antichrist, but with the Lord and his Christ.

5. The introductory statement of verse 1 is now expanded in the vision of the seven angels to whom the seven bowl-cups of God's wrath are given (vv. 5–8). John sees **the temple ... in heaven ... opened** to allow the angels to step forth and carry out their task. But *the temple* is qualified in an unusual way. It is called the temple **of the tent of witness.** The additional phrase denotes the tabernacle in the desert, and it was so named because of the 'witness' to God's covenant law (the ten commandments) inscribed on the tablets placed within the ark, which was housed in the 'tent' or tabernacle. The full name therefore means either 'the temple, namely a tent of witness' (Bousset) or 'the temple in which the tent of witness stands' (Lohmeyer). The former interpretation is to be preferred. The temple is viewed as the tabernacle which contains the testimony to God's abiding covenant and his moral demand of mankind. The chastisements about to be described are in harmony with both aspects of God's holiness. They judge the rebellious of earth and fulfil God's redemptive purpose for earth.

6, 7. The angels who emerge from the heavenly temple are dressed in a manner similar to the appearance of the risen Christ in the opening vision of the Revelation (1 : 13). They bear the marks of royal dignity and of holiness (cf. 19 : 8),[1] a further sign that the judgments which the angels are about to execute are expressive of the sovereign and holy purpose of God in his creation. As the four living creatures called forth the four horsemen at the opening of the seals (6 : 1ff.), so it is one of these supreme representatives of the holy God who gives **the seven angels seven golden bowls full of the wrath of God.** The description abbreviates the concept of seven golden bowl-like cups full of wine, which symbolizes God's wrath (cf. the discussion introductory to chs. 15–16).

8. When the preparations for the judgments were completed **the temple was filled with smoke.** The smoke is signicative of **the glory of God and ... his power,** and its manifestation

---

[1] For *linen* (Greek *linon*) some MSS read 'stone' (Greek *lithon*), a more difficult reading, which is favoured by some critics for that very reason, and which is thought to be supported by Ezekiel 28:13. The confusion, however, is a simple one for a scribe to make, and in the uncertainty most critics agree with the verdict of the *RSV* translators.

denotes the presence of the glorious and powerful God himself (cf. Isa. 6 : 4, and especially the appearance of the glory at the consecration of the tabernacle; Exod. 40 : 35; and of Solomon's Temple, 2 Chr. 7 : 1ff.; and of the temple of the new age, Ezek. 44 : 4). It is the awful holiness of that Presence which forbids any to venture an approach, as the previously cited passages indicate. The mention of this feature here suggests not so much that no angel can approach the Lord to intercede for earth now that judgments are about to fall (Charles, Farrer, Caird), as that God himself is present in his majesty and glory to perform that action which will execute his judgments and establish his kingdom in power. The angels with the bowl-like cups are instruments in the hands of the almighty Judge and Redeemer. They empty the cups. He acts.

THE SEVEN BOWLS 16 : 1–21

The similarities between the judgments of the seven trumpets and the seven bowls are sufficiently striking to warrant setting down the two series in tabular form:

Trumpets	*Bowls*
1. Hail, fire, and blood fall on the *earth*, one third of which is burned up.	A bowl is poured on the *earth*. Malignant sores come on men who had the mark of the beast and worshipped his image.
2. A blazing mountain falls into the *sea*. One-third of the sea becomes blood, a third of sea-creatures die, and a third of ships are destroyed.	A bowl is poured on the *seas*. This becomes blood, and every living thing in it dies.
3. A blazing star (Wormwood) falls on a third of *rivers and fountains*; their waters are poisoned and many die.	A bowl is poured on *rivers and fountains*, and they become blood.
4. A third of *sun, moon, and stars* are struck. Darkness results for a third of a night and day.	A bowl is poured on the *sun*, which scorches men with fire.

5. The shaft of the pit is opened. Sun and air are *darkened* with smoke from which locusts emerge to *torment* men without the seal of God.

A bowl is poured on the throne of the beast. His kingdom is *darkened* and men are in *anguish.*

6. Four angels bound at *the Euphrates* are released, with their 200 million cavalry. A third of men are killed by these.

A bowl is poured on *the Euphrates,* which dries up for kings from the east. Kings of the world assemble for battle at Armageddon.

7. *Loud voices in heaven* announce the coming of the kingdom of God and of Christ. *Lightning, thunder, earthquake,* and *hail* occur.

A bowl is poured into the air, *a loud voice from God's throne* announces, 'It is done'. *Lightning, thunder,* and an unprecedented *earthquake* occur, and terrible *hail* falls.

The differences between these two series are but variations on common themes. True, the variations are not without significance. The difference in content of the first trumpet-judgment and that of the first bowl supplies a hint as to the nature of the bowl-judgments generally. Whereas the earth is affected by both initial judgments, no mention is made of the effect upon humanity of the burning of grass and trees following on the first trumpet, but the description of the first bowl-judgment is concerned solely with its consequences for men who submit to the Antichrist. Thus the bowl-judgments are directly related to the rebellious of mankind who reject the Christ and follow the Antichrist.

It is also evident that the bowl-judgments extend the area afflicted by the corresponding trumpet-judgments; e.g., the first four trumpets describe judgments affecting one-third of earth, of the sea, of fresh waters, and of the sun, etc., while the first four bowls initiate judgments on the earth as such, the sea, the rivers and fountains generally, and the sun. This enlargement has given rise to the suggestion that the bowl-judgments belong to a later point of time than the trumpet-judgments. The deduction is plausible but unnecessary. It is sufficient to recognize the greater extent of the bowl-judgments over those of the trumpet-judgments.

The dominant theme, emphasized alike by the similarities and differences between the two series of judgments, is the representation of the bowl-judgments as divine intervention in history like that at the first exodus. The introduction to these judgments in chapter 15 has already made that plain. John provides a last delineation of the messianic judgments, with such repetitions and modifications of the trumpets series to emphasize the conviction, already present in the earlier descriptions, that the generation of the Antichrist will experience on a vaster scale the judgments of the Lord which befell Pharaoh and his subjects in Egypt in the time of Moses. The repetition is fully comprehensible, since John could not relate this theme to his generation as closely as he wished without first giving the account of the activities of the Antichrist and his allies which he has provided in chapters 11–13. To this account he constantly relates the succession of judgments in chapter 16.

It is this dominant motif of the exodus which caused John to reflect, in a manner not elsewhere observable in his prophecy, the meditations in the so-called Wisdom of Solomon relating to the plagues and blessings of the exodus. There we find an emphasis on the Lord in his judgments arming 'all creation to repel his enemies' (5 : 17). The author dwells again and again on the way God makes his judgments suit the sins of men: 'In return for their foolish and wicked thoughts, which led them astray to worship irrational serpents and worthless animals, thou didst send upon them a multitude of irrational creatures to punish them, that they might learn that *one is punished by the very things by which he sins*' (11 : 15f.). It is likely that this conviction impelled John to change the content of the first trumpet-judgment when recounting his first bowl-judgment. While in both cases it is the earth which is smitten, John omits the Egyptian plague of hail and lightning and chooses instead the immediately preceding plague of boils. It was fitting that men who received in their body the mark of the beast should receive in their body 'foul and evil sores'. The declaration of the angel after the changing of water into blood at the third bowl (vv. 5f.) clearly echoes Wisdom 11 : 5ff. Contrasting the spurting of water from the rock for the Jews in the desert, the writer comments that the Egyptians found their river no unfailing stream of water, but 'stirred up and defiled with blood, in rebuke for the decree to slay the infants'. So the Jews through their experience in Egypt and in the desert 'learned how the ungodly were tormented when judged in wrath' (Wis. 11 : 9).

A further motif in the bowl-judgments probably owes its place to the second-exodus theme, namely, the perpetual refusal of men to repent in spite of their experience of the divine judgments.

Three times it is mentioned (after the fourth, fifth, and seventh bowls, vv. 9, 11, 21) that far from repenting, they who felt the weight of the messianic judgments cursed God for their pains. This in contrast to the narration of the two witnesses in 11 : 2ff. (cf. especially 11 : 13) and the proclamation of the eternal gospel in 14 : 6f. The purpose of judgments is evidently not alone the divine requital of evil but the production of human repentance for it. The followers of the Antichrist, however, are like Pharaoh and his people in the time of Moses. Their hearts remain obdurate through all the divine chastisements. So the wrath comes on the last generation to the uttermost, as it did on Pharaoh and his generation.

1. In view of the statement in 15 : 8, that none could enter the temple until the seven plagues were finished, it would seem that the **loud voice from the temple** is that of God, as in verse 17.

2. The judgments ensuing on the outpouring of the first **bowl** (= cup of wrath, as in v. 19; see introduction to ch. 15) repeats the Egyptian plagues of boils which broke out into sores, Exodus 9 : 1of. (but the language also echoes Dt. 28 : 35). Just as the boils came on men and beasts in Egypt, apart from the Hebrews, so these **foul and evil sores** afflicted only **the men who bore the mark of the beast and worshipped its image.** The observations as to the wickedness and impenitence of those affected by the bowl-judgments in verses 4f., 9, 1of., 21 (i.e., following the third, fourth, fifth, and seventh bowls), together with the fact that the seventh bowl results in the destruction of Babylon, suggests that this whole series of judgments is primarily directed against all in the Antichrist's realm who acknowledge his authority.

3, 4. The turning of sea and sources of fresh water into **blood,** after the second and third bowls, distributes into two the single Egyptian plague, Exodus 7 : 19ff. (as in the second and third trumpet-judgments, 8 : 8ff.). These universalize the Nile plague into a catastrophe affecting the sea and all rivers and fountains of the *oikoumenē.* For the prophet **the sea** naturally would have denoted the Mediterranean, and **the rivers and the fountains** those of the lands surrounding it. He has in view the Roman Empire and its adjacent territories, which constituted the *oikoumenē,* the inhabited earth.

5, 6. The angel of water is he who has control over the waters, like the angels in control of the winds (7 : 1ff.) and of the fire

(14 : 18). In apocalyptic literature all the elements of nature have
angels assigned to their care (see e.g., *Enoch* 60 : 11ff.). We have
observed (introduction to ch. 16) that the sentiment expressed in
the angel's cry echoes the observation in Wisdom 11 : 5ff. as to the
fitness of the Nile plague in view of the Egyptian's murderous
treatment of the Hebrew children. As the Egyptians killed the
Israelite infants and were punished by water 'stirred up and
defiled with blood', so the subjects of the Antichrist throughout
his empire are requited for shedding the blood of the saints and
prophets of the Church.

7. The cry from **the altar** is perhaps viewed as uttered by the
angel who came out from the altar in 14 : 18, and who called for
the final messianic judgment to take place. The altar in heaven is
above all the place where prayers are offered. In 6 : 10 the souls of
the martyrs beneath the altar plead for their speedy vindication,
and in 8 : 3f. the prayers of the saints on earth ascend from the
altar and are answered by the signs which accompany the end of
the age. The prayers of the people of God in heaven and on earth
now find expression in a great Amen to the **judgments** of God.
That these are **true and just** is the theme of the victors song sung
by the heavenly Red Sea (15 : 3) and of the multitudes in heaven
after the judgment of Babylon (19 : 2). The character of God, as
revealed in his acts of judgment and redemption, is the great
theme of the worship of heaven in the book of Revelation.

8–11. As the smiting of the Nile waters was distributed by John
into the two judgments of the second and third bowls, so the
Egyptian plague of darkness, reproduced after the fourth trumpet
by the smiting of the sun and other luminaries (8 : 12), becomes
extended into the judgments of the fourth and fifth bowls. On the
one hand the pouring of the fourth bowl on the sun intensifies its
heat instead of extinguishing it, and on the other the darkness is
confined to the area of the beast's sovereignty (= **the throne of
the beast and its kingdom**). In reality both judgments are
directed against the subjects of the Antichrist. That the sun was
allowed to scorch men with fire is in contrast to the blessedness of
the followers of the Lamb, of whom it was written, 'the sun shall
not strike them, nor any scorching heat' (7 : 16f.). In some way
the subjects of the Christ are exempted from this judgment, just as
the darkness in the kingdom of the beast, with which is linked
anguish through pain and sores, afflicts the subjects of the Anti-

christ alone. The question of how these things are possible is not
to be raised. John knew well that in the Egyptian plague of darkness the people of Israel had light (Exod. 10:23), even as they
were exempted from the other plagues on Egypt. John's whole
writing is a conveyance of parables, and this we must never forget.[1]

It is consonant with all this that the men affected by these
judgments **cursed the name of God ... and ... did not
repent and give him glory.** This stands in contrast with the
scene in 11:13 (see note for its language), but more immediately
with the cry of the angel of the water in verses 5f. and of the altar
in verse 7, as well as the ascriptions of glory to God by the hosts of
heaven and the redeemed in chapter 19. It is basic to the Revelation that the judgments of God should quicken the consciences of
men as to the gravity of their rebellion against the God of creation
(the God who had power over these plagues) and that they
should bring men to repentance and submission to the Lord God
Almighty. Remarkably, the total effect of the messianic judgments
is stated to have precisely this effect, and it is celebrated in song by
the victors over the beast (15:4). These, therefore, who curse God
for his judgments are the obdurate. The mark of the beast on their
bodies has penetrated their souls, instilling in them the hostility
towards God and his holiness which is characteristic of the beast
himself.

12-20. The parallel between the judgments of the sixth bowl
and the sixth trumpet should be observed. At the sounding of the
latter the four angels bound at the Euphrates are loosed to lead a
vast demonic army, by which one-third of mankind is killed. At
the outpouring of the sixth bowl the river Euphrates is dried up to
enable the kings from the east to cross with their armies and join
forces with the kings of the whole world for the confrontation of
Armageddon. The parallel is more than verbal, for in the events
of the sixth trumpet we perceive a highly mythological application
of the Roman fear of invasion by the Parthian kingdom which lay

[1] Charles would dissociate the judgment of the fifth bowl from the Egyptian
plague of darkness and view it as an abbreviation of the judgment of the fifth
trumpet. The darkness is caused by the smoke from the pit, and the anguish
and pains of men are due to the torture inflicted by the locusts (9:1-11). The
dissociation from the exodus-typology is almost certainly mistaken, for this is
the dominating motif of chapters 15-16, but the parallels between the trumpet-
and bowl-judgments are so consistent as to make it possible that John has in
mind the demonic instruments of pain as he writes of the fifth bowl in verses 10f.

east of the Euphrates (see notes on 9 : 13ff.). In the sixth bowl this
expectation is given a more realistic expression, but it is obscured
through the compression of the story in verses 13–16. From 17 : 16
it would appear that the object of the kings from the east is the
destruction of 'Babylon'. Only after that takes place do the kings
of the whole earth assemble for Armageddon. John's brevity has
been compelled through the close-knit structure of the seven
bowl-judgments. He will explain the implications of the sixth
bowl more fully in chapters 17–19.

12 invites comparison with Isaiah 11 : 15, wherein it is promised
that **the river Euphrates** will be **dried up** to enable the remnant
of Israel to return from the Assyrian captivity to their own land,
just as the Lord made a way for their forefathers through the Red
Sea on the way from Egypt to the promised land. In verse 12
therefore a miracle of redemption has become an eschatological
miracle of judgment. Observe, however, that the drying up of the
Euphrates makes possible the march of **the kings from the east,**
but provides no necessary motivation for an invasion of the west.

13, 14. The impulse is provided by the evil trinity of the
dragon, the **beast,** and the **false prophet.** Out of their mouths
issue **three foul spirits like frogs.** These fitly represent the
lying propaganda associated with the worship of the emperor,
behind which stands the malignant forces of the spiritual world.
But why are they represented as *foul spirits like frogs?* It has been
observed (Moffatt) that in the ancient world sinister associations
attach to frogs. In Iranian religion they are viewed as agents of the
evil spirit Ahriman in the final contest of history. Their mention
here would be particularly favoured through their featuring in the
plagues of Egypt (Exod. 8 : 1ff.). Farrer views the sixth trumpet
as an allegory on the plague of frogs. Whereas, however, the frogs
of the Egyptian plague were merely a nuisance, the frog-like
spirits lead men to destruction. The **signs** wrought by them have
already been anticipated in the description of the work of the
false prophet (13 : 13f.). Here they are employed to persuade **the
kings of the whole world** to assemble their forces, and these
will include not alone the kings from the east (v. 12) but rulers in
the rest of the *oikoumenē*. The deception which draws them doubtless lies in the nature of their coming together. They think in
terms of the annihilation of the helpless people of God, but it
proves to be a confrontation with their champion, the Word of

God (19 : 11ff.). They fail to understand that their assembly is for
the great day of God the Almighty.

15. Accordingly the warning is given as to the unexpectedness
of the **coming** of Christ. This echoes the parable of Jesus about
the **thief** who comes at night (Mt. 24:43f., cf. 1 Th. 5:2ff.,
2 Pet. 3:10). John has already given such a warning in the letter
to the church at Sardis (3:3). Its repetition in this passage is
eminently suitable. It is precisely because the followers of the
Antichrist are not awake to God and his gospel that the day of
God for them is a day of doom instead of a day of redemption.
Like captives of war in ancient times, they will then **go naked and
be seen exposed** (cf. the grim use of this figure in Ezek. 23:24–9,
and Paul's application of it to shame in the judgment, 2 C. 5:3).
The beatitude contains an implicit warning to believers to maintain spiritual alertness so as not to suffer the fate of the godless.

16. The name for the place of assembly of the kings of the
world, **Armageddon,** presents an even more perplexing puzzle
than 666. It is a Greek transliteration for the Hebrew *Har-Meggido,*
the mountain of Megiddo. This little town is in the plain of Esdrae-
lon in Israel, and it has no mountain. The nearest mountain is
Carmel in the north, though some think in terms of the range of
hills in southern Galilee. Carmel would be an attractive identification, since it witnessed Elijah's contest with the prophets of
Baal, when the Lord gave a signal revelation of his presence and
power, and the false prophets were put to the sword. Unfortunately there is no indication in ancient literature that Carmel was
ever referred to as *Har-Megiddo.* Numerous attempts have been
made to explain the name by derivations from allied forms. One
most widely favoured viewed *Har-Megiddo* as a corruption of the
Hebrew *Har-Mo'ed* = mountain of assembly. This term appears in
Isaiah 14:13 to denote a mythical mountain of the gods which the
king of Babylon in his pride determined in his heart to ascend, but
in vain. It is suggested that this mountain became viewed as the
demonic counterpart to the heavenly mount Zion, on which the
city of God stands (Heb. 12:22ff.; cf. Rev. 21:10), and so a
fitting symbol for the gathering of the rebellious hosts of earth
against the God of heaven. The notion is interesting, but no one
has satisfactorily explained why *Har Mo'ed* should become corrupted to *Har-Megiddo,* and so the speculation must be viewed as
dubious.

Whatever the origin of the term, we are not to think in terms of a geographical locality in Israel (the Holy Land does not really feature in John's prophecy). Indeed it is doubtful that any single locality is in mind at all. The name stands for an event. Like the number 666, it will have had a history in the apocalyptic tradition, lost to us but known to the prophet, and for him it will have been a symbol for the last resistance of anti-god forces prior to the kingdom of Christ.

17. After bowls had been poured on earth, water, and sky, the seventh is poured **into the air** in order to produce a storm of cataclysmic proportions, which is matched by an earthquake of unprecedented severity (vv. 18ff.). Everything—from the voice in heaven to the storm in the sky and the quaking of the earth—combines to proclaim that the end has arrived. The **great voice** which proceeds **out of the temple, from the throne** is that of God himself. With divine holiness and authority it declares the good news, **It is done!** We are reminded of the observation in 15:1, that with these plagues the wrath of God is ended. The seventh bowl signifies the *end* of the end, but at the same time the beginning of the kingdom which knows no end (note how the song after the seventh trumpet celebrates in one breath the beginning of God's reign in glory and the exercise of his judgment on the destroyers of the earth, 11:17f.).

18. The **lightning, thunder, earthquake,** and **hail** (v. 21), which in 8:5 and 11:19 appeared at the conclusion of the seals and trumpets as concomitants of the end, come together also at the conclusion of the bowl-series, but with a measure of detail which enables us to understand the earlier cryptic references made to them. They are instruments of the divine wrath on rebellious men. Having featured in God's judgments at the time of the exodus, they now come on the generation of the Antichrist to the uttermost.

The lightning and thunder of the storm are separated from the hail in order to bring the series of plagues to a climax in a judgment which terrifyingly surpasses its counterpart in the exodus-narrative. Curiously, however, the language relating to the earthquake, that it was **such as had never been since men were on the earth,** repeats a sentiment which appears as a refrain in the descriptions of the Egyptian plagues, and it is first used in relation to the plague of hail (Exod. 9:18; cf. 10:6, 14, 11:6). This

language passes into the apocalyptic tradition through Daniel
12:1, where it applies to the last tribulation (cf. Mk 13:19). It
evidently was taken up into ordinary speech, for Josephus uses
it three times of the sufferings of the Jews in the Roman war.
(*Wars, Proem.* 4, VI. ix. 4, and note especially v. x. 5, 'Neither did
any other city ever suffer such miseries . . . from the beginning of
the world.')

19. Earthquake as an accompaniment of the divine appearing
at the end of the age is a standing element of eschatological expectation (see Isa. 13:13, Hag. 2:6, Zech. 14:4, Mk 13:8,
Heb. 12:26f.). John invokes the expected earthquake as God's
means of judging **the great city,** which is **great Babylon.** With
her **the cities of the nations** which followed in her ways are also
destroyed. The shattering of Babylon is the culminating, not the
exclusive element in her draining **the cup of the fury of his
wrath.** The fuller story of what is involved in this event is related
in chapters 17-18. For John it was a just judgment, since Babylon,
like a prostitute among men, had corrupted nations with her wine
for fornication, which in turn had led to their drinking the wine of
God's wrath (cf. 14:8). Babylon herself is therefore now made to
drink the cup of wrath to its dregs.

20. As an accompaniment, if not consequence of the earthquake, the **islands** and **mountains** flee from their place. The
scene has already been described at the opening of the sixth seal
(6:12ff.). Despite assertions to the contrary it is unlikely that
John wished to be taken literally, as though he thereby signified
the destruction of the universe, for he looked for the earth to be
the scene of the kingdom of Christ (5:10, 11:15, 15:4, 20:4ff.).
John's employment of this traditional language is characteristic of
his impressionist pictures of the last things. Through it he depicts
the unspeakable grandeur of the awe-fulness of the revelation of
God's judgments and deliverance at the end of history.

21. A like observation should be made on his transformation of
the Egyptian plague of hail into the appalling horror depicted in
verse 21. John will have found warrant for such an expectation in
the prophecy of Isaiah 28:2, but still more pertinently in Ezekiel
38:23, in the prophet's description of the overthrow of Gog and
his hosts through an earthquake and a storm of hail, fire, and
brimstone. The first exodus is the type of the last exodus, but the
latter infinitely surpasses the former, and this applies to both the

judgments and the deliverance. In conformity with this typology and the drift of the whole chapter we should view the **men** who **cursed God for the plague of the hail** as the subjects of the Antichrist. Elsewhere John tells of men repenting as they see the judgments of God in the earth (so explicitly 11: 13, and by implication 15: 40). Here he has in mind the obdurate who have no room for repentance, whether through experience of God's kindness (Rom. 2: 4) or the suffering of his judgments. Having received the mark of the beast on themselves, they have assumed his character also.

THE REIGN AND RUIN OF THE CITY OF THE ANTICHRIST 17: 1–19: 10

This section, which flows without a break into a description of the parousia of Christ (19: 11ff.), is a unity. It expands and explains the judgment of the seventh bowl, which was briefly described in 16: 17–21. Under no circumstances should it be interpreted as recounting events that take place after the conclusion of the seventh bowl-judgment. The seventh bowl concludes the messianic judgments. Babylon's draining of the cup of God's wrath is a major cause for announcing that all has now happened ('*It is done!*' 16: 19). How Babylon is made to drain that cup is the theme of chapter 17. The finality and significance of that event are underscored in the lamentation for Babylon in chapter 18 and the worship of the hosts of heaven in chapter 19.

The love-hate relationship between the city and the beast compels the prophet to concentrate attention in chapter 17 on the latter rather than the former, since it is the beast which becomes the agent of the city's destruction. The seven-headed monster has already appeared in various guises in earlier chapters. He comes on the scene without introduction in 11: 7 as 'the beast that ascends from the bottomless pit', and apparently is viewed as an individual ruler of the world. In chapter 12 the monster is described in greater detail, but he is there explicitly identified with the Devil (v. 9). In chapter 13 the beast referred to in chapter 11 is called from the sea by the dragon. He is again presented as an individual ruler, but the identity of his appearance with the dragon suggests that he is to be viewed as an incarnation of the spirit of evil. The

picture in chapter 17 is more complex. The woman who is the
harlot city, Babylon (v. 18), reclines on the monster. In the
ancient myth from which this cartoon is drawn the monster itself
is female. The two figures of monster and woman are really
alternative representations of a single entity, but in this context
they yield an appropriate means for depicting the antichristian
city in relation to the antichristian empire. The beast is therefore
the empire. In verse 11 however the beast is identified with an
eighth king, who at the same time is one of the seven kings symbolized by the monster's seven heads. How is it that within a single
vision a significant change like this should take place in the meaning of its symbolism? Some have solved the problem by suggesting
that two originally distinct sources have been fused in this chapter,
one in which the beast is the empire and another in which he
represents a line of emperors. Other scholars regard the second
individualizing section (vv. 8ff.) as an interpolation by a later
editor into John's text. The majority appear to see no change in
the symbolism. They maintain either that the whole prophecy has
in view rulers only, or that it is controlled throughout by a corporate conception.

The denial of a shift in the use of the symbolism is surely mistaken. If we did not possess the latter half of the chapter, none
would interpret the woman and the beast as representing other
than the city and the empire. This is so plain it ought not to be
modified by verse 11, for in any case the latter is concerned only
with a single head as representative of the seven-headed monster.
In view of John's use of sources in some of his earlier prophecies,
notably in chapters 11 and 12, wherein the monster also figures,
there can be no *a priori* reason for excluding the possibility of his
employing separate sources in chapter 17. Indeed, a glance
through the chapter will show that apart from verses 6*b* and 14 the
whole prophecy could have been penned by a Jewish apocalyptist,
for every line reflects Old Testament prophecy and Jewish apocalyptic tradition. Moreover after the terrible Jewish war, culminating in the destruction of Jerusalem, the Jews would have
looked for just such a judgment of God on Rome as this chapter
delineates. John could have taken up a current Jewish prophecy
and modified it to become a vehicle for his own message. Nevertheless it is equally possible that John himself independently
moulded contemporary traditions to make them yield the Lord's

message he had to proclaim, and in that case he would have felt wholly free to adapt the images to make them convey his meaning more adequately. Whether or not he did use sources, it should be observed that a fluctuation in the use of images to represent king-doms and their kings is observable in the work which was of greatest importance to John, namely Daniel. In Daniel 2:36ff. the head of gold is said to denote Nebuchadnezzar, but the other parts of the image are spoken of as kingdoms which succeed his. In Daniel 7:17f. the four beasts from the sea are interpreted as four kings, but in 7:23ff. the fourth beast is defined as 'a fourth king-dom on earth which shall be different from all kingdoms'. So in Revelation 17 a similar oscillation appears between kingdom and kings. In the opening paragraph the beast depicts the empire, in the latter its rulers who represent it.

The question of sources in chapter 17 therefore may be con-sidered as of uncertain solution, but of secondary importance. It is of greater moment to recognize that John has laid under tribute traditional images and, as elsewhere in his prophecy, dealt with them freely for the sake of his message.

As for the woman portrayed in chapter 17, it seems certain that John is at pains to present her in colours that contrast in the strongest possible manner with his picture of the woman who in chapters 12 and 21 represents the community and city of God. We are reminded of the sustained contrast in chapter 13 between the Antichrist and the 'lamb' of the Devil on the one hand, and the Christ of God who is the Lamb of God on the other. Babylon has her seat in the desert, the home of the demons; Zion belongs to heaven (12:1ff.), and is set on the mount of God (21:10). Babylon reposes on the beast, the incarnation of the Devil; Zion is the throne of God and the Lamb. Babylon is characterized by earthly pomp and luxury—purple, scarlet, and costly jewels; Zion wears the adornment of heaven—the sun, moon, and stars, and the fine linen which is the righteousness of the saints (12:1, 19:8). Babylon has a cup of abominations which brings death to all who drink it; Zion invites all to drink the water of life (22:17). Babylon is the mother of harlots; Zion is the mother of the Messiah and of the faithful of all ages. Babylon is drunk with the blood of saints and brings ruin to the earth; Zion brings to the world life and salvation. Babylon ends in eternal destruction (19:3), and becomes a dwelling of demons and hateful creatures (18:2); Zion belongs to the new creation, in which God and his people will dwell forever. These contrasts will have been readily perceived by John's original readers, and will have served to emphasize the necessity that they should 'depart' from Babylon, so as not to share in its fate, and that they maintain their lot in the city which will endure for ever (cf. 18:4).

1, 2. The judgment of the great harlot announces the theme of the entire section 17:1–19:10. Not surprisingly, therefore, the judgment is not immediately narrated. Its deferment till after the portrayal of the history whereby the beast comes to be her adversary, enables the doom song of chapter 18 to follow immediately upon that narration. *Harlot* is a term applied by Old Testament prophets to various apostate cities. It is used with respect to Tyre (Isa. 23:16f.) and Nineveh (Nah. 3), but above all with regard to Jerusalem (e.g., Isa. 1:21, Jer. 3, Ezek. 16 and 23). We recall the identification in 11:8 of the antichristian city with Sodom, Egypt, and Jerusalem. That the woman is **seated upon many waters** echoes Jeremiah 51:23. There it relates to the actual geographical situation of Babylon, for the river Euphrates flowed through the city, which was also surrounded by many canals and had a thorough irrigation system. This circumstance afforded the city both a source of wealth and its sense of security. The **kings of the earth** who **committed fornication** with the harlot, and the dwellers on earth who became **drunk** with her wine represent the apostate nations generally. 'Babylon' was a source of corruption to all the people who came into contact with her. They participated in her idolatries and evils.

3. The opening two verses convey the angel's invitation to view the woman. The vision proper now commences. When the prophet states that he was **carried ... away in the Spirit into a wilderness,** this is not to indicate that he is transported to a better vantage-point from which to view the city, but rather that he now sees Babylon's true situation. The harlot-city on the waters is actually set in the desert. It is hardly likely, as many assume, that the symbolism is inspired by the title of the prophecy against Babylon in Isaiah 21, 'The oracle of the wilderness of the sea'. The desert features in several of John's visions, but it is an ambiguous symbol. In chapter 12 the mother of the Messiah escapes from the dragon into the wilderness, there to be cared for in safety by God. When the mother of harlots is represented as residing in the wilderness, it is then conceived as the dwelling place of the Devil and evil spirits (cf. Tob. 8 : 3, Lk. 11 : 24). The **beast** on which the woman sits is described as **scarlet**. If the colour relates to the beast himself, it shares the likeness of the dragon (12 : 3), but its description as scarlet rather than red could indicate the materials with which it is draped—the scarlet of royalty and of conquerors, beloved of Rome. Whereas in 13 : 1 the **blasphemous names** were stated to be inscribed on the heads of the beast, referring to the emperors' claims to divinity, the beast is here said to be **full** of them, i.e., it is covered all over with them. The empire embraced a multitude of forms of idolatry, not the least of which were Rome's own claims to be divine.

4. It has already been pointed out that **the woman** and the beast go back to a single origin, for in the Babylonian mythology the monster Tiamat was female. The transformation of a beast into a woman belongs to a common development in paganism, wherein gods were frequently conceived of as having animal shape and then were refined to possess the appearance of humans. It was not uncommon for the two kinds of representation to be preserved alongside each other, and in such cases their relations varied. The divinity could lead the beast, carry it, sit on it, stand on it, or even merely hold an image of it.[1] In our passage the woman and the beast are both clothed in scarlet. Since the woman represents the anti-christian city, it is natural to interpret the beast on which she sits, and which supports her and shares her nature, as symbolizing the antichristian empire. Her gorgeous array suggest her luxury and magnificence. Her possession of **a golden cup** echoes Jeremiah 51 : 7, except that in the latter passage Babylon herself is a cup in the Lord's hand, whereas here she hands the cup to others; but the meaning is not very different. The **abominations** within the cup are not so much horrible practices, from the moral point of view, as idolatrous practices. Abomination was a characteristic Jewish term for an idol.[2] A cup which implicates those

---

[1] See Gunkel, *Schöpfung und Chaos*, pp. 365 ff.

[2] The Jewish use of the term 'abomination' for the idol is reflected in some interesting changes of name in the Old Testament. Compounds featuring the name of Baal (= lord) were changed by substituting the term *bosheth* (= abomination) for Baal; e.g., Ishbaal in 2 Samuel 2:8 becomes Ishbosheth in 1 Chronicles 8:33. The most striking example of this change is seen in the refusal of the Jews to give the heathen idol and altar which Antiochus Epiphanes placed on the altar in the temple of Jerusalem its proper name. Whereas

who drink it in abominations and fornication is therefore a consistent idea, for idolatry is spiritual fornication.

5. As harlots in Roman society had their names on the headband customarily worn by Roman women, so this most notorious of all prostitutes has **a name of mystery** on her forehead, i.e., a name which is a symbol (*mystery* in the apocalyptic tradition = *secret*). **Babylon the great, mother of harlots and of earth's abominations.** What ancient Babylon was to the world of its day so the city represented by the woman is to John's day, the cause of earth's apostasy from God and devotion to devilish ways.

6, 7. The woman is **drunk with the blood of the saints and ... of the martyrs of Jesus.** These could denote the members of the Church of Jesus alone. It is feasible, however, that the double expression includes the saints of the Old Covenant, whose blood was shed in loyalty to the eternal God, and the witnesses to Jesus who died in earlier persecutions and in the last great trial (cf. Heb. 12 : 1f., which brackets the witnesses of Jesus with the witnesses of former ages). If John has employed an earlier Jewish source in this chapter, the reference to the martyrs of Jesus would have been added by him, to be grouped, as by the writer to the Hebrews, with the Jewish confessors of earlier centuries.

The sight of the glory of the risen Lord sent John into a swoon (1 : 17), that of the harlot into great admiration. There is no need to seek hidden motives or causes for John's reaction. It is consonant with the experiences of apocalyptists, and provokes the explanation of the angel-guide as to the meaning of what he has seen.

8. The beast that you saw is the beast of verse 3, which represents the antichristian empire. In verse 10 the identification of its seven heads with seven kings presupposes that in this paragraph also the seer is conscious that the beast represents the empire, of which the heads are rulers. Yet in verse 11 'the beast that was and is not' is identified with the eighth king. He so represents

---

Antiochus called his idol Baal Shamaim, 'Lord of heaven' (the title given to Zeus), the Jews contemptuously termed it *shiqquz shomem*, 'the abomination that appals' (1 Mac. 1:54, Dan. 11:31). So arose the well-known term for the idolatrous representation of the Antichrist, the 'abomination of desolation' (Mk 13:14), or better, 'the shocking abomination', the appalling idol. The associations of this term make its use in Revelation 17:4f. and 21:7 very suitable.

the empire-beast that he is called the beast *simpliciter*. How then are we to interpret verse 8? Has the transition from beast-empire to beast-king already been made, so that the ruler alone is subject of the statement? If so we must interpret verse 8 as meaning, 'The beast that you saw will be represented in a ruler who will perfectly embody its spirit. He will arrogate to himself divine claims, but they are the reverse of true divinity, for unlike Him who is, and was, and is to come (1 : 8) the beast was, but is not, and he is to ascend from the pit but go to destruction. Nevertheless the world will marvel at him during his brief hour, since he was, and is not, but is to come.' With this interpretation most exegetes are content. The reversal of the divine name carried with it an imitation of the redemptive acts of the risen Lord (1 : 17f.), but implies an end in destruction. The language clearly reflects the Nero-*redivivus* myth, which has featured in the description of the beast in 13 : 3f. (see notes).

That the attributes of God and the redemption of the Lamb and the expectation of a Nero-Antichrist provide the materials for the formulation of verse 8 is reasonably certain, despite the denials of some. But it is possible that there is more. The beast of verse 3 is not merely a society characterized by a permissive morality. It is a kingdom in which the spirit of the primeval dragon is incarnate (ch. 12); i.e., it shares the nature of the chaos-monster which in the ancient myth defied and fought the gods of heaven. This is the creature in whose likeness Daniel portrayed the empires of world history and above all the fourth antigod-kingdom of his day. It had provided the earlier prophets with images which could be applied to the political powers of their own times. Egypt was characterized with especial frequency by this figure, for her subjugation by God was a particularly apt parallel to the lineaments of the myth, since it had involved the drying up of the waters of the sea (cf. Isa. 30 : 7, 51 : 9f., Ezek. 29 : 3ff., 32 : 2ff.). Isaiah 27 : 1 conveys another vivid, if enigmatic, example of the use of the myth, and expositors have been uncertain whether the prophet had in view specific political powers (some identify Assyria, Babylon, and Egypt in the text), or whether the figures were meant to denote rebel powers generally. In any case a conscious application of the myth to eschatological expectations of God's triumph in the world is evident. The survival of the eschatological use of the myth beyond the limit of the Old Testament writings

and into the first century AD is attested by its appearance in
2 *Enoch* 60 : 24, 2 *Baruch* 29 : 4, 4 *Esdras* 6 : 49ff., although in these
passages the myth is non-political (the monsters will be food for the
faithful in the new age). Interestingly John's consistent representation of the monster as having seven heads is a direct reminiscence
of the primitive myth, for it does not occur in the Old Testament
references to it.

Now the basic presupposition of the eschatological application
of the myth to political powers is that the monster who had reared
up against God in primeval times and been subdued by him would
do it again, with the same result. In this connection certain
deviations of the myth are of interest. Whereas in some versions
the monster was slain and its body used in the creation of the
world, in others the monster was simply subdued. The former is
reflected in Isaiah 51 : 9. As Rahab was cut in pieces, so Egypt
was overcome when the ransomed of the Lord crossed the sea. The
latter is reflected in Isaiah 30 : 7. As Rahab was reduced to helplessness, so Egypt is an ally that can do nothing: 'Therefore I have
called her "Rahab who sits still" ', or as *NEB* renders it, 'Rahab
quelled'. This latter representation could be expressed by saying
that the monster **was, and is not.** If it appears again, it will
naturally **ascend from the bottomless pit,** the abyss (= the
ocean), as in Revelation 13 : 1 and Daniel 7 : 3ff., but it will per-
force **go to perdition.** Revelation 17 : 8, therefore, is a perfect
representation of the eschatological application of the creation
myth to a political power.

A peculiar circumstance however combined to strengthen John's
attribution of this figure to Rome. It was in his time that the
expectation arose that Nero would return from the dead to wreak
vengeance on Rome. In apocalyptic circles Nero-*redivivus* had
become a demonic figure. It was extraordinarily opportune for
John, for it enabled him to combine the traditional representation
of the chaos-dragon of primeval times with the current myth of
Nero returned from the dead. This resulted in the unusually
powerful representation of an antichrist-ruler of an antichrist-
kingdom. Both of them participated in the nature of the evil
spiritual power which had inspired the evil political powers
through the ages, and the fear of them was sharpened through the
dread of a demonic adversary from hell.

In view of this it does not seem fanciful to interpret verse 8 as describing the antichrist-ruler in whose nature and history are embodied the nature and history of the antichristian empire he ruled. Both share in the likeness of the dragon; both have opposed the Lord in his people; both belong to the abyss of the pit; both are to unite in an onslaught on the followers of the Lamb; both are doomed to share the fate of the monster of the deep.

The dwellers on earth ... will marvel to behold the beast. They will admire the ruler of the empire for his astonishing powers (see note on 13 : 3), even as they admire the empire for its embodying the splendour and might of former ages.

9. This calls for a mind with wisdom. The reader is in need of guidance that he may understand the mystery of the beast. The clue to the monster lies in his heads. A double interpretation is provided, the first of which is of importance, since it instantly identifies the location of the beast. From early times Rome was known as the city of the seven hills. Its literature frequently refers to it, and an annual festival celebrated it (the so-called *septimontium*). That **the seven heads are seven hills** illustrates yet again that John is conscious of the essentially corporate nature of the beast. It is a world-power centred in the renowned city with the seven hills.

10, 11. A further interpretation of the seven heads is given. **They are also seven kings.** Of these **five** belong to history. They **have fallen.** The sixth is reigning at the time of writing. He **is.** The seventh **has not yet come,** but when he does appear **he must remain only a little while.** But there is to appear **an eighth,** which yet **belongs to the seven;** i.e., one of the seven kings is to come on the scene again and sum up in himself the characteristics of the beast. The beast is an eighth king.

Students of the Revelation have needlessly bemused themselves over this second clue to the identity of the beast. They have worried over the five kings, whereas John was concerned only with the eighth. The awkward fact is that no arrangement of the line of emperors yields a satisfactory solution to the problem which John unintentionally set us. The full list of emperors to the time of Domitian is as follows: Julius Caesar, Augustus, Tiberias, Gaius, Claudius, Nero, Galba, Otho, Vitellius, Vespasian, Titus, Domitian. If one begins with Julius Caesar, then the sixth emperor, in whose reign John writes, is Nero. Could John have been writing in his time? Some have thought so. Certainly his death

ushered in a chaotic period for the empire, with three emperors
tumbling from their thrones in less than two years. But this setting
for the Revelation does not tally with what we have seen of John's
teaching on the Antichrist as another Nero, nor with the tradition
of John's writing in the time of Domitian. A more popular reckoning begins with Augustus (following the precedent of Tacitus) and
omits the three brief reigns of Galba, Otho, and Vitellius, since
they were viewed as rebels rather than emperors. The sixth emperor is then Vespasian, whose son Titus reigned only for two
years. On this basis the choice is either to consider that John wrote
under Vespasian and awaited the coming of the seventh and eighth
emperors, or to regard verse 10 as written in the style of a prophecy after the event, and to conclude that John viewed Domitian
under whom he wrote as a second Nero, the Antichrist inspired by
hell.

Of the two possibilities the former is the more plausible, but it is
more likely that this whole procedure should be viewed as misguided. The symbolism of the beast's seven heads was not created
by John to suit the Roman historical situation, but was an eschatological dogma with roots reaching into past millennia. That
Rome was situated on seven hills was a happy coincidence of
which John gladly availed himself. It was, however, too much to
expect that the Roman empire would conveniently have seven
emperors only; nor was any such limitation necessary. When
apocalyptic traditions are applied to history, precision is not to be
looked for. The next item in John's interpretation of the beast
illustrates that, for the ten horns are also derived from the eschatological tradition. But John applies them differently from Daniel,
and their number does not precisely fit the circumstances he has in
view. We, therefore, interpret as follows. *Seven* in the Revelation is
a number of completeness. Of the complete line of emperors that
fall into view the majority have appeared (five), the sixth is now
reigning, and the seventh, when he comes, *must remain only a little
while*—not through any presumption of his ill-health, but because
the end is at hand (1:3, etc.). The coming of the eighth king then
is future to John (he *is not*), but it is not far off.

12. The feature of **the ten horns** of the beast is derived from
Daniel's vision of the fourth beast (Dan. 7:7). In the interpretation they are said to denote a line of **kings** who precede the Antichrist, and some of them are overthrown by him (Dan. 7:24). In

John's vision, however, they are confederate with the Antichrist. Where are they located? If this passage stood alone, we should assume that they held rule in various parts of the empire, for the horns are on the beast (it has been suggested that they represent governors of the senatorial provinces). Nevertheless, since chapter 17 explains the concluding vision of chapter 16, we should have regard to what is there written. At the outpouring of the sixth bowl the Euphrates dries up and the kings from the east respond to the bidding of the dragon, the beast, and the false prophet to invade the west (16: 12ff.). *The ten horns*, therefore, are probably to be identified with these kings from the east, beyond the empire's borders. In that case the ten horns are thought of as on the head of the beast-emperor. It is not impossible that the Parthian satraps are specifically in view. There were fourteen of them, but the eschatological tradition of ten horns was sufficiently close to represent them. Perhaps, however, we should not be over precise. The powers of the mysterious east, beyond the border of the empire, put themselves at the Antichrist's behest. Their **authority ... with the beast** is short, **for one hour.** Naturally, for the Antichrist himself speedily goes to perdition (v. 11).

13. The **one mind** of the ten kings is explained in verse 17. It is God who puts unanimity of purpose into their hearts **to give over** their royal **power and authority to the beast.** This is characteristic of John's teaching. When the Antichrist and his allies reach the height of their impiety and folly, even to the extent of making war on the Lamb as well as on the antichrist-city (v. 14) they subserve the will of God (cf. 13: 5ff. and notes).

14. The single mind of the allies of the Antichrist, like that of their leader, is ultimately antigod in character. Accordingly their resistance to the Lamb is mentioned prior to their devastation of the harlot city. But how are we intended to conceive of this **war on the Lamb**? The parallel with 13: 7 suggests that it is through waging war on the saints. It is likely that verse 14 compresses a whole complex of ideas. In chapters 11, 12 and 13 the **called and chosen and faithful** are not represented as standing behind the Lamb while he fights alone on their behalf. Rather they are **with him** in the fight, and they conquer by the blood of the Lamb and the word of their testimony, and they love not their lives even unto death (12: 11). Yet this 'war' is short, and it is ended by the appearance of the Lamb as the mighty Word of God (19: 11ff.).

When he wields the sword of his mouth, all resistance immediately
comes to an end (19 : 20f.). Then those who were with him in their
hour of testimony will be with him in the hour of his triumph
(19 : 14).

Was John aware of the fact that in the Babylonian tradition the
title **Lord of lords and King of kings** was accorded to the god
Marduk, the conqueror of the monster Tiamat? Apart from
Egypt it does not appear to have been claimed by other sovereigns
in the Mediterranean countries. If John did know it, he will have
adopted the same procedure as in chapter 12 and claimed for the
Lamb of God the sole right to use the title, since the Lamb alone
is the conqueror of evil and redeemer of the world.

15. Comment is made on the picture of the harlot city in verse
1. There the 'many waters' referred to the literal 'waters of Babylon', for which the city was famed. The transference of this
feature to the city of the seven hills made it desirable to give it a
relevant meaning. This John does after the manner of Isaiah
8 : 7, which may well have been in his mind at this point. Under
the figure of 'the waters of the River, mighty and many' (i.e., the
river Euphrates) which are to overflow their banks and sweep into
Judea, Isaiah depicts 'the king of Assyria and all his glory' coming
like a flood into the land. The original application of this figure
would suit the context of verse 15 (i.e., vv. 12ff. and 16f.) perfectly.
As the overflowing of the waters of the Euphrates into Palestine
signified an overwhelming invasion of the land, so the many
waters on which 'Babylon' sits represent **peoples and multitudes and nations and tongues** who join forces with the invading powers and attack the godless city. This alliance of the
nations with the ten kings repeats in a fresh way the events of the
sixth bowl, when the kings of the east march to the west and join
forces with 'the kings of the whole world' for their fight against
Babylon and against God in the event of Armageddon (16 : 12ff.).
In 6 : 14 the kings of the world include the nations they represent.
In 17 : 15 the nations include their kings, but the situation that is
depicted is the same.

16. The fears of Nero returning, alive or risen from the dead,
with armies of the east to destroy the empire's capital are amply
fulfilled: **the ten horns . . . and the beast will hate the harlot.**
The language takes up phrase by phrase Ezekiel's prophecy of the
destruction of faithless Jerusalem through the Babylonians and

Assyrians (Ezek. 23 : 25ff.). In that prophecy the Jews' apostasy
from her covenant-God is allegorized as the behaviour of an
adulterous woman, who receives the punishment reserved for such
conduct. The city is destroyed through her former lovers turning
against her in **hate** (Ezek. 23 : 29). They strip her of her clothes
and jewels and leave her **naked** in shame (23 : 26). The flames
devour her children (23 : 25), and they **burn up** their houses
with fire (23 : 47). Such is the fate appointed for the harlot city of
God. And if Jerusalem is so judged, how much more the city of the
beast?

17. The single mind of the kings, the beast, and all who unite
with them, is the work of **God,** who uses the wrath of men to
praise him. In wreaking their vengeance on the anti-christian
city these enemies of God have no thought that they are fulfilling
his purpose. This is more strongly expressed by John than the
translations indicate, for in Greek the terms 'purpose' and 'mind'
are one, so that we may render, 'God has put it into their hearts to
carry out his mind by being of one mind . . .' Their **mind** is to
give over **their power** and authority **to the beast,** who wills to
destroy the city he once ruled and to annihilate the followers of
the Lamb. But it is precisely the mind of God which impels them
to move against Babylon, and even against the called and chosen
and faithful of the Lamb. Babylon must be judged, and so also
must the beast and his consortium, even as the Church must be
refined and the world made ready for the kingdom. Hence **the
words of God**—made known through the prophets of the old
covenant and of the new—are **fulfilled** also through those who
hate him, alike in their action against the empire and in their resistance to heaven. Evil is destroyed by evil, and in turn reaps
its own harvest. That the agents of the Devil execute the will of God
vividly illustrates that there is no real dualism in the Revelation.
The beast and his allies remain in the hand of the God they defy,
and by the impulse of the Devil they unitedly fulfil the words of
God. It can never be otherwise, if there is but one Lord of lords
and King of kings, and none but he shares the throne of his
Father.

18. Finally the identity of the woman on the beast is made
known—at least as openly as the mode of apocalyptic writing permitted. **The woman . . . is the great city which has dominion
over the kings of the earth.** If verse 9 also be taken into account,

there was one city only in the first century to which this description could refer, namely Rome, whose rule reached virtually to the limit of the world of western and mid-orient man.

Rome, then, was the Babylon of her age. She was to be desolated and left in ruins as a perpetual memorial of the judgment of God on human and demonic wickedness (19:3). What are we to say of this prophecy in face of the fact that no Nero-*redivivus* appeared on the scene after the decease of the seventh emperor, and that in the irony of history, Rome instead of becoming the seat of the Antichrist eventually capitulated to the Lamb of God and commanded all her citizens to acknowledge his supremacy? Was John a false prophet? At best pious and sincere, but completely misguided in his view of the outcome of history? Only they will answer in the affirmative who are prepared to place Isaiah, Jeremiah, Ezekiel, and the rest of the Old Testament prophets in the same category; for they also related their own generations to the day of the Lord. From the gospels and epistles it would seem that John the Baptist and our Lord and his apostles did likewise, although their modes of expression differed from John's.

Here it is necessary to distinguish between the content of John's prophecy and its presentation; or, if you will, between his doctrine and his application of it. The burden of the Revelation is one with that of Old Testament prophecy, but transposed into a key determined by the new covenant. This transposition is all important, for at its heart is the gospel of the crucified and risen Lord. John mediates the eschatology of the judgment and redemption of the Lamb of God, and he is conscious that both the judgment and the redemption have to do with history. He was led to apply this insight to the history of his time, believing, like all prophets, that 'the appointed time has grown very short' (1 C. 7:29). For this he had ample reasons. On the one hand the Redeemer's work in the bringing of God's new world is one and indivisible. The redemption having been achieved, the completion of its effect was at hand (so ch. 5). On the other hand the 'mystery of lawlessness' is plainly at work in the world (2 Th. 2:7). John's exile was evidence of that, and the signs of the times betokened its speedy extension. His prophecy sets forth the nature and the outcome of the opposition between these two processes, namely, God's purpose for the redemption of the world, already realized in Jesus Christ our Lord, and the mystery of lawlessness, which is also at work in the world. The time scale used by John was too short, but his interpretation of the ultimate issues of this conflict is at one with the rest of the Bible.

Some wise and frank words of Adolf Schlatter are in place here: 'God's ways with Rome and the nations ruled by it were other than the prophecy described them. But this did not weaken the Church's conviction that the word spoken to it by John is a precious gift of God, and that it performs a great service for the knowledge of his ways. For so long as the prophetic word was a living force in the churches it remained apparent to all that the prophet sees God's work as it is capable of perception by human sight, and that he receives God's word as it corresponds to the place in which he is set in human history. Therefore along with attention to the prophecy there was always conjoined a readiness to be shown further by God's sovereign rule how he fulfils his promise. And gratitude for the visions given to the prophet was based on the fact that they inspire Christian people to observe God's work in their own situation and to understand his ways.'[1]

A DEATH SONG FOR BABYLON 18 : 1–24

Having portrayed the fate of the harlot-city through the on-slaught of the Antichrist and his allies, John composes a dirge over the city in the style of the doom-songs of Old Testament prophets. One cannot but notice that the song of the ruin of Babylon is a good deal longer than the story of it narrated in 17 : 15ff. Yet the song is really part of the story, and greatly adds to its effectiveness. For the news that John has to tell was almost unbelievable to his contemporaries. To declare to them the total overthrow of the city that ruled the world was like foretelling the end of the world. And in its way so it was. It signified the end of an old world, too much subject to the powers of evil, and the revelation of another, under the sway of the prince of peace. The song which celebrates the city's fall drives home the reality of the prophet's message and its significance.

It will be observed that the stance adopted in the song fluctu-ates at various points. The song begins with an angel's announce-ment of the stupendous event which has just taken place: 'Fallen, fallen is Babylon the great!' This little oracle of three verses in

1 *Erläuterungen*, p. 299.

length is followed by a second declaration from heaven (from another angel?), which views the fall of the city as future (vv. 4–8).
Then come three lamentations over the ruin of Babylon, uttered
by the kings of the earth (vv. 9f.), the merchants (vv. 11ff.) and
sea-captains and sailors (vv. 17ff.). Each little threnody ends with
a virtually identical utterance: 'It all happened in a single hour!'
In contrast to these cries of woe, a call sounds out for heaven and
the saints of God to rejoice over the judgment which has been
accomplished on Babylon (v. 20). Finally, an angel enforces by a
symbolic action a prophecy that Babylon will be overthrown
without remedy (vv. 21–4). These modifications of viewpoint in
the song are due to variations in the mode of presenting its single
message. But in any case, whether viewed as past, present, or
future, the whole is a prophecy, which celebrates a day of judgment when evil will be requited and God's cause vindicated in a
world which has never ceased to belong to him.

Every line of the song reflects earlier compositions, and it has not
unfairly been described as a cento of doom-songs of the prophets
(Kiddle). Charles went further than this, and maintained that the
song could not have been composed by John, even though he saw
fit to employ it, since its view of Babylon's fall differed from his
own. In 19 : 3, which is John's own composition, it is assumed that
Babylon will be overthrown by fire and will remain a burning
heap for ever, whereas in chapter 18 Babylon is described as a
desolate ruin, occupied by every kind of foul bird and evil spirit
(v. 2). This contention is an odd one for so experienced a commentator as Charles to make, for it appears to overlook that the
composition of chapter 18 is as truly symbolic as the story of
Babylon's fall in the highly coloured chapter 17, despite the
differences in styles of imagery (ch. 17 employs the cartoon
characteristic of apocalyptic writing, ch. 18 the imagery of the
earlier prophets). In drawing from the prophetic doom-songs John
has as freely mixed his metaphors as they did. The demon-
possessed ruin of verse 2 becomes in verse 7 a wanton woman, a
queen who refuses to be a widow. In verse 6 she is to drink a
double draught in the cup she mixed for others, but in verse 8 the
city is to suffer from plagues, pestilence, famine, and fire. It is not
surprising, therefore, that the variety of viewpoint to which
Charles draws attention is observable in this very chapter. For
in contrast to the description of the lonely ruin in verse 2, the

lamentations of the kings, merchants, and sailors are introduced each time, with references to the smoke of the city's burning, on which they gaze from afar (vv. 9, 15, 18). Moreover, the same dual representation of destruction occurs within a single paragraph of Isaiah 34:8ff., on which John has drawn in this passage. In reality the remarkable feature of this song of death is its magnificent unity of composition despite its multiplicity of sources. The chief quarries to which John has gone for his structure are the prophecies against Babylon in Isaiah 13 and Jeremiah 51, and that against Tyre in Ezekiel 26-7, together with significant snatches from the prophecies against Edom in Isaiah 34 and Nineveh in Nahum 3. John's employment of these doom-songs, directed against the tyrannies of former ages, is itself significant in the way he viewed Rome. This city summed up in itself and surpassed the wickedness of the tyrant-powers of the past. Hence in his song which celebrates her desolation he concentrates into one the prophecies against them all.

1. The opening paragraph supplies an introduction to the song and states its chief themes. The **angel coming down from heaven,** announcing Babylon's doom, has **great authority** and divine **splendour.** In the Revelation the greatness of an angel accords with the greatness of his proclamation (cf. 10:1ff.). The description of this angel is unusually impressive, for it cites Ezekiel 43:2, which tells how the glory of the Lord, having departed from the old temple prior to its destruction, returned to the temple of the new age. Thus in announcing Babylon's fall the angel manifests the glory of God in a manner similar to its revelation in the coming kingdom. The judgment of God and the redemption of God are a unity. They are integral to the coming of his kingdom. They alike manifest his glory, and both are for the good of his universe.

2, 3. The **mighty voice** of the angel befits the majesty of his appearance and the critical nature of his message. What men had thought impossible has happened: **Babylon the great** has **fallen!** Its occupation by **demons** and **every foul and hateful bird** (so Jer. 51:37 of ruined Babylon, and Isa. 34:11-15 of Edom) emphasizes the totality of its desolation; the city has taken on the character of the sinister desert to which it inwardly belonged even in its glory (cf. 17:3, and note). The reason for Babylon's fall is summarized, and expanded later in the chapter: **all nations**

have drunk the wine of her impure passion, or rather, the wine which leads to immorality (= false religion) and which symbolizes God's judgment (see 14 : 8) and note). **The kings of the earth** have shared in her evil idolatries, leading their people to do likewise, and **the merchants of the earth** have profited from her limitless **wantonness,** so becoming partners in her worship of Mammon. The whole earth has been corrupted by Babylon, therefore Babylon is destroyed from the earth.

4. The second **voice from heaven,** which declares a second oracle, may be presumed to be that of an angel, in view of the transition to the third person in verses 5 and 8. The use of the first person in verse 4 may then be taken to be a citation of the divine command. Swete observed that the cry, **Come out of her, my people,** rings through Hebrew history, from Abraham and the exodus through the centuries of prophetic witness; see especially Jeremiah 50 : 8, 51 : 6, where the call is made to flee from Babylon before it is destroyed, and Isaiah 48 : 20, 52 : 11, where appeal is made to the exiles to leave Babylon and return to their homeland. Paul applies it in a purely spiritual sense in 2 Corinthians 6: 17. It is not impossible that in his citation of the cry John may have had in view both the literal and spiritual meaning of the words.

5, 6. Her sins are heaped high as heaven, so they cannot be overlooked by God. Not only their number, but the brazen openness of Babylon's sins may be in view. **God has remembered her iniquities,** but they are punished by none other than the Antichrist (19 : 16f.). The call, therefore, to **render** to Babylon **as she herself has rendered** could be addressed to the Antichrist and his helpers. Or the reference may be general, in recognition that heavenly, earthly and demonic powers must needs play a part in the judgment that falls on the city. Observe that this is not a demand for indiscriminate slaughter, but for a judgment on the city in accordance with the *lex talionis*. Rome was notoriously ruthless in her conquests of nations and treatment of any who tried to free themselves from her control. She is therefore to experience what she has repeatedly meted out to others. For the sentiment, cf. Jeremiah 50 : 15, 29; and for the double punishment for sins, cf. Jeremiah 16 : 18, Isaiah 40 : 2 (the former in prospect of Israel's receiving it, the latter in retrospect of Israel's experiencing it in Babylon).

7, 8. The latter half of verse 7, with its sequence in verse 8, paraphrases the prophecy against Babylon in Isaiah 47 : 7ff. In the world of the biblical writers a widow was the type *par excellence* of poverty and helplessness—a condition as far opposed to Rome's splendour as the imagination could conjure. But **in a single day** her position will change. While the language of this passage reflects Isaiah 47 : 9, this feature of the suddenness of Babylon's fall runs through the whole chapter (cf. the refrain in the lamentations of the kings, merchants, and sailors, vv. 10, 17, 19, and the acted prophecy of v. 21). The judgment which faces Babylon, however incredible it may appear to the world, is inescapable. Though the Antichrist and his minions are its agents, it is the divine decree which has determined it, and **mighty is the Lord God who judges her.**

9–19. This central passage, recording the lamentations of the kings, merchants, and sailors, is especially indebted to Ezekiel's extended doom-song over Tyre, Ezekiel 26–8. While the earlier prophet's compositions are not structured like John's, which is divided into three stanzas with virtually identical refrain, he too includes expressions of distress from the princes of the sea (Ezek. 26 : 16f.), mariners and pilots (27 : 28f.) and merchants of the peoples (27 : 36), as he has a passing reference to the horror of the kings of the coastlands (27 : 35).

9, 10. The kings of the earth naturally do not include the kings confederate with the Antichrist, and who were jointly responsible for the destruction of the great city (17: 12, 16). They are to be envisaged as rulers of countries subject to Rome, within its empire, and others allied to Rome beyond its borders. They had **committed fornication and were wanton with her** in a religious sense. They had not hesitated to adopt Rome's idolatries and her blasphemous emperor-worship, nor resisted her restrictive policies against the people of God. As kings they represent the nations over which they rule. And because they are kings they mourn the passing of the **mighty city, Babylon** (contrast vv. 17 and 19, where the merchants and sailors grieve for the *wealthy* city). Their weeping and wailing is not entirely altruistic, for if the mighty city is overthrown **in one hour,** who can hope to stand?

11–16. The merchants of the earth are given more space than the kings (vv. 11–17), doubtless through the precedent of Ezekiel's song, whose longer list of wares in which Tyre traded inspired John's catalogue in this passage (see Ezek. 27: 12-24). While Ezekiel included in his list of goods names of countries from which they came, John is silent on them. His contemporaries, however, on reading this passage would be able to identify the areas from which many of them came. Rome's trade was world-wide, and even this modest enumeration of its imports entails many lands. The **gold, ivory,** and **costly wood,** for example, came from North Africa, the **jewels** and **pearls** from India, **spices** from Arabia, **cinnamon** from South China, **myrrh** from Media, **wheat** from Egypt, **horses** from Armenia, **chariots** from Gaul, and **slaves** from all areas of the world. John's double mention of the last item is revealing, since the term for slaves is 'bodies', and the phrase **human souls** in ordinary speech was synonymous, but it virtually carried the meaning of human live-stock. 'The world of St John's day,' commented Swete, 'ministered in a thousand ways to the follies and vices of Babylon, but the climax was reached in the sacrifice of human life which recruited the huge familiae of the rich, filled the *lupanaria* (brothels), and ministered to the brutal pleasures of the amphitheatre.'

17-19. The merchants, however, are concerned neither for the miseries of the innocent nor for the sufferings of the city, but solely for loss of trade. **'Alas, alas ... In one hour all this wealth has been laid waste.'** Their spirit was one with sister Babylon.[1] The cry and signs of mourning from **all shipmasters** (= captains) **and seafaring men, sailors and all whose trade is on the sea** imitate the words and actions of the mariners and pilots in Ezekiel 27: 29ff. As with the merchants, their concern over the city's ruin is not for the city itself, nor for those who

[1] It has frequently been maintained that verse 14 ill suits its present context, for it apparently interrupts the description of the merchants' wares and their laments, the passage reads smoothly without it, and it is addressed to Babylon in the second person in a context set in the third person. Since the final paragraph is also set in the second person the verse could have fallen out of the text from there. Charles therefore placed it after verse 21, Lohmeyer and others favoured a position after verse 23. While this is a reasonable conjecture, the content of verse 14 does not suit the final paragraph in either of the positions mentioned, but it is related to the paragraph of the merchants. It would seem best to leave it where it is. John has interrupted his merchants' lament through the expansion of verse 11 into a list of wares which they sold to the city. In verse 14 he declares in direct prophetic style that these fruits, dainties, and splendour are things of the past. He then takes up again the merchants' song where he left it.

have perished in it, but for their own loss of revenue. At Babylon's port (the differences between Rome and Tyre in their relation to the sea is dismissed) **'all who had ships at sea grew rich by her wealth!'** Mammon again! As Caird rightly observed, there was nothing sinful in the commodities of the merchants and sailors: 'Every object of worth which seafaring men had ever carried to Rome to grace the life of the imperial capital, whether in its natural state or enhanced by the craftsmanship of man, belonged to the order of God's creation which must be redeemed by the overthrow of Babylon, and would find its proper place in the new Jerusalem.' The sin of Babylon was its use of these things to seduce mankind to adopt the kind of gross materialism and mammon-worship which is illustrated in the songs of the merchants and seamen.

20. It is misleading to include (with *RSV*) verse 20 in the lament of the sailors. The saying should be viewed either as an independent declaration of the prophet or as the completion of the angel's statement beginning in verse 4, which then includes the prediction of the lamentations of the kings, merchants, and sailors. It finds its response in the songs of joy which open chapter 19. The cry is addressed to **heaven, saints, apostles and prophets.** Are the *saints* the whole company of God's people in heaven and on earth? In that case the *apostles* would be representative of the saints of the new covenant and the *prophets* those of the old—fittingly so, since both find their significance in their testimony to Jesus. If the saints are they who have suffered at the hands of the great whore, the apostles and prophets would be exclusively those of the new covenant—again singled out because of their representative testimony to Jesus. In any case the company of heaven and the saints are called to **'Rejoice ... for God has given judgment for you against her!'** In 12:12 the citizens of heaven are bidden to rejoice for the victory of the Lamb over the Devil's claim to his people and their own participation in it through confession of faith in his name even to the death. Here they rejoice because of God's vindication of their cause in the lawsuit of the evil city. She had condemned them to death, but God reversed her verdict as he passed judgment upon her.

21, 22. The final paragraph of the doom-song leads off with a prophecy in action, such as was common among the great Old Testament prophets (v. 21; cf., e.g., Isa. 20, Jer. 13, Ezek. 4). The

casting of **a stone like a great millstone** into the sea recalls a
comparable action of Jeremiah. He tied his prophecies against
Babylon to a stone and threw the stone into the Euphrates,
declaring, 'Thus shall Babylon sink, to rise no more' (Jer. 51 : 63f.).
Similarly, the action of the mighty angel confirms the spoken
word. As surely as that monstrous stone sank to disappear from
sight for ever, so certainly and completely will Babylon perish.
The imagery of the closing stanza balances that of the opening
paragraph. There the city's desolation is emphasized by the description of the strange and repulsive creatures which lurk in its
ruins. Here it is underscored by a description of its total silence. To
do this John recalls language used by Jeremiah of Jerusalem's
overthrow (25 : 10) and that used by Ezekiel of the ruin of Tyre
(26 : 13). No strains of music will be heard among the city's ruins,
no sound from craftsmen plying their crafts, no noise from the
household-mill grinding corn, and no more happy voices of
bridegroom and bride at weddings. All will be still, and every
light will be extinguished. Babylon's total silence and total darkness will signify its total desolation.

23, 24. The reason for so severe a judgment is repeated in summary form, again echoing the final sentence of the introductory
paragraph, verse 3. Her **merchants** were as kings in the earth,
the **nations** were led astray by her, and her hands were stained
with the **blood of prophets and of saints.** The traders are
singled out, not simply because they were successful, but because
their activity was part of that corrupting influence whereby the
soul of the world was being destroyed through the harlot city.
They were part and parcel of the city's deception of the world
through her **sorcery.** By this term is indicated not so much the
magic used for the murder of the innocent (as indeed was common) as the bewitchment that beguiles men to adopt false religion.
This is Babylon's greatest sin (cf. 17 : 2), and its condemnation is
one with the protesting voices of the Old Testament prophets.
John's words come very close to the sentiment of Nahum's in-
dignant oracle against Ninevah: 'Woe to the bloody city, all full of
lies and booty! . . . And all for the countless harlotries of the harlot,
graceful and of deadly charms, who betrays nations with her
harlotries, and people with her charms' (3 : 4). The ultimate be-
trayal is to lead the nations to a false religion which ends in the
adulation of an Antichrist and the murder of the followers of the

true Christ. In her persecution of prophets and of saints Babylon has numbered herself with her predecessors in the slaughter of the saints of God, so that her bloodguiltiness includes **all who have been slain on earth.** It is a hyperbole, applied by our Lord to Jerusalem, the city which kills prophets and stones them sent to her (Mt. 23 : 35ff.). The city of the Antichrist fulfils the role of every Babylon of history, and pays the price for every Babylon.

A 'TE DEUM' ON THE RIGHTEOUS JUDGMENT OF GOD 19 : 1–10

The title is taken from Arethas' description of this passage. Prompted by the fall of Babylon, as narrated in chapters 17–18, it formally supplies a response to the cry in 18 : 20,

> 'Rejoice over her, O heaven,
> O saints and apostles and prophets,
> for God has given judgment for you against her!'

The praises of 'heaven' are those recorded in verses 1–4, and those of 'saints, apostles and prophets' in verses 6f. Such is a reasonable interpretation of the passage, since the great multitude of verse 1 is explicitly said to be 'in heaven', while that of verse 6 is made up of the servants of God—'you who fear him, small and great'. On this understanding the heavenly host is described in a series of concentric circles, commencing in verses 1–3 with the 'myriads of myriads and thousands of thousands' of angels about the throne (5 : 11), passing to the twenty-four elders and the four living creatures (v. 4), and finally to the voice from the throne (v. 5). At the bidding of that voice the worship of the redeemed follows (vv. 6–8a).

The *Te Deum* relates to the judgments of God. Interestingly this is the theme of the worship of 'heaven', while the 'saints' sing of the coming of God's kingdom and the marriage of the Lamb (vv. 6f.). It is heaven which is concerned with the justice of the divine judgments on the power which corrupted earth and murdered the saints, and the Church which rejoices in the triumph of the divine sovereignty. The two processes are, of course, two aspects of a single reality. Their interweaving in this passage may be linked with another strain of thought, which is a feature of the whole Revelation. It arises from the fourfold use of 'Hallelujah' in the worship here described. Surprising as it may appear, the term

Hallelujah occurs nowhere else in the New Testament outside this paragraph. Its familiarity to Bible readers is due to its appearance in certain Old Testament psalms. Its adoption into the Church's vocabulary of worship appears to have been influenced especially by its use at Easter, wherein the Church saw our Lord's dying and rising as fulfilling the typology of redemption in the passover and exodus. The description of verses 1–8, therefore, as 'a liturgy of Hallelujahs, reminiscent of the Hallel Psalms' (Farrer) is very apposite. This group of psalms (113–18), while sung at the three pilgrim-festivals of Jerusalem, was especially associated with the passover. The first two psalms (113, 114) were sung prior to the passover-meal, and the rest were sung after it. The Hallel of heaven and earth, then, comes fittingly at this point in the Revelation. Heaven gives praise to God for the deliverance from the oppressor tyrant of Babylon—the contemporary 'Pharaoh'—and the saints give praise for the inheritance of the kingdom, and for that special fulfilment of the passover and the Christian eucharist in the marriage-supper of the Lamb.

The section is rounded off by a little epilogue (vv. 9f.), in which the truth of the foregoing visions, notably in chapters 17–18 and 19 : 1–6, is affirmed.

1. The **great multitude in heaven** (cf. 5 : 11 and Heb. 12 : 22) ascribe praise to God first in terms already used in relation to God's establishment of his sovereignty through the sacrificial redemption of Christ (12 : 10; cf. 7 : 10). God's **salvation** comes through judgment, even as God's judgment of evil is for the salvation of the world.

The preservation of the term **Hallelujah** (= 'Praise Yah(weh)') in language other than Hebrew was due to Greek-speaking Jews, who transliterated the term into Greek, and from them it passed into Christian circles. The same thing occurred with *Amen* and *Hosanna*, and among Christians *Abba* (= 'Father!') and *Marana-tha* (= 'O Lord, come!'). For the significance of *Hallelujah* in this passage, see the introduction to verses 1–8.

2. Praise is offered to God because **his judgments are true and just.** So sing the redeemed hosts by the heavenly Red Sea (15 : 3), and so declare the martyrs beneath the altar (16 : 7). The justice of God's judgments is seen in his wrath on the great harlot for her two cardinal sins. She **corrupted the earth with her fornication** and she shed **the blood of his servants.** To

corrupt is to destroy (cf. 11 : 18), and that in the most comprehensible way possible—morally, spiritually, and physically. In
corrupting the earth Babylon was undoing the work of the Creator
and frustrating the purpose of creation. In waging war on the
saints she fought the *God* of heaven. Her works accorded with her
nature as the incarnation of the spirit of evil and its instrument in
the world (ch. 13). The time had to come for the destroyer to be
destroyed (11 : 18), and when it came the judgment was acclaimed
by heaven as *true and just.*

3. A second **Hallelujah** is called forth by the perpetuity of
Babylon's destruction. The language recalls the descriptions of
Babylon's fires in 17 : 16, 18 : 8, 9, 18. But the imagery goes back
to the prophecy of Edom's desolation in Isaiah 34 : 9f., which in
turn recalls the overthrow of Sodom and Gomorrah (Gen.
19 : 24–8). Babylon by her deeds showed herself to be another
Sodom (cf. 11 : 8). She now shares the fate of her ancient pre-
cursor, except that her destructive fires are never to be extinguished. We have already observed that this symbol is qualified by
the different picture of desolation implied in 18 : 2. For the understanding of apocalyptic imagery it is noteworthy that the phrase
for ever and ever (literally 'to the ages of the ages') also requires
qualifying in the light of John's description of the new creation in
21 : 1ff., for Babylon's ruins will have no place in that setting. The
meaning of the phrase clearly is determined by the nature of its
context.

4. Whether intentionally or not, the praise of **the twenty-four
elders and the four living creatures** cites the concluding
words of the fourth book of Psalms (**'Amen! Praise the Lord!'**
Ps. 106 : 48). Their occurrence in this context is significant, and
invites comparison with other descriptions of the worship offered
by these highest angelic beings in the Revelation. In 5 : 9f. the
elders and living creatures add an *Amen* to the adoration of God
and the Lamb by the whole creation. In 11 : 17f. the elders worship God for commencing his reign and judging the world. In
14 : 3 the elders and living creatures silently observe the singing of
the song which only the redeemed could learn. Now their silence
is broken. As they ratified the praise of the universe for the salvation of the Lord, so they confirm the praise of heaven for his
true and righteous judgment.

5, 6. The **voice from the throne** is unlikely to be that of God, and it cannot be that of Christ (with **our God** contrast 'my God' of 3 : 12, and Jn. 20 : 17). It must be that of one of the elders or living creatures nearest the throne. The inclusive description of those addressed, **all you his servants, you who fear him, small and great,** forbids relating them to a group within the Church, e.g., the martyrs. They are the whole company of God's people (cf. 11 : 18). Their shout of praise is overwhelming, as the roar of a vast **multitude,** as the **waters** of a Niagara, or as peals of **thunder.**

7, 8. They celebrate not the destruction of Babylon but the coming of God's reign and the **marriage of the Lamb.** The figure of the marriage of the Christ is deeply rooted in the history of the people of God. The idea of Israel or Zion as the wife of God is frequently met in the prophets, but it is significant that in every context where it is used Israel is depicted as a *faithless* wife. Hosea's use of it to press home the call to repentance is well known (Hos. 2), and the same idea is vividly developed by Ezekiel (ch. 16), who roots it in God's covenant with Israel in the desert, and by it he portrays Israel's faithlessness to the covenant God as harlotry (such also is the presupposition of Isa. 1 : 21 and Jer. 2 : 2). The prophets, however, looked for God to deal tenderly with his people as he did in former years. Accordingly the new exodus-typology enables them to look for Israel to be betrothed anew to God, thenceforth to enter upon felicitous relationships (this is again expressed most clearly in Hos. 2 : 14f., 19ff.; cf. also Ezek. 16 : 59ff.). This dual conception of a covenant relationship rooted in history but to be perfected in the future is taken up in a fresh way in the New Testament and applied to Christ and the Church. Here the emphasis falls on the Christ, the Lord and Saviour, as the Bridegroom, but since his sovereignty and his salvation alike are eschatological, belonging essentially to the new age, the figure is never used to illustrate the apostasy of the people of God. In this respect Ephesians 5 : 25 mirrors the prevailing concept: 'Christ loved the church and gave himself up for her, that he might sanctify her ...' She is even now a pure bride, having been cleansed by the nuptial bath. But the writer continues, '. . . that he might present the church to himself in splendour, without spot or wrinkle or any such thing'. The perfection in glory of the bride belongs to the eschatological future. In this figure, therefore, the *now* and the *not yet* of the New Testament doctrine of salvation in the kingdom of God is perfectly exemplified. The Church is the Bride of Christ now, but her marriage lies in the future.

The eschatological aspect of the figure is emphasized here through its conjunction with another image for the kingdom of God, namely, that of a feast prepared by the Lord for the world, in which his people will be the guests. It is expressed most clearly in Isaiah 25 : 6 (observe its eschatological context), and is echoed in our Lord's parable of the great feast (Lk. 14 : 15ff.) and his sayings at the Last Supper (Mk 14 : 25, Lk. 22 : 28ff.). The two concepts are brought together in Matthew's version of the parable of the great feast (= the wedding of the king's son, Mt. 22: 1ff.) and in the parable of the virgins (Mt. 25: 1ff.). By this means a whole wealth of associations relating to salvation are brought together: the prior love of God for man, revealed in deeds of grace which win the love of the bride; the depth of fellowship between God and man, established in the love of God and the grace of Christ and mediated through the Holy Spirit (2 C. 13 : 13); the joy of that relationship, when the trials of the former days are forgotten in laughter and happiness around the table of the Lord in his kingdom. Its concentration in relationship between Christ and the Church is consonant with the Christian doctrine of Christ as mediator of the divine revelation and redemption for man.

A typical duality of Christian thought on salvation and sanctity is expressed in the two lines:

> **his Bride has made herself ready;**
> **it was granted her to be clothed with fine linen, bright**
> **and pure.**

The Bride *made herself ready* through repentance and faith and continuance in righteous deeds which are the fruit of faith (cf. the emphasis on 'works' in the seven letters, e.g., 2: 2ff., 9, 13, 19, etc.). Yet *it was granted her* to be clothed with fine linen. Holiness is the gift of God. It is the holy life of the Redeemer in the redeemed. This duality characterizes the Christian life through all its stages (Phil. 2 : 12f.) and finds its ultimate manifestation in the salvation and judgment which the kingdom of God brings.

9. Blessed. The beatitude verse, the fourth in the book, in some respects represents a climax beyond which none can go, since its elucidation involves an exposition of the blessedness described in the final vision of 'the Bride, the Wife of the Lamb'

(21 : 9ff.).[1] But who are the **invited**? They are believers in Christ, who have heard and responded to the invitation of the Lamb to exercise repentance and faith. Accordingly a double symbolism is employed in this picture. In verse 7 the followers of the Lamb constitute the Bride, whose marriage the feast will celebrate. In verse 9 they are the guests at the feast. We have noted that a similar mode of thought is implied in the gospels, above all in Matthew's parable of the marriage feast of the king's son (Mt. 22: 1ff.). Lohmeyer finds in it a parallel to the concept of the heavenly and the earthly Church, such as appears in 1 : 20 and the letters to the churches (see note on 1 : 20). The question, 'When will the marriage supper take place?' has caused embarrassment to some expositors, prompted especially through their conviction that in the Revelation the martyrs alone participate in the kingdom of Christ. On the basis of this understanding, for example, Charles interprets verses 5ff. as relating solely to the martyrs, and he is then led to believe that the marriage supper of the Lamb, though spoken of here as 'come', in fact takes place at the close of the millennial reign, when the rest of the faithful combine with the martyrs to form the perfected Church. This interpretation can scarcely be reconciled with the intention of the text, namely that the Church will be united with its Lord when he is revealed in glory and will share with him the joy of the kingdom. That is salvation as John understands it.

The angel's asseveration of the truth of **these... words of God** relates not to the whole Revelation, still less to the immediately preceding paragraph, but to the section of which 19 : 1ff. forms the climax, i.e., chapters 17–18, with 19 : 1–8. A similar affirmation occurs in the epilogue to the book (22 : 6). Its occurrence at this point indicates the importance to John of the prophecy contained in 17 : 1–19 : 8.[2]

10. Was the account of the angel's refusal to permit the prophet to worship him included so as to discourage a like practice among

[1] Hence Schlatter's comment: 'To participate in it (the marriage supper) is the sum of every promise, the completed gift of God.'

[2] As to the implications of this for the modern reader, see the note on 17:18, and compare Swete's comment: 'This solemn claim to veracity does not of course require belief in the literal fulfilment of the details. Apocalyptic prophecy has its own methods and laws of interpretation, and by these the student must be guided. Under a literary form Divine truth expresses itself and fulfils itself "in many and various ways"; it is only in the Son that it reaches finality.'

others? So it is often thought (cf. Col. 2 : 18). We should perhaps rather view the narration as an artless statement of John's instinctive reaction to bow down before one who had shown him so great a vision as that in 17 : 1–19 : 8. He learns that the glory of the revelation belongs to the Revealer and not to lesser intermediaries. Angels who mediate a revelation, prophets who pass it on, and Christians who live by it, are brothers. Naturally, for an angel can pretend to no other revelation, a prophet can preach no other, and a believer can have no other hope. In this setting no doubt should attach to the meaning of the phrase **the testimony of Jesus.** It means 'the testimony which Jesus gives'. The thought is closely related to that in the opening paragraph of the Revelation, which describes the book as John's witness to 'the word of God and the testimony of Jesus Christ', i.e., the word given by God and the testimony borne by Jesus Christ (a similar parallelism occurs in 12 : 17, where 'the commandments of God' and 'the testimony of Jesus' are commandments from God and testimony from Jesus). Accordingly the final sentence must mean, 'The testimony given by Jesus is the spirit of prophecy.' It is tempting to interpret this as meaning that the testimony which Jesus bore is the principle which dominates prophecy, but that is too impersonal. In view of John's knowledge of Jewish traditions he could not have been ignorant of the fact that the concept of the Spirit which was uppermost in the minds of his fellow Jews was that he is the inspiration of prophecy. Their favourite name for the Spirit of God was precisely 'the Spirit of prophecy'.[1] We should, therefore, interpret verse 10 as meaning that the testimony borne by Jesus is the concern or burden of the Spirit who inspires prophecy. Such is the chief thrust of the teaching on the Paraclete in John 14–16 (see especially Jn 16 : 12ff.).

But what is the reason for adding this observation? Presumably it strengthens the command, **Worship God.** It either emphasizes the relative unimportance of the angel, since his function is to pass on the message which Christ has brought from the Father (1 : 1), or it carries an indirect reference to the fact that the testimony of Jesus directs men to the Father. If the latter thought is in mind, it would bear the further implication that since prophecy inspired by the Spirit is exposition of the revelation from Jesus, Spirit-inspired prophets will do as he did: point men to God.

[1] See the illustrative material in Strack-Billerbeck, ad loc.

THE REVELATION OF CHRIST AND OF THE CITY OF GOD 19:11–22:25

The vision of 17:1–19:10 expanded the prophecy of the seventh bowl-cup of divine wrath (16:17ff.), which told of Babylon's draining the cup of God's wrath. In the course of this expansion John also utilized the prophecy of the sixth bowl (16:12ff.), which described the invasion by the kings of the east and the assembling at Armageddon of the kings of the earth. In a similar manner the visions of 19:11–22:5 are prompted by the necessity to explain the reference to Armageddon after the sixth bowl, and the implications of the cry following the seventh bowl, 'It is done!' (16:17). This entails a description of the parousia of Christ (19:11–16), with the consequent subjugation of the evil powers at Armageddon (19:17–20:3), the revelation of Christ's kingdom in this world (20:4–10), the last judgment (20:11–15), and the new creation (21:1–5). These prophetic oracles lead on to the final visions of the new Jerusalem, and again a parallel is observable in the group of prophecies in 17:1–19:10. Just as John in those passages had dwelt on the appearance of the harlot-city Babylon, so he elaborates his brief allusion to the marriage of the Lamb (19:6ff.) by his description of 'the Bride, the Wife of the Lamb', which is none other than the city coming down out of heaven from God (21:9–22:5). The contrasts between the two cities are deliberate and striking, and repay careful attention by the reader.

THE PAROUSIA OF CHRIST 19:11–20:3

The description of the Lord's coming in this passage is one of the most powerful and impressive portrayals in the Revelation. Its delineation of Christ draws on elements of description scattered throughout the book, but it is yet more notable for its use of hyperbolic symbols with apparently little regard for their consistency. The Christ who comes appears as Field-Marshal of the armies of heaven, riding as to battle on a white horse. But he stands in the wine-press of God's wrath, and he treads it alone (v. 15). He has a name inscribed which no one knows but himself (v. 12), yet his name is inscribed on his robe for all to read (v. 16),

and the name by which he is called is the Word of God (v. 13).
His robe is dipped in blood (v. 13), but the battle has not yet
taken place, nor has the winepress of God been trodden. The representation of the Lord sweeping down at the head of the armies
of heaven is majestic, but that of the vultures gorging themselves
on human flesh, enjoying a grisly counterpart to the supper of the
Lamb, shocks our sensibilities (vv. 17ff.). Both pictures, however,
are surrealist. There is no cavalry kept in heaven, and 'the great
supper of God' (v. 17) is as pictorial as the marriage-supper of the
Lamb (v. 9). Yet more important, although the stage is set for an
encounter between the army of heaven and the massed forces of the
Antichrist on earth, there is no battle. The trinity of ringleaders of
revolt are seized, the beast and the false prophet being thrown into
the lake of fire (v. 20) and the dragon chained in the bottomless
pit (20 : 1ff.), while 'the rest' are slain by the sword which issues
from Christ's mouth (v. 21). The 'battle' resolves itself into a
judgment uttered by the Word of God, and it is not easy to be
confident as to how John intended his readers to interpret this
word-picture. The ultimate reality depicted is plain enough. The
Christ is revealed in majesty and authority to fulfil both his
promise of deliverance from all evil powers and his promise of
judgment on all evil-doers. The heightened symbolism emphasizes
his power to perform both acts, for when he appears in his glory,
evil is helpless before him, and earth must submit to his judgment.

One further lesson may be gathered from this portrayal of the
parousia. Not even in this book of highly imaginative pictures is
there a greater concentration of symbolic representations of a
single event than here. When John comes to describe the parousia
of the Lord, he is forced like all others to resort to sheer picture-
thinking. The coming of the Lord is an event which transcends the
thought and imagination of man. It is not so much a movement in
space as a revelation of him who is there, a transcendent deed in
which grace and judgment are combined as truly as they are in the
cross of Christ. In the context of the Revelation it is important as
focussing hope on a Person, on him who alone can perform what
man needs above all things else, namely, redemption from the
powers which destroy the world and judgment upon the agents of
destruction. This message the Church of John's time sorely needed
for its encouragement in faith and obedience, as indeed the Church
of all ages needs it. For the scene on earth takes on a different

aspect when viewed in the light of the coming of the Lord. If the
glory of that event has power to transform present living and inspire continuance in well doing to the end, the Church can afford
patiently to wait to learn the nature of the great unveiling. The
day itself will declare it.

11. At the beginning of John's vision of the end he saw a door
opened in heaven through which he could enter the transcendent
realms (4 : 1). Now it is no mere door but **heaven** itself which
stands 'wide open' (*NEB*) to reveal the Christ in his glory, accompanied by the hosts of heaven. But first **behold, a white horse!**
For the bridegroom is Commander of heaven's armies, setting out
to conquer (cf. 6 : 1). His name is called **Faithful and True.** The
origin of the name is indicated in 3 : 14, where it is an exposition
of the term *Amen*, which in Isaiah 66 : 16 is a title for God. It is a
singularly appropriate name for him who is called the Word of
God (v. 13), for it indicates that unlike the deceivers of mankind,
who lead men to ruin (vv. 19ff.), his speech embodies the faithfulness and truthfulness of God, and therefore is to be trusted.
Accordingly **in righteousness he judges and makes war.** For
John, as frequently in the Old Testament, these two activities are
synonymous, hence the sole weapon of Christ is the word he speaks
(v. 15). The attribute of *righteousness* in judgment is a direct reminiscence of the portrayal of the Messiah in Isaiah 11 : 3ff., and
reminds us of the constant insistence in this book that God's
judgments are righteous and true (15 : 3, 16 : 5, 19 : 2). The
judgments of Christ are indeed the judgments of God.

12. In this setting of judgment the **eyes ... like a flame of
fire** are suitably recalled from the opening vision of the risen
Christ (1 : 14; cf. 2 : 18), for they connote the Lord's ability to
'see through' all pretence and to penetrate the depths of the
human heart. By contrast the **many diadems** belong not to a
judge but to a king. The dragon has seven of them (12 : 3), the
beast ten—one for each of the ten subservient kings (13 : 1,
17 : 12). But Christ has *many*, for as God's representative he is
King of kings and Lord of lords (v. 16; cf. 1 Tim. 6 : 15), master of
the Devil and all his agents, and sovereign lord of the universe.
That **he has a name ... which no one knows but himself** is
formally contradicted by verses 11, 13 and 16. Symbolically, however, it is thoroughly fitting. Throughout the ancient world a
name revealed the nature of an individual, who he is and what he

is. The unknown name of the Christ comports with the fact that his nature, his relationships to the Father, and even his relationship to humanity, transcend all human understanding. Accordingly 'only the Son of God can understand the mystery of his own Being' (Swete)—a thought closely related to Matthew 11 : 27.

13. How is it that the Christ wears **a robe dipped in blood?** Patristic writers interpreted this as meaning that the robe was stained with the blood of Christ's own sacrifice, a view which may claim support from 1 : 5, 5 : 9, and 7 : 14. Most modern commentators hold that the blood is intended to be that of his enemies. Some (e.g., Swete) would refer it to both Christ and his enemies, while Caird understands it as stains of martyr blood. The context, however, above all verse 15, demands our recognition that the figure is drawn from Isaiah 63 : 1ff., and that it is used in a similar manner as in its Old Testament source. The Conqueror tramples his enemies beneath his feet as a farmer treads down the grapes in his vat. It is because the picture has been drawn from Isaiah 63 : 1ff. that the robe of Christ can be viewed as blood stained even before the battle takes place or the wine-vat is trodden. It indicates his function as executor of the divine wrath.[1]

That his **name** is called **the Word of God** brings a variety of associations together. As bearer of the word of God in his speech the Christ also embodies that word in his deeds of redemption and judgment, and his parousia will bring that revelation to a climax. The description of the all-powerful Word, leaping from the royal throne to execute judgment on Egypt's first-born, could have been in mind (Wis. 18 : 15). More pertinently, perhaps, in view of the circulation in the early Church of the logos-type Christology (attested in Col. 1 : 15ff., and echoed by John himself in 3 : 14), it would seem likely that some notion of the role of cosmic mediator will have been present to John's mind in using the term. Since the parousia initiates the eschatological process completed in the new world, it may be held that the title *the Word of God* is fitting for him who both initiates the creation and fulfils its purpose in the new creation.

[1] The above interpretation is supported by the rabbinic use of Isaiah 63:1ff. The rabbis systematized representations in the *OT* as to the various garments of God therein described. In this connection it was affirmed that the blood-red garment of Isaiah 63:1ff. will be assumed by the Lord on the day of his vengeance on 'Edom' (= Rome). See Strack-Billerbeck, ad loc.

14. The armies of heaven who follow the Lord are composed not of the saints (as in 17 : 14) but of angels. The phrase is the equivalent of the Old Testament 'host(s) of heaven', which denotes both the ordered array of the starry heavens and the angelic hosts who wait upon God (e.g., 1 Kg. 22 : 19, Ps. 103 : 21, Dan. 4 : 35). Accordingly the New Testament descriptions of the parousia represent Christ as accompanied by the angelic hosts who wait upon him (e.g., Mt. 25 : 31, Mk 13 : 27, 2 Th. 1 : 7f.). Their **fine linen, white and pure** suggests, as in verse 8, the clothing of those who are on the way to a joyful occasion. The angelic attendants of the Lord in his parousia are not about to engage in mortal combat, but are to witness their Commander exercise authority in judgment to which the mightiest forces of earth and hell must yield. They, therefore, have no need of armour, but are clothed in the apparel of festivity. They are on their way to a wedding.

15. The judgment of Christ is depicted under three figures, drawn from Old Testament passages beloved of John. The Lord wields **a sharp sword** which issues from his mouth (cf. 1 : 16 and Isa. 11 : 3ff.). He is to rule with **a rod of iron,** as the Messiah in Psalm 2 : 9 (cf. Rev. 2 : 27, 12 : 5). **He will tread the wine press** of God's furious wrath (Isa. 63 : 1ff.; cf. v. 13). Observe that in each of these figures the Christ acts alone. The armies of heaven who accompany him are witnesses of his judgments, not contenders along with him. The three figures are three representations of the word of Christ by which he executes with indisputable authority the judgment of God.

16. That Christ's **name** is inscribed **on his robe and on his thigh** has provided commentators with an exegetical puzzle. Attempts have been made to show either that the reference to the robe is secondary, and that the name was written only on the thigh (so Charles), or that the name was not on the thigh but on the place where the robe covers the thigh (Swete), or on a sword which normally is worn on the thigh (Grotius), or that the thigh stands for the sword (Caird), etc. On the contrary, the symbolism is not so difficult as is represented. A robe or mantle can in itself represent dignity or status, and it is not surprising that a name signifying worth should be thought of as embroidered upon it. We recall the description of the beast as covered with blasphemous names (17 : 3), which may be thought of as woven into a scarlet cloak thrown over the creature. The beast thus displays devilish names, but the Christ displays a divine name. Moreover, the idea of a name inscribed on the thigh was not unknown in ancient society. Examples have been mentioned by Wettstein of statues in classical times inscribed on their thighs with the names of the individuals represented. Lohmeyer cites the Egyptian notion, according to which the titles and signs of kingship are inscribed on every limb of the royal prince, and a representation in Alexandria of a god Aion which bore five divine 'seals' on forehead, hands, and knees. The significant element in the symbol here is that the Christ bears on his person and on his garment the sign of universal sovereignty (for the name, see note on 17 : 14).

17. An angel is seen **standing in the sun,** i.e., in the highest point of heaven, where all the birds that fly in midheaven (cf. 8 : 13) can see and hear him. The summons of **the birds** (= vultures) to attend **the great supper of God** cites Ezekiel 39 : 17, where they with the beasts are invited to come together for the destruction of the hosts of Gog. Observe, however, that John employs at this juncture only the imagery of that passage. Conformably with Ezekiel's prophecy, the onset of Gog is placed by John at the end of the millennial rule (20 : 8f.). What for Ezekiel is a sacrificial feast, prepared by the Lord on the mountains of Israel— an ironic reversal of the natural order, when beasts and birds eat human sacrifices instead of men eating sacrificial beasts and birds —in the Revelation becomes a terrible counterpart to the marriage supper of the Lamb (v. 9). The triumph of God's kingdom over its adversaries is celebrated by a joyful feast for the righteous and by a nightmare feast for the scavenging birds of prey.

18. Ezekiel's list of doomed mighty men is extended by John to include **all men, both free and slave, both small and great.** This is taken by Lohmeyer to relate literally to all on the earth apart from the Church. History thus attains its end in a complete division of the human race into two groups, namely, the Church which is loyal to the Christ of God, and the world which fights for the Antichrist.[1] This is surely pressing John's language beyond his intention. He does not wish to imply that the total population of earth outside the Church is gathered for battle against the Christ,

[1] So apparently Rissi, who interprets verse 21 as indicating that all unbelievers on earth will be slain by the returning Christ (*The Future of the World*, p. 33). Bousset avoids the difficulty by assuming that the armies of the Antichrist are wholly demonic, as in 9 : 13ff.; cf. 16 : 13.

for the closing paragraphs of this short section (20 : 1ff.) states that the dragon is chained in the pit 'that he should deceive the nations no more', i.e., the nations surviving Armageddon. Moreover the conquerors by the heavenly Red Sea have sung in exultant anticipation of the submission of all nations to God (15 : 4). That hope is no merely secondary idea, irreconcilable with John's real beliefs, but it stands at the heart of his eschatological teaching. It would seem, therefore, that John, very much in the spirit of Ezekiel, adopts and elaborates the earlier prophet's symbolism in order to emphasize the greatness of Christ's conquest. *All men* clearly excludes the followers of Christ. The term here means 'all kinds of men', just as Ezekiel speaks of 'mighty men and all kinds of warriors' in Ezekiel 39 : 20 (the latter phrase significantly being rendered in the Septuagint as 'every warrior'). The point of the announcement to the birds, made before the armies are even assembled, is to underscore the senselessness and futility of rebellion against God. When man resists God, he can do no more than advance to his judgment.

19, 20. The inspiration of this rebellion is indicated once more, verses 19ff., namely, **the beast, the false prophet** (cf. 13: 11ff.), and **the dragon** (20: 2). This trinity of evil has already been linked with the gathering for Armageddon in 16: 13. As in John's favourite psalm, **the kings of the earth** also set themselves against the Lord and his anointed (Ps. 2 : 2). These presumably include the kings of the east, who fight against Babylon (16: 12, 17: 16f.), and the remaining 'kings of the whole world' (16: 14), who join them after Babylon's fall. Observe that it is these forces of the Antichrist which **make war** against the Christ and his retinue. The army of heaven has no need to fight. It simply witnesses the judgment executed by the Christ on the leaders of the revolt. The antichristian forces have no opportunity even to make a show of strength. **The beast** and **the false prophet** are **captured** and thrown into the lake of fire, and the dragon is seized and bound with a chain and confined in the bottomless pit (20: 1ff.).

21. The rest are **slain by the sword** of the Christ. It is a picture of the total helplessness of the foes of God when confronted by the Christ revealed from heaven. The symbolic nature of the whole description is evident from the fact that the forces of the Antichrist are **slain by the sword of him who sits upon the horse.** The *sword* is a symbol for the powerful utterance of

Christ, with particular reference to its expression in judgment. The representation of Christ as one *who sits on a horse* is also purely pictorial, emphasizing the dignity and power of the Lord of heaven and earth. The precise signification of the picture, however, is less clear. The leaders of revolt are swept away from the earthly scene, the beast and false prophet being condemned to a judgment which is final, but the dragon to an imprisonment which has a term set to it. What is meant by the slaying of *the rest* by the sword from Christ's mouth? Some are inclined to interpret the picture in the light of the representation in Hebrews 4 : 12 of the divine word which is sharper than any sword, and of the power of Christ's reconciliation to slay the enmity of man towards God (Eph. 2 : 16). Hence Swete, while recognizing the element of judgment in verse 21, comments: 'The vision of the victorious Word fulfils itself in any movement which leads to conversions on a great scale, such as that which attended the preaching of Boniface; and it may find a more complete accomplishment at the time yet future, when Christ will work through some new Apostle of the Gentiles for the "obedience of the Gentiles" (Rom. 15 : 18).' This is hardly to be received. The context is one of judgment, not conversion of the rebellious, hence the invocation of **the birds** of prey to the scene. It is most natural to assume that the judgment here portrayed implies the death of the rebels, after which they await the last judgment (20 : 11ff.). Yet we cannot be sure that this is intended, for the picture is a symbolic portrayal of what is essentially a judicial procedure. We do well to recognize that John does not write to satisfy our curiosity about the details of the future. By his symbolic representations he conveys his message of the victory of the Lamb over those who war against him and the judgment upon all who allow themselves to be led astray by the enemies of God and man. Beyond that we cannot with confidence say more on the basis of this passage.

20 : 1–3. After the judgment on the beast, the false prophet, and the multitude whom they led astray, the ultimate enemy is dealt with—the dragon. It is noteworthy that no great and terrible struggle takes place between the supreme antagonists of history, i.e., between the Christ from heaven and the dragon from hell. A nameless **angel** suffices to reduce the Devil to impotence when God so decrees. Admittedly **a great chain** is used to bind the powerful enemy, but the chain is a symbol for the word of God,

which reduces Satan to impotence. As with the hosts of evil
(19: 19ff.), so with their leader: 'A word shall quickly slay him'
(Luther). The angel has not only a chain. He holds also **the key
of the bottomless pit.** The *pit* (Greek *abyss*) is the abode of
demonic forces (see 9: 1ff.). Satan, therefore, in being thrust into
the pit, is removed from the sphere of man to be chained among
his own kind. After consigning him to the pit, the angel **shut it,**
i.e., locked it by using the key, and **sealed it over him.** A seal on
a prison door ensured that prisoners could not escape unobserved.
Only he who authorized the imprisonment could authorize
release from it (see Dan. 6: 17, Mt. 27: 66). Thus the incarceration of the Devil is trebly circumscribed. He is bound up, locked
in, and sealed over. The writer could hardly have expressed more
emphatically the inability of Satan to harm the race of man.

The various names for the Devil in verse 2 are recounted, as in
12: 9, partly to enhance the greatness of the victory over him
which the Christ has won, and partly to emphasize its significance
for man. As the **dragon** he is the primeval foe of heaven who has
inspired the tyrannical powers of history, but whose destruction
has been assured from the beginning. As **that ancient serpent** he
is the deceiver of mankind, who has brought ruin to man from
Eden onwards. As **the Devil** and **Satan** he is the accuser or
slanderer of men, a perpetual reminder to God of the guilt of the
race that he has successfully perverted. But the time has come
when he can no longer fulfil the functions denoted by his names.
His role of accuser was finished when the great reconciliation was
wrought by Christ, for through that redemption there is forgiveness for man which no slanderer from hell can reverse (cf. Rom.
8: 34). Consequently Satan was ejected from heaven to earth
after the death and resurrection of the Lamb (12: 9). No longer
able to work mischief in heaven, Satan intensifies his efforts on
earth, raging because his time is short (12: 12). His calling the
Antichrist on the scene and initiating the great rebellion (13: 1ff.,
16: 13) are the supreme and climactic examples of this activity.
Once more, however, the deeds of Christ put an end to his evil
works. At the Lord's revelation from heaven he is removed from
earth and incarcerated in the depths of the abyss.

Since the Christ puts into effect the will of God, only that same
divine will can change the situation. So when it is said that at the
end of the thousand years **he must be loosed for a little while,**

the *must* expresses God's purpose (see Mt. 26 : 43, Mk 8 : 31, 13 : 7, Lk. 24 : 26, 44, Rev. 1 : 1, 4 : 1). Satan's release from his prison as truly subserves God's design for the world as his being thrust into prison.

As the myth of the slaying of the dragon by the child (see introduction to ch. 12), so the image of the binding and imprisonment of the Devil has a long and diffuse history in the religions and folk lore of the nations. The Zend religion of Persia has a clear relation to it, but from the point of view of the Revelation it is curiously topsy-turvy. In the Bundehesh it is related that the wicked serpent Azi-Dahaka is overcome by Thraetaeona and chained in a mountain for 9,000 years. He is released by the evil spirit Ahriman to reign for 1,000 years, but is finally slain, and the new world arrives. Other parallels have been noted in the Egyptian myth of Osiris, the Mandaean traditions, and the Scandinavian and Germanic myths.[1] Nearer at hand than these are the precedents in the Old Testament and in Jewish apocalyptic literature. The essential idea of Revelation 19 : 19-21 : 3 is present in brief compass in Isaiah 24 : 21f.:

> On that day the Lord will punish
>   the host of heaven, in heaven,
>   and the kings of the earth, on the earth.
> They will be gathered together
>   as prisoners in a pit;
> they will be shut up in a prison,
>   and after many days they will be punished.

The binding of evil spirits is a prominent motif in the book of *Enoch*. In particular command is given that Azazel be bound hand and foot and cast in the darkness for ever, i.e., till the day of judgment, when he will be thrown into the fire (*En.* 10 : 4ff.). The *Prayer of Manasseh* has the closest verbal agreement of all literature with our passage. In verse 3 the prayer is addressed to the Lord Almighty,

> 'who hast confined the ocean by the word of command,
> who hast shut up the abyss and sealed it with thy fearful
>   and glorious name',

an invocation which appears to echo the ancient myth of the conquest of the sea-monster.

[1] See Charles and Lohmeyer, ad loc.

The important thing to observe is that the symbolism common to these myths is made a medium by John for a message which was conveyed to him alike through the Old Testament prophets and by the apostolic traditions of the teaching of Jesus, namely, that the powers of evil are doomed by the word of God. The subjugation of the Devil and his removal from the sphere of man's existence is characteristic of the biblical monotheistic religion of redemption, which cannot endure the notion that evil will be prevalent for ever. The removal of Satan, therefore, is integral to the good news of Jesus Christ. It is a complement of that teaching which lies at the heart of the Christian gospel, that the kingdom of God comes through the Christ and will triumph in history through him. The defeat of Satan and the triumph of the kingdom are essential elements in the acts of judgment and redemption which God accomplishes through the Christ.

THE MILLENNIUM

The essential element in the idea of the millennium is the appearing of the kingdom of the Messiah in history, prior to the revelation of the kingdom of God in the eternal and transcendent realm of the new creation.

The conception of a limited kingdom of the Messiah is not found in the Old Testament, but its nature as the divine sovereignty manifested within history and in the earthly scene is basic to the prophetic hope. For almost all descriptions of the kingdom in the Old Testament picture it in terms of this world. They not only set the kingdom in the context of this earth, but frequently and characteristically represent it as centred in the Holy Land, and above all in Jerusalem. On the other hand the concept of new heavens and a new earth as the scene of the kingdom is found in Isaiah 65–6, even though the depiction of life in the kingdom is still given in terms of this world. This conception of new heavens and new earth become dominant among later Jewish apocalyptic writers, not least because it harmonized with their tendency towards a pessimistic view of life in this world. A reconciliation of the two expectations of the kingdom as within history and beyond the boundaries of time was natural, especially since the Messiah was commonly viewed as a second David who would rule over Israel in a manner comparable with the glorious rule of the first David.

The anticipation of the preliminary kingdom of the Messiah was by no means universal among Jews in the era of the primitive Church, but it was widespread and was held with an extraordinary diversity regarding the duration of the messianic kingdom.[1] Akiba, combining Deuteronomy 8:3 with Psalm 90:15, viewed it as a counterpart to Israel's sojourn in the wilderness, and so he thought that it would last for forty years (so also the *Apocalypse of Elijah*). Rabbi (*c.* AD 217) however, on the basis of Micah 7:15, thought it would be for the same length of time as Israel's stay in Egypt, and so gave it as 400 years (similarly 2 Esd. 7:28). R. Jehuda, taking Deuteronomy 11:21 as his authority, thought that the kingdom would last for a period as long as from creation to the present, i.e., 4,000 years. More modestly, R. Jose the Galilean (*c.* AD 110) set the figure at sixty years (cf. Ps. 72:5), while R. Eleazar b. Azaria (*c.* AD 100) suggested seventy years, on the basis of Isaiah 23:15. R. Dosa observed that Isaiah 65:22 compared the days of God's people in the messianic kingdom with those of a sycamore. A sycamore lasts for 600 years, therefore the kingdom of Messiah will be for 600 years.

Isaiah 63:4 influenced many teachers in their reflection on the messianic kingdom: 'I resolved on a *day* of vengeance; the *year* for ransoming my own had come.' On the basis of a day representing a year, some reckoned the kingdom as 354 years, viewing the year as lunar. Others took the year to be solar, and so extended the kingdom to 365 years. One rabbi fixed it at 365,000 years since with God a day is as a thousand years (Ps. 90:4). This last scripture, however, was seen to be susceptible of yielding other possibilities. R. Eliezer b. Jose the Galilean, comparing Psalm 90:4 with Isaiah 63:4, reckoned that the messianic kingdom will be for a thousand years. Abbahu (*c.* AD 300) read in Isaiah 62:5 that God will delight in his people as a bridgroom in his bride. A wedding-feast lasts for seven days, accordingly the days of the Messiah will last for seven thousand years. More significantly, the thought of a day as a thousand years was combined with the idea that the world's history would last for a 'week' of years. This led to the popular division of history into two thousand years without the law (i.e., from creation to Moses), two thousand years with the

[1] See the detailed review by Strack-Billerbeck, op. cit., III, pp. 824ff., from which I have freely drawn in this paragraph.

law (from Moses to the present), and two thousand years for
Messiah's kingdom, followed by one thousand years of sabbath for
the world. A variant of this interpretation viewed history as a
recapitulation of the week of creation. As the six days of divine
work were followed by God's sabbath rest, so the six days of man's
history will be followed by the sabbath of Messiah's kingdom,
which in turn will give place to an eighth day without end—the
timeless age of the eternal kingdom. This view is found in a Jewish
apocalypse of uncertain date (*2 Enoch* 32–3), and it is also preserved in the *Epistle of Barnabas* (ch. 15) and by later Christian
writers. It is highly probable that this idea was in circulation in
John's time. In contrast with the preoccupation (one is inclined to
write *mania*) of apocalyptically minded Jews at this time with the
dates in God's eschatological timetable, it is likely that John's
adoption of the figure 1,000 for the messianic kingdom is intended
to indicate not so much its length as its character, namely as the
sabbath of history. Such a view harmonizes with the notion,
of importance to John, that creation prefigures new creation,
and it links with the idea, attested in Hebrews (ch. 4), of God's
sabbath-rest as a type of the kingdom.

The source of John's concept of the millennium, however,
almost certainly lies elsewhere than in contemporary Jewish
speculations on the messianic kingdom, even if it has connections
with them. The imagery of the closing chapters of Ezekiel is continually employed by John in his delineation of the kingdom, and
in them John will have found the basic elements of his interpretation. Ezekiel 36–7 describes the 'resurrection' of Israel and the
restoration of the nation to its land under the rule of the new
David. After an unspecified period the rebellion of Gog and
Magog occurs (chs. 38–9), followed by the promise of a new
Jerusalem with a new temple in the bliss of an untroubled kingdom (chs. 40–8). The pattern of this prophecy appears to have
determined the presentation of John's vision of the kingdom in
chapters 20–2, above all in chapter 20. It may not, however, have
been the sole or even ultimate source of the theology which lies
behind it. For we have seen that at the heart of John's doctrine of
redemption lies the belief that in the life, death, and resurrection
of Christ the turn of the ages took place. That is, in and through
Christ the promised kingdom of God came among men. The
kingdom, therefore, which is to be revealed in the power and

glory of the parousia will not be something totally new to this world, but the revelation of that kingdom of the Messiah which has been among men in the world from Easter onwards.

Cullmann rightly stresses the unity of the kingdom of Christ, binding as it does the two great ages of the universe, as the New Testament along with Judaism views it. He sees this unity especially exemplified in the element of recapitulation which is observable in John's description of the millennium.[1] Rissi makes much of this point, and urges that herein lies the reason for and the partial justification of Augustine's interpretation of the millennium as the age of the Church. The first resurrection, consequent on the parousia, is already known in the Church's experience of life from the risen Lord. The reign of the saints is characteristic of the Church's eschatological existence in this age (cf. 1:6, 9), and the attack of Gog and Magog at the instigation of the Devil answers to the opposition of the Church through the forces of the Antichrist (chs. 12, 13, 17). The millennial reign therefore signifies 'the unveiling of the secret realities of faith'.[2]

How widespread this interpretation was in the first-century Church it is impossible to state. Scholars differ in their understanding of 1 Corinthians 15:22-5, but there is little doubt that the whole paragraph in which those verses are set (vv. 20-8) is closely related to the theology embodied in John's vision, and it may well indicate that it was an established tradition in the primitive Church. John doubtless will have been encouraged in his interpretation by the current use of the prayer which Jesus taught his disciples to pray:

> Thy kingdom come,
> Thy will be done
> On earth as in heaven.

There are indications in the gospels that the *teaching* of Jesus coincides with the implications of this *prayer* for the kingdom, not least the beatitudes with which the Sermon on the Mount begins. We think especially of Matthew 5:5, 'Blessed are the meek, for they shall inherit the earth', and the next beatitude, which the *NEB* surely correctly understands, 'Blessed are those who hunger and thirst *to see right prevail*; they shall be satisfied.' Schniewind remarks that Matthew 5:5 speaks quite definitely of a hope for the

---

[1] *The Early Church*, p. 113.   [2] *The Future of the World*, p. 34.

earth, and 'not only a hope for something invisible, which stands beyond all earthly realities. The hope of the Bible carries throughout a double aspect. It embraces a hope for the earth, which is usually named after Revelation 20:4, the "thousand-years kingdom", and besides and beyond that a hope for the final comsummation, when "God will be all in all" (1 C. 15:28).'[1] To make such a recognition is not to claim that Jesus taught a doctrine of the millennium, but it does suggest that the latter is harmonious with his teaching. One can comprehend how, in the light of the apostolic exposition of the relation between our Lord's redemptive action and the kingdom of God, it readily became developed in this manner. It was reasoning of this kind which led Visser t'Hooft to state, 'Because he reigns already we may and must see the world and all that is in it as the theatre in which that glory is to be manifested',[2] a sentiment which would have secured John's unqualified approval.

One more question should be raised in this connection, since it arises in verse 3 of chapter 20, and still more in verse 7ff. If the millennial reign represents the revelation of the glory of Christ in this world, why does John depict its end in disaster, and why in particular is the Devil released so as to precipitate such an end? A sufficient reason could be that John found it so represented in Ezekiel, for Scripture was authoritative for him, and Ezekiel was especially influential in his thinking. While this is so, there must be further motives which impelled John so to interpret Ezekiel, for he considerably adapts the Gog-Magog prophecy and uses various motifs from it to characterize the period prior to the parousia as well as the conclusion of the millenium. It is likely that Genesis will have taught John as truly as Ezekiel, since its pictures of the first paradise are used by John to depict the last paradise. Genesis will have suggested that as Satan was allowed to enter the first paradise to expose the nature of man's heart, so in the restoration of paradise he will be permitted to do so again. 'All enmity must come out into the open and be annihilated before God's reign is made absolute' (Farrer). It is further almost certain that John believed, and wished to convey the thought, that the full potentialities of human existence cannot be attained within the limitations of this world, even in the most idyllic conditions, in view of

---

[1] *Das Evangelium nach Matthäus* (*Das Neue Testament Deutsch*), ad loc.
[2] *The Kingship of Christ*, London, 1948, p. 95.

the unceasing possibilities for evil which exist within it. Ultimately it is the transfiguring grace of God, revealed in the resurrection, which alone can enable man to reach the goal of his creation. Of this the last rebellion of redeemed history is the final demonstration.[1]

THE REIGN OF CHRIST 20 : 4–10

It is extraordinary that after the portrayal of the coming of Christ in glory and his subjugation of the forces of evil, no real description of the rule of Christ is given, only a statement relating to the blessedness of those who participate in it with him (vv. 4–6). Not till the following chapter is the nature of the kingdom described (21 : 9ff.), but the allusion at this point is sufficient to identify the reality. John's mode of representing the messianic kingdom by depicting the place which Christ's confessors have in it is determined by his pastoral purpose, namely, to encourage his fellow believers to remain firm in faith and testimony, whatever the cost demanded of them.

4, 5. The opening sentence freely cites and adapts the description of the judgment scene recounted in Daniel 7 : 9ff. There the rampaging of the antigod-power is halted by the coming of the Ancient of Days to execute judgment upon it: 'As I looked thrones were placed, and one that was ancient of days took his seat.' The identity of those who sat on the thrones is not stated in Daniel, but they will be viewed as assessors who assist the judge when 'the court sat and the books were opened' (v. 10). By divine decision the kingdom was taken from the earthly powers and given to 'one like a son of man' (vv. 13f.). In the later exposition of the vision this is explained. 'The kingdom and the dominion and the great-

---

[1] Caird has expressed this admirably: 'The myth of Gog enshrines a deep insight into the resilience of evil. The powers of evil have a defence in depth, which enables them constantly to summon reinforcement from beyond the frontiers of man's knowledge and control. However far human society progresses, it can never, while this world lasts, reach the point where it is invulnerable to such attacks. Progress there must be, otherwise God is neither Lord of history nor Lord of creation. But even when progress issues in the millennium, men must remember that they still have no security except in God. This is, in fact, the mythical equivalent of the Pauline doctrine of justification by faith alone, which teaches that from start to finish man's salvation is the work of grace, and never at any time his own achievement' (op. cit., p. 257).

ness of the kingdoms under the whole heaven shall be given to the people of the saints of the Most High ... and all dominions shall serve and obey him' (v. 27). John interprets Daniel's statement in the light of a tradition in the Church which goes back to Jesus (see Mt. 19:28, Lk. 22:30, 1 C. 6:3). The occupants of the thrones are followers of the Messiah Jesus. Daniel had stated (7:22) that when the Ancient of Days came, 'judgment was given for the saints ... and the time came when the saints received the kingdom', i.e., their cause was vindicated in the court, and they were given the kingdom. In accordance with the principle that the Christ in his parousia is the executor of the divine judgment and that he himself brings the kingdom, John associates the saints with Christ in the judgment and they commence their rule with him at once.

In his vision of the heirs of the kingdom John immediately singles out the martyrs, **the souls of those who had been beheaded for their testimony to Jesus and for the word of God.** The language is consciously reminiscent of the vision of the martyrs who cry beneath the altar for vindication. 'I saw ... the souls of those who had been slain for the word of God and for the witness they had borne' (6:9ff.). In chapter 6 they are given a white robe and told to be patient a little longer. Here their prayer is answered, and they are raised to reign with Christ in his kingdom. For Christians of John's day this assurance was of importance. It held out the prospect that even if they were called to yield up their lives for Christ in the last great conflict, their sacrifice would issue in God's vindication of them in the kingdom of his Son.

Are they, **who had not worshipped the beast ... and had not received its mark,** the martyrs more particularly defined; or are they the wider company of Christ's confessors who remained faithful to him, even though they had not been called on to surrender their lives? The former interpretation appears to be the most natural way of reading the text. The martyrs are then defined first in terms of their positive witness and then in terms of their refusal to conform to the popular obedience to the Antichrist. On the other hand, 13:8 states that all will render that obedience except those whose names are written in the Lamb's book of life. This indicates that the Church alone, but the Church in its entirety, is distinguished by its rejection of allegiance to the beast, and this corresponds to the fact that the whole company of the

Church receives the seal of God, in contrast to 'all who dwell on the earth', who receive the mark of the beast. John, therefore, would have had adequate reason to distinguish between the martyrs and Christ's loyal confessors, and yet conjoin them as together constituting the confessing Church of Christ. The possibilities of interpretation are so evenly balanced, it is difficult to be confident as to the author's intention. With great hesitation the present writer, who formerly registered his vote for the distinction of two groups, in verse 4bc inclines to feel that the simplest understanding of the text is preferable, and to see that the martyrs alone are in view here.

What then are we to make of the next two sentences of the text? The martyrs **came to life, and reigned with Christ ... The rest of the dead did not come to life until the thousand years were ended.** Is the kingdom of Christ reserved for the martyrs only? Commonly the answer given is 'Yes', on the ground that the passage demands such an interpretation. It is further urged that this view is comprehensible if John anticipated that the whole Church would be martyred before the end came. All would be martyred and all rise for the triumph of Christ. Admitting the plausibility of this exegesis, it should nevertheless be observed that it contradicts the drift of the Revelation from beginning to end, for this view restricts the kingdom to one generation only of the Church. The opening doxology gives glory to the Christ who by his redemption has made the Church as such kings and priests to God (1 : 6). This is echoed in the song of redemption, sung when the Lamb takes the book of destiny from God's hand, and which celebrates the Church as a kingdom and priests to our God, 'and they shall reign on earth' (5 : 9). The fulfilment of that expectation appears to be recorded in the concluding sentence of our paragraph (20 : 6): 'They shall be priests of God and of Christ, and they shall reign with him a thousand years.' Assurance of participation in the kingdom of Christ is the burden of the promises to the conquerors which conclude the letters to the churches (chs. 2–3). Most conclusively, chapter 19 records the praise of a vast crowd, following on the judgment of the antichristian city and empire: 'Hallelujah! for the Lord our God the Almighty reigns. Let us rejoice and exult and give him the glory, for the marriage of the Lamb has come, and his Bride has made herself ready' (19 : 6f.). The marriage of the Lamb takes place immediately following the deliverance of the Church from the assault of the Antichrist and at the commencement of the messianic reign. The bride is a symbol for the whole Church and not for a segment of it. In 21 : 9f. the bride, the wife of the Lamb and the city of God are complementary concepts. The Church itself therefore is viewed as entering with its Lord into the eschatological joy of the kingdom revealed in the glory of the parousia.

This teaching is by no means necessarily inharmonious with 20 : 4–6. If verse 4*bc* is rightly interpreted of the martyrs, we must assume that verse 4*a* relates to the Church generally. In this initial statement John declares that Daniel's vision now receives its fulfilment. The promised kingdom is given to 'the people of the saints of the Most High', i.e., the Church of the Son of man and Messiah Jesus. The martyrs are then singled out for particular mention because of the situation of the Church for which John writes. On this understanding **they came to life, and reigned with Christ** relates to the whole company of the Christian dead. As to the relationship between the saints of the old covenant and the messianic kingdom John is silent. But what of the members of the Church who have not passed through the portals of death? John is silent about them too. He does not state whether he anticipates that they will enjoy a privileged association with Christ in the kingdom while still in life, or whether he awaits the transformation of the living with the resurrection of the dead in Christ, as Paul expresses it in 1 Corinthians 15 : 51f. and 1 Thessalonians 4 : 16. Again, however, if we look back on his vision, we observe that the promises to the conquerors spell out various aspects of the life in the kingdom which is Christ's gift to the victors (e.g., 2 : 7, 11, 17), and this will have been conceived of in terms of resurrection. It is likely that Paul's teaching on the resurrection will have represented convictions generally shared in the primitive Church, and that John in common with the rest will have held them also. These convictions will almost certainly have been influenced by the traditional expectation of the 'gathering of the elect' for the messianic kingdom, as expressed, e.g., in Mark 13 : 27, and will therefore have assumed importance for John. Accordingly we may assume that John looked for the transformation of the whole Church at the resurrection of the dead saints.

5. The resurrection for life in the messianic rule is termed **the first resurrection.** The expression is not found elsewhere, but

the doctrine may well be intended by Paul in 1 Corinthians
15:22–4. Certainly Paul's teaching on the Holy Spirit as the
pledge or 'down payment' of the kingdom of God (2 C. 1:22,
Eph. 1:14, 4:20) implies a distinction between the resurrection
of those in Christ and those not so united with him. On this understanding the Holy Spirit is both the first of the gifts of the
kingdom of God, and mediates to the Church in this age the life of
the new creation, seen in the resurrection of Christ (2 C. 5:17),
and so he will bring it to its fruition in the kingdom of Christ
(cf. Rom. 8:9–11). The distinctiveness of resurrection in Christ is
assumed in the New Testament generally (e.g., Mk 12:24ff.,
Jn 5:28ff., Phil. 3:11, Heb. 9:27f., 1 Pet. 1:3–5), but its separation in time is John's own contribution.[1]

6. A benediction is pronounced on him **who shares in the
first resurrection.** He is **holy** as well as **blessed,** since he
belongs to the Christ of God. **Over such the second death has
no power;** see note on 2:11. As **priests of God and of Christ,**
privileged to reign with Christ, it may be presumed that these have
ministry to perform on behalf of Christ in the world. John's
brevity of expression, to which he has adhered throughout this
chapter, forbids his enlarging on the nature of that ministry.
Caird has suggested that the most helpful analogy to it is in the
ministry of the risen Christ himself, who walks among the seven
lamps of his world-wide Church and sends out the seven spirits of
God into all the world: 'For them, as for him, resurrection means
that they have been "let loose into the world".'[2] The thought of
the Church continuing to be an instrument of Christ's blessing for
mankind in the age to come is encouraging, even if the mode of

---

[1] See further H. Bietenhard, *Das Tausendjährige Reich*, 1955, pp. 54f. It is to
be observed that this inward connection between the Holy Spirit and the
resurrection of man in Christ is quite different from the doctrine which
became established in later rabbinic teaching. In contrast to earlier views,
which reserved the resurrection to the eternal age which follows the messianic
kingdom, the view became established from the third century on that the dead
in the land of Israel would rise in the messianic kingdom. The righteous who
were buried outside the Holy Land would have to roll in underground tunnels
to the promised land, there to join in the resurrection of the blessed, but the
rest of the dead would not rise till the day of the world's judgment. Strack-
Billerbeck see this as primarily determined by the glorification of the land of
Israel, op. cit., III, pp. 827ff.

[2] Commentary, ad loc.

this ministry eludes our comprehension. The vision of 21 : 9ff. will give some hints of its scope and need.

7, 8. After the thousand years **Satan** is **loosed from his prison ... to deceive the nations ... Gog and Magog,** and assemble them for battle. The motif is ancient. Ezekiel tells of an invasion from the north of 'Gog of the land of Magog', where Gog is the prince and Magog the name of a people (Ezek. 38 : 1; cf. 39 : 6). As early as the Tell el-Amarna tablets *Gog* was used as a name for the nations of the north. Ezekiel sees in the attack on Israel by Gog the fulfilment of earlier prophecies (38 : 17). He depicts this as an invasion of the Holy Land and attack on Jerusalem after the Jews return from their exile among the nations and dwell in the peace of the messianic age under the new David (see especially 38 : 8). Gog comes at the head of many peoples 'like a cloud', but the Lord will create confusion amongst the invaders, so that every man's sword is against his brother. Ezekiel declares in the name of the Lord, 'I will rain upon him and his hordes and the many peoples that are with him torrential rains and hailstones, fire and brimstone' (38 : 22). As Ezekiel sees in Gog's invasion the fulfilment of earlier prophecies of Gentile attacks on Israel, so John sees in the hosts of Gog and Magog a symbol of the evil in the world of nations which resist the rule of God. For him, therefore, the attack of Gog comes not from one corner of the earth—the north—but from all four corners. It is doubtful that John wished by this means to point to the nations beyond the Roman empire which had been untouched by the rebellion under the Antichrist (Schlatter). Wherever the theme of Ezekiel 38–9 is taken up in Jewish apocalyptic writers (e.g., 2 *En* 56 : 5ff., 2 Esd. 13 : 5ff., *Sib. Or.* 3 : 662ff.) it is the nations generally which combine in assault on Israel, and it is likely that John had a similarly undefined company in view. On the other hand it is unlikely that John thought of the entire world of men, women, and children, as massed together under the leadership of Gog against the city of God, resulting in the end of history as the destruction of every living soul on earth (as Charles thought). We have already observed the mistake in overpressing the language of 19 : 17ff. in this manner, and the same applies to verses 8f.

9. The hordes of Gog and Magog surrounded **the camp of the saints and the beloved city.** The language befits Jerusalem, viewed however first as the focal point of the pilgrim people on the

march through the desert to the promised land, and then as the
city which God loves (cf. Ps. 87). But Jerusalem in the Revelation
is equated with Sodom and Egypt, 'where their Lord was crucified'
(11 : 8). The city which John has in mind is 'the holy city Jerusalem', which comes down from God out of heaven (21 : 10). Its
mention at this point indicates that John sees the beloved city as
descended from God out of heaven in the messianic age and so
views it as the centre of the kingdom of Christ. The brevity of the
description of that kingdom in verses 4–6 is at least partly due to
John's intention to describe its nature in the vision of 21 : 9ff. The
assault on the city, therefore, represents an attack on the manifestation of the divine rule in the world, comparable to the attack
on the Church in the present age.

10. As the opponents of the Christ in his parousia were slain by
the sword of his mouth (19 : 21), so the army that seeks the
destruction of the city of God is consumed by fire from heaven
(v. 9, cf. Ezek. 38 : 22). **The Devil,** having accomplished his work
of manifesting the hidden rebelliousness of man, is no longer
tolerated to work further mischief. He is **thrown into the lake of
fire and brimstone,** to join his accomplices in the evil work of
seducing mankind from the Creator. The passage is significant as
suggesting that the function of the Devil is not to originate sin but
to reveal it and develop its latent possibilities in man. Since sin is
directed against the will of God, it is most characteristically to be
seen as rebellion against God, a rebellion which would destroy the
works of God (here the beloved city) and even the Christ and God
himself. But the Devil is not God, nor is he in any real sense a rival
to God. He cannot stray beyond the permission of God for his
action, and at the appointed time it will cease. The mystery of the
Devil, like the mystery of evil itself, lies hidden in the depths of the
mystery of God's purpose for his creation. In the last analysis the
Devil has to contribute to that purpose. It is beyond his power to
frustrate it. For the original readers of the Revelation that will
have been a source of no little comfort. It should provide that for
the people of God in all ages.

THE LAST JUDGMENT **20: 11–15**

The greater part of the Revelation (chs. 6–19) is concerned with
the judgments of God within history. This passage has as its

theme the judgment of God upon history, for earth's story has
now reached its end. The executor of the divine judgments on
man in the world has been the Christ, hence the judgments of the
seals, trumpets, and cup-bowls are 'messianic' judgments. The
identity of the Judge on the throne in verse 11 is not stated, but the
allusion to Daniel 7:9 (and possibly Isa. 6:1) is plain, and
Revelation 4:2ff. lies yet closer to hand. The criteria of judgment
are afforded by the *books*, i.e., records of deeds performed, and by
the book of life, which is the Lamb's book (21:27). This latter
provides in symbol an equivalent to the synoptic picture of the
Christ bearing testimony before the Father in the judgment (Mt.
10:32f., Mk 8:38). Thus John represents God as the Judge and
Jesus as the supreme witness, whose testimony determines the
decision. Comparison is often made with the conception expressed
in John 5:22, 'The Father judges no one but has given all judgment to the Son.' The difference should not be pressed as though
the divergence were absolute, for in John 5:22 the Son goes on to
say, 'As I hear, I judge' (5:30), and later represents the judgment
of the Father and the Son to be coincidental (8:16), subsequently
declaring that the judgment is that of the Father in accordance
with the word he has given to the Son to speak (12:47ff.). Such a
duality of thought as to the person of the judge is frequently to be
observed in the New Testament; cf., e.g., Matthew 6:4, 18:35
(God as Judge) with Matthew 7:22f., 25:31–46 (Christ as
judge), and Romans 14:10 ('the judgment seat of God') with
2 Corinthians 5:10 ('the judgment seat of Christ'). Similarly, in
the Revelation, John has already alluded to Christ as sharing the
Father's throne (3:21, 5:6ff.), and in his descriptions of the New
Jerusalem he depicts God and the Lamb as seated together on the
throne (22:1, 3; cf. 21:22, 23). We are again constrained to recall that throughout this book we are dealing with parables and
symbols which point to ideas beyond their verbal expression.
John's concern is to paint an awesome picture of the Judge on his
throne and the judged who are summoned to appear before him.
The relations of the Father and the Son in the judgment are not
under consideration at this point.

11. The **throne** of God was the first object which had caught
John's attention in his opening vision of heaven (4:2). Now it is
portrayed as not alone the dominating feature of heaven, but as
the sole, awful reality in the universe, from which all else flees

away in terror. Its description as **great** and **white** emphasizes the glory and holiness of him who occupies it.[1]

That **earth and sky fled away** from the presence of the Lord may indicate the total disappearance of the old creation; i.e., it vanishes in the sense of ceasing to exist. In favour of this it is observed that the clause **no place was found for them** cites Daniel 2:35, with reference to Nebuchadrezzar's image, which disappeared without trace, to be replaced by the stone which 'filled the whole earth'. On that understanding, however, verse 13 provides a puzzle, since the sea can hardly be said to give up its dead if the world has passed away. Charles therefore proposed to strike that statement out from verse 13 as an unauthentic addition, but this is a needless expedient. John could have neglected to observe due order at this point, assuming that his readers would understand that resurrection to judgment precedes the disappearance of the heavens and earth. But it may be that his thought proceeded along quite different lines. His subject at this point was not geophysical and astronomical changes in the universe, but the majesty of God in the judgment. An instructive parallel is afforded by 6:1ff., where the terrors of the closing messianic judgments are enhanced by the description of cosmic signs—the sun turns black as sackcloth, the stars fall to earth, the sky vanishes like a scroll that is rolled up, mountains and islands are hurled from their places, and the wicked call on the mountains to hide them from the face of him who sits on the throne and from the Lamb, 'for the great day of their wrath has come'. Commentators frequently

---

[1] Cf. the vivid picture in 2 Esdras 7:39ff:

> 'Thus shall the day of judgment be:
> (A day) whereon is neither sun, nor moon, nor stars;
> neither clouds, nor thunder, nor lightning;
> neither wind, nor rainstorm, nor cloud-rack;
> neither darkness, nor evening, nor morning;
> neither summer, nor autumn, nor winter;
> neither heat, nor frost, nor cold;
> neither hail, nor rain, nor dew;
> neither noon, nor night, nor dawn;
> neither shining, nor brightness, nor light,

save only the splendour of the brightness of the Most High, whereby all shall be destined to see what has been determined for them.'

Charles, (*Pseudepigrapha*, p. 584) cites Gunkel's comment that the verses breathe the spirit of the mystic before which all that hides the vision of God disappears.

interpret that passage as implying the destruction of the physical universe, but that is far from John's intention, for the events of the sixth seal give place to the inauguration of the kingdom of Christ in power and glory on the earth. The traditional language of cosmic signs has been employed chiefly to identify this event as the time of the parousia, and to expose the terror of the wicked on earth when the messianic judgments reach their climax. And such, it would appear, is John's motive in 20 : 11. It is not the earth and the heavens but 'those who dwell upon the earth' and the angelic, or rather demonic, powers which seek to flee from the overwhelming glory of the presence of the Lord.

12. But they are not allowed to escape that awful presence. **I saw the dead, great and small, standing before the throne.** The description is inclusive, embracing all humanity. None are conceived of as alive in the body, for it is no terrestrial scene in mind, such as Daniel 7 : 9ff. describes. Nor is there any suggestion that the wicked alone of humanity have been summoned for this occasion, as though it had been convened solely to demonstrate the justice of their sentence to the lake of fire (so Lohmeyer, Rissi). Humanity appears before God for judgment, that all may hear the just declaration of God concerning them, whether for acquittal and welcome into the kingdom, or condemnation and exclusion from the eternal city. Consistency may demand that *the dead . . . standing before the throne* are all at this point raised for judgment, and hence that the company which 'came to life and reigned with Christ a thousand years' (v. 4) is excluded. On such a view the Church is envisaged as exempt from the last judgment. On the other hand, 3 : 5 assumes that the believer in Christ will appear before the tribunal of God for judgment, exactly as in this scene. If the Church is excluded from the last judgment, it can only be because it has already appeared before God in judgment. John himself gives no hint that such an event has taken place. It is wiser to recognize that John teaches that all must submit to the judgment of God, saints and sinners alike. Differentiation of order or locality have no room in such a scene as verses 11ff. describe.

The judgment of men according to **what was written in the books** demonstrates the justice of the divine decision, since what stood written was **what they had done**—not evil things alone, but the good also. The symbol of books in heaven, wherein men's deeds are recorded, reflects the practice of certain oriental monarchs (notably the Persians) to keep such records of the activities of their subjects. It embodies the idea that no element in a man's life, whether good or evil, is forgotten by God, and in pronouncing according to such a record it is revealed not alone that God is just, but also that a man prepares his own destiny. The declaration by God of that destiny is in harmony with what a man has both willed and performed. This, however, is not the whole story of judgment. Along with the books which record a man's deeds there appears **the book of life.** It is kept by the Lamb (21 : 27), which suggests that the book is a register of those whom the Lamb acknowledges as his (3 : 5, and see the comment thereon for the significance of the symbol). They in their turn have recognized their own inadequacy before God and gratefully confessed that the Lamb has wrought a redemption which embraces them (5 : 9f., 7 : 9f.). They have further come to understand that all they have ever possessed or performed, including their decision for God and their continuance in faith, comes from the gracious giving of God, who sovereignly works his will among men (cf. 17 : 8). The joint testimony of the books of men's deeds and the Lamb's book of life accordingly gives a final expression to that duality of religious conviction and experience which sees God as sovereign in his guidance of history and man as responsibly free in his action. In the judgment God's justice and grace are neither divorced from one another, nor set in conflict with each other, but are harmonious, uniting in a single voice in their declaration of the destiny of every child of man.

13-15. The yielding up of the dead for judgment, alike by **the sea** and **Death and Hades,** emphasizes that no man is left out of account in the last judgment. Ancient ideas as to the relation of soul and body after death and the desire to be with one's own people in the realm of the dead caused great importance to be attached to burial, so that to remain unburied after death was a terrible fate (cf. 1 Kg. 13 : 21f., 14 : 11, Jer. 8 : 1f.) and to bury a corpse left in the open was a kindly and pious act (see Tob. chs. 1–2). Those who died at sea, therefore, were regarded as in a terrible situation, having been forever denied the privilege of burial and separated from their kin in the world of the dead. So John makes explicit mention of them. They are not overlooked by God at the end of the times, but they will join all the rest of the departed in the resurrection tc judgment. *Death and Hades* are

declared in 1 : 17f. to be under the control of the risen Lord. In
6 : 7f. they are personified, as here, but there they represent agents
of judgment—death stalking the land in the wake of sword,
famine, pestilence, and wild beasts, and the underworld opening
its jaws to receive the dead. John therefore views *death* as evil and
an adversary which only the Lord can subdue, and *Hades* as a part
of the old order of existence which must give way to the life of the
new creation, very much in the same way as Paul in his exposition
of resurrection (cf. 1 C. 15 : 26, 54f.). Death and Hades therefore
are **thrown into the lake of fire.** Their power over man has
ended, since they who are acknowledged by the Lamb have risen
for participation in the life of the new creation, and those whose
deeds condemned them suffer **the second death,** i.e., **the lake
of fire** (vv. 14f.; cf. 21 : 8, and see note on 2 : 11).

The terrible symbol *the lake of fire* should be distinguished from
the more common expression for hell, *Gehenna*, although the use to
which the two concepts are put is the same. *Gehenna* is the Greek
form of *Ge-hinnam*, the Aramaic equivalent of the Hebrew name
Ge-Hinnom, 'valley of Hinnom', which lay south of Jerusalem, immediately outside its wall. The assumption that the city's rubbish
was burned in this valley appears to go back to the Jewish scholar
Kimchi (*c.* AD 1200), but it is not attested in any ancient source.
The valley was notorious as the scene of human sacrifices, burned
in the worship of Moloch (2 Kg. 16 : 3, 21 : 6). Jeremiah, therefore, prophesied that the valley would later be called the Valley of
Slaughter, because of the judgment that would overtake it (Jer.
7 : 32f.). This combination of abominable fires and divine judgment led to the thought of the valley as a place of perpetual
judgment (Isa. 66 : 24), and at length as a symbol for divine judgment by fire, without any thought of location beside Jerusalem
(the earliest examples of this latter use are in the *Book of Enoch*;
e.g., 27 : 1ff., 54 : 1ff., 56 : 3f., 90 : 26ff.). While the term appears
frequently in the gospels (e.g., Mt. 10 : 28, 25 : 41, Mk 9 : 43ff.),
it is absent from the Revelation. Its place is taken by *the lake of fire*
the origin of which is thought to be in the idea of the primeval sea
as the home of the sea-monster, the enemy of God. For this the
term *abyss* (*RSV*, 'bottomless pit') was used, and it was differenti-
ated into various sections, e.g., as the home of evil spirits and the
place where fallen angels were punished. In *Enoch* 18 : 12ff. it is
described as 'the end of heaven and earth . . . a prison for the stars

and host of heaven', but in 108:3ff. (a fragment of the *Book of Noah*) it is spoken of as 'a chaotic wilderness . . . not a heaven but only the flame of a blazing fire', and an angel declares, 'Here are cast the spirits of sinners and blasphemers, and of those who work wickedness, and of those who pervert everything that the Lord has spoken through the mouth of the prophets.' Thus the place of demonic spirits has become the place of their temporary punishment, and finally the place to which Satan and his evil agencies and the wicked of mankind are condemned perpetually after the judgment.

John's use of the symbol shows that he views it as the alternative to the city of God, the new Jerusalem (see 21:7f.). Its significance for humanity thus begins with the new creation. That it does not have the meaning of annihilation is indicated by 20:10. The lake of fire signifies not extinction in opposition to existence, but torturous existence in the society of evil in opposition to life in the society of God. For which reason John is able to represent the same reality by the very different symbol of life outside the city (21:27) in contrast to life inside the city (21:24ff.), the separation being effected by the city's wall (21:14). It is the conviction of some exegetes[1] that John anticipated that the multitude which had rejected the rule of God will ultimately find their way through the gates into the city in the new world (21:24ff. is of importance to this view). Candour compels us to state that John has given no clear indication of any such teaching. He simply presents stark alternatives before mankind of life for or against God in the here and now, and its consequences in the age to come. With his eye on the impending climax of history in the life and death struggle of the forces of Christ and the Antichrist among the nations, and its issue in the judgments of God within and beyond this world, John was not worried by the problems which perplex us in our more detached reflections on time and eternity. Without doubt John would have affirmed as readily as any that the last word on the ultimate destiny of man remains with God, who has revealed himself in our Lord Jesus Christ, and whose grace and truth are equally present in his judgment of man as they were united in the judgment of the cross. When we have stated all our arguments, we too finally have to rest in that acknowledgement.

[1] See Rissi, *Time and History*, pp. 123ff., and *The Future of the World*, pp. 36ff., 67ff., and references to literature supporting this view.

THE NEW CREATION 21 : 1-8

With the two paragraphs which form this section John's vision of
the future reaches its climax. He had described under varied
forms the messianic judgments of the last times, the collapse of the
antichristian empire and overthrow of evil powers which inspired
it, the coming of the Christ and his kingdom on earth, and the last
judgment wherein God's verdict on mankind is made known.
Now follows the unveiling of a new order not subject to the
ravages of time. It is, in Farrer's words, 'the last of the Last
Things and the end of the visionary drama'. Nothing more than
this can follow, beyond the attempt to explain it.

It is characteristic of John's prophetic style that he has com-
pressed his vision of the transcendent order for which creation and
the history of man has prepared into a single paragraph consisting
of about a hundred words. Its essential feature is the appearance
of a new creation and the descent of the new Jerusalem (vv. 1–2).
A voice from the throne declares the significance of this for mankind (vv. 3–4). A further paragraph then follows, closely related to
the first, but having primarily a pastoral purpose. It guarantees
the truth of the prophecy contained in the first paragraph,
promising participation in the blessings of the new world to all
who exercise faith and maintain it in face of discouragements, and
warning of the doom which will overtake all who apostatise and
persist in the ways of the Antichrist. The mood of the whole is
positive, despite the solemn note of warning on which it ends.
Indeed it is inexpressibly joyful, for here are depicted the ultimate
goal of the suffering Church and the only reward which Christ's
confessors really want, namely, God himself in the company of all
who love him. Since this vision is set on the far side of the last
judgment, that company is greater far than the Church. The vision
therefore, may be viewed as the climax not only of the book of
Revelation, but of the whole story of salvation embodied in the
Bible. The comfort of the Church, as it faces the contest with the
forces of the Antichrist, is nothing less than the realization of God's
purpose in creation.

1. John's economy of words in his description of the ultimate
attainment of God's will for creation has caused difficulties for his
interpreters. In particular it is by no means clear how we are to

understand his statement that he saw **a new heaven and a new earth.** The text which forms the inspiration of John's exposition, namely, Isaiah 65 : 17ff., provides a description of the new earth almost wholly in terms of the present order of things. The earlier prophet has in view not a different world, but an earth freed from the sorrows of sin and renewed for the joy of the people of God. The Isaianic passage is a very late text, and the Jewish writers who pondered it not long afterwards elaborated its teaching in two different directions. Some emphasized the ruinous effects of the sin of man on life in this world, and this was seen as evoking the merciful and powerful operation of God in cleansing the earth from sin, quickening it to new life and transforming it to become the scene of his glory. In such a tradition the expressions 'new world' and 'new creation' meant a transformed world or creation. This tradition is to be found alike in certain of the apocalyptic writings and in sayings of later rabbinic teachers.[1] On the other hand some Jewish writers considered that the concept of new heavens and earth is to be understood literally, and that it pre-supposes the prior destruction of the old order. The latter was thought of either in terms of a return of the world to its primeval chaos or its destruction by fire. In such cases a new heaven and earth meant the creation of a completely new universe. Again, these interpretations of 'new creation' are to be found within Jewish apocalyptic literature and in the Talmud.[2] The question arises how John understood this matter, and what he wished to convey to his readers. We have already noticed the obscurity of his language in 20 : 11ff. (the fleeing of earth and sky from the Lord in the judgment), with the probability that his cosmic figures there relate primarily to living creatures rather than the 'material' heaven and earth. In 21 : 1 the emphasis appears to lie

[1] In 2 *Baruch* 3:4ff. the question is asked whether Jerusalem will be destroyed and the world revert to chaos, the great multitude of living beings destroyed, and mankind cease to be. The answer is given that the city will be delivered up for a time and the people chastened for a time, but the world will not be des-troyed. Consequently in a later vision it is said that in Abraham's time the unwritten law was named among men, belief in the judgment was generated 'and hope of the world that was to be renewed was then built up', 57:2. See further *Jubilees* 4:26, 23:18, and for examples in rabbinic writings see Strack-Billerbeck, III, pp. 843f.

[2] See especially 2 *Esdras* 7:29ff., *Sibylline Oracles* 5:476ff., *Enoch* 83:3f. 91:14ff.; and for the rabbinic literature, Strack-Billerbeck, III, 843ff.

not on the inhabitants of heaven and earth but on heaven and earth itself. This is made clear in the second clause, **for the first heaven and the first earth had passed away,** echoing language which had become traditional in the Christian Church (cf. Mt. 5 : 18, Mk 13 : 31, 1 C. 7 : 31, 1 Jn 2 : 17), and also by the third clause, **and the sea was no more.** In the ancient cosmology a world which possesses no sea is even more vastly different from the present order than it appears to modern views. John's *language*, therefore, seems to demand the recognition that he viewed the new heavens and earth as newly created, in the strictest sense of the term, and that they replace a creation which has ceased to exist.

2. While John's statement undoubtedly possesses that form it should be observed that the question as to whether it is to be understood literally is not thereby settled. The dominating feature of the new heaven and earth is **the holy city.** It is defined as **new Jerusalem ... prepared as a bride adorned for her husband,** and the description of the city-bride which follows in verses 9ff. is symbolic from first to last. Indeed, John's chief interest in the new heavens and earth is precisely its setting for the city of God. For this reason Rissi could write, 'The new Jerusalem is a part of this new world, or, to put it better, *the holy city is its concrete form.*'[1] Moreover it is extremely difficult to be confident of the meaning of *the sea is no more.* There is little doubt that the statement is motivated by more than a mere distaste for or fear of the sea. Rather, we have here the climax of that connection between the sea and evil which runs through much of the Revelation. As Daniel's terrible beasts rose from the sea (Dan. 7 : 3ff.), so John's Antichrist-beast comes from the sea (13 1ff.), and the antichristian empire has the identical appearance as the Devil, namely, the lineaments of sea-monster (17 : 3; cf. 12 : 3). But in the ancient myth, with which John is clearly acquainted, the sea-monster is the sea personified, and it has to be quelled before creation can take place. It is little wonder that Rashi, the famous Jewish teacher, once actually equated the sea with Gehenna.[2] Oman thought that John in this passage meant by it the sea of separation in heaven, mentioned in 15 : 2 and linked in 20 : 13

---

[1] *The Future of the World,* p. 55.
[2] In a comment on *Shab.* 104a; see Strack-Billerbeck, III, 847.

with Death and Hades[1], and Caird similarly defines it as the
cosmic sea out of which the first heaven and earth were made.

Perhaps John's statement is to be taken at its face value. He
means the sea which laps the shores of the land, but his general
use of the term points to the fact that he is speaking parabolically.
We cannot be sure how he viewed the new heaven and new
earth, but the context of this statement suggests that his real concern is not with physical geography, but to describe a context of
life for God's people which accords with the great and glorious
purpose God has in mind for them. If that be so, the closest parallel
in literature to verse 1 also has an inward affinity to it: 'If anyone
is in Christ, there is a new creation; the old has passed away,
behold the new has come' (2 C. 5:17). In Paul's view the new
creation came into being in the death and resurrection of Christ,
so that to step into fellowship with Christ is to participate in that
new world. John's vision could well signify its extension to embrace all that God has made, but the emphasis is on the creatures
rather than the creation of God.

The sole reality which John is given to see in the new heaven
and earth is **the holy city, new Jerusalem.** The city fills his
vision since it is the centre of existence for the redeemed and
renewed mankind in the new creation. For John the importance of
the new creation is precisely its setting for the city of God, even as
the significance of the city is its provision of a context for the holy
fellowship of God with his creatures. The city is seen **coming
down out of heaven from God.** It is therefore no earthly metro-
polis, rebuilt in magnificence in the Holy Land, but a creation of
God which is to fulfil for the glorified humanity the role which the
prophets saw for the earthly Jerusalem in relation to Israel (and in
a less degree the Gentile nations).

John's symbol of the city of God in the new creation however is
not simply a raising to a higher plane of prophetic anticipations of
Jerusalem's glory in the kingdom of God, but the product of
traditions from various sources flowing together. The teaching of
the Old Testament prophets about the destiny of Jerusalem
naturally was of prime importance to John. The exaltation of the
city in the new age combined the thought of God's glorious rule
over the world with his acknowledgement by the nations in true
worship (e.g., Isa. 2:1ff.). With this the vindication of God's

[1] *Book of Revelation*, p. 162.

people oppressed by the nations was combined, especially after
the fall of Jerusalem. As the ruined city was to be restored to a
glory greater than it had known, so the nation was to be exalted
above all others in the world (e.g., Isa. 60). In the visions of
Ezekiel the restoration of Jerusalem was almost wholly subordinated to the theme of the restored worship of the temple, and hence
to the exaltation of God in holy acknowledgement by his people
(chs. 40–7). Jerusalem's glorification naturally featured in the
visions of apocalyptic writers. It is notably exemplified in Tobit
13 : 16ff. and in the Qumran writings (see especially the psalm in
1QM. XII, 13ff.). In Deutero-Isaiah the prophet's compassion
reveals itself in his emphasis on the restoration of 'Zion', i.e., the
people rather than the city (but not to the exclusion of the latter,
cf. Isa. 49 : 14ff., 50 : 1ff., 54 : 1ff.). This emphasis reaches its
height in Isaiah 54, wherein the prophet speaks of Zion as the
wife of Yahweh, who will show compassion on her with everlasting
love (vv. 5ff.), and then describes the future glories of Jerusalem,
whose walls and buildings are to be adorned with precious stones
and whose security is in the Lord (vv. 11ff.). The pertinence of
this for John's vision is apparent, for the city which descends from
God is prepared as a bride adorned for her husband. A striking
parallel to the combination of city and bride occurs in the near
contemporary 2 Esdras 10: 25ff., wherein the woman who
addresses the seer is transformed before his eyes into 'a city of large
foundations'. She too is Zion, not the earthly Jerusalem but a
heavenly city, pre-existing and hidden with God (see 2 Esd.
8 : 52f., 10: 49).[1]

This notion of a pre-existent Jerusalem in the heavens readily

[1] The same conception appears in 2 *Baruch* 4:2ff. in unmistakable terms:
'This building now built in your midst (= Jerusalem) is not that which is
revealed with me, which was prepared beforehand here from the time when I
took counsel to make Paradise and showed it to Adam before he sinned ...
Behold, it is preserved with me, as also Paradise.' This conception takes its
rise from the conviction that earthly institutions are copies of heavenly realities
and the features of the age to come are created by God before all time. The
employment of this conception in Hebrews 12:22ff. lays emphasis on the
eschatological aspect of the heavenly Jerusalem. The Church of Christ belongs
even in this age to the city of God, and in its worship it has freedom of access
through Jesus, mingling in spirit with the citizens of the heavenly Jerusalem in
heaven and on earth. Paul has a similar idea in Galatians 4:26f. The redeemed
children of Abraham rejoice in 'our mother' the Jerusalem above, even in this
age.

links with two other related ideas which have quite different sources, namely, that of the mythical 'mountain of God' (Ezek. 28:16), or 'the mountain where the gods meet' (Isa. 14:13) in the north, where the starry constellations revolve, and the city of the gods in the heavens, which featured in the astral religion of the Babylonians. John undoubtedly pondered Ezekiel's use of the mythical story about the attempt by the morning star to scale the mountain of God and become king of the stars (it occurs in Isa. 14 as well as Ezek. 28), for Ezekiel 28 is one of the sources from which he draws his account of the heavenly Jerusalem. It is also evident that certain features in his description of the new Jerusalem are traceable back to Babylonian ideas about the city of the gods, and there are grounds for thinking that John was fully aware that he was drawing on concepts from other religions. We shall observe these in our exposition of verses 9ff., but here we content ourselves with noting that the twelve gates of the city with their twelve angels may go back to the twelve figures and divisions of the heaven in the zodiac, the city's precious stones to the twinkling stars of heaven, the river running through its street (and possibly the street itself) to the Milky Way, and the wall of jasper to the night horizon. John's employment of these elements of pagan belief should be compared with his use in chapter 12 of the widespread myth or myths of the redeemer who destroys the dragon. As in that passage John employs the myth to declare the fulfilment by Jesus of the hope of the world for redemption, so in these final visions he appropriates the pagans' dream of a city of the gods and combines it with the Old Testament prophetic descriptions of restored Jerusalem (and those of later Judaism) to show that all these intimations of immortality reach their fulfilment and realization through Jesus, and through Jesus alone. The uniqueness of the Christian revelation concerning the city of God is indicated through the modifications John makes of the traditions, e.g., the gates are inscribed not with the figures of the zodiac, but with the names of Israel's tribes; the foundations are inscribed with the names of the apostles of the Lamb, who bear witness to Jesus as the sole redeemer of the world; the city is the dwelling place of the Father of our Lord Jesus Christ, but it does not remain remote in the heavens. Rather it descends to earth, that the multitude for whom Christ died and rose might enter and enjoy holy fellowship with God for ever.

3. Accordingly **a great voice from the throne** (cf. 19:5) sounds out the wonderful news, **Behold, the dwelling of God is with men.** That is the supreme blessing of God for man and the climax of man's aspirations. The unveiled presence of God with man signifies unhindered and unbroken fellowship between God and man and the fullness of God's grace for man. It is not without reason that the closing words of Ezekiel's vision of restored Jerusalem in the kingdom of God are, 'The name of the city henceforth shall be, The Lord is there.' All John's descriptions of its features expound the consequences of this feature of its life.

The statement of verse 3 resounds with echoes of the Old Testament history and prophecy. For the term *dwelling* literally means tent (Greek, *skēnē*). In the LXX it translated the Hebrew *mishkan*, which is used of the tabernacle in the wilderness. We recall that the pillar of cloud and fire rested on the tent, and this association of God's manifest glory, the *Shekinah* (from the Hebrew *shakan*, to dwell), with the tabernacle caused the Jews to view the tabernacle as the manifestation of God's presence among his people. The statement of Leviticus 26:11, 'I will make my abode (Heb. *Mishkan*) among you', is paraphrased in the Targum, 'I will set the *Shekinah* of my glory among you.' The Jews looked for the return of the *Shekinah* in the kingdom of God. Greek-speaking Jews were conscious that the term *Shekinah* has the same consonants as the Greek *skēnē*, and this enabled them to associate with *skēnē* the conceptions of the *Shekinah*. A notable example of this occurs in John 1:14, 'The word became flesh and pitched its tent (Greek *eskēnōsen*, from *skēnē*) among us, and we beheld his glory.' In the incarnate Lord the hope of the return of God in his *Shekinah* glory was fulfilled. This same revelation of divine glory reaches its consummation in our text. The dwelling of God among men means God in all his gracious glory, present among his people in the desert, manifest from time to time in the history of the chosen people, revealed to eyes of faith in the incarnate Son, and now unveiled for all to see. But the presence of God is not simply to be gazed at. It is to be enjoyed. **He will dwell with them, and they shall be his people.** Man will see God, and live. Indeed, he will live because he sees God, for this holy fellowship is the fount of life for man. Moreover, *his people* no longer means the chosen people in a restricted sense of one nation, for the elect are renewed humanity.

And all that Immanuel connotes comes to perfect fulfilment. **God himself will be with them** (cf. Isa. 7:14).

4. Since God is among men in fullness of grace and glory, all the unhappy concomitants of the old order disappear—**every tear, death, mourning, crying** and **pain.** This is not an automatic effect. It is God, the gracious Comforter, who wipes away the tears, gives life which death cannot touch, and affords joys with which sadness cannot subsist. For the thought, cf. Isaiah 25:8, 1 Corinthians 15:24, Isaiah 35:10, 51:11.

5–8. The succeeding paragraph is distinctive in that here alone in the Revelation God is represented as the speaker. It is conceivable that the vision of the new creation continues in these statements without a break, but the command of verse 5*b* and the pastoral intention of verses 6–8 suggest that God now speaks through his servant in the light of the revelation of the new order of existence described in verses 1–4.

5. The word order should be observed: 'Behold, new am I making all things!' The emphasis is on the newness which God imparts to his creation, and therefore to his creatures. He is not discarding them, but granting them to know the newness of life manifest in the risen Christ, and operative even in this age in all who are in Christ (2 C. 5:17; cf. Gal. 6:15). The present tense **I make** is prophetic of God's future new creative action, but it is rooted in the Easter of redemption and present in all who respond to the Gospel's invitation to life.

He who has so acted, is now acting, and will act in his new-creative power, affirms the truth of the vision. **These words are trustworthy and true.** They are guaranteed by the faithfulness and omnipotence of him who sits upon the throne. For this he has wrought through the ages, to this he has borne testimony through his prophets, and for this the Son of God died and rose and reigns and comes.

6. Accordingly, the cry rings out from the throne, **It is done!** Uttered as from the conclusion of the story in the new world, it is declared in the present, for the character of God is expressed in that word. As **the Alpha and the Omega,** the Lord God Almighty is the initiator of creation and its end, and in his hands lies the whole intermediary process, which he guides to its desired conclusion (see note on 1:8). So truly as God is Alpha and Omega, so certain is his affirmation that he will make all things new.

That leads directly to the pastoral adjunct of verses 6b–8. Since the end depicted in verses 1–4 is guaranteed by the nature and character and word of God, the destiny which man chooses, and which is to be revealed in the last judgment (20 : 11ff.), is equally sure. Promise is made that God himself **will give** to the thirsty **water . . . from the fountain of the water of life.** The language is conditioned by the well-known invitation in Isaiah 55 : 1 that the thirsty man procure from the Lord water, wine, and milk without price. In the light of the revelation of the new creation in verses 1–4 this has a fullness of meaning imparted to it of which the prophet could not have dreamed: life in that fullness of measure which proceeds from unclouded fellowship with God in his new world (observe that the river of water of life proceeds from the throne of God and the Lamb, 22 : 1). While the saying doubtless extends to all who will come forward and take the water in the future (22 : 17), its primary application is to the believer who has come, who trusts in the Christ, and who faces the testing described in the earlier chapters of this book (see especially chs. 12–13). The reward of faith no persecutor can wrest, for it is in the hand of him who sits on the throne.

7. The promises to the conquerors, declared in the seven letters of chapters 2–3, therefore find their summary expression at this point. **He who conquers shall have this heritage** namely that described in verses 1–4. He will participate in the blessedness of God's people in the new creation. The term *heritage* is paraphrastic. Literally it is 'these things', but the *RSV* translators are justified in so rendering it, for in this context the declaration **I will be his God and he shall be my son** views the victorious believer as an heir of God. It expresses the same sentiment as Romans 8 : 15–17 ('if children, then heirs, heirs of God and fellow heirs with Christ'). Characteristically the thought is put into the language of a key messianic prophecy of the Old Testament, viz., 2 Samuel 7 : 14. Its orginal reference is to the son of David, although its echo in Psalm 89 : 26f. is applied to David himself, and inevitably in due time it came to be interpreted of the Messiah (as in Heb. 1 : 5). This is comprehensible, for these passages, along with Psalm 2 : 7, are alone in the Old Testament in referring to a single individual as Son of God. John makes a significant modification when citing the language, for he replaces the term *father* with *God*. To John the uniqueness of Jesus as Son of the Father is expressed by reserving to Jesus alone the right to regard God as Father. Believers are God's sons, but derivatively through their relation to the Christ, who is the unique Son of the Father.

8. The assurance of the truth of the vision concerning the new creation carries with it the certainty that those who persist in active opposition to God will meet with the judgment of God. The list of those whose lot will be in **the lake that burns with fire and brimstone** is determined by the earlier accounts of the rebellion fostered by the Antichrist. **The polluted** have been rendered so through the pollutions arising from the worship of the beast (cf. 17 : 4f.; *polluted* = Greek *ebdelugmenoi*, from *bdelugma*, an abominable thing, an idol). The **murderers, fornicators, sorcerers, idolaters** have been encouraged in their activites by the movement fostered by the Beast, described in 13 : 12–15. **Liars** are not so much men guilty of speaking untruth as those who promote the great lie of the Antichrist, as is indicated in the parallel passage 22 : 15. The Devil is the father of lies (Jn 8 : 44), and in the apostasy of which he is author a supreme attempt is made to deceive the earth into believing and following the lie (cf. 12 : 9, 13 : 4, 5–8). Nevertheless this list was not produced in order to be nailed up in public. It was intended especially for the man of faith, who is warned not to be of their number. Accordingly, the list begins with the **cowardly,** i.e., those who fear the threats of the beast more than they trust the love of Christ, and the **faithless,** who in this context are less likely to be men without faith than men who renounce faith. This sure word of judgment is added as a plea to the followers of Christ to make their calling and election sure. The prophecy of the new world in verses 1–4 is guaranteed by God. The promise of inheriting the new world is assured to believers by God (vv. 6a–7), and the prospect of exclusion from that new world is equally affirmed by God. Everything of worth is at stake for the man of God. Therefore, in the coming contest, one action alone is appropriate: endurance (Mk 13 : 13).

THE CITY OF GOD **21 : 9—22 : 5**

In the exposition of the preceding section, verses 1–8, we observed that John's description of the new creation and the holy city in verses 1–4 forms the climax of his visions of the end. It is, there-fore, natural to assume, with the majority of commentators, that

21 : 9–22 : 5 supplies an extended exposition of that paragraph. The passage certainly makes sense when so interpreted, and from one point of view it has to be so understood, for the central feature of the new creation in verses 1–4 is precisely the city of God, which is the theme of 21 : 9ff.

On the other hand, it is also evident that 21 : 9ff. is related to other texts besides verses 1–4. The introductory sentence of verse 9 not merely echoes but uses identical language to that in John's introductory statement to the vision of the harlot, the antichristian city (17 : 1). The Revelation as a whole may be characterized as *A Tale of Two Cities*, with the sub-title, *The Harlot and the Bride*. 21 : 9 is written in order to make that theme crystal clear. The harlot-city reposes on the beast from hell—she partakes of the character of the devil, and the bride-city descends from heaven— she is the creation of God. But one thing they have in common. They stand alike on the earth, and invite humanity to come to them. The vision of 21 : 1–4 shows the city of God coming down to earth in the new creation. The question arises: Which city rules the earth in the period between the destruction of the harlot-city and the appearance of the bride-city in the new creation? That is not intended to be an apocalyptic puzzle, but rather calls attention to John's purpose in writing his book, namely, to inspire in his readers the faith that the empire of the Antichrist and his minions is destined to be replaced by the rule of the Christ and his saints. He could not but believe that the overthrow of the harlot- city and the Antichrist would be followed by the establishment of the bride-city in the rule of the Christ.

That John did so believe is shown by two passages. First, in chapter 19 the destruction of the harlot city is celebrated in song by the angelic hosts and the triumphant Church. The theme of the Church's song is that the marriage of the Lamb has come and his bride has made herself ready (19 : 7). The vision is immedi- ately followed by that of the parousia of Christ and by the des- cription of the kingdom of Christ (19 : 11ff., 20 : 4ff.). John clearly wishes to indicate that the bride will appear in splendour along with the bridegroom, and that the marriage supper will then be celebrated. The marriage supper is, of course, an adapta- tion of the traditional symbol of the kingdom of God as a feast. The people of God share in the joyous table-fellowship provided by their Lord. Likewise, the symbolism of the bride and the city

depict fundamentally the same thing, namely, God's people in
fellowship with their Redeemer. 21:9ff., therefore, virtually
identifies the bride with the city—they appear together. To say
then that the saints rule with Christ and that the city of God
comes down from heaven to earth is to portray a single reality.

The second passage to which we allude is the enigmatic 20:7ff.,
which describes the final rebellion against God in terms of an
attack on 'the camp of the saints and the beloved city' (v. 9).
Despite pleas to the contrary,[1] there is no question that John is
thereby describing a literal attack of hostile forces on Jerusalem in
Palestine. It is true that John's imagery is derived from precisely
such a picture, but he is as certainly allegorizing it, as he has
earlier allegorized the kindred expectation of a battle at Armageddon (see note on 16:16). The city called by the Jews 'holy' (11:2)
has become, in John's teaching, one with Sodom and Egypt
(11:8) and, therefore, a fit symbol for the world which crucified
its Lord (see notes on these passages). The prophetic expectations
of Jerusalem's role in the kingdom of God, therefore, is fulfilled in
the bride-city which descends out of heaven from God. The
cryptic reference in 20:9 indicates that John assumes that that
city of God will be revealed in the kingdom of Christ, in this
world and not alone in the next.

It accords with this understanding of John's writing, as Charles
argued in his commentary, that certain features in John's description of the city are more readily applicable to life in this world
than to conditions in the new creation; e.g., 21:24f. (the nations
walk in its light, kings bring their glory into it, and the nations
convey their glory and honour into it, but nothing unclean passes
through its ever open gates), and 22:2 (the leaves of the tree of
life heal the nations). One should go further and recognize that
the whole description of the city in 21:9–22:5 is eminently
appropriate to the concept of the kingdom of Christ revealed in
this world. It is equally to be recognized that the whole description
is applicable to the concept of the city of God in the new heaven
and earth, even though that entails a shift in the application of
some of the symbols (notably the idea of life 'outside' the city).
Accordingly the notion that parts of John's description of the city
in 21:9ff. belong to the millennial rule alone and part to the new
world alone, and that the present text which does not make that

[1] H. Bietenhard, *Das Tausendjährige Reich*, pp. 90ff.

distinction presents a confused disarray due to an incompetent
editor[1] is needless. The Revelation as we possess it yields a consistent representation of God's acts in Christ: the messianic
judgments in chapters 6–16, the overthrow of the antichristian
city detailed in 17–18, the parousia, kingdom of Christ, last
judgment, and new creation in 19: 1–21: 8, are successively narrated. Then, as the overthrow of the harlot-city had been related
in recapitulatory fashion for the encouragement of the saints, so
the appearance of the bride-city is portrayed in 21 : 9ff., again for
their comfort. It is emphasized however that the city endures not
merely for an age, but for the ages of eternity which none can
comprehend. It is the *new* Jerusalem, belonging to that new
creation which was brought into being in Christ's redemptive
activity. Since his Easter exaltation to the right hand of God, it is
true to say that it 'comes down' from heaven to earth, for Easter
means the kingdom of Christ in the world and life eternal for man.
Life in the city, life in the kingdom, life in Christ, life eternal, all
represent the same thing. But it is all hidden reality until the unveiling at Christ's parousia. No one who has pondered the
redemptive theology of chapter 5 should be surprised at the
thought that John looked for the city of God to be revealed in
history as well as in the eternal world that is to come. The kingdom of God and of Christ is meaningless if it does not include
God dwelling with man; and Christ's redemption is a chimera if
it is not operative in the world.

[1] See Charles' commentary, vol. 2. pp. 144ff.: 'We stand aghast at the hope-
less mental confusion which dominates the present structure of these chapters'—
a statement which embraces chapters 20–2 in their entirety. Charles assumed
that the author of the Revelation intended to present a continuous chronological
description in chapters 20–2, as he has in chapters 6–19—an assumption which
is as difficult to substantiate in the one section as in the other. On his premises
he reconstructs the order of text as follows: 20:1–3, the chaining of Satan;
21:9–22, 2, 14–15, 17; 20:4–10, the millennium; 20:11–15, the last judgment;
21:5a, 4d, 5b, 1–4c, 22:3–5, the new creation; 21:5c, 6b–8, admonitions of
God; 22:6–7, 18a, 16, 13, 12:10, declarations of Christ; 22:8–9, 20, John's
closing testimony; 22:21, benediction. It never seemed to occur to Charles
that John may have viewed the city of God as the revelation of God's rule alike
in the kingdom of Christ and in the new world. He is compelled to believe
that the city manifest in this world has to be 'made new' for the world to come,
so that 'this new city is either wholly new in every respect or it is the former
city transformed' (p. 158). Such an interpretation is unjust both to the text and
to the theology of John.

The city of God is no strange place to the children of God. It is home, today and in the morrow of Christ's appearing, and to eternal ages.

THE DESCENT OF THE CITY 21 : 9–11

The identity of language regarding the angel-guide in verse 9 and that in 17 : 1 is deliberate. The angel commissioned to show the prophet the harlot-city in the desert now conducts him to the bride-city on the mountain of God.[1] It is noteworthy that it is none other than an agent of the divine wrath, who first bade John to gaze on the horror of a society sunk to the limit of degradation under the Devil, who brings him to contemplate the wonder of a fellowship raised to the height of divine splendour. This is one of the many illustrations of John's unswerving conviction as to the unity of the justice of God and the grace of God in his portrayal of the execution of the divine purpose in history and beyond it.

9. John is invited to look upon **the Bride, the wife of the Lamb.** Should a *bride* be termed *wife*? In western societies hardly so, for the two words represent different relationships. Some commentators, therefore, would eliminate the second term as having originated in an explanatory gloss in the margin.[2] In Hebrew society, however, betrothal was a more serious affair and more closely related to the married state than it is among western peoples. This was reflected in the habit of referring to a betrothed woman as a wife (it has in fact, already happened in 19 : 7, where the *RSV* has rendered the term *gunē*, wife, as bride, presumably to avoid misunderstanding by modern readers).[3] The imagery of God's people standing in relation to God as a wife to her husband is rooted in the Old Testament (cf. especially, Isa. 54 : 5, 'Your Maker is your husband', and Hos. 1–2). In the New Testament it is freely applied to the Church and Christ (cf. the parables of Mk 2 : 19f., Mt. 22 : 1ff., 25 : 1ff., Jn 3 : 29, and 2 C. 11 : 2, Eph. 5 : 25ff.). At all times, in both Testaments, the emphasis in the symbol lies on the choice and the love of the Husband or Bride-

[1] For the contrast which John draws between the two cities, see the introduction to chapter 17.

[2] So Bousset, Charles.

[3] See further the informative discussion in Jeremias's article on bride (*numphē*) in Kittel, *TWNT*, IV, pp. 1092f. (*ET* IV, p. 1099).

groom, never on that of the wife or bride. Erotic suggestions in the relationship have no place.

10. John's rapture to **a great, high mountain** is described in language reminiscent of Ezekiel 40:2, wherein Ezekiel commences his description of the restored Jerusalem and its temple. In that passage the prophet is transported in vision to a high mountain 'on which was a structure like a city'. It would appear here also that John is carried away to a mountain, not to view the city from above, but to survey it on the site to which it descends. In representing the city as situated on a mountain, John has characteristically combined two ancient religious traditions, namely, that which sprang from Babylonia regarding the 'holy mountain of God' (Ezek. 28:14), which was thought of as a heavenly Garden of Eden or Paradise (Ezek. 28:13) wherein the gods lived, and the prophetic tradition of the mountain of the house of the Lord, raised above the hills, to which all peoples flow to worship the Lord of hosts (Isa. 2:1ff.). In this way he relates the fulfilment of God's purpose in history to both pagan aspirations and the prophetic word of the Old Covenant. For John, as for all Christians, there is but one God, the Father, and one Lord, Jesus Christ (1 C. 8:5f.). The heavenly city accordingly is the dwelling of God, made accessible to men through Christ the Redeemer. Its descent to earth for the blessing of the nations at once fulfils the word of prophecy and meets the profoundest need of all men.

11. The city has **the glory of God.** As the glory rested on the tabernacle in the wilderness (see on v. 3), so it fills the city. Its **radiance** (virtually = the glory) was as the reflection of light in **a most rare jewel,** every facet of which sends out a ray of differing brilliance. Its appearance **like a jasper, clear as crystal** recalls the description of the divine appearance on the throne in 4.3, which is said to be 'as jasper and carnelian', i.e., both transparent and fiery red, as the light. The whole city, therefore, is conceived of as glowing with the glory of God, reflecting the divine nature in its every part. No wonder John subsequently states that the city has no need of sun or moon to shine upon it: 'for the glory of God is its light, and its lamp is the Lamb' (v. 23). To the extent that this may be translated into terms of personal relations, the thought is akin to that expressed by Paul in 2 Corinthians 3:18 (cf. 1 Jn 3:2).

THE WALL OF THE CITY 21: 12-14

12, 13. In ancient times a wall was the characteristic feature of a city, distinguishing it from smaller settlements. It determined the city's bounds, and above all afforded protection from invaders. Zechariah in a vision is told that the rebuilt Jerusalem will have too large a population of men and beasts to be enclosed by a wall. Hence the Lord decrees, 'I will be to her a wall of fire round about' (Zech. 2:4f.; cf. Isa. 26:1). The **great, high wall** in John's vision accordingly symbolizes the eternal security of the city's inhabitants. At the same time a wall inevitably excludes those who are outside the city, and this function of the wall is recognized in 22:15. Nevertheless access to the city from without and egress from within are provided by **twelve gates.** The number accords with **the twelve tribes of the sons of Israel,** the names of which are inscribed on the gates. It is apparent from verse 13 that John has in mind the apportionment of Jerusalem's gates among the tribes of Israel in Ezekiel's vision (48:30ff.). Presumably the earlier prophet thought of these as gates assigned to the various tribes for their own individual use.[1] If such a thought was present to John, he would have gone further, for unlike Ezekiel he did not view the city as confined to the holy people, but saw it as the city of the new humanity with blessings for all the world, hence the kings and the nations stream through its gates (vv. 24ff.).

Here we recall that John's vision of the city of God is compounded of Old Testament prophecy and the aspirations of the nations. Like many other Jews, John was familiar with the twelve divisions of the heavens, which in the astrological religion stemming from the Babylonians were regarded as standing under the authority of twelve gods. Jewish apocalyptists before John had variously deployed this mode of viewing the skies in ways agreeable to monotheistic religion. In the lengthy description of phenomena of the heavens in *Enoch* 72–82 the twelve divisions of the zodiac are replaced by twelve 'portals', six to the east and six to the west, and in chapters 33–6 the (different) author speaks of them as twelve gates of heaven, which face the four directions of

---

[1] Similarly *Midr. Ps.* 48:§4 (138*b*) raises the question, 'How many gates will there be in the future Jerusalem?' and the answer is given, '144, for each individual tribe twelve' (Strack-Billerbeck, III, p. 848).

the compass, and through which the stars and winds and snow, etc., pass. John has no interest in this kind of speculation, still less can he admit the idea of twelve gods ruling the heavens. One God alone is sovereign Lord of the universe, and he has committed all rule and authority and power to the Christ-Redeemer. John nevertheless recognizes that the Lord delegates authority to created spiritual powers, alike in heaven and on earth, hence he states here that **at the gates** are **twelve angels.** These befit the city which descends from heaven to earth, but their mention in this passage hints of the dual origin of John's description, as also of his motive in combining the two traditions. The city from heaven is not for one nation alone, but for all men who desire to dwell with God and the Lamb.

14. The city's wall has **twelve foundations,** inscribed with **the twelve names of the twelve apostles of the Lamb.** The repetition of the number is deliberate. It features in every measurement of the city as the number of the people of God. We are to understand that the foundations are partially visible, lying as a chain of stones round the base of the walls, but interspersed by the twelve gates. Their inscription with the names of the apostles of the Lamb invites comparison with the inscription of the gates with the names of Israel's twelve tribes. The unity of the people of the old and new covenants is thereby immediately suggested. But more than this will be in mind, for strictly speaking the names of the twelve tribes alone suffice to represent the Church of both covenants (cf. 7:1-8, and see notes thereon). The twelve apostles stand at the beginning of the Church's story, as Israel's patriarchs at the beginning of Israel's story, and they fittingly represent the Church, even as the patriarchs serve as Israel's representatives. More significantly, however, the Twelve were the bearers of 'the testimony of Jesus Christ' in a unique way, so that whoever builds on their testimony to Jesus and from Jesus rests on the Christ himself. This conviction is embodied in the tradition which circulated in the Church of John's day, represented in Matthew 16:17ff. and Ephesians 2:19ff., and it finds its ultimate expression in his vision of the eternal city.

As the twelve tribes represent the people of God in its completeness, so the twelve apostles represent the apostolic company in its totality. Discussions as to whether Judas is excluded or Paul is included have no place in the use of this symbolism.

THE DIMENSIONS OF THE CITY **21 : 15–17**

15. In a manner reminiscent of Ezekiel's vision (40 : 3ff.), John's angel guide takes **a measuring rod of gold** to indicate to him the extent of **the city and its gates and walls,** a feature which could not be conveyed by mere sight.

16. The city lies foursquare. Whether John was aware that the Greeks viewed the square as a symbol of perfection, or that Babylon was built as a square, as scholars remind us, is doubtful. He certainly knew that the square dominated Ezekiel's description both of the temple (45 : 2) and of the rebuilt Jerusalem (48 : 20). John, however, went further in emphasizing that the **height** of the city is the same as its length and breadth, and thus that the city is a cube. With his interest in the Old Testament he could not have been ignorant that the holy of holies in the ancient temple was a cube (so explicitly 1 Kg. 6 : 20). This helps to explain John's insistence, which is unparalleled in Jewish writings, that the city of God has no temple. It is all temple, filled with the presence of the Lord God Almighty and the Lamb (v. 22).

The vastness of the city is beyond grasp: **twelve thousand stadia,** i.e., 1,500 miles. The measurement in fact should not be translated into miles. It represents the ordinary unit of distance (the furlong) multiplied by the number of God's people (twelve) and extended indefinitely. Such a city beggars the imagination, yet the symbolism conveys a message which would have been grasped by at least some of John's readers. There is evidence that in John's day, when Jerusalem lay in ruins, the Jews were speculating about the kind of city by which God would replace it. They found Scriptures to suggest that it would extend to Damascus in the north and to the ocean on the west, and that it would stretch up to the heights until it reached the throne of God.[1] A couplet in *Sibylline Oracles* v, lines 251–2, similarly states that the Jews will build about Jerusalem a ring wall as far as Joppa, and that it (or they) will be 'exalted on high up to the darkling clouds'. Such representations depict *a city which reaches from earth to heaven.* That conception accounts for John's staggeringly large measurements. The city of God and the Lamb will extend far over the territories of men and unite earth and heaven into one. The concept will

[1] See Strack-Billerbeck, III, p. 849.

have been even sharper for John than for his particularist Jewish contemporaries, since he unhesitatingly appropriated for the city of God ideas relating to the city of the stars which were beloved by the pagan astrologers of his day. They believed that the basis of the vault of the heavens was equal in length and breadth, i.e., that it was square, and the greatness of size of the heavenly city would have been self-evident to them. John declares that the reality which corresponds to their imperfect vision is to be found in the city of God and the Lamb. And if any of his readers knew that the Babylonians modelled their temple-tower on such a conception, the same message would hold good for them also: the holy temple of earth and heaven is the dwelling of God and the Lamb.

17. The measurement of the wall is perhaps to be viewed from the same dual viewpoint as that of the city itself. **A hundred and forty-four cubits** was its measure. Again the number is a multiple of twelve. A city-wall of that height is undoubtably **great,** but in relation to the height of the heavenly Jerusalem it appears to be ludicrously small. Attempts have been made to evade the difficulty, for example by suggesting that the figure relates to the thickness, not the height, of the wall; or that an angel's measurement is different from that of a man (cubit originally = the length from a man's finger tip to his elbow. How much bigger will the measurement be of a mighty angel's forearm!). Possibly we are not meant to make comparisons of this sort. The wall is great enough to symbolize the security of God's people within the city, and big enough to exclude the evil from it. Nevertheless, one is constrained to ask whether John reflects the ancient idea that the wall of the city of the heavens is formed by the crown of the night horizon.[1] It would be characteristic of his whole description of the city of God if he linked the Jewish and the comparative religious concepts about the city's wall in this way. On any reckoning, the Lord God needs but a small wall for the protection of his saints.

THE FABRIC OF THE CITY 21: 18-21

18. The wall was built of jasper. According to verse 11 the whole city shines with the radiance of 'a most rare jewel, like a jasper', thereby indicating that the city is suffused throughout

[1] So Strathmann, article *polis, TWNT,* VI, p. 533.

with the light of the glory of God (cf. 4 : 3). Here we learn that the
fabric of the wall surrounding the city glows with the same divine
splendour. Again verse 11 defines the jasper, to which the city is
compared, as 'clear as crystal'. Here the material of the city is said
to be **pure gold, clear as glass.** A jasper clear as crystal is comprehensible, gold of this order is not. Does John wish to convey an
impression of a heavenly reality which transcends the qualities of
its earthly counterpart? Or does his symbolism hark back to an
earlier model? He may have recalled that the temple of Solomon,
both in its most holy place and in the rest of the sanctuary, was
covered completely with gold (1 Kg. 6 : 20ff.). The transference of
this feature to the city would harmonize with John's characterization of it as a holy temple, shimmering with the glory of the divine
presence in its every part.

19, 20. The descriptions of the jewels adorning the city's
foundations (or of which they consisted, vv. 19-20) was initially
inspired by Isaiah 54: 11ff., but the fullness of John's statement is due
to other sources. The dirge over the king of Tyre in Ezekiel
18 : 12ff. casts the king in the role of one who walked on the holy
mountain of God, in the midst of 'stones which flashed with fire',
but he exalted himself in unholy pride. The list of precious stones
with which the king's clothing was covered (v. 13) is almost
certainly intended to correspond with the list of the jewels on the
high priest's breastplate, and which were inscribed with the names
of the tribes of Israel (Exod. 28 : 17ff.). The Hebrew text of
Ezekiel 28 : 13 contains only nine jewels, but the Septuagint has
twelve, and this is probably original. Scholars are divided as to
how to explain this link between the two passages but that is hardly
our concern. For our purpose it is significant that Ezekiel's song
links these twelve stones with the paradaisical dwelling of God.

Now John is unlikely to have been ignorant of speculations
among his contemporaries concerning the stones of the High
Priest's breastplate. Both Philo and Josephus viewed them as
denoting the twelve signs of the Zodiac. In harmony with this
Charles cited a correlation of John's list of stones with the signs
of the Zodiac drawn up by Athanasius Kircher in the seventeenth
century, and claimed by Kircher to be based on ancient Egyptian
and Arabic sources. The table is as follows: **jasper** represents the
Fish; **sapphire,** the Water-carrier; **chalcedon,** the Goat;
smaragdos, the Archer; **sardonyx,** the Scorpion; **sardius,** the

Balance; **chrysolite,** the Virgin; **beryl,** the Lion; **topaz,** the
Crab; **chrysoprase,** the Twins; **hyacinth,** the Bull; **amethyst,**
the Ram. Charles perceived that on this basis the signs of the
Zodiac, as represented by John's list of jewels, occur in precisely
the reverse order of the path of the sun through the signs! Not
unreasonably he comments: 'This cannot be an accident.' Given
Kircher's correlation of signs and jewels, it is difficult to disagree.
Charles drew the conclusion that John's reversal of the order of
Zodiac signs, together with his linking the jewels with the tribes
of Israel and the apostles, demonstrates that John rejected any
connection between the ethnic speculations of the city of the gods
and the City of God and the Lamb. This is doubtful, for the connection is too striking for a rejection to be communicated in this
way. It is more likely that John's listing of the jewel signs *plus his
connecting them with the people of God and apostles of the Lamb* is intended to suggest that *the reality after which the pagans aspire is found
in the revelation of God in Jesus Christ.*[1] The inscription of the stones
with the apostles' names ultimately signifies that the city of God
reposes on the testimony of Jesus committed to his followers. Or
in the words of a book closely related to John's prophecy, the
Lamb of God is the Way, the Truth and the Life, and men enter
the Father's house through him (Jn 14:2–6).

21. The statement **the twelve gates were twelve pearls** is
dependent on Isaiah 54:12. When describing the precious stones
of the future Jerusalem the prophet declares in the Lord's name,
'I will make . . . your gates of carbuncles.' John, like other Jews
of his time, interpreted 'carbuncles' as pearls. The same scripture

---

[1] Objection has been raised to this interpretation on the ground that no such
correlation of stones and signs has been found in ancient records. F. T. Glasson
claims that Kircher is an unreliable guide, and suggests that he may have based
his list of correspondences on John's and reversed the order to disguise where
he got it from! (The Order of Jewels in Revelation xxi. 19–20, *JTS* XXVI
(1975), p. 99). A. P. Stone is more charitable and suggests that Kircher's *source*
was dependent on John (*A Christian looks at Astrology,* 1974, p. 76). Until it is
demonstrated that Kircher was in error his testimony should be treated with
seriousness. *If* grounds for rejecting his correlation are forthcoming, the suggestion of Una Jart is worthy of consideration, that John reflects a common
astrological geographical view which links the zodiac signs with the nations;
the Jewish division of the nations into *seventy-two* would lend itself to this, and
in that case the jewels would represent the new Israel drawn from all the
nations of the world (The Precious Stones in the Revelation of St. John xxi.
18–21, *Studia Theologica* 24 (1970), pp. 169f.).

led R. Jochanan (third century AD) to affirm, 'One day God will procure precious stones and pearls, whose size will be thirty cubits square; and he will make an opening in them of ten cubits wide and twenty cubits high and then set them up as the gates of Jerusalem.'[1] It is interesting to observe that where the rabbis voice expectations in hope of literal fulfilment, John consciousiy uses the language of symbolism.

In verse 18 the whole city is said to be 'pure gold, clear as glass'. Why then does John single out **the street of the city,** and emphasize that this, too, is **pure gold, transparent as glass?** His motive may simply be to add to the impression of the overwhelming glory of the city, and on this assumption *the street* is commonly viewed as a generic term for the streets of the city. While this is possible, it would harmonize with John's consistent intention in his description of the new Jerusalem if he thought primarily of the main street which traverses the city from one end to another. In that case the model for his street is none other than the Milky Way. The heavenly way is transformed into a golden High Street of the *Jerusalem which comes from above,* and made conformable to the nature of the whole city—*pure gold, transparent as glass.* It is not the gods who tread this way, but the multitudes of redeemed humanity who rejoice in God and the Lamb (vv. 24ff.).

THE HOLINESS AND GLORY OF THE CITY 21:22–27

22. No element in John's vision of the future more strikingly differentiates him from contemporary Jewish writers than his statement **I saw no temple in the city.** 'For the old Synagogue the future Jerusalem without a temple was an inconceivable idea,' commented Billerbeck. 'The building of the sanctuary was the most self-evident element of the old Jewish hope of the future.'[2] In this respect John has faithfully developed a feature of the teaching

[1] *Baba Bathra* 75a. The saying occurs with variations in many other places in the Talmud. See Strack-Billerbeck, III, pp. 851f.

[2] Strack-Billerbeck, III, p. 852. The seventeenth benediction of the eighteenth prayer in the *Aboda* is cited: 'Look with favour, Yahweh our God, on your people Israel and on their prayer. And bring back the ministry of sacrifice in the most holy place of your house. And receive with favour Israel's burnt offering and its prayer in love. And let the daily offering of Israel, your people, be accepted with favour. May our eyes see your return to Zion in pity. Praise be to you, Yahweh, for you cause your *Shekinah* to return to Zion!'

of Jesus, who in prophetic fashion announced both the ruin of the
Jerusalem temple (Mk 13 : 2) and its replacement by a different
order of worship (Mk 14 : 58). No word of Jesus seems to have
infuriated the Jewish religious leaders more than the latter saying,
hence the attempt made at his trial to incriminate him through it.
The Fourth Evangelist has followed up the Marcan phrase in
Mark 14 : 58, 'not made with hands', relating to the new temple,
by observing that the temple is really the body of the risen Lord
(Jn 2 : 21). He thereby suggests that the risen Christ will be the
'place' wherein God meets man in grace and man offers acceptable worship to God. Whether consciously or not, John the prophet is in the direct line of the symbolism when he represents that
the temple of the new Jerusalem *is* the Lord God Almighty and the
Lamb. Everything for which the temple stood is transferred to the
life of the city. All is sacred, the *Shekinah* glory fills the entire city
(cf. Ezek. chs. 10–11 and 43 : 1–7), and God is everywhere
accessible to the priestly race.

One feature of this symbolism, however, should not escape us.
The temple-function is fulfilled not simply by the Lord God
Almighty but by God **and the Lamb.** Such an association of God
and the Lamb in the eternal city inevitably suggests their unity of
being. Yet it is possible that the language has in view a more
specific concept, namely that the Lamb of God, who has wrought
redemption for the world (1 : 5f., 5 : 6ff., 12 : 11), retains his role
as mediator in the eternal city. The symbolism of Christ as the
light of the world (v. 23), his possession of the book of life (v. 27),
his continued exercise of kingly authority (22 : 3), and the fact
that the blessings of life in the city are subject to his bestowal (see
the promises to the conquerors, especially 2 : 7, 17, 26ff., 3 : 12, 21)
confirm this impression.

23 summarizes, and characteristically modifies Isaiah 60 : 19f.
The **sun** and **moon** have not ceased to exist. 'Their splendour
is simply put to shame by the glory of God himself' (Charles).
Bossset hazarded the suggestion that the light of sun and moon
is replaced by the radiance of God as the sun, and the Lamb
as the moon. This is doubtful, for the contrast between the brightness of the luminaries of creation and the greater splendour of
God and the Lamb is similar to the implicit contrast between
the ancient temple and the new presence of God (v. 22), and one
with other features of life in the city of which God and the Lamb

are the source (22 : 1, 3). In this context the **lamp is the Lamb**
recalls the saying, 'I am the Light of the world' (Jn 8 : 12),
uttered at Tabernacles, and which implies that what the *Shekinah*
was to Israel in the desert and shall be in the coming kingdom, so
Christ is for the whole world, the source of salvation and the
manifestation of the divine glory for all mankind.

24. The thought of Isaiah 60 (especially vv 3–11) is again
dominant here, but with a difference. In the Isaianic passage the
nations flock to Jerusalem primarily to restore its exiles and to
offer tribute to Israel. The nations bring their wealth to the Jews,
and 'the nation and kingdom that will not serve you shall perish'
(v. 12). No such thought is present in John's vision. When **the
kings of the earth shall bring their glory into it,** that is for
the glory of God and the Lamb. Bousset admittedly was puzzled
by this feature, for the symbolism seems to be out of harmony with
the context of verses 1–4, namely the new heavens and earth. He
considered that the depiction of nations outside the city and the
unclean who are not allowed access to it (v. 17) is a survival of
earlier representations out of keeping with the vision as a whole.
On the contrary, the whole picture is an element of vital importance to John. His earlier visions have shown **the nations** (= those
who dwell on the earth, 13 : 14, etc.) as deceived by the Devil and
subservient to the Antichrist, and *the kings of the earth* as the vassals
of the antichristian empire and ruler (e.g., 17 : 2). But the ancient
serpent, the deceiver of the whole world, has been defeated (12 : 9)
and finally removed (20 : 2f.). Now is the time when the song of
the redeemed is fulfilled: 'All nations shall come and worship
thee' (15 : 4). The primary application of verses 24ff. is in the
kingdom of Christ on earth, but it is equally true of the kingdom of
God and the Lamb in the transcendent order of the new creation.
It is important to retain both the positive and the negative aspects
of this view of the kingdom.

The encouragement which this expectation would afford the
original readers of the Revelation, and its pertinence to their
situation, should not be overlooked. It indicates that their
opponents, whose hostility is to grow to murderous proportions,
are yet to render up their sword to God and the Lamb and offer
him the tribute of their adoration. It suggests more. The nations
who once offered their riches to the city of the Antichrist will
yield them instead to the city of God and the Lamb (vv. 24 and

26), and that implies a sanctification of the whole order of this created world and its products.[1]

25–27. Its gates shall never be shut by day cites Isaiah 60 : 11. **And there shall be no night there** is John's addition, following on verse 23 and encouraged by Zechariah 14 : 7.[2] Similarly verse 26 reproduces the thought of Isaiah 60 : 5, 10–12. But an important caveat is entered respecting the nations: **Nothing unclean shall enter it,** for the new Jerusalem is constituted a holy sanctuary by the presence of God and the Lamb. The sentiment is that of Isaiah 52 : 1: 'There shall no more come into you the uncircumcized and the unclean.' In its context, however, that is a promise of Israel's freedom from the oppressor nations, whereas John has in view access into the city by all the nations—except the **unclean,** whether Jew or Gentile. **Any one who practises abomination or falsehood** is excluded, for he partakes of the nature and the ways of the city of the Antichrist (cf. 17 : 4f., and see note on 21 : 8). They who desire entrance into the city of God and the Lamb require conformity to the nature and will of God and the Lamb; i.e., they must be **written in the Lamb's book of life.**[3]

THE BLESSEDNESS OF THE CITY **22 : 1–5**

1. In this paragraph John seems to be conscious of adding a fresh section, which serves both as a summary and culmination of his description of the city of God. The opening words of verse 3, **Then he showed me . . .** recall the commencement of his account

---

[1] So Caird: 'Nothing from the old order which has value in the sight of God is debarred from entry into the new. John's heaven is no world-denying Nirvana, into which men may escape from the incurable ills of sublunary existence, but the seal of affirmation on the goodness of God's creation.' He adds, in relation to the whole paragraph, 'Nowhere in the New Testament do we find a more eloquent statement than this of the all-embracing scope of Christ's redemptive work.' (Commentary, pp. 270f.)

[2] The rabbis had a similar concept, but differently based. *Exod.R.* 18 (81*a*): 'In this world God did a miracle for the Israelites in the night (= the slaying of the firstborn in Egypt) . . . but in the future the night will be as the day, as it stands written, "The light of the moon will be like the light of the sun . . .", Isaiah 30:26.'

[3] See note on 3:5, and cf. the prayer in *Odes of Solomon* 11:33 (cited by Lohmeyer), 'There is much room in your paradise, but there is nothing unclean in it.'

of the city in 21: 9–10. Moreover, one or two important new elements of symbolism occur. The throne of God and the Lamb, not
mentioned previously, dominates the scene, and the imagery of
the paradise of Eden, linking the end of history with its beginning,
appears for the first time. In verses 3–5 certain elements of
21: 22–7 find repetition, but in such a manner as to convey a
sense of climax, which finds a supreme expression in the last
clause of 22: 5.

The river of the water of life recalls a variety of Old Testament pictures. The conjunction of the river with the tree of life
(v. 2) shows that the author has in mind in the first place the river
which flowed through Eden (Gen. 2: 9f.). The return at the end of
history of features which characterized the beginnings of time
gives expression to an important principle of biblical and extra-
biblical prophecy, stated in all clarity in *Barnabas* 6: 13: 'Behold I
make the last things as the first.' Not that the end is thought of as
simply a reversal to the beginning, but the circumstances of the
beginning are viewed as prophetic of the nature of God's purpose
in history. In all respects, however, the last things surpass the first
in overwhelming measure, as we see in this paragraph.

Along with Genesis 2, Ezekiel's description of the river in the
vision of the new temple is also before John's eyes.[1] While Ezekiel
47 does not speak of the river as 'living' water the prophet ap-
proaches closely to the idea; e.g., 'everything will live where the
river goes' (v. 9), the Dead Sea teems with fish when the river runs
into it, and the trees by the river-bank bear fruit every month
'because the water for them flows from the sanctuary' (v. 12). But
whereas Ezekiel's river issues from beneath the threshold of the
temple, John sees it **flowing from the throne of God and of
the Lamb.** The reality is not far removed from Ezekiel's picture,
for to the prophet the temple was the locus of God's holy presence,
and in the city wherein God and the Lamb are the temple the
counterpart to that is the throne of God. Observe, however, that
the throne is *of God and the Lamb*. The river, therefore, has its
source in 'God and the Lamb'. This may well be a conscious echo
of the saying in John 7: 37f., itself based on Ezekiel 47: 'If any one
thirst, let him come to me, and let him who believes in me drink.

[1] Doubtless John would have been mindful of other portrayals of fountains
and streams which the Lord provides for the thirsty, e.g., Isaiah 41:18, Joel
3:18, Zechariah 14:8; cf. Jeremiah 2:13, Psalm 36:9.

As the scripture has said, "Out of his heart shall flow rivers of living water" ' (*RSV* margin; *NEB* gives a like rendering in its text). The river of living water here flows from the Christ, who has taken the place of the temple. The Fourth Evangelist interprets it of the Holy Spirit, whom the Christ is to bestow consequent on his 'glorification', and so in anticipation of resurrection life in the consummated kingdom. Revelation 22:17 constitutes a bridge between John 7:37f. and Revelation 22:1; the theology is virtually identical.

2. The punctuation adopted in the text of *RSV* is preferable to alternative interpretations. The river flows **through the middle of the street of the city.** *RSV* margin records the possibility of commencing a fresh sentence with the cited phrase, thus: 'In the midst of the street of the city, and on either side of the river, was the tree of life.' The picture is of an avenue of 'trees of life' (the singular taken for plural) lining the river's banks, but the opening clause seems superfluous on this rendering. It is possible to interpret the statement in yet a third way. In the midst of the city's street stands a single tree, the tree of life, *situated between either side of the river*, which at this point has diverged into two branches. This is then thought to reflect the dependence of the concept on the Milky Way with its two branches (so Behm, and in part Bousset). If this is what John had in mind he has not expressed himself plainly. It is simplest to interpret his language as in the *RSV*. The river runs down the city street, flanked by trees of life on both banks. The imagery combines that of Genesis 2:9 and Ezekiel 47:7ff. The twelve kinds of fruit yielded by the 'tree' each month, are such as Ezekiel mentions: 'On the banks on both sides of the river, there will grow all kinds of trees for food . . . they will bear fresh fruit every month' (Ezek. 47:12). From the same passage comes the statement, **the leaves of the tree were for the healing of the nations.** There is no question of John taking these images literally. As elsewhere they represent spiritual realities. The **fruit** of the tree of life, like the manna (2:17), symbolizes life in fullest measure and delight. The **river** of living water even more powerfully expresses the idea of life in inexhaustible supply. The thought would be the more impressive to all who saw behind the symbol the mighty Milky Way of the heavens. *The healing of the nations* may have in view especially the healing of the hurt caused by the Antichrist's reign and possibly the effects of the judgments of God in the earth. The symbolism is more suitable to the order of life in the kingdom of Christ than in the new creation.

3. There shall no more be anything accursed is a citation from Zechariah 14:11, and in this context it indicates a reversal of Genesis 3:14ff., 17ff. The reference is to existence in the city. Nothing in it will be cursed, for there will be within it no cause for curse. Rebellion against the will of God is unthinkable within the city's walls, therefore there are no springs of ruin among men and no judgment from God. This thought is in harmony with that expressed immediately afterwards: **the throne of God and of the Lamb shall be in it.** God and the Lamb dwell there in manifest glory and sovereignty, his will is everywhere acknowledged, and therefore only blessing is known within the city. **His servants shall worship him.** This is paraphrase, and it is better to render the verb literally, *shall serve him* (cf. Dt. 10:12, Rom. 12:1, Phil. 3:3). If worship is the highest form of service, it is nevertheless desirable to maintain the contrast between the life of service which the servants of God render in the city, and their activity as kings who 'reign for ever and ever' (v. 5). In truth the service of God's people is royal, and their reign is service. But observe: *his* servants serve *him*. Whose servants, and who is served? God, or the Lamb, or God and the Lamb? It is difficult to interpret the statement in reference to the Lamb alone, who is the immediate antecedent of *his*. Still more difficult is it to refer it to God alone. We must assume, therefore, that the third alternative is correct: God and the Lamb are viewed as a unity in so real a fashion that the singular pronoun alone is suitable to interpret them.[1]

4, 5. They shall see his face, and so attain the ultimate hope cherished by the people of God through all ages. It is expressed in various passages of the Old Testament (e.g., Isa. 52:8, 60:2, Zech. 9:14), and is aspired after by the worshippers in the temple as they seek the presence of God (e.g., Ps. 11:7, 27:4, 42:2). A beatitude of Jesus declares that the pure in heart 'shall see God' (Mt. 5:8). Schniewind believes that such a blessing relates not to

[1] So Holt, who observes that the same phenomenon is observable in 11:15, 'The kingdom of the world has become the Kingdom of our Lord and of his Christ, and *he* shall reign for ever . . .' The unity is the reason why the Christ is seated on the throne with God. 'The Christ stands in God's place, without thereby removing God himself to an unapproachable distance; they melt into a unity of function. God's role as Lord over the world and Regent of the end of time has at the same time become that of the Christ' (op. cit., pp. 202f.).

a mystical experience of God's presence, but to freedom to look into the eyes of the Almighty Judge without shame, in contrast to those from whom God hides his face in wrath against their misdeeds.[1] Perhaps we should recognize in John's picture the fulfilment of all the experience given to God's people of the salvation of God, including their anticipated final deliverance from death into the resurrection life of the new world, together with the consummation of all their experience of his presence in worship.

His name shall be on their foreheads. As the people of God were sealed on the forehead in time of tribulation as a sign that they belonged to God (7:3), so the whole populace of the New Jerusalem are marked as belonging to God and the Lamb (*his* in the same sense as in v. 3).[2] The conjunction of this statement with verse 5 could well be due to the fixed association of receiving the name of God and living in the light of God, preserved in the ancient benediction of Numbers 6:22ff. The second clause of that benediction reads, 'The Lord make his face shine upon you, and give you peace', after which is added, 'So shall they put my name upon the people of Israel.' The coincidence of language in our passage is closer than the *RSV* reveals, for the clause **the Lord God will be their light** should literally read, 'The Lord God will shine upon them.' If this be in John's mind the thought of verse 4a comes to yet more forceful expression in verses 4b–5. The age-long benediction, called over the people of God through succeeding generations, now reaches its complete answer from God, namely, eternal life in the light of the immediate presence of God and the Lamb.

And they shall reign for ever and ever. Here is the ultimate reach of the bliss of God's people in the city which descends from heaven: participation in the sovereignty of God and the Lamb, not alone for the duration of the kingdom of Christ on earth but in the eternal kingdom of the new creation. It signifies the final fulfilment of the promise in 3:21, the status of joint sovereignty with Christ in God. That is an extension of the grace of God in Christ beyond the grasp of the human mind. As such it brings to a fitting conclusion John's vision of the city of God and the Lamb, leaving the reader dazzled, not to say dazed, with the glory of the prospect before him.

[1] *Das Evangelium nach Matthäus*, p. 47.
[2] This thought has already appeared in 3:12.

EPILOGUE 22 : 6–21

The concluding paragraphs of the Revelation sum up and press home on the reader's conscience the foremost practical lessons of the book. The two themes of the opening paragraph, verses 6f., namely, the authenticity of the work as a revelation from God and the nearness of the fulfilment of its message, reappear in the various utterances which follow and bind them into a kind of unity (for the concept of authenticity, see vv. 8f., 16, 18f.; and for the nearness of the end, see vv. 10, 12, 20).

In contrast to the prologue, however, the epilogue creates an impression of haphazardness. The sayings appear to be comparatively unrelated, and distributed among a variety of speakers whom it is difficult to identify. Charles held that in this section, more than anywhere else in the final chapters of the Revelation, we have the mere *disjecta membra* of the Seer. He bracketed 21 : 6*b*–8 with 22 : 6ff., and changed the order of the sayings so as to present the following picture: 21 : 6*b*–8 contains the declaration of God; 22 : 6f., 18*a*, 16, 13, 12, 10 (11), (18*b*–19), the testimony of Jesus; and 22 : 8f., 20f., the testimony of John.[1] Few are prepared to go along with Charles in his proposals, but most succumb to the temptation of trying to assign the various utterances to different speakers. Rissi for example holds that in verse 6 the speaker is the angel, in 7 it is Jesus, in 8f. John, 10 the angel, 12–14 Jesus, 15 John;[2] while Lohmeyer spoke for the majority in assigning verses 6f. to Jesus, 8f. to the angel, and 10–16 again to Jesus. In contrast to this procedure it is needful to recall that the whole work is represented by John as the revelation of Jesus Christ made known to him through the angel (1 : 1–3). Certainly it is natural to assume that the speaker in verse 6 is the interpreter angel, who has shown John the city of God described in the immediately preceding passages (21 : 9–22 : 5). The utterances of the risen Lord in verses 7*a*, 12f. may be viewed as conveyed through the same angel. Further the relation of 21 : 7f. to 21 : 1–6, and of 21 : 24–7 to 21 : 9ff., encourages the idea that 22 : 14f. bring the epilogue to a climax.[3] In that case it is most plausible to regard the epilogue proper as consisting of verses 6–15 and to assume that it is medi-

[1] See Commentary, vol. II, pp. 211–15.
[2] *The Future of the World*, p. 84.   [3] So Rissi, ibid.

ated throughout by the angel-guide. A concluding paragraph is composed of two oracular sayings, from the risen Lord (v. 16) and from the Spirit (v. 17), a warning concerning the inviolability of the book (vv. 18f.), a final word of assurance from the Christ (v. 20) and a benediction (v. 21).

6. The statement **These words are trustworthy and true** occurs in 21 : 5, and both passages echo 19 : 9*b*. It is noteworthy that in all three passages the affirmation follows a statement relating to the gift of God's final salvation to man. But in view of the general reference of verse 7*b* it is likely that the application of these words should extend beyond 22 : 1–5 (and beyond 21 : 9– 22 : 5) to the whole revelation. The coincidence of language between the title **the Lord, the God of the spirits of the prophets** and the frequent name for God in the *Similitudes of Enoch* 'the Lord of spirits', is almost certainly fortuitous (*contra* Bousset). The phrase may have been suggested (unconsciously?) by 19 : 10 —'the testimony of Jesus is the spirit of prophecy'—but it has in view *the spirits of the prophets*, i.e., the prophets themselves, who are subject to the Spirit who inspires prophecy (cf. 1 C. 14 : 32 for a close parallel). There is no need to restrict the scope of *the prophets* here. The Lord sends the Spirit upon the prophets of all ages, under the old covenant and under the new. The mention of the **angel** in this passage, however, relates the concept to the inspiration of this particular revelation given to John. We are thus presented with the idea of a fourfold inspiration of prophecy, comparable to that which appears in the opening paragraph of the book, but going beyond it. That inspiration is derived from the Lord God who gives the word, the Christ, who is the word, the Spirit who inspires the prophets, and the angel who communicates the word.[1]

7. The content of the revelation (v. 6) is **what must soon** (Greek *en tachei*) take place. This prompts the assertion, **I am coming soon** (Greek *tachu*). The addition of the beatitude, the sixth in the book, **Blessed is he who keeps the words of the prophecy of this book** (cf. 1 : 3) makes it plain that the flow of thought in verses 6f. reproduces that which appears in 1 : 1–3. Since the earlier passage may well have been penned after the conclusion of the whole work, it could be that the former is a systematization of this one. Yet there is a fitness in the book ending

[1] After Farrer, ad loc.

as it began, with an emphasis on the burden of the revelation ('*I am coming soon*') and on the blessedness of those who maintain faith in Christ and loyalty to him at all costs. The glory of the city of God is prepared for such as these. Accordingly, the benediction upon the faithful is pronounced not by John (as in 1 : 3) but by the regnant Christ, who sends his word through the angel to the prophet (for a fuller consideration of the concepts which appear in vv. 6f. see the exposition of 1 : 1–3).

8, 9 call to mind the similar scene in 19 : 10. It has been suggested that John found such an episode at the conclusion of one of his sources and that he used it twice over (so Bousset). Alternatively Charles believed that the earlier passage was due to the hand of the final editor, but this was authentic. Neither postulate is compelling. John could as easily have recounted his own experience more than once, or he could have known the ecstatic experience more than once. It is more important to determine the motive and significance for including the vision at this point. Its repetition may have been occasioned by John's desire emphatically to repudiate tendencies to angel-worship among the churches known to him. Colossians 2 : 18 attests the existence in his day of such a propensity among some Christians in Asia Minor.[1] On the other hand, there is nothing in John's earlier visions to suggest that he was concerned about such a danger among the churches known to him. Possibly he had certain positive lessons in view in this passage. He commences the paragraph with an attestation of his identity as the prophet who has received the revelation, **I John am he who heard and saw these things** (cf. 1 : 9). The overwhelming greatness of the Revelation led him to do obeisance to the angel who mediated it, but in forbidding the worship the angel affirms his oneness with John and with **your brethren the prophets.** The act and the statement together have the effect of confirming the authoritativeness of the word attested by John. On the angel's confession he is one with the angel and with the prophets. But further: the angel is one also with **those who keep the words of this book.** God's people as a whole are raised to the dignity of angels. As heirs of the eternal kingdom they have been exalted to share the royalty of Christ (3 : 21, 20 : 4, 22 : 5). The praise, therefore, belongs to God alone.

[1] For evidence of Jewish and later Christian tendencies to angel worship see Charles, ad loc.

10. The command **Do not seal up the words of the prophecy of this book** reverses the procedure adopted in Jewish apocalyptic literature generally. For when a work of this character was written in the name of a saint of ancient times, as was usually the case, the distance between the prophet of old and the circumstances which the writer really had in view was explained by representing that the prophecy had been 'sealed' from the eyes and understanding of men until the period to which it referred, i.e., the present. In this respect John forsook the apocalyptic tradition. He had no need to appeal to authorities of earlier days, for he had been commissioned directly by the risen Lord, the Holy Spirit was upon him, and the angel of God was his guide in the things that were to come. He, therefore, openly spoke to his contemporaries in the name of the Lord. There was no question of sealing the prophecy from the eyes of men, **for the time is near.** All must hear, in hope that all will take heed, for judgment and redemption are at hand (v. 11).

11. John's mode of expressing this tacit appeal is admittedly ambiguous, but his interpreters have not served him well at this point. It is commonly maintained that verse 11 describes a situation in which fixity of character, and therefore of destiny, have been reached, the hour of the shut door has arrived (Mt. 25:10, Lk. 13:25), and repentance has become impossible to men. Such an interpretation is possible only if one ignores verse 17, or arbitrarily limits its application. Charles saw this clearly, but he felt that the two sayings are irreconcilably opposed, and so he put verse 11 to the account of the editor who is supposed to have muddled his way through the final chapters of this book. The truth is surely simpler. John's thought has been determined primarily by Daniel 12:9f., where the prophet is commanded, 'Go your way . . . for the words are shut up and sealed until the time of the end. Many shall purify themselves . . . and be refined; but the wicked shall do wickedly; and none of the wicked shall understand . . .' Now John has not followed the LXX in citing this passage, but he has agreed with it in one crucial point, for the LXX makes the 'until' of verse 9 govern verse 10 also. It has the effect of linking the 'sealing' of the prophecy with the deeds described in verse 10, as though the prophecy read, 'the words are sealed until . . . many purify themselves and are refined, and the wicked do wickedly and fail to understand . . .' For John those

days are at hand—**the time is near.** In sharpening Daniel's
thought he may have been influenced by Ezekiel 3:27, 'I will
open your mouth, and you shall say to them, "Thus says the Lord
God"; he that will hear, let him hear; and he that will refuse to
hear, let him refuse.' John's provocative utterance assumes the
circumstances described in his book. Evil is rampant in the world,
and is heading for a climax, in which men will raise their fist to
God in heaven and endeavour to crush the Church on earth. But
those who hold the testimony of Jesus will obey God rather than
men, and will continue in the way of holiness. As Daniel has said,
the wicked do not understand, they do not realize that God's
Christ is already on the throne of the universe, and that he is to
put forth his power in judgment and redemption, but the righteous
know it, and they should take heart. In the light of the approaching denouement, let men ponder their ways and contemplate the
end to which they are moving. **Let the evildoer** who so chooses
still do evil, and the filthy still be filthy. His judgment is
assured. But let **the righteous still do right, and the holy still
be holy,** so as not to miss the recompense of the kingdom. This
may not be orthodox missionary preaching, but it is a solemn
warning to every reader, to whom the implicit appeal should be
plain. As such it is an element in the 'eternal gospel' which must
be proclaimed to all the nations (14:6f.).

12. I am coming soon has already been uttered by the Christ
in 3:11 and 22:7. But the association of that coming with a
judgment which differentiates between the evil and the righteous
(v. 11) causes John to recall the majestic picture of God's coming
to judgment in Isaiah 40:10: 'Behold the Lord God comes with
might, and his recompense before him.' The power of God, represented by the exercise of his mighty arm, is to be wielded by
the coming Christ, when he will **repay every one for what he
has done.** The declaration is eminently suitable to its context, but
it closely conforms to Proverbs 22:12b (cf. Jer. 17:10, Ps.
62:1), which Paul also cites in his exposition of judgment in
Romans 2:6ff. It should be observed that the same terms for
describing the basis of judgment have appeared in 20:13, relating
to the last judgment executed by the Lord on the great white
throne. In our passage this function of judgment is ascribed to the
Christ at his coming.

13. Accordingly as judge of the world the Christ claims the divine title affirmed by the Lord God Almighty in 1 : 8, i.e., **the Alpha and the Omega.** The Christ exercises the judgment which belongs to God alone because he shares the nature of God. *Alpha and Omega* is fittingly defined as **the first and the last, the beginning and the end.** The former phrase is taken from Isaiah 44 : 6, and has already been appropriated by the risen Lord in 1 : 17 and 2 : 8. It is noteworthy that while 1 : 8 expounds Alpha and Omega in terms of the Jewish exposition of the divine name in Exodus 3 : 14 (see notes on 1 : 8 and 1 : 4), its reference to Christ as *the beginning and the end* has contact with the ancient Orphic confession of God as 'the beginning and the end and the centre of all things that exist'.[1] Certainly that formula conveys the meaning of Alpha and Omega, as John understands it, whether he knew the formula or not. The same essential affirmation appears on the lips of the risen Lord in 1 : 17, but there the central point of history appears to be the cross and resurrection: 'I am the first and the last and the living one: I died, and behold I am alive for evermore.' This accords with our understanding of the *Sator-Rotas* word square, which appears to be constructed on the basis that the Alpha and Omega is he who died on the cross (see additional note, pp. 60–63). The purport of adducing the symbol in verse 13, however, is to affirm the authority and power of the exalted Christ to execute the divine function of judgment at his coming.

14. The last beatitude of the Revelation (for the previous six, see 1 : 3, 14 : 13, 16 : 15, 19 : 9, 20 : 6, 22 : 7) renders in the form of a blessing what is essentially a declaration of acquittal in judgment (the second clause, **that they may have the right to the tree of life** is juridical language). The imagery of washing robes has appeared in 7 : 14 (see notes thereon). It applies the idea of cleansing soiled clothes to the removal of a man's guilt through the blood shedding of a sacrifice. In a Christian context it signifies participation in the redemption of Christ. The opening doxology of the book (1 : 5) indicates the importance to John of the typology of the second exodus for the understanding of Christ's

---

[1] It is first cited by Plato, *Leg.* iv. 7. Charles points out that the formula appears to have been familiar to Palestinian Jews. Not only was it adopted by later Talmudists, but Josephus quotes it both in its fuller form (*c.Ap.* ii. 22, 'God ... is ... the beginning and centre and end of all things'), and in an abbreviated form, almost identical with John's statement in verse 13 (*Ant.* viii. ii. 2, 'God ... is the beginning and end of all things').

redemptive action. To participate in the benefit of Christ's atonement is to enter upon renewal of life through entry into the saving sovereignty brought about by the divine action in Christ, and so to share the glory of the divine holiness. It is an apocalyptist's equivalent of the Pauline teaching on the unity of justification, sanctification, and glorification (cf. 1 C. 1 : 30, Rom. 8 : 30).

Forgiveness of sins has in view **the right to the tree of life,** i.e., life in fullest measure and delight in 'paradise', the kingdom of God (see notes on 2 : 7 and 22 : 1f.). Such life is a gift of God and the Lamb in fellowship with his people, hence they who wash their robes also have the right to **enter the city by the gates.** There is indeed no other way by which the city may be entered (see 21 : 12, 21, 24f., and notes on those passages). But the mention at this point of life in the city serves as a reminder that it is the context wherein God's gracious purpose for man finds its fulfilment. Nothing less than that is the goal of Christ's redemptive deed. That may be one reason why the right to the tree of life forms the first of the promises given to the victors in the letters to the churches (2 : 7). It is a further reason for doubting that the promises to the victors are directed to a select group within the Church, namely, the martyrs.[1] On the contrary this beatitude implies that all whose robes are unclean may seek that cleansing from him who died and rose for them, and they who find that forgiveness are assured of the right to enter the city. The sole division of persons in this oracle, as verse 15 makes plain, is that between the righteous and the wicked, the heirs of God and the rejected of God.[2]

As after the vision of the new creation (21 : 8) and the description of the city of God (21 : 27), so after the last beatitude, a final warning is given concerning the alternative to the blessedness of life in the city of God, namely life outside the city. The identity of those excluded is made known as an implicit appeal to the readers not to permit themselves to be numbered with them.

15. The terms in which the reprobate are described are closely

[1] Both Lohmeyer and Caird explicitly relate the beatitude of verse 14 to the martyrs.

[2] It is strange that Lohmeyer, who described verses 14–15 as 'a cameo of judgment of the world under Christ the Judge', did not recognize the implications of such an insight. The correct perspective on this beatitude is given by Swete, who characterized it as 'another version of "Blessed are the pure in heart, for they shall see God", interpreted in the light of the Cross'.

similar to those used in 21 : 8 and 27. **Dogs** however are mentioned here alone. In the ancient east these were scavengers of the streets rather than pets, and they were viewed by the Jews as the most despicable of all creatures. To call a man a dog (or, what was virtually the same, to call a dog by the name of an individual) was to express the utmost contempt for him. The term was applied by the Jews to the godless in general,[1] and especially to the heathen.[2] It is evident that for John the term relates not to the heathen over against the Jew, but to the godless of any nation in contrast to men of all nations who have washed their robes and made them white in the blood of the Lamb (7 : 14, and 22 : 14). **Sorcerers and fornicators and murderers and idolaters** designate in the first place those who participate in the evil practices fostered by the Antichrist (see 13 : 12ff.). In this context, therefore, **every one who loves and practises falsehood** denotes the man who promotes the lie of the Antichrist. That he *loves* the lie, as well as acts in accordance with it, suggests that such a man has entered into an affinity of character with the Antichrist, and therefore with the father of lies himself (Jn 8 : 44). That represents the antithesis of what is imaged in the washed robe of the citizen of the heavenly kingdom.

It is to be observed that whereas in 21 : 8 those rejected by God are said to have their lot in the lake of fire, they are here stated to be **outside** the city. How are the two pictures to be related? Some insist that they refer to wholly different conditions, verses 14f. applying to the millennial age alone, when the nations have free access to the city, apart from the unclean (21 : 27), while 21 : 8 depicts the existence (or annihilation) of the godless in the eternal world. This is questionable exegesis. The beatitude of verse 14 and warning of verse 15 form part of John's summing up of his message to the Church. The implied warnings of verses 10f. and 12f. are various ways of setting forth the judgment which the parousia of Christ will initiate and the varying destinies of mankind to which it will lead. The portrayal of man's final destiny as life within the city of God or life outside it is one way among others of expounding the alternatives which confront man in this world, and it has precedents in the gospels (Mt. 8 : 12, 22 : 13,

---

[1] According to *Sotah* 9:15 the generation which will precede the age of the Messiah will, by virtue of their impiety, look like dogs.

[2] See Strack-Billerbeck on Matthew 15:26 (I, pp. 722–26).

25:30). That John can use such divergent images to represent a single reality, illustrates yet again his flexibility in the imagery by which he conveys 'the word of God and the testimony of Jesus Christ' (see notes on 1:1f.).

16. In the first of the final sayings of the book (cf. introductory note on the Epilogue, p. 334) the opening sentence takes up the statement of verse 6 and puts it into direct speech. Observe however that while verse 6 states, 'The Lord God . . . has sent his angel', this declaration reads, **'I Jesus have sent my angel'.** This accords with the description of the book in the introduction to the Revelation (1:1), but following so closely after verse 6 it provides yet another instance of John's habitual attribution of the action of God to Jesus, thereby implying by this unity of action a unity of being. Jesus has sent his angel **to you:** the term is in the plural, and so does not denote John. Which persons then are in view? If we may interpret verse 16 by verse 6, *you* will have the same reference as 'his servants' in verse 6. In that verse the 'servants' of God can hardly be the prophets, but God's servants in the widest sense, i.e., his people, believers in Jesus (such is the meaning in 1:1; cf. 2:20, 7:3, 19:5, 22:3). If this be correct, the persons addressed as *you* in verse 16 are probably the members of the seven churches, to whom the Revelation is addressed in 1:4 (cf. 1:11), and **the churches** for whom the testimony is provided will be the churches generally, as in the conclusions of the seven letters (2:7, etc.).

Two titles are now brought together in the self-designation of Jesus, each having an Old Testament source, but each characteristically modified by an expansion of their original meaning. The messianic prophecy in Isaiah 11:1 begins:

> There shall come forth a shoot from the stump of Jesse,
> And a branch shall grow out from his roots.

The Messiah is viewed as growing from the stump or root of Jesse, and so a descendent of David's line (the LXX renders both 'stump' and 'roots' by the single term 'root'). The risen Lord however, speaking in verse 16, reverses the concept of Isaiah 11:1. He is **the root** from which David grew, and so the source of David's line; and he is the 'stock' (rather than offshoot) of David, in whom the whole family is comprehended. It is the same kind of thinking as occurs in the discourse on the vine in John 15:1ff.,

where 'I am the true vine' virtually means, 'I am the true Israel',
and 'you are the branches' means, 'you are members of the true
Israel inasmuch as you are united to me'.[1]

As **the bright morning star** Jesus fulfils the hope declared in
the prophecy of Balaam, Numbers 24:17 (echoed in *Test. Levi*
18:3, *Test. Jud.* 24:5, and traditionally regarded as messianic by
the Jews). In that passage it is said,

> A star shall come forth out of Jacob
> and a sceptre shall rise out of Israel.

The star is not described as the *morning* star, i.e., Venus. This
identification has a different origin. In our comment on the
promise to the conqueror in 2:28 we showed the relevance for the
promise of the ancient belief in Venus as the symbol of victory and
sovereignty over the nations (the Roman generals courted her
favour in their campaigns). By declaring that he himself is the
morning star, the risen Son of God claims that in his acts of redemption and judgment he fulfils the biblical hope of Messiah's
rule and gives actuality to the pagans' notion of the sovereignty
they ascribed to the gods. The sole Lord of history is the crucified
and risen Christ, in whom the dawn of the new age of righteousness and peace has already broken and whose coming is to bring to
the world the full glory of the day of God.

17. To whom is the repeated **'Come'** addressed? To the exalted
Christ, in entreaty that he may manifest himself to the world? Or
to men and women in the world, that they may come to him and
receive the life he bestows now and in the hereafter? It is undoubtedly simpler to interpret it in the latter sense, and so give to
the verb the same reference in each sentence of this verse.[2] But

---

[1] Charles, therefore, rightly comments, 'In his own person Christ is at once
the root, and the stem and branches that spring from the root, and this combines all the messianic claims of the Davidic family.'

[2] Charles thinks that this understanding is demanded by the use of the term
bride, since (in his view) that can relate solely to the Church united with Christ
at his coming. Naturally there can be no question of the Church in the new
Jerusalem appealing to her Lord to 'come' to her, and since the bride is thought
to be the Church in the city of God (as in 21:9), the call to the world to 'come'
is held to relate to the Church's missionary activity in the millennial kingdom.
This is hardly to be received. Most who interpret the call as addressed to the
world view it as a present invitation to come to the Lord in prospect of his
coming, and the term bride is regarded as the Church viewed in prospect of
her union with Christ at his coming.

while this interpretation yields an acceptable sense, it is more
likely that John intends us to view the call in the first two sentences as directed to the Lord. The preceding Epilogue is made up
of a succession of declarations and responses. This is especially
clear in verse 7, but the same pattern is also to be seen in verses
10f., 12f., 14f. It seems plausible to read the same pattern in verses
16f., as it certainly is present in verse 20. The reiteration in verse 16
of Christ as the Messiah of the Jews and Lord of the world embodies once more the promise of final redemption. Verse 17,
therefore, commences with the responsive cry of the Spirit and the
Bride to Christ, that he may come and complete his beneficent
work for the world. The hearers of the book, as it is read to the
assembled congregations, are bidden individually to take up the
cry. And since the end of the book has now been reached, an appeal
is made by the prophet to men and women who have not yet
responded to the gospel to 'come' and taste the salvation of God,
which is available now in this world, and is to flow in its fullness in
the age to come.

How are we to interpret **the Spirit** in this context of prayer to
Christ? Despite the hesitancy of the commentators in this regard
there seems no adequate reason why John should not have meant
quite unambiguously the Holy Spirit.[1] In considering the letters
to the churches we saw that the concept of the Spirit assumed in
the closing statements of the letters is closely related to the doctrine
of the Paraclete in the Fourth Gospel (see note on 2:7). One
passage relating to the Paraclete's ministry is especially relevant
here, viz. John 15:26f.: 'When the Counsellor comes . . . even the
Spirit of truth . . . he will bear witness to me; and you also are
witnesses . . .' The Spirit and the Church bear a joint witness to
Christ in the world. If it be so that the Spirit inspires the Church's
witness to Jesus, it is also true that the Spirit himself bears witness
within men's consciences and exposes them to the reality of sin,
righteousness, and judgment revealed in the preached gospel
(Jn 16:8ff.). The idea of the Spirit engaging in intercessory

[1] On the basis of the relation between the Christ who speaks in the letters
and the Spirit who conveys the message, Charles thinks that in 22:17 the
Spirit = Christ. Commonly the Spirit is here viewed as the Spirit of prophecy,
hence the Spirit and the Bride = the Prophets and the Saints (Swete). Lohmeyer considers the Spirit to be the inspirer of fellowship; that makes an easy
transition to the frequent opinion that the Spirit and the Bride = the Spirit-
inspired Church at prayer (e.g., Farrer).

prayer is not strange to the New Testament. It occurs in Romans 8 : 36f., significantly in an eschatological context. The motive for such a conception in our passage is not difficult to perceive. The Spirit inspires prophecy, the burden of which is the testimony borne by Jesus (19 : 10). The end of that testimony is the unveiling of the day of God, which Christ as the morning star leads on (v. 16). In that day the goal of all Spirit-inspired prophecy will be attained, hence the Spirit impels the bride to appeal to the Son of God to come, and joins the bride in the entreaty.

The Bride is the Church viewed in the light of her destiny to share life with her divine Bridegroom in the city of God (19 : 7ff., 21 : 9ff.). The term does not necessarily connote the consummation of the future age, as 21 : 9ff. could be held to imply, but it does at least denote the Church destined for the bliss of relation to Christ in the world to come, as 19: 7 suggests. In the present context the Church, anticipating her glorious future with her Redeemer, may be viewed in a manner comparable to the way in which the congregations 'in Jesus' are addressed as 'angels', i.e., from the viewpoint of their heavenly existence in Christ, which determines their empirical life on earth (see note on 1 : 20). The Church in Christ is already essentially that which she is destined to be in the day of Christ. The revelation of his glory will be the revelation of hers also.

Not only the Church as a whole but the individual member of the congregations assembled to hear the Revelation read should take up the prayer to Christ: **let him who hears say, 'Come',** for in the answer to that prayer lies the Christian's hope of participation in the salvation of the world to come. It represents the concentration into a word of the prayer which Jesus taught his disciples, the heart of which is *Thy kingdom come.* Its inclusion at this point suggests that the Spirit is more desirous that we should set our hearts on Christ than that we should fill our heads with apocalyptic lore, more concerned that we should be prepared for the day of Christ than that we should be capable of passing an examination about it.

The last word of this oracle is directed not to the Church member but to the stranger to grace:

Let him who is thirsty come,
let him who desires take the water of life without price.

It is unlikely that two classes of people are in mind, the parallelism is synonymous. The invitation is extended to any who have not yet responded to the appeal of Christ in the gospel:

> If any one thirst, let him come to me,
> and let him who believes in me drink (Jn 7:37f.).

The river of living water, which flows from the throne of God and the Lamb in the eternal city (22:1f.), flows from the heart of Christ even now to all who will **come ... take ... without price** (cf. Isa. 55:1). He who drinks this water slakes his thirst for ever (Jn 4:14), but it will require the day of the unveiling to reveal the wealth of that grace by which God and the Lamb will satisfy the soul of man for ever and to the utmost (Heb. 7:25).

18, 19. The warning appended by John to his book to discourage those who would 'add' to it or 'take away' from it is as characteristic as his apocalyptic cartoons and has a history almost as long. Before the invention of the printing press authors were at the mercy of those who copied their works, and it was common for authors to add a strong note inculcating faithfulness in transcription.[1] Needless to say, John's concern was not simply to ensure the precise reproduction of the terms he used, but to see that the message he had received from the Lord was delivered to the churches entire, without diminution and without perversion. The history of Gnosticism, which was gathering momentum in John's day, illustrates the need for such a concern. The *Gospel of Thomas* reproduced the teaching of Jesus in such a way as to make of him a Gnostic. Marcion's edition of Luke (the only gospel he circulated among his followers) systematically eliminated from the text everything which suggested that Jesus had a real body. Tatian's *Diatessaron*, which superseded the four gospels in Syria, had a

---

[1] The best known example is that referred to in the *Letter of Aristeas*, relating to the translation of the Old Testament into Greek. 'After the books had been read, the priests and the elders of the translators and the Jewish community and the leaders of the people stood up and said that, since so excellent and sacred and accurate a translation had been made, it was only right that it should remain as it was and no alteration should be made in it. And when the whole company expressed their approval, *they bade them pronounce a curse in accordance with their custom upon any one who should make any alteration either by adding or changing in any way whatever any of the words which had been written or making any omission.* This was a very wise precaution to ensure that the book might be preserved for all the future time unchanged' (310-11).

similar bias in the selection of passages he used. And according to Tertullian, Valentinus perverted the text of the whole New Testament by the verbal additions and alterations he made.[1] Apart from the contemporary scene, the relation of John's statement to the scriptures should be observed, for it has been determined by Deuteronomy 4:1ff., a significant passage for the thought of Judaism:

> And now, O Israel, give heed to the statutes and the ordinances which I teach you, and do them; that you may live, and go in and take possession of the land which the Lord, the God of your fathers, gives you. You shall not add to the word which I command you, nor take from it, that you may keep the commands of the Lord your God which I command you.

There follows a reference to the destructive judgment of God on the Israelites who departed from the Lord at Baal-Peor, and a reiteration that this word is given that Israel may observe it and live. Historically and theologically the passage is of importance, for it reflects the consciousness that in the Torah the will of God stands revealed in completeness and authority, and the so-called 'canonization-formula'—'not add nor take away'—which had been traced back as far as 2450 BC in Egypt,[2] came to have a decisive influence in the Jewish attitude to the Scriptures. By a natural process of extension it came to be applied to the whole Old Testament Scriptures, but it also led to the view that the word of God stands fully revealed in the Law of Moses, so that everything in the Prophets and Writings is already to be found in the Law.[3] The use of the formula led Bousset to believe that in verses 18f. John canonizes his own writing. It is more likely that John's employment of the formula constitutes an assertion of the authority of his book as conveying in its totality and in full measure 'the word of God and the testimony of Jesus' (1:2). John has no thought of adding his work to the Old Testament, and the New Testament is not yet in sight. But he knows that he has received a word from the Lord for a crucial hour in history. It is imperative that that word be delivered in its integrity to those for whom it was intended. The

[1] *Praescr. Haer.* 38.
[2] See G. von Rad on Deuteronomy 4:1ff., and further, his *Old Testament Theology*, vol. 1, pp. 221ff.
[3] See Strack-Billerbeck on Matthew 11:13 (1, pp. 610f).

curse, which was usually added for the warning of copyists of doubtful morality, he transforms into an eschatological warning, and he underlines the link between the judgment threatened and the sin of destroying the word of God by a play on the formula. He who perverts the message concerning the acts of Christ and the Antichrist by *adding* to it joins forces with the Antichrist, and therefore he will be among those to whom God will **add the plagues described in this book,** since they are directed to the Antichrist's kingdom.[1] Similarly, from the man who destroys the message by *taking away* essential elements, God will **take away his share in the tree of life and in the holy city,** since that is for those who acknowledge the Lamb, whose testimony this book declares.

20. It is impossible to read the closing affirmation from the risen Lord, **'Surely I am coming soon',** and the responsive cry, **Amen. Come, Lord Jesus!** without being aware of the link thereby made with the faith and worship of the primitive Church. For *Come, Lord Jesus* translates *Marana-tha,* which occurs in 1 Corinthians 16:22 and in the eucharistic prayer recorded in the *Didache* (10:16):

> May grace come and may this world pass away.
> Hosanna to the God of David.
> If any man is holy, let him come;
> If any man is not, let him repent.
> Marana-tha. Amen.

This link could have bearing on the interpretation of our passage. In 1 Corinthians 16:22 *Maranatha* appears to enforce the preceding utterance: 'If any one has no love for the Lord, let him be anathema. Maranatha.' The appeal to the Lord to come appears to be for the purpose of exercising judgment on the sinner. There is evidence that the conjunction 'anathema maranatha' was a fixed one,[2] and while the anathema is not present in *Didache* 10:6 and our passage, that train of thought could have been present, especially in the latter. A solemn warning on any who mutilates the word of God has been pronounced by John in verses

---

[1] It is assumed that the day is not far distant.

[2] A Christian grave-inscription from Salamis (*C.I.G.* iv, 9303) calls down a curse on any who interfere with the remains, with the words, 'Let him be anathema, maranathan'; cited by Moule (see next note).

18f. The Lord who testifies to these things (the judgment described in vv. 18f.?) declares that he will speedily come—to
execute the sentence. The prophet adds his assent to the declaration: 'Amen. Come, and render to the sinner his due!'[1] While this
is a plausible interpretation, it seems preferable to recognize a
more positive note in John's statement. There is no anathema in
the prayer of the *Didache*. The context is one of joyful anticipation
of the coming of the kingdom, to which the Lord's Supper looks,
and the keynote of the passage is, 'May grace come!' *Maranatha*
will originally have expressed a like sentiment—a yearning by the
Church for the coming of her Lord. And the cry will have sounded
out above all in the Supper, wherein the Lord's presence was
thankfully recognized and the promise 'till he come' vividly
remembered.[2] That association of the term will surely have pre-
dominated when it was used on occasions other than the Supper,
and it is likely to have been in John's mind as he echoes it at the
conclusion of his book. If any link exists between verse 20 and its
preceding context, it is likely to be with verse 17. The Spirit and
the bride, joined by the hearers of the book read in the churches,
call on the Lord to come. Concluding his testimony to the revelation of the triumph of God and his saints in this book, the Lord
gives a final affirmation that the prayers of his people will be
answered: 'Surely I am coming soon.' The prophet responds on
behalf of his fellow believers with the formula of confirmation,
Amen, and with the ancient prayer, *Maranatha*, 'Come, Lord
Jesus'. 'That promise', wrote Schlatter, 'is the sum of all promises.
And that prayer is the sum of all living hopes.'[3]

21. The benediction reminds us that the Revelation was intended to be read to congregations gathered for worship, and that
while it has the form of an apocalypse it conveys a message
addressed to churches from which the writer is forcibly separated,
and beyond them to **all the saints** throughout the world. The

---

[1] This interpretation is favoured by C. F. D. Moule in 'A Reconsideration
of the Context of Maranatha', *NTS* 6 (1959–60) pp. 307ff. He thinks it likely
that in 1 Corinthians 16:22 and *Didache* 10:6 the language reflects the use of
maranatha to 'fence the table', and so warn the unworthy of the dire consequences of participating wrongfully in the Lord's Supper.

[2] Such is the conviction of the majority of commentators. For a full discussion
on *Maranatha*, see K. G. Kuhn's article on the term in Kittel, *TWNT* IV, pp.
470ff.

[3] *Erläuterungen*, ad loc.

occurrence of the benediction immediately after verse 20 strengthens the suggestion that the prayer for the Lord's coming, voiced in
the *maranatha*, has the same nuance as the prayer in the *Didache*,
May grace come. In the revelation of God in Christ grace has the
last word, as it has the first. As in revelation, so in history: **grace**
shall have the last word!

INDEX OF MODERN AUTHORS

INDEX OF SUBJECTS